TRAVEL ACROSS THE UNITED STATES AND EXPERIENCE AMERICA'S FASCINATING NATURAL WONDERS.

From glacier-covered peaks to windswept red-rock canyons, and moss-draped rainforests to sun-soaked coasts, *Otherworldly America* reveals the country's most breathtaking landscapes. Join nature photographer Jake Guzman as he explores hidden backcountry spots, iconic national parks, and overlooked state parks waiting to be discovered.

Journey from Alaska's icy wilderness to Hawaii's tropical landscapes, through the dense forests of the Pacific Northwest, the towering Rockies, the dramatic Southwest, and the vibrant Northeast and Southeast. Each location comes alive with stunning imagery, hike recommendations, captivating stories, and photography tips, making the adventures to these places as compelling as the landscapes themselves. This is a perfect book for outdoor enthusiasts, armchair travelers, and anyone seeking landscapes so extraordinary they feel otherworldly—no spaceship required.

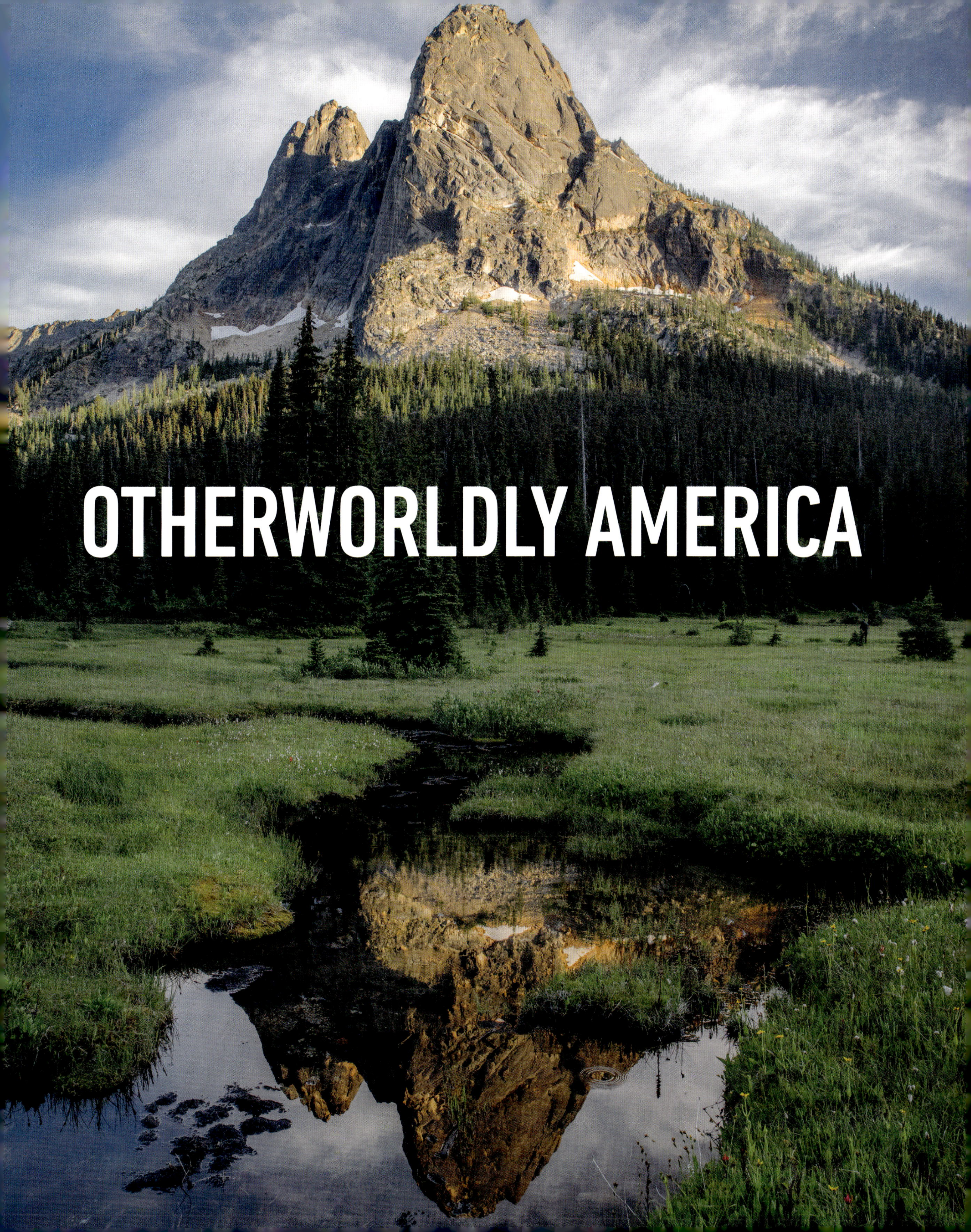

OTHERWORLDLY AMERICA

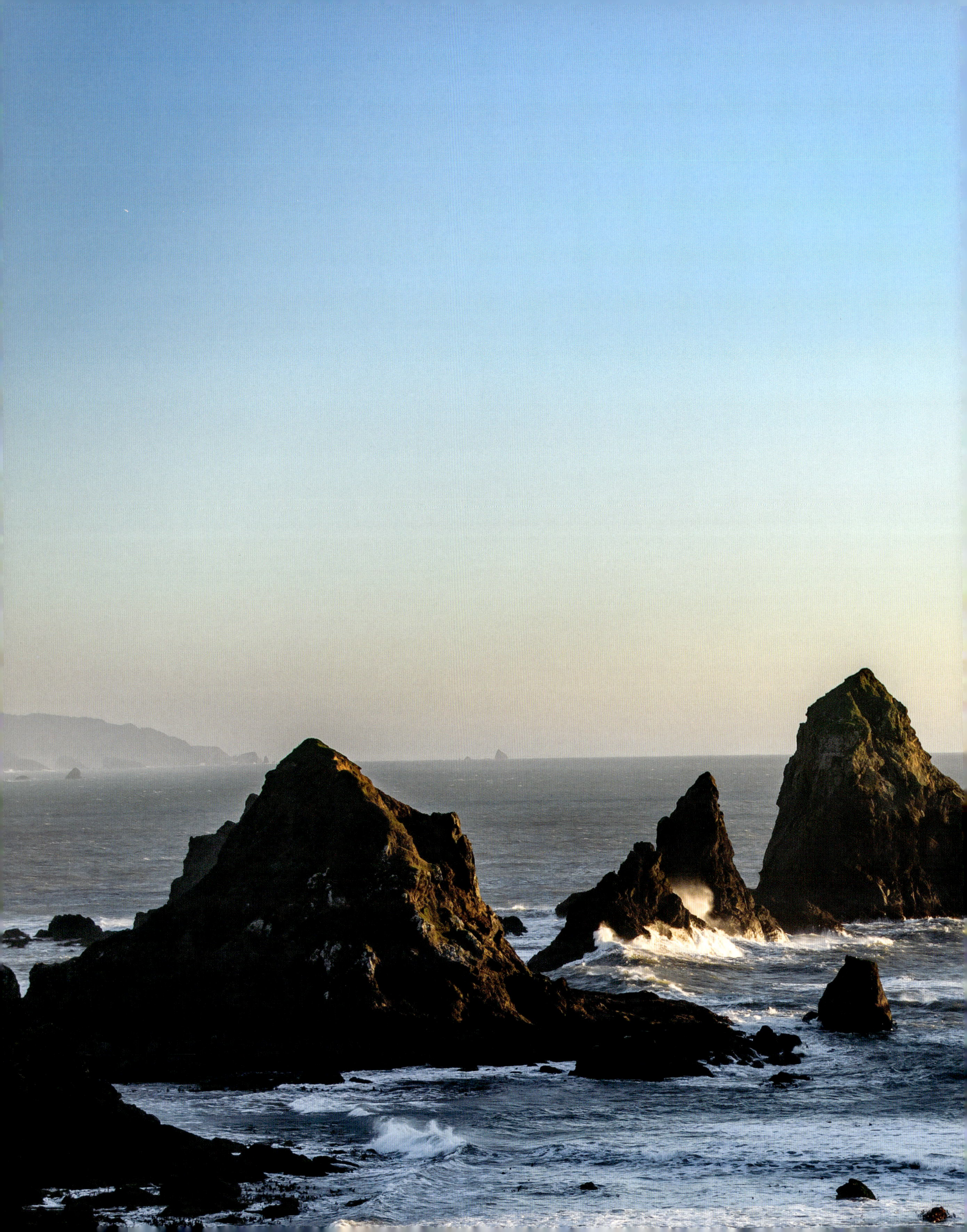

OTHERWORLDLY AMERICA

EXPLORE THE MOST UNIQUE
NATURAL WONDERS OF THE UNITED STATES

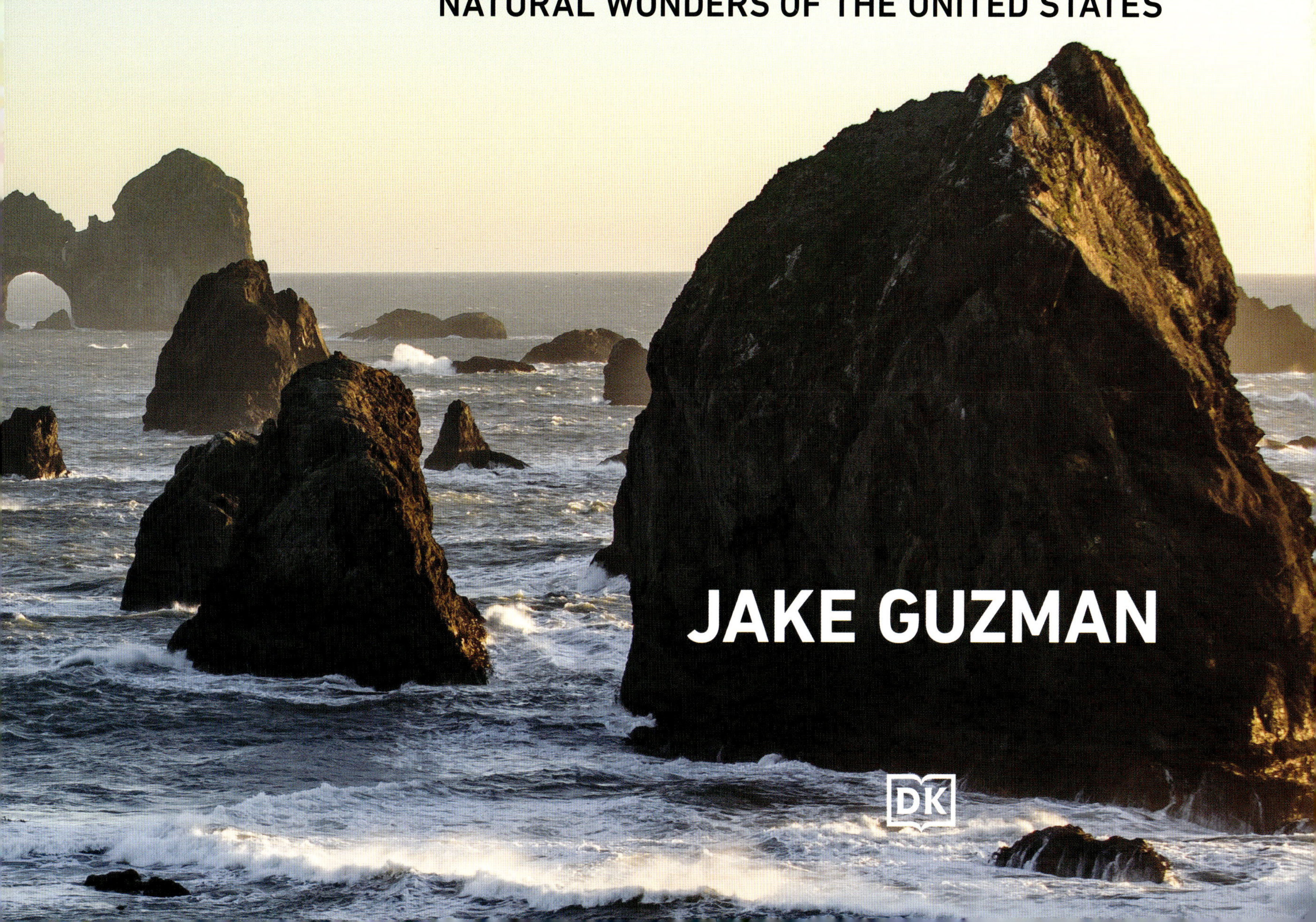

JAKE GUZMAN

DK

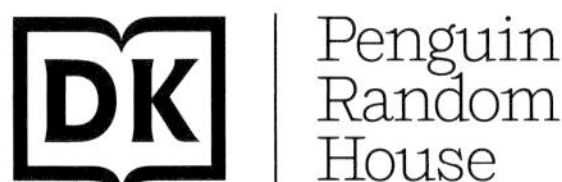

Publisher Mike Sanders
Executive Editor Alexander Rigby
Editorial Director Ann Barton
Art & Design Director William Thomas
Designer Ryan Scheife
Photographer Jake Guzman
Developmental Editor Tiffany Taing
Copy Editor & Fact Checker Devon Fredericksen
Proofreaders Bianca Bosman, Mira S. Park
Indexer Celia McCoy

First American Edition, 2026
Published in the United States by DK Publishing
1745 Broadway, 20th Floor, New York, NY 10019

The authorized representative in the EEA is Dorling Kindersley Verlag GmbH. Arnulfstr. 124, 80636 Munich, Germany

26 27 28 29 30 10 9 8 7 6 5 4 3 2 1
001-348880-MAY2026

A catalog record for this book is available from the Library of Congress.
ISBN 978-0-5939-6772-0

Printed and bound in China

www.dk.com

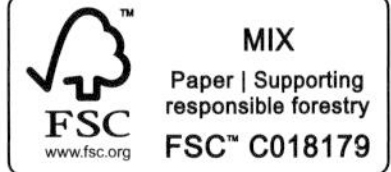

This book was made with Forest Stewardship Council™ certified paper – one small step in DK's commitment to a sustainable future.
Learn more at
www.dk.com/uk/information/sustainability

Page 1: Liberty Bell Mountain, North Cascades, Washington

Pages 2–3: Crook Point, Oregon Coast

Page 5: Mars Desert Research Station, Utah

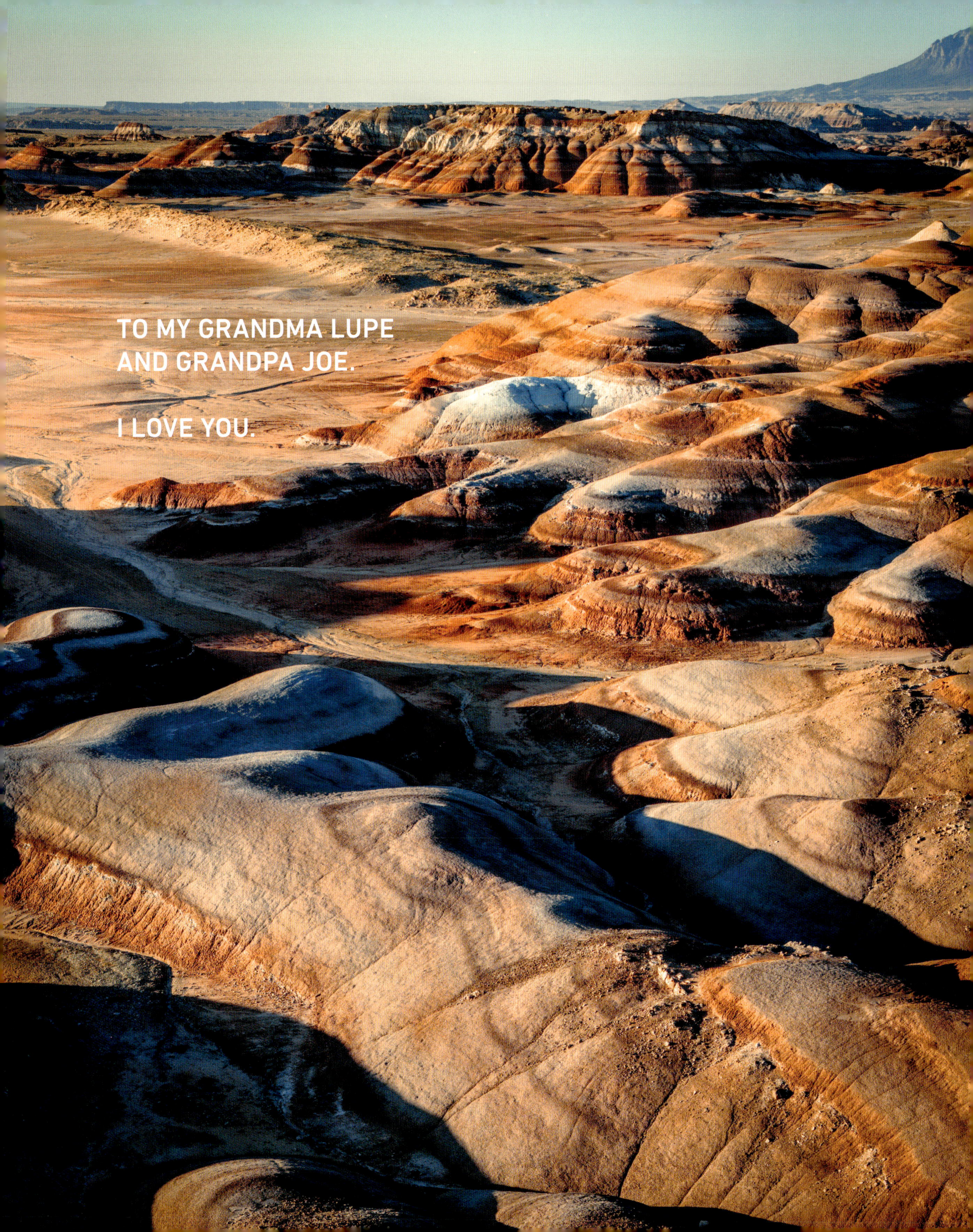

TO MY GRANDMA LUPE
AND GRANDPA JOE.

I LOVE YOU.

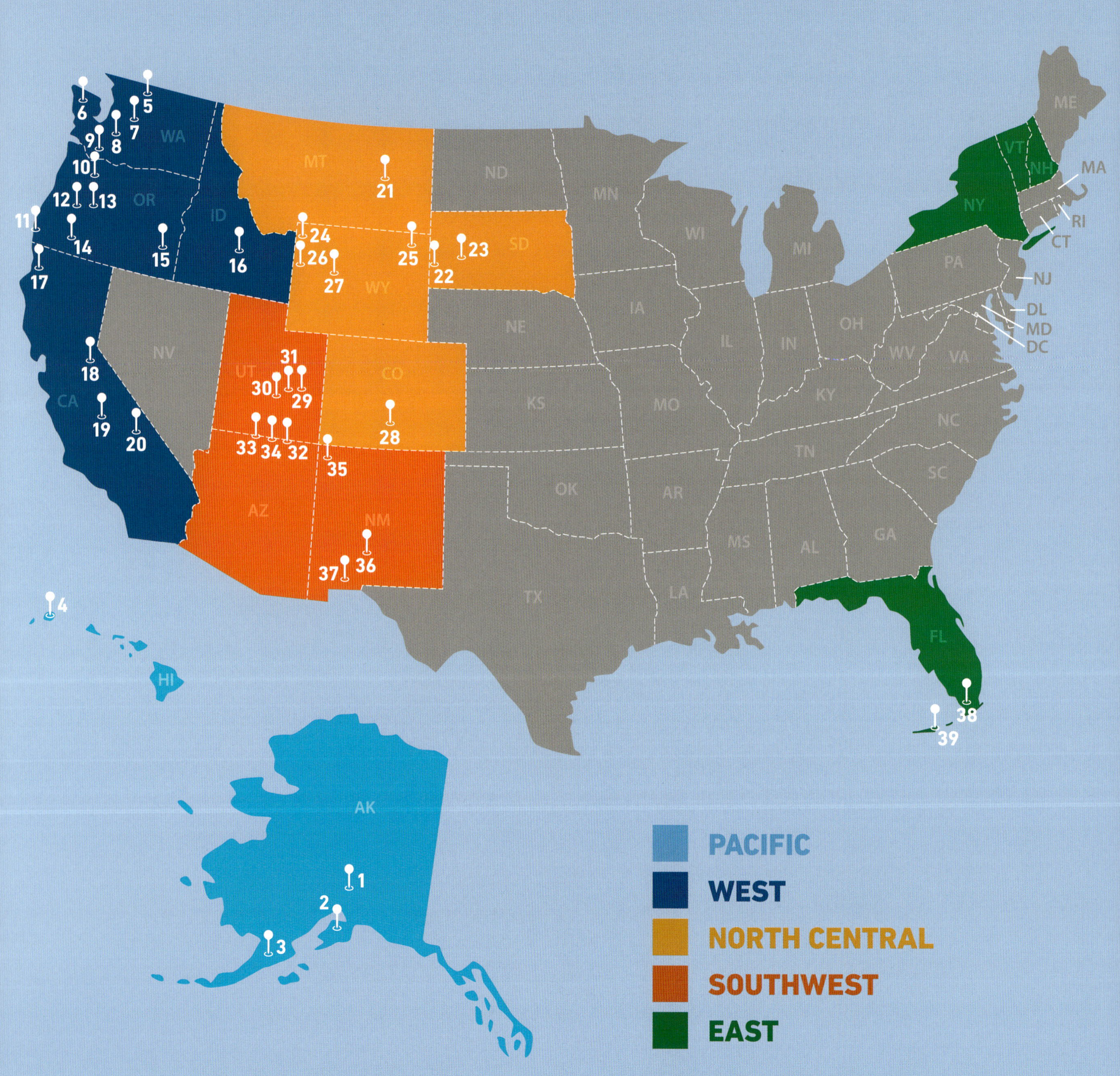
PACIFIC
WEST
NORTH CENTRAL
SOUTHWEST
EAST

Contents

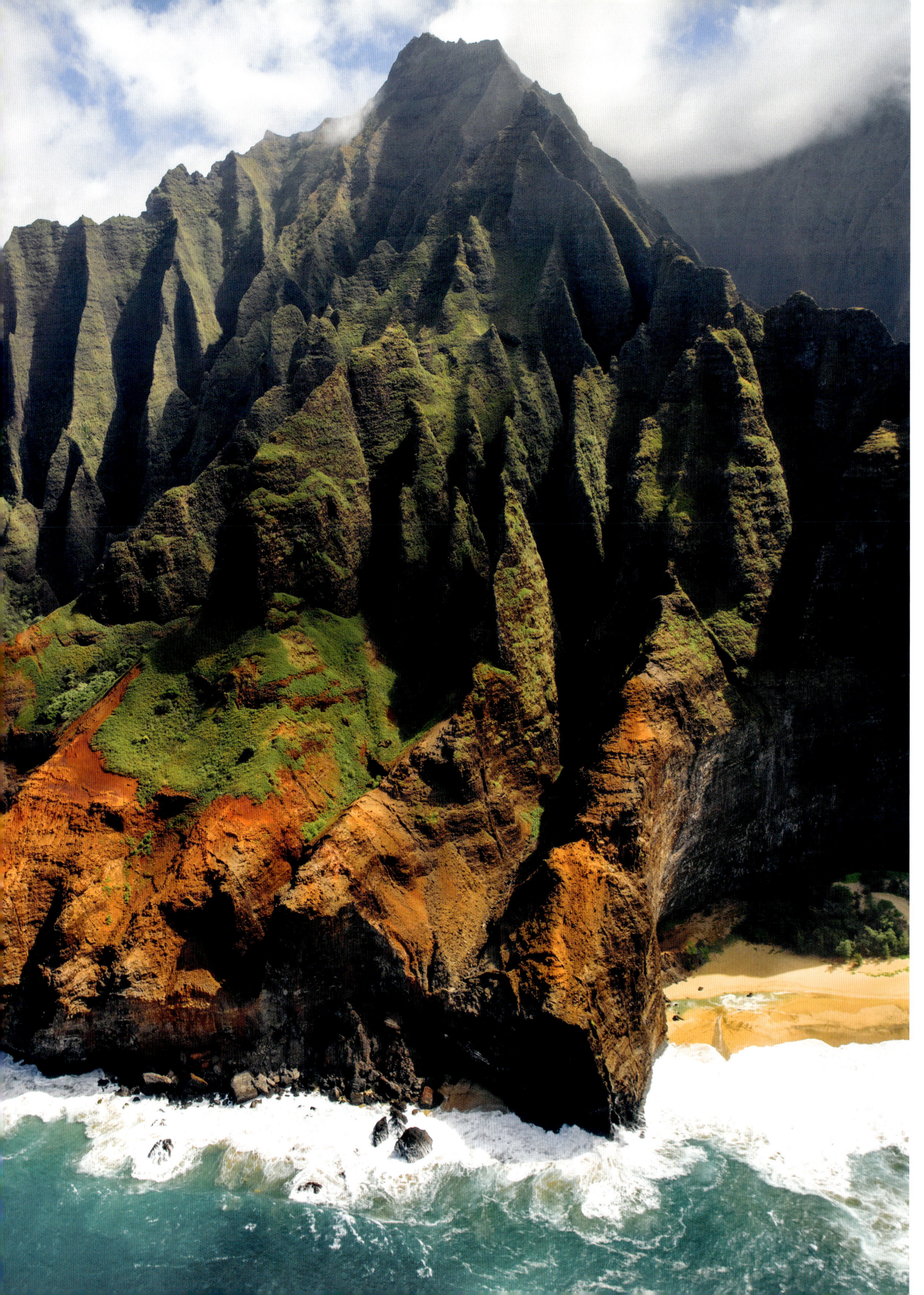

Introduction

I grew up in Washington State, where the Cascade Mountains were the first landscapes that ever made me stop and look closer. On childhood trips into Seattle, Mount Rainier would rise in the distance—towering above the horizon, impossibly huge, like a gateway between the everyday world and something far more mysterious. I was drawn to places that felt otherworldly, and the outdoors became an open invitation to explore them. When I eventually picked up a camera, I realized that documenting those places wasn't just a hobby—it was something I genuinely loved.

Otherworldly America is built around that feeling. This book brings together the locations and photographs that pulled me back to that early sense of curiosity and wonder. For two years, I traveled across the United States with a simple goal: to find landscapes that felt unlike anything I had experienced before. Not necessarily the most famous places—just the ones that made me pause and think, *I've never seen anything like this.*

Those travels led me through remote stretches of Alaska, where the sheer scale of the land made time itself feel slower, and into the steep, rain-soaked terrain of Kaua'i in Hawai'i. I wandered through the rugged mountains and deep forests of the Pacific Northwest, then continued south to explore California's iconic national parks, shaped by granite, desert, and ancient trees. Crossing the Rocky Mountains, I sought out unique geological wonders—from the geothermal landscapes of Yellowstone to the sculpted formations of the Badlands in South Dakota. In the Northeast, I chased the explosion of fall colors deep into the Adirondacks. And in the far Southeast, I traveled through the water-drenched islands of the Everglades and the Florida Keys, where the boundary between land and sea seems to dissolve entirely.

Each place taught me something—about America, about photography, and about myself. This book is my way of sharing those experiences and the moments that shaped them. My hope is that these images encourage you to look a little closer at the world we live in, because there is far more out there than we often realize.

Opposite: Nā Pali Coast, Kaua'i, Hawai'i

PACIFIC

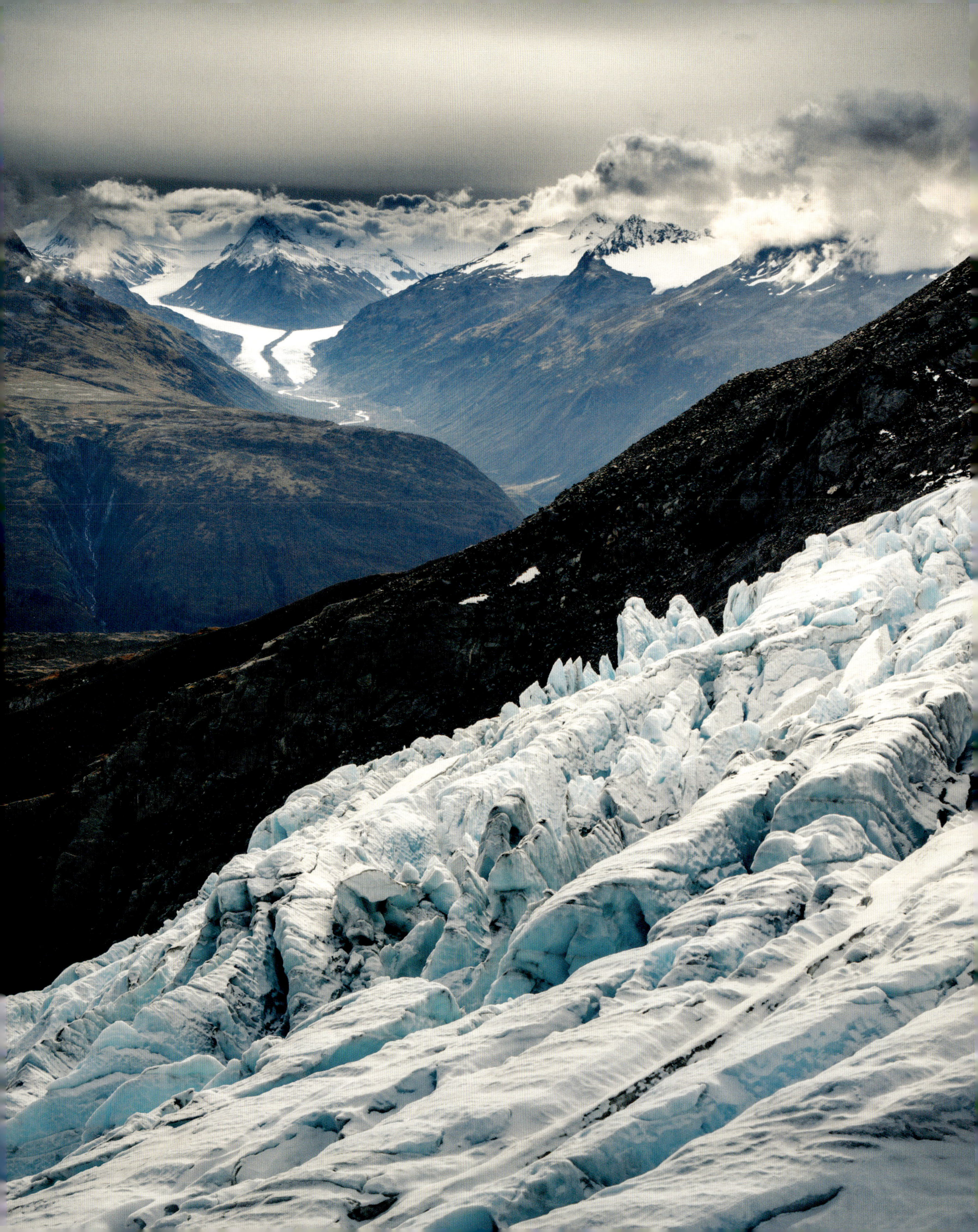

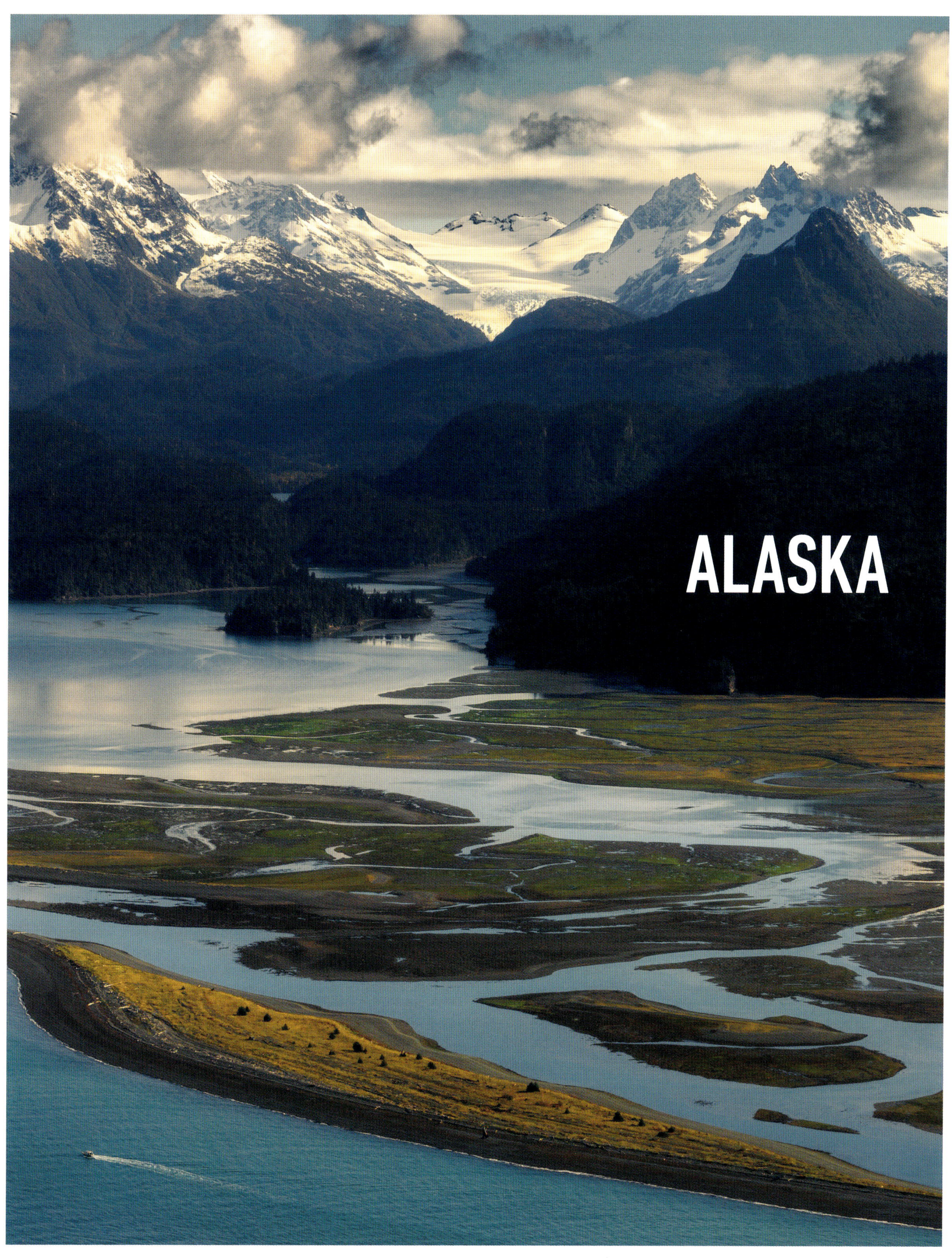

ALASKA

DENALI NATIONAL PARK & PRESERVE

Visit North America's highest peak and step onto Earth's grandest stage, with towering granite cliffs, sweeping tundra, fast-moving rivers, and glaciers larger than cities. Denali's vast wilderness humbles and inspires, offering an unforgettable encounter with raw Alaskan beauty.

Region: Pacific

State: Alaska

Coordinates: 63°04'10.0"N 151°00'30.0"W

Focal feature: Denali, which stands at 20,310 feet (6,190m) tall

Formation attributes: Carved by tectonic uplift and glacial erosion along the Alaska Range and spanning nearly 6 million acres, this park is larger than the state of Massachusetts!

Fun fact: Only about 30 percent of visitors ever see the full mountain due to its frequent cloud cover. Denali's name means "the High One" in the Athabaskan language.

Best time to visit: Mid-May to mid-September for the best weather, wildlife viewing, and accessibility. Shoulder seasons (May–June, late August–September) provide fewer crowds and dramatic tundra colors.

How to access: Access the park by car from Anchorage or Fairbanks via the Parks Highway or take the Alaska Railroad's Denali Star route. Private vehicles are allowed only up to Mile 15; beyond that, park shuttle or tour buses are required.

Things to consider: Weather changes quickly; dress in layers, and bring rain gear and sturdy footwear. Wildlife is abundant—bears, moose, caribou, and wolves roam freely. Maintain safe distances and observe from shuttles or marked viewing areas. Most of the park is trailless; be prepared for off-trail hiking and backcountry navigation. Shuttle buses can pick up hikers along the road.

RECOMMENDED TRAILS:

Savage River Loop: *2.1-mile (3.4km) round trip; 600 feet (183m) elevation gain; easy.* A scenic walk along the river through rocky terrain and tundra.

Horseshoe Lake Trail: *2.1-mile (3.4km) loop; 400 feet (122m) elevation gain; easy–moderate.* Forested trail with views of a glacial lake and frequent beaver sightings.

Eielson Alpine Trail: *2.2-mile (3.5km) round trip; 1,100 feet (335m) elevation gain; moderate–strenuous.* Ascend a ridge for panoramic views of the Alaska Range and Denali on clear days.

Tips for taking a great photo

- Photograph Denali at dawn or dusk from Wonder Lake or Polychrome Overlook for soft lighting and possible mountain views.
- Use a telephoto lens for wildlife shots and a wide-angle lens for sweeping tundra and mountain scenes.
- Incorporate foreground elements like wildflowers or fall-colored shrubs to add depth and scale.
- Bring a tripod and shoot with fast shutter speeds to capture sharp images of moving wildlife or low-light landscapes.

Page 12: Twenty-Seven Mile Glacier, Chugach Mountains

Page 13: Near Homer

Opposite and pages 16–17: Along the Denali Highway

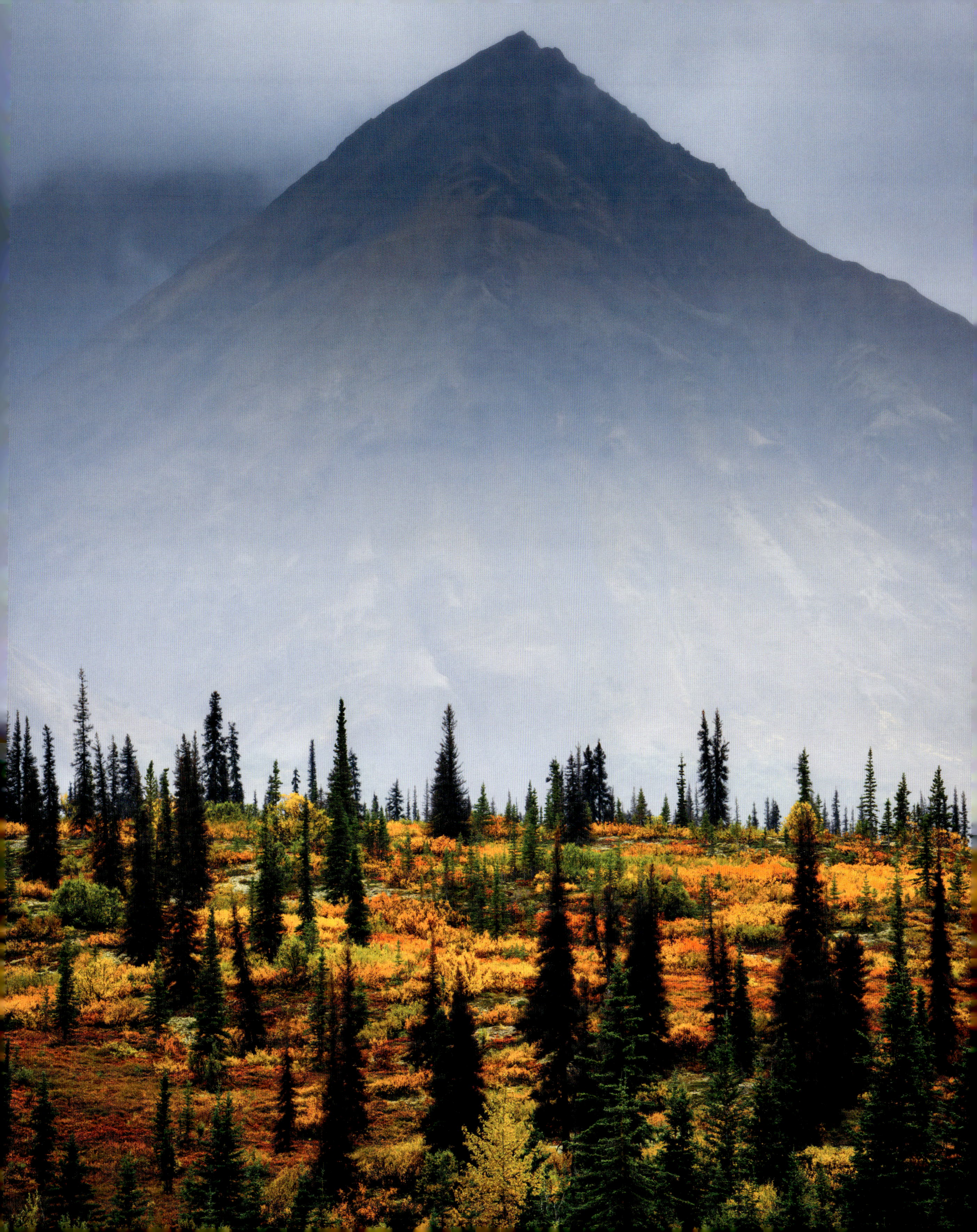

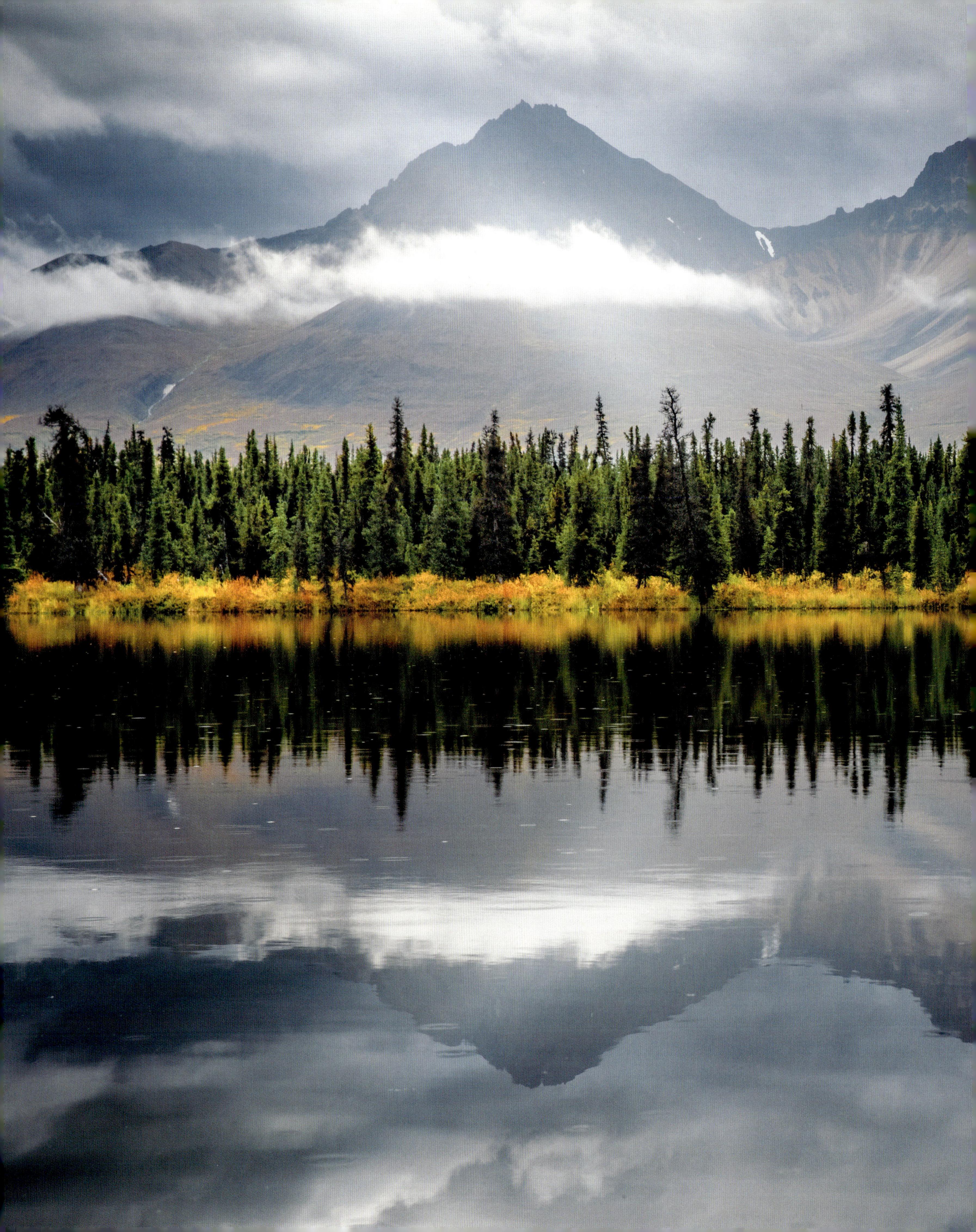

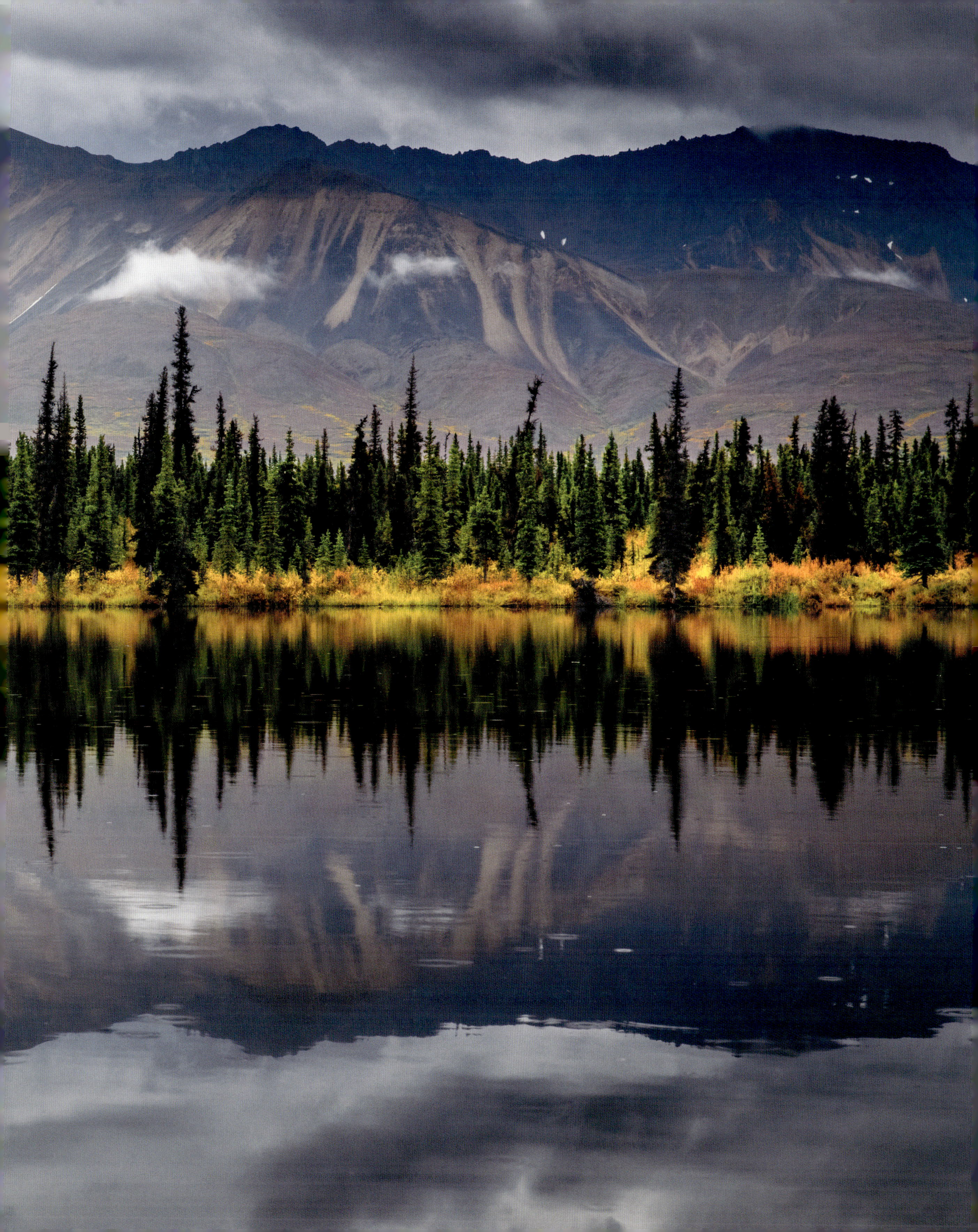

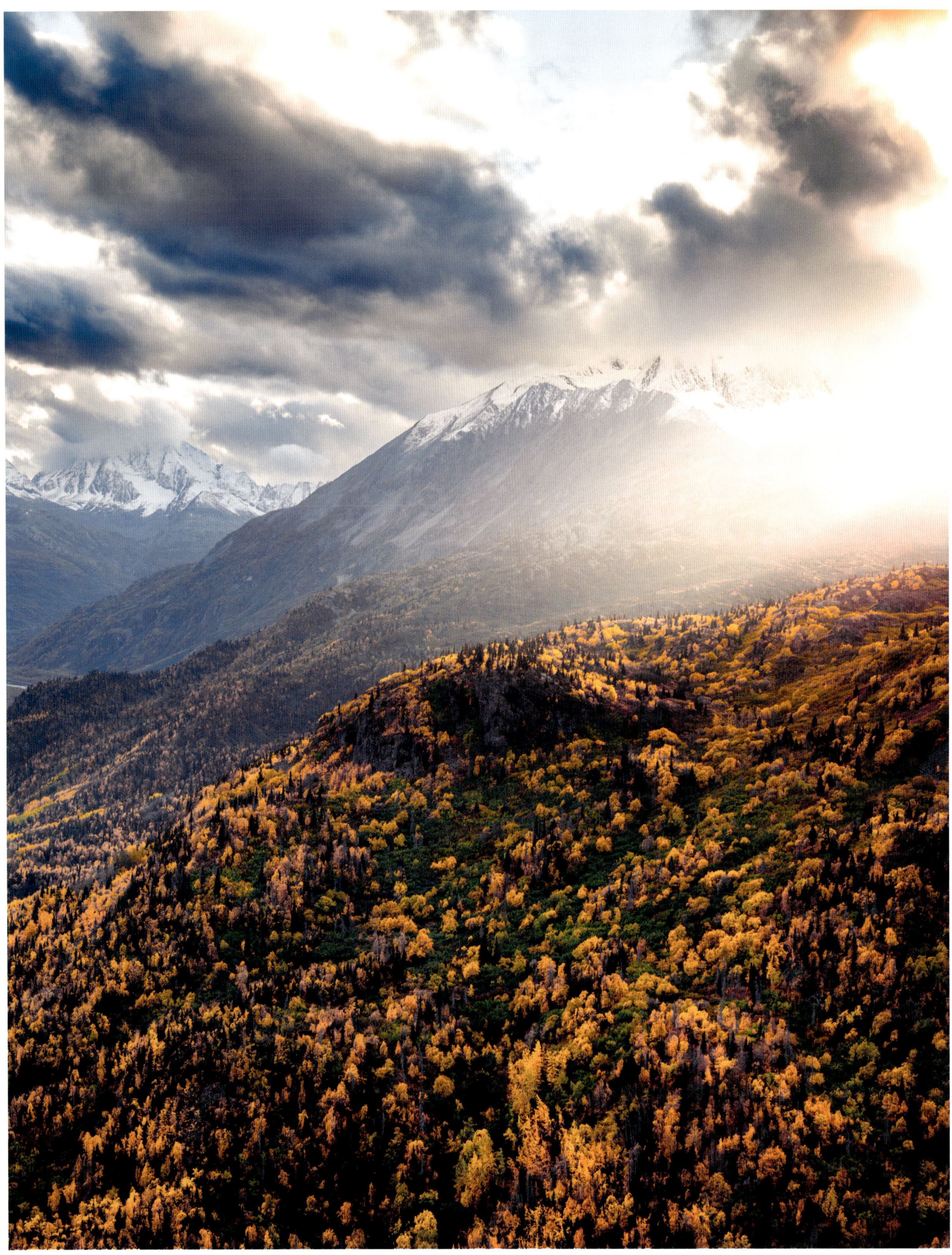

Above and opposite: Along the Richardson Highway

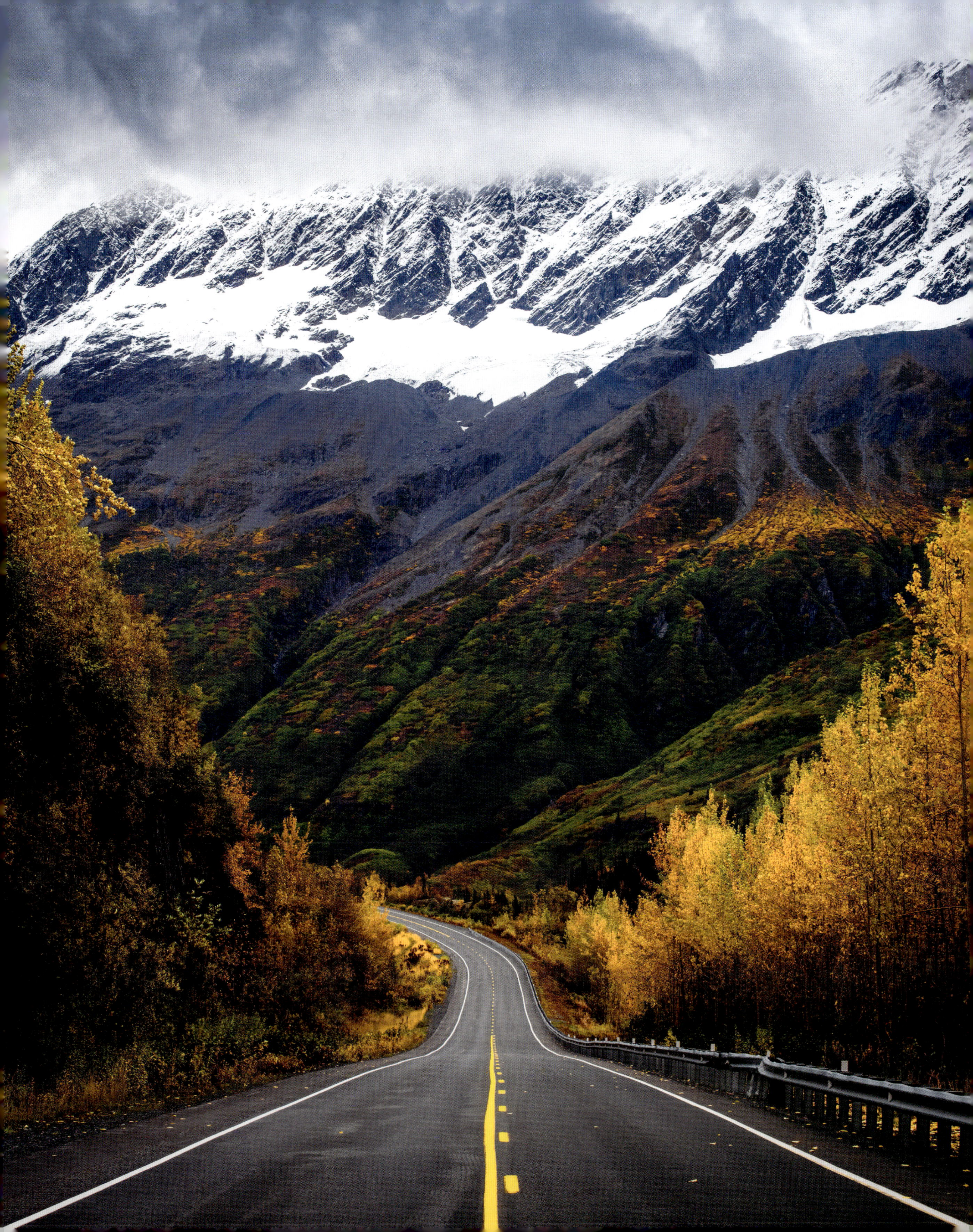

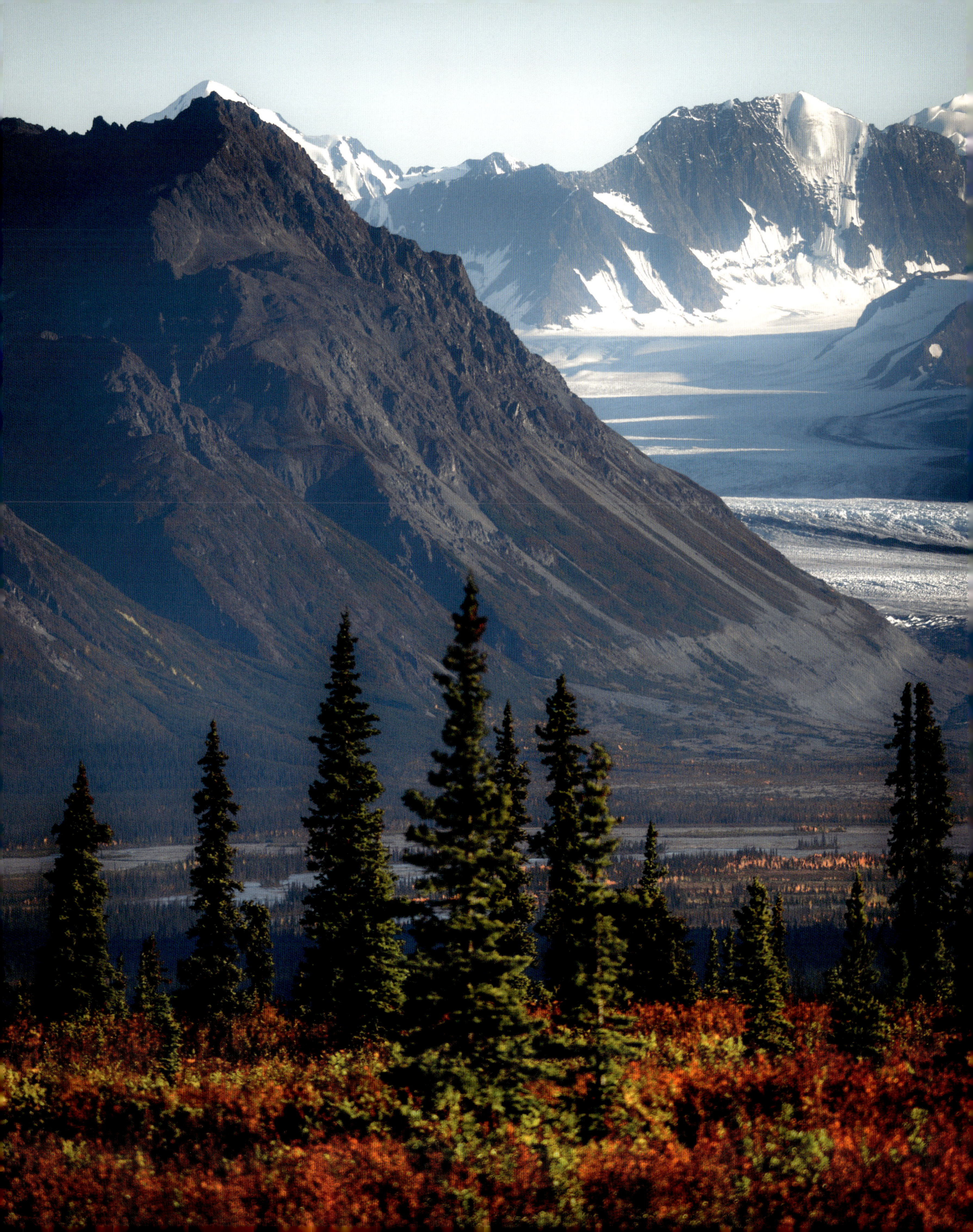

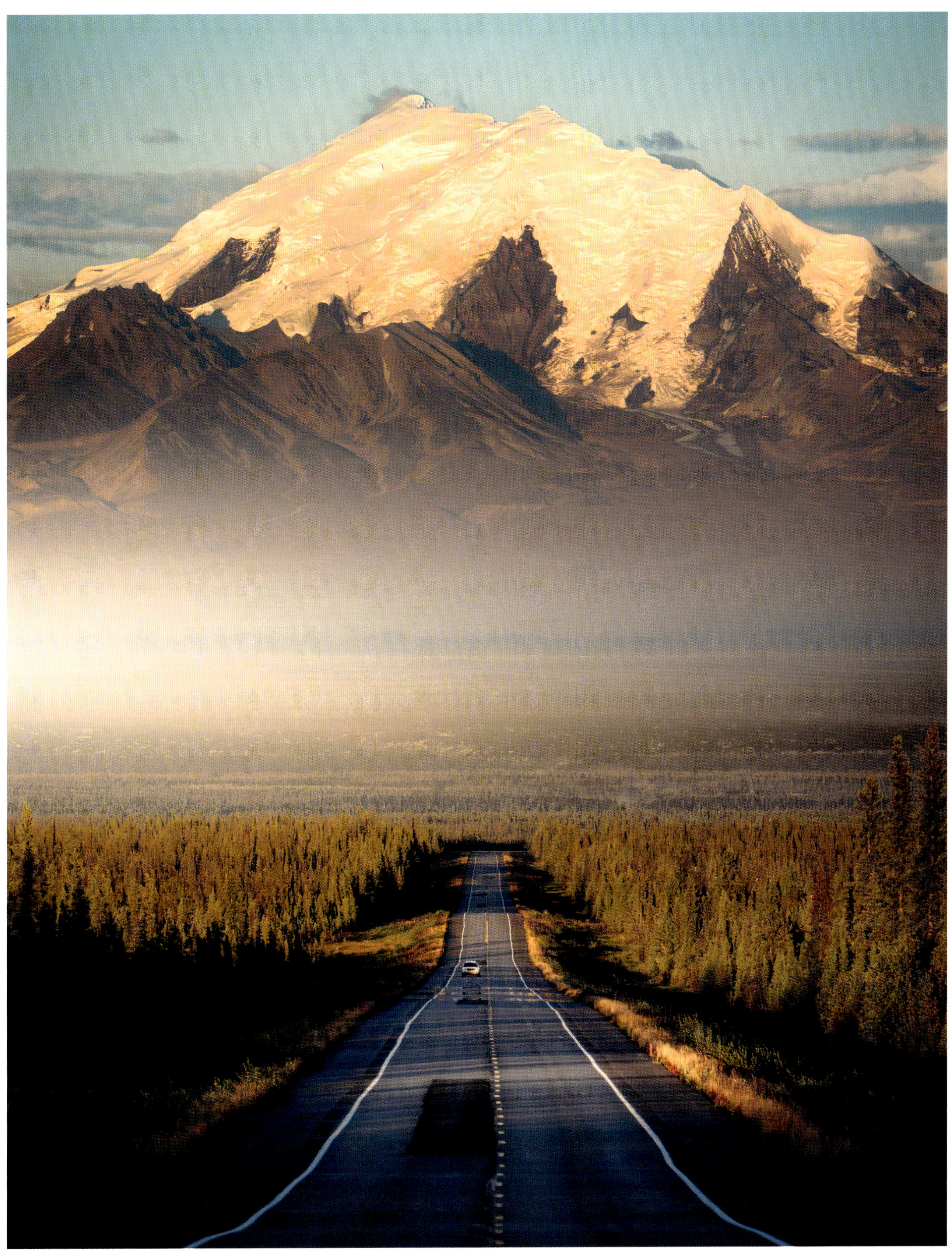

Above: Mount Drum | Opposite: Along the Glenn Highway

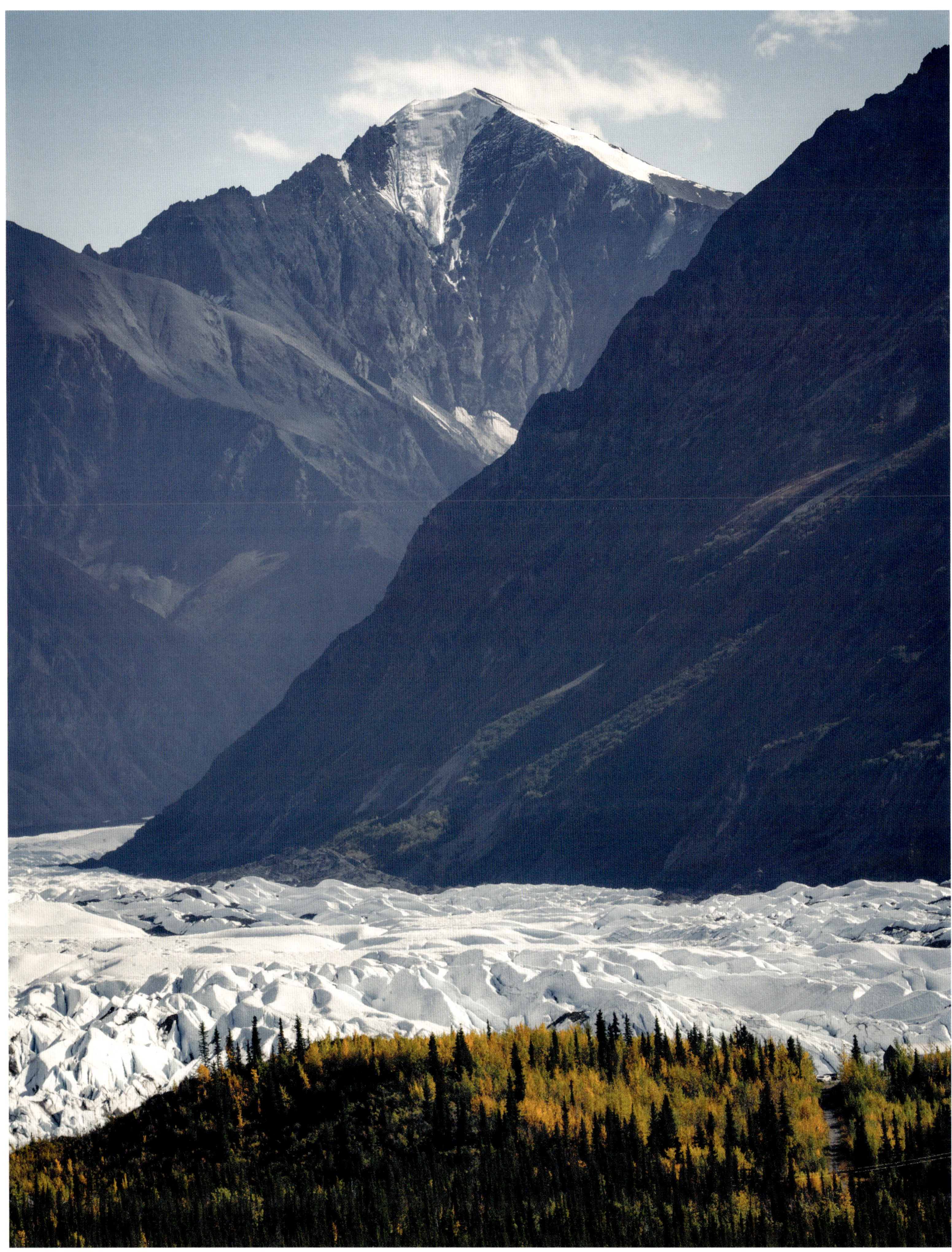

Above: Matanuska Glacier along the Glenn Highway | Opposite: Nelchina River flowing toward Tazlina Lake

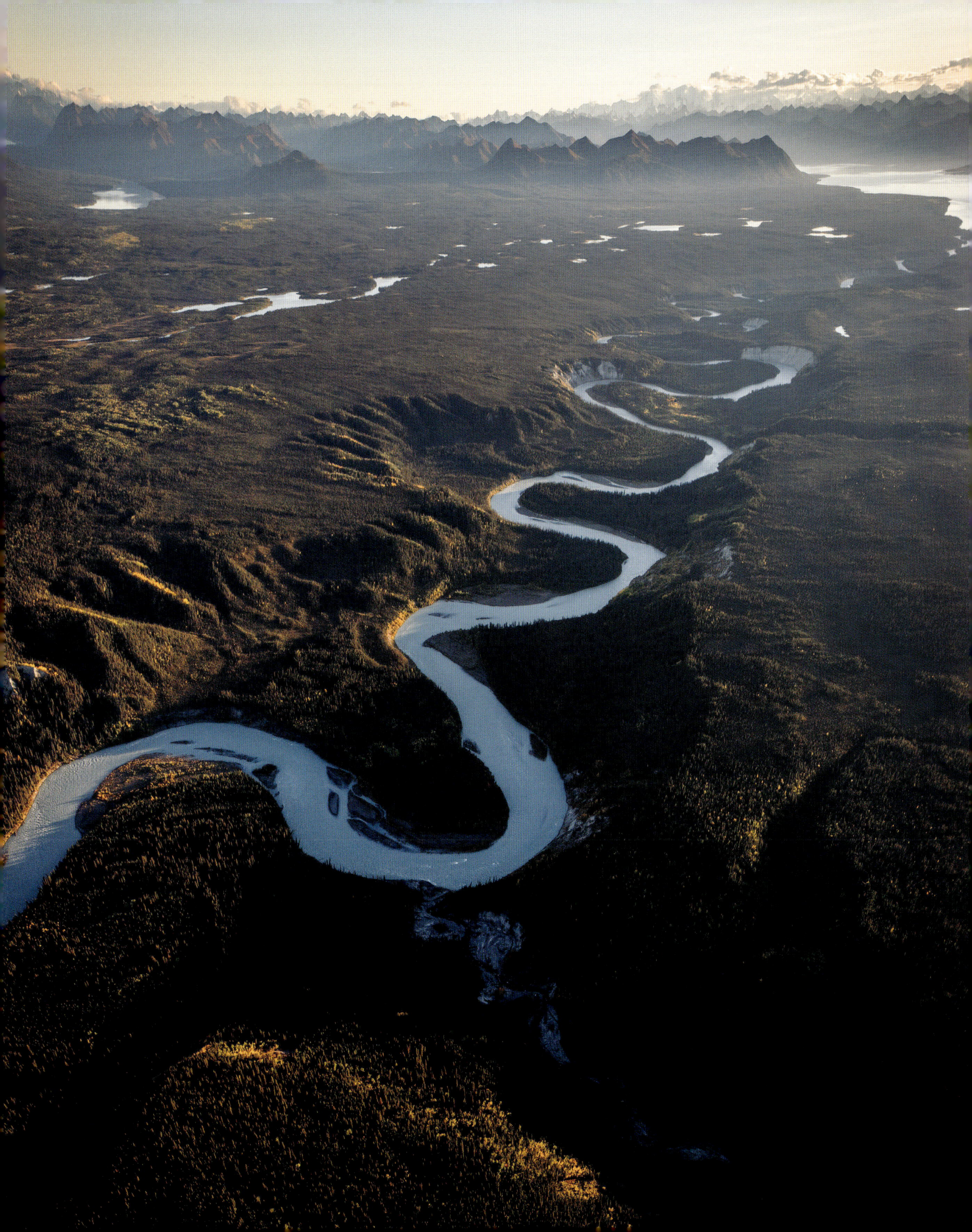

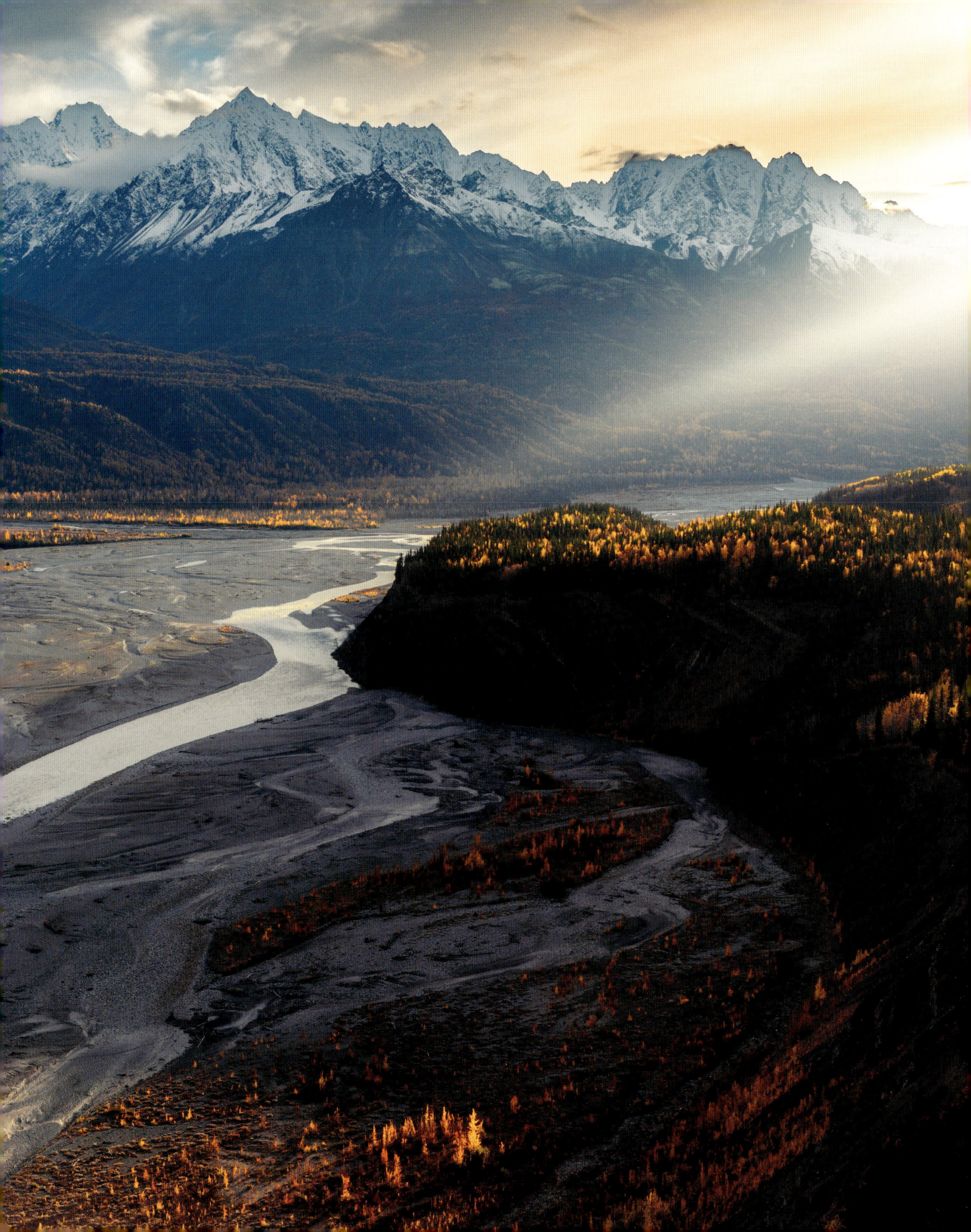

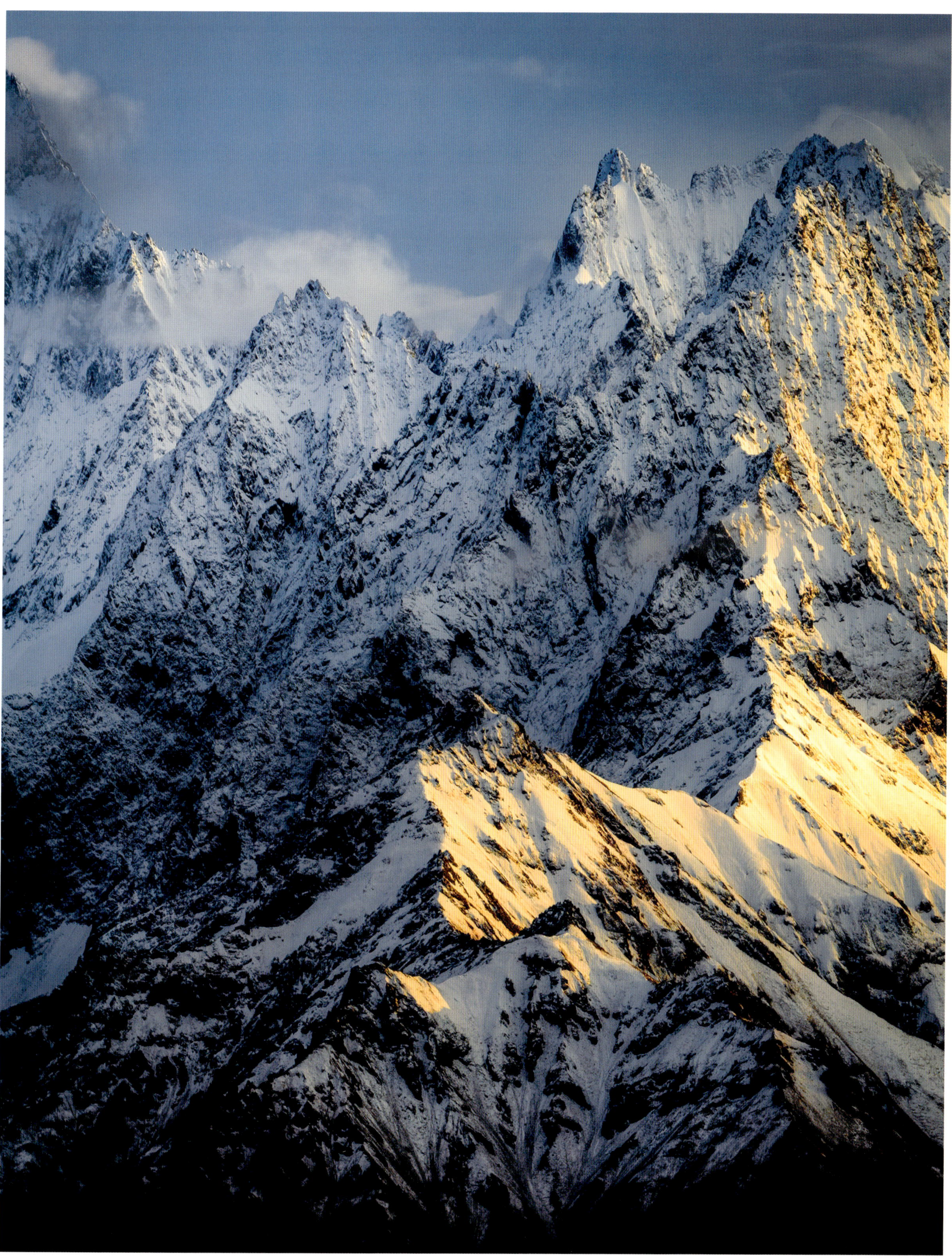

Above and opposite: Sunset in the Chugach Mountains

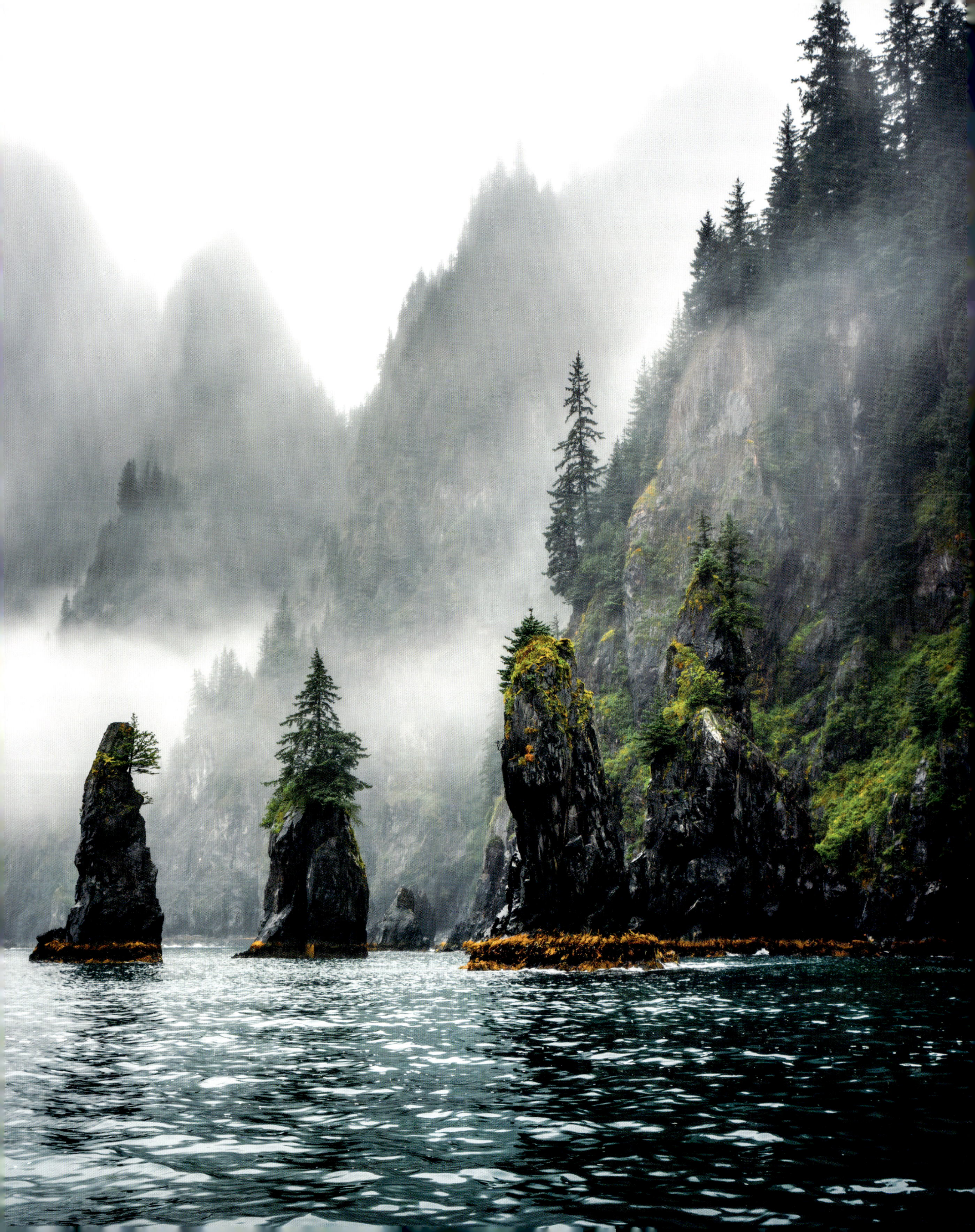

KENAI FJORDS NATIONAL PARK

Sail through the icy waters of Kenai Fjords, where tidewater glaciers crash into the sea, mountains rise straight from the ocean, and sea otters float through fields of ice. This coastal wilderness is a dramatic meeting point of land, ice, and sea in which wildlife thrives and glacial movement continues to shape the landscape.

Region: Pacific

State: Alaska

Coordinates: 59°55′00.0″N 149°39′00.0″W

Focal feature: Rugged coastline carved by glaciers, featuring fjords, tidewater glaciers, and rich marine ecosystems

Formation attributes: Shaped over thousands of years by retreating glaciers, the park includes the massive Harding Icefield—one of the largest ice fields in North America—and nearly forty glaciers that flow from it.

Fun fact: Nearly 51 percent of the park is covered in ice year-round, with the Harding Icefield feeding glaciers that descend to the sea.

Best time to visit: Late May to early September for boat tours, hiking trails, and wildlife sightings under long daylight hours.

How to access: Drive or take the Alaska Railroad to the town of Seward, the gateway to the park. From Seward, access the park via boat tours, kayaking, or hiking. Exit Glacier is the only area accessible by road, located about 12 miles (19km) from Seward.

Things to consider: Coastal weather can shift rapidly; pack warm layers, waterproof clothing, and gloves, even in summer. Marine tours may encounter rough seas, so if you're prone to motion sickness, come prepared. Wildlife is abundant; look for puffins, sea lions, orcas, humpback whales, and black bears along the coast and shores.

RECOMMENDED TRAILS AND ACTIVITIES:

Exit Glacier Overlook Trail: *2.2-mile (3.5km) round trip; 300 feet (91m) elevation gain; easy.* A popular path leading to a close view of the retreating glacier.

Harding Icefield Trail: *8.6-mile (14km) round trip; 3,200 feet (975m) elevation gain; strenuous.* A steep alpine hike with panoramic views of the massive icefield. Bring bear spray and plenty of water.

Coastal kayaking: *Varying distances and difficulty.* Paddle near calving glaciers and sea stacks, often accompanied by seals or porpoises.

Tips for taking a great photo

- Calving glaciers are most photogenic in midday light. Use a fast shutter speed to freeze the motion.
- A telephoto lens helps capture distant wildlife on the water or cliffs.
- Use a polarizing filter to cut glare and bring out the blues in the ice and sea.
- Early-morning and evening light add depth and drama to the fjords, especially from boat decks or elevated coastal overlooks.

Opposite: Spire Cove, Kenai Fjords National Park

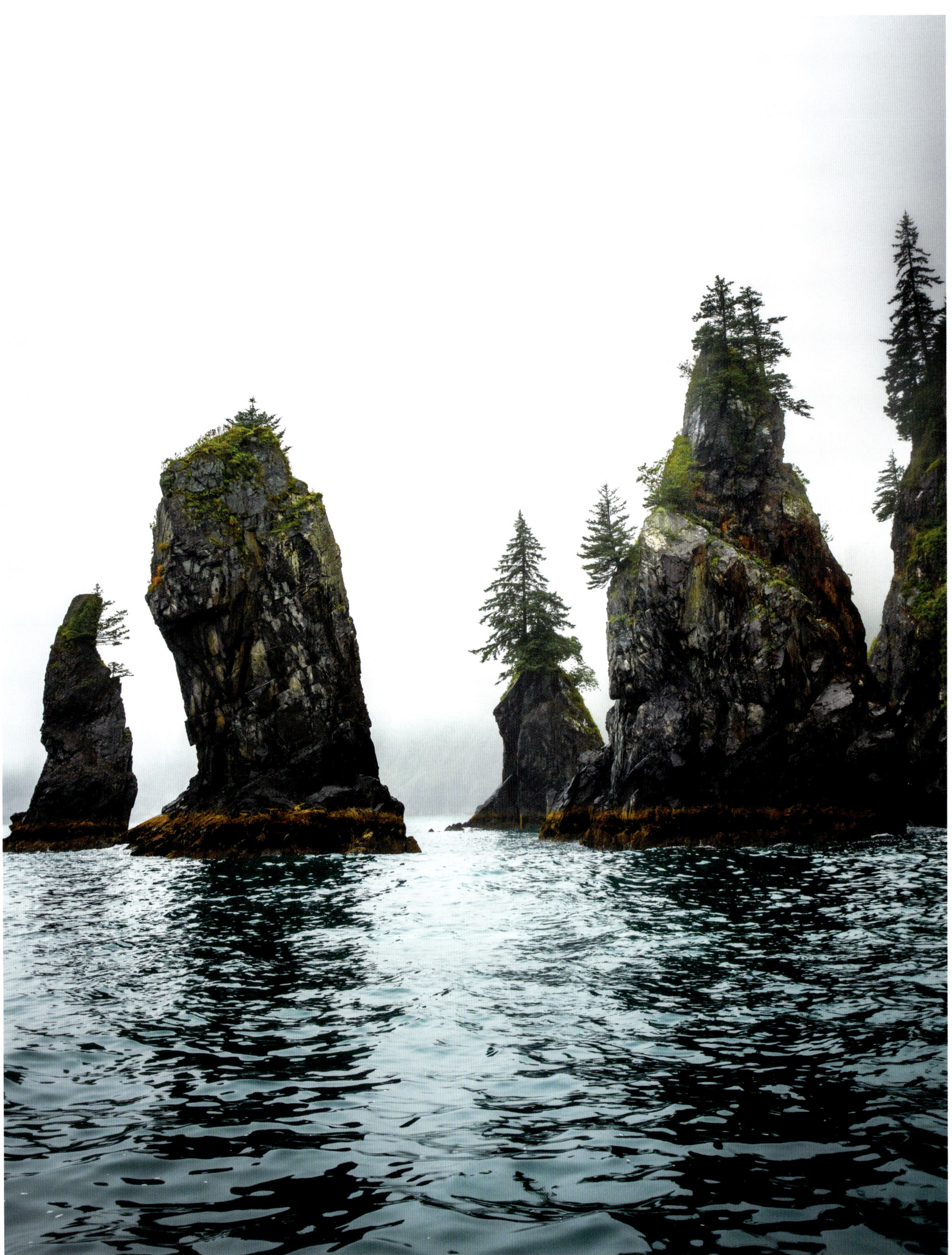

Above and opposite: Spire Cove, Kenai Fjords National Park

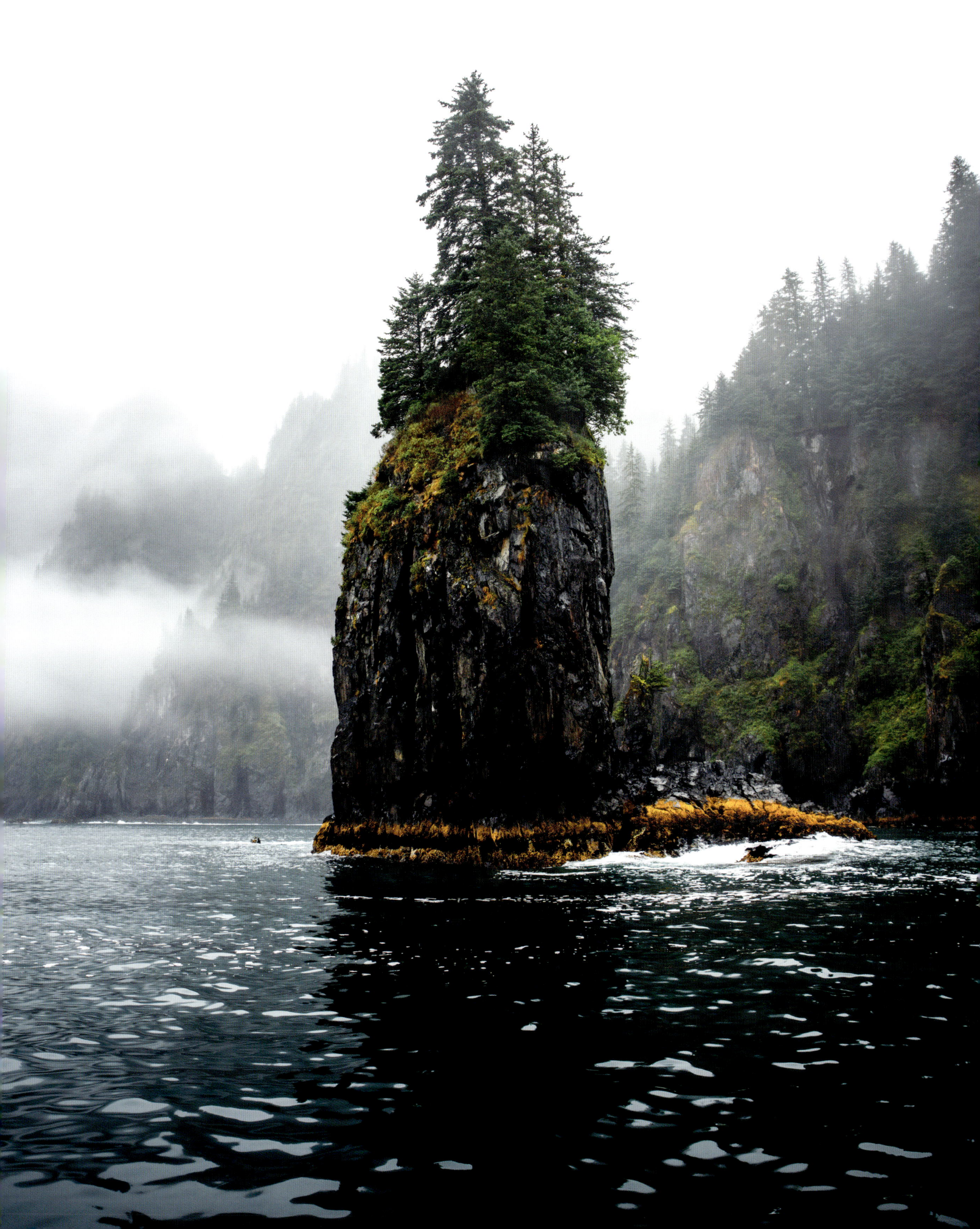

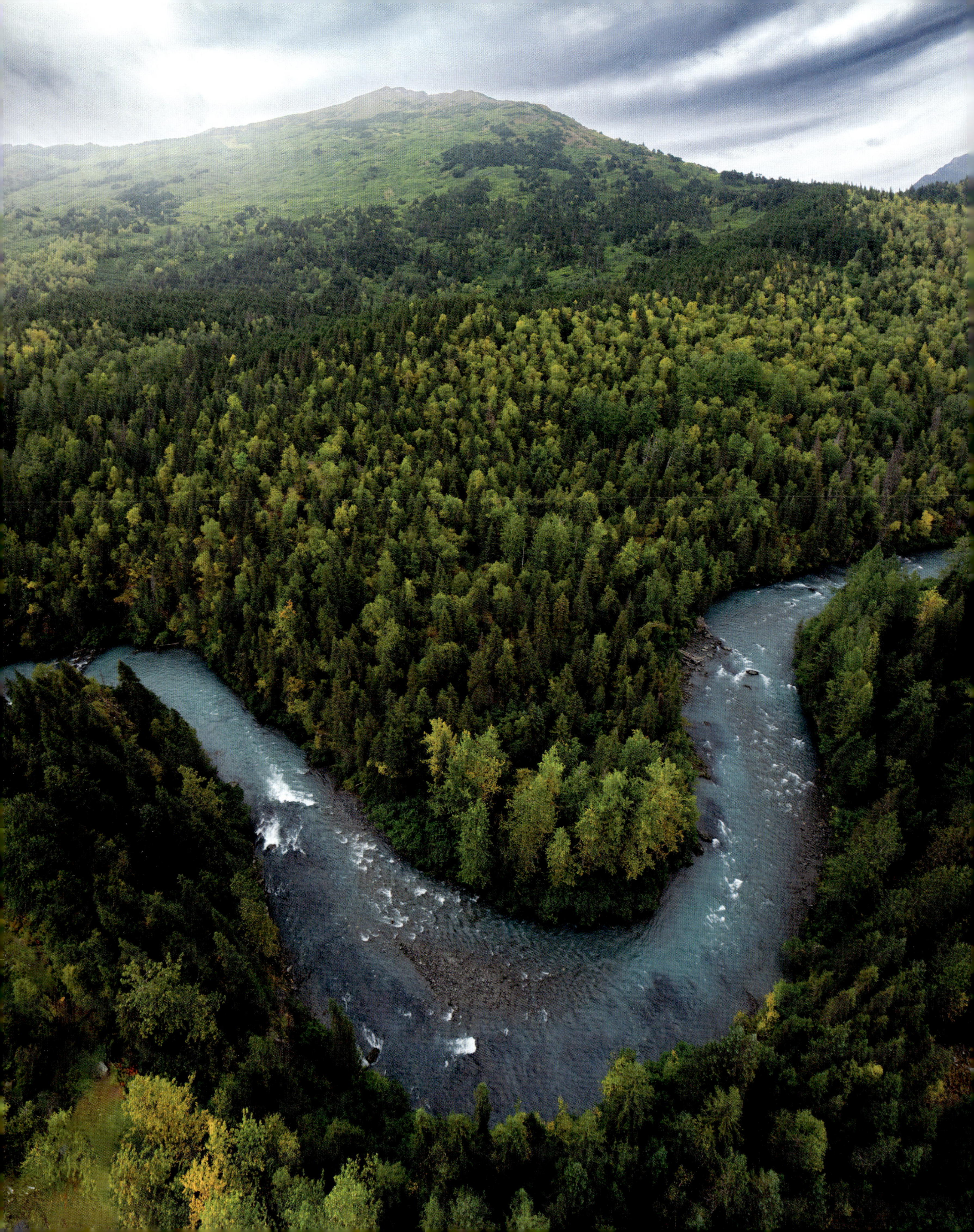

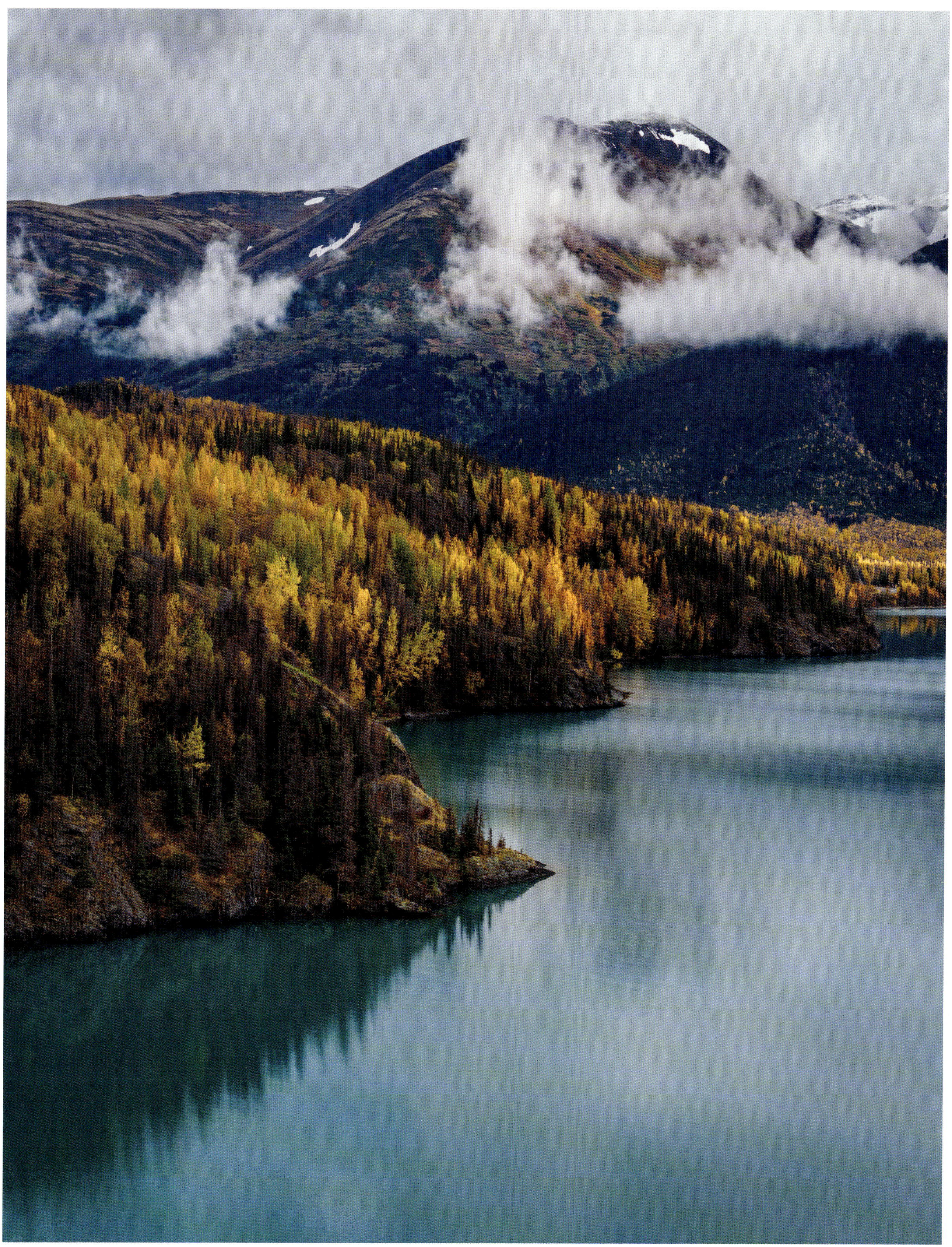

Above: Kenai Lake | Opposite: Along the Seward Highway

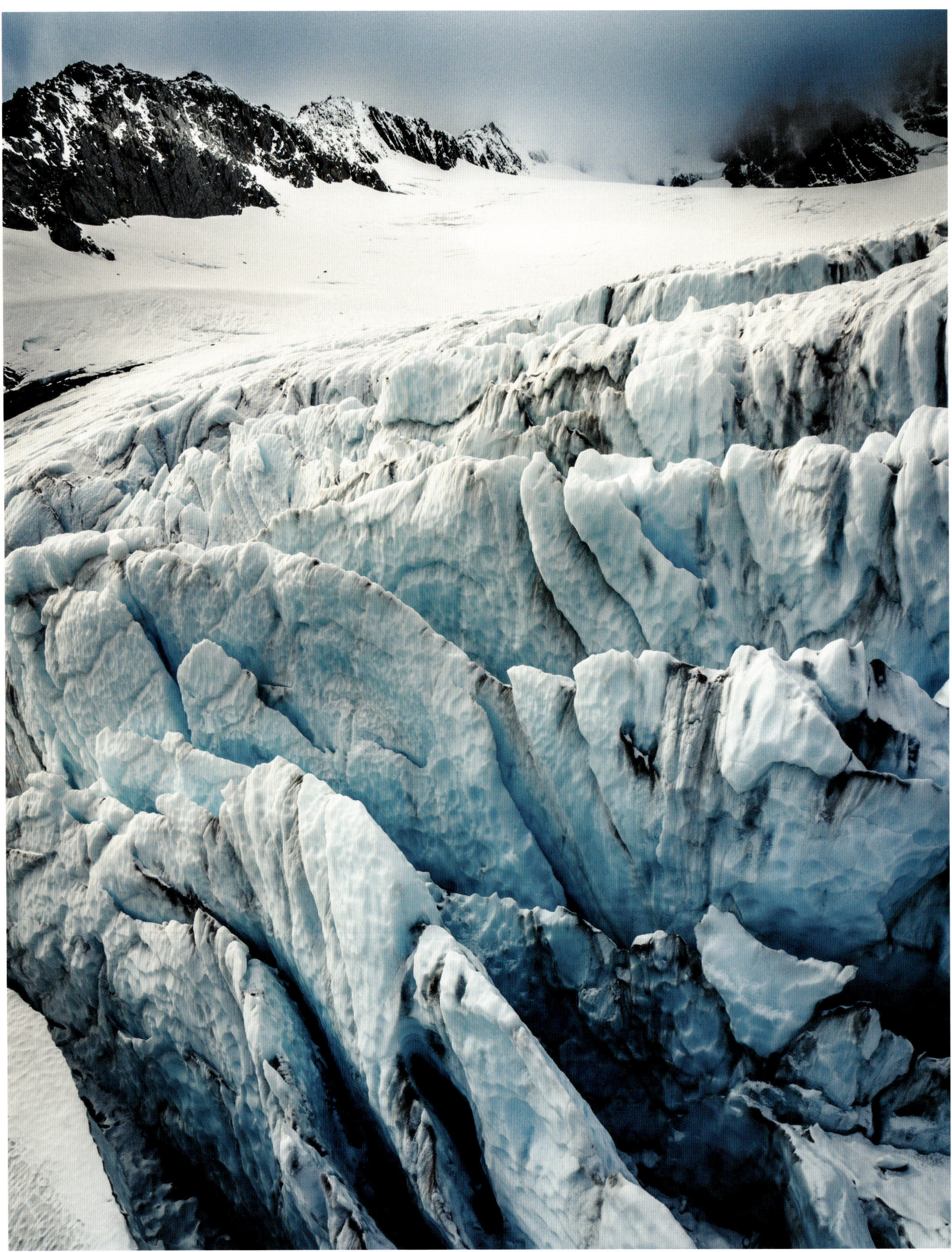

Above: Twenty-Seven Mile Glacier, Chugach Mountains | Opposite: Kenai River along the Sterling Highway

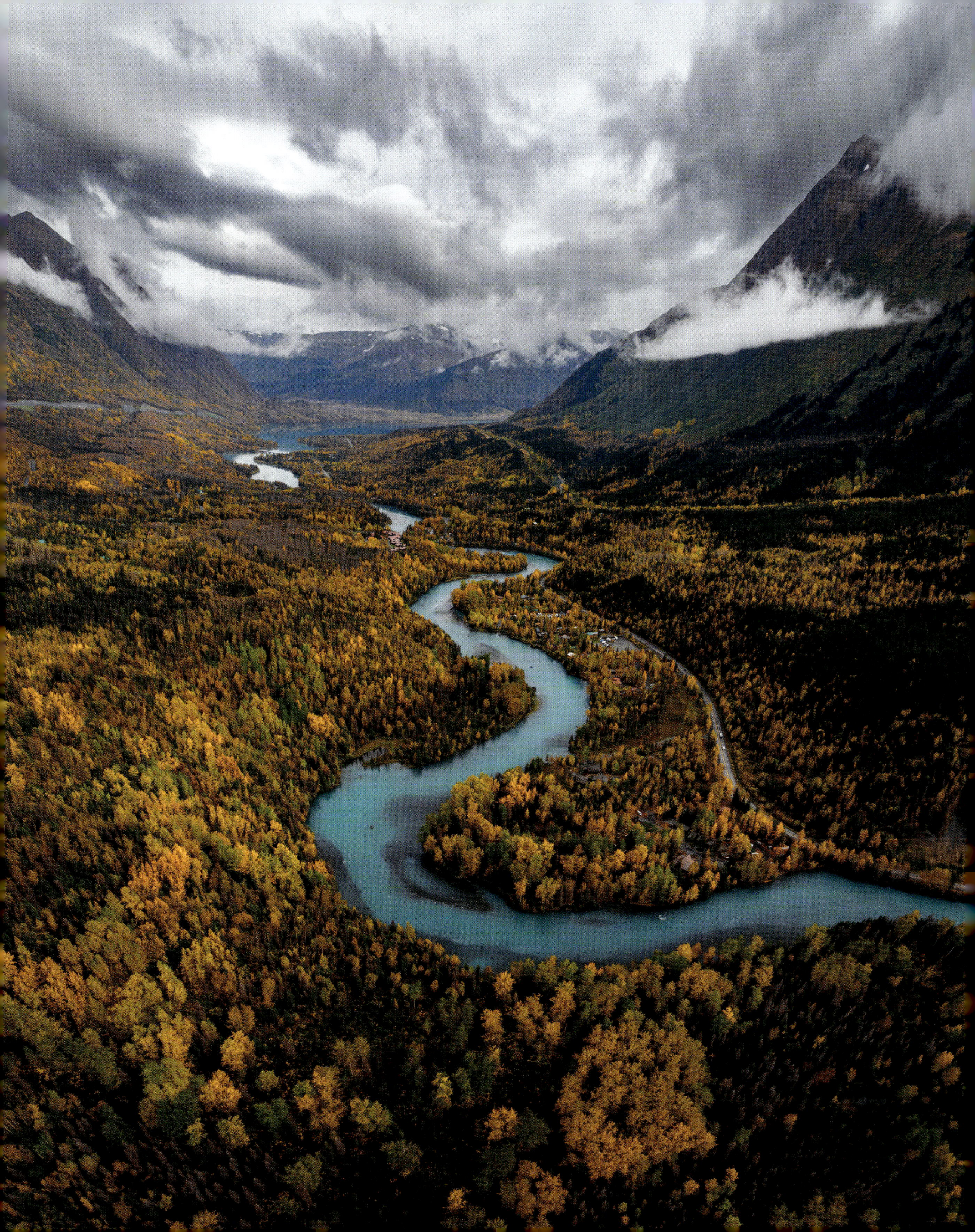

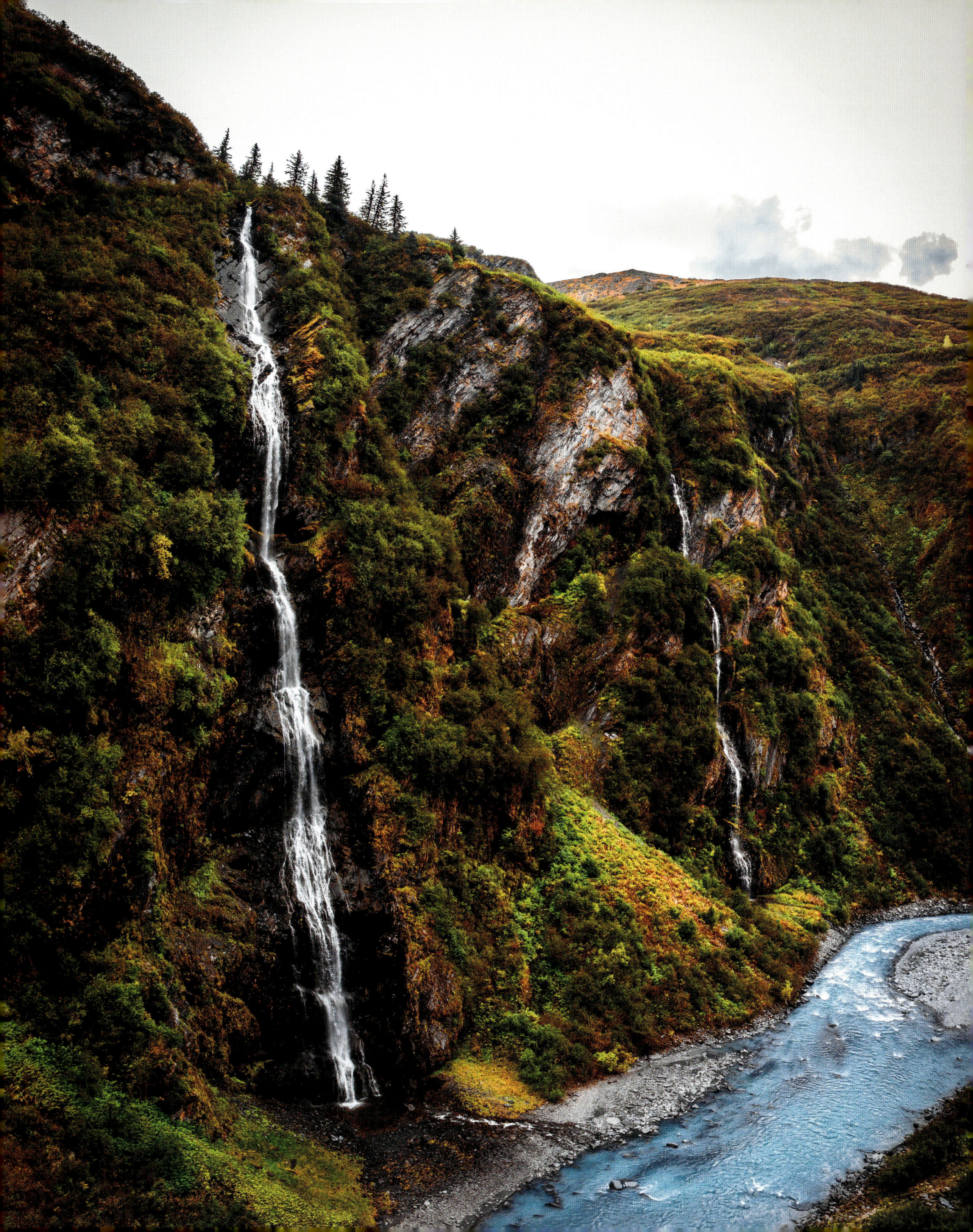

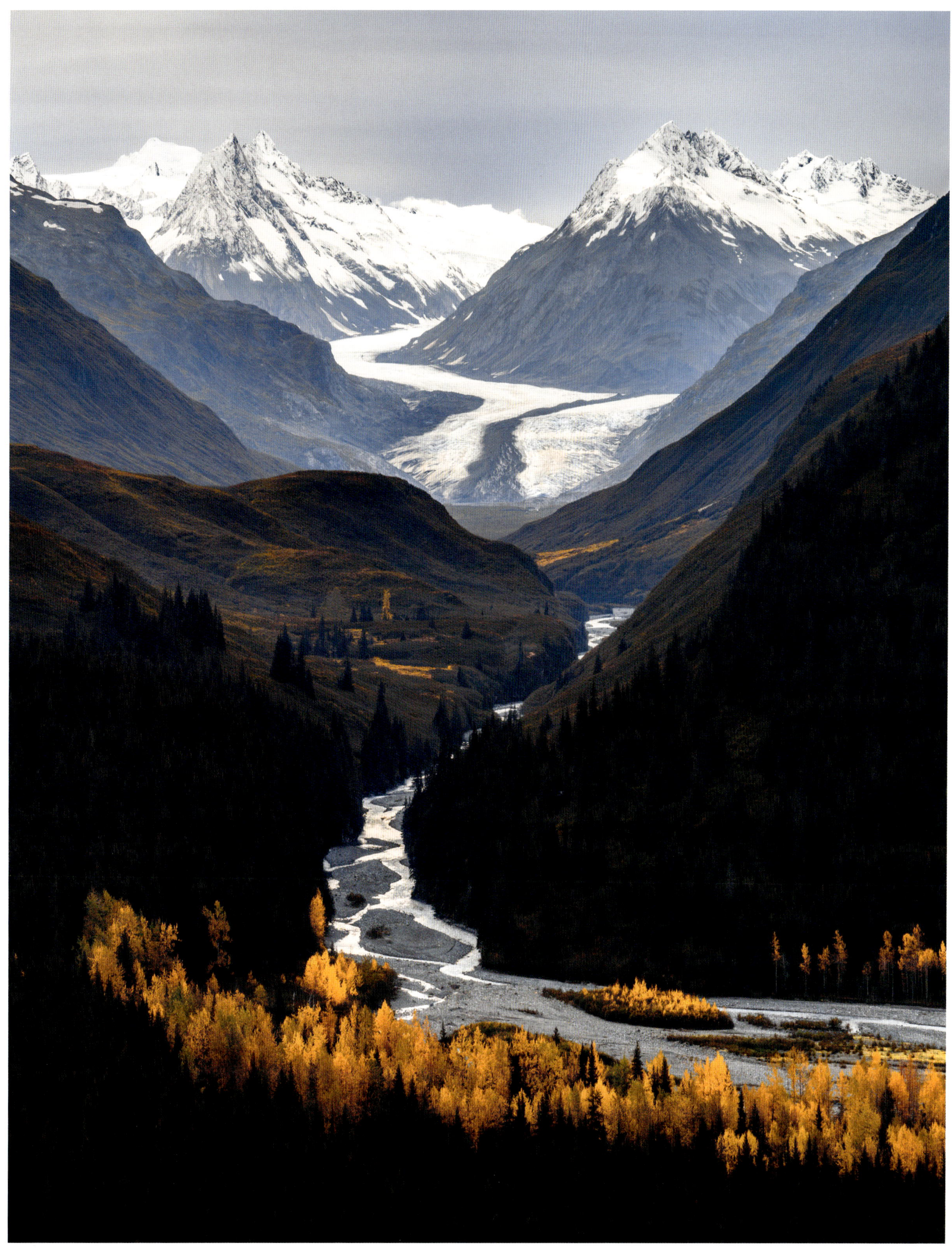

Above: Wortmanns Glacier and Creek | Opposite: Bridal Veil Falls, Richardson Highway

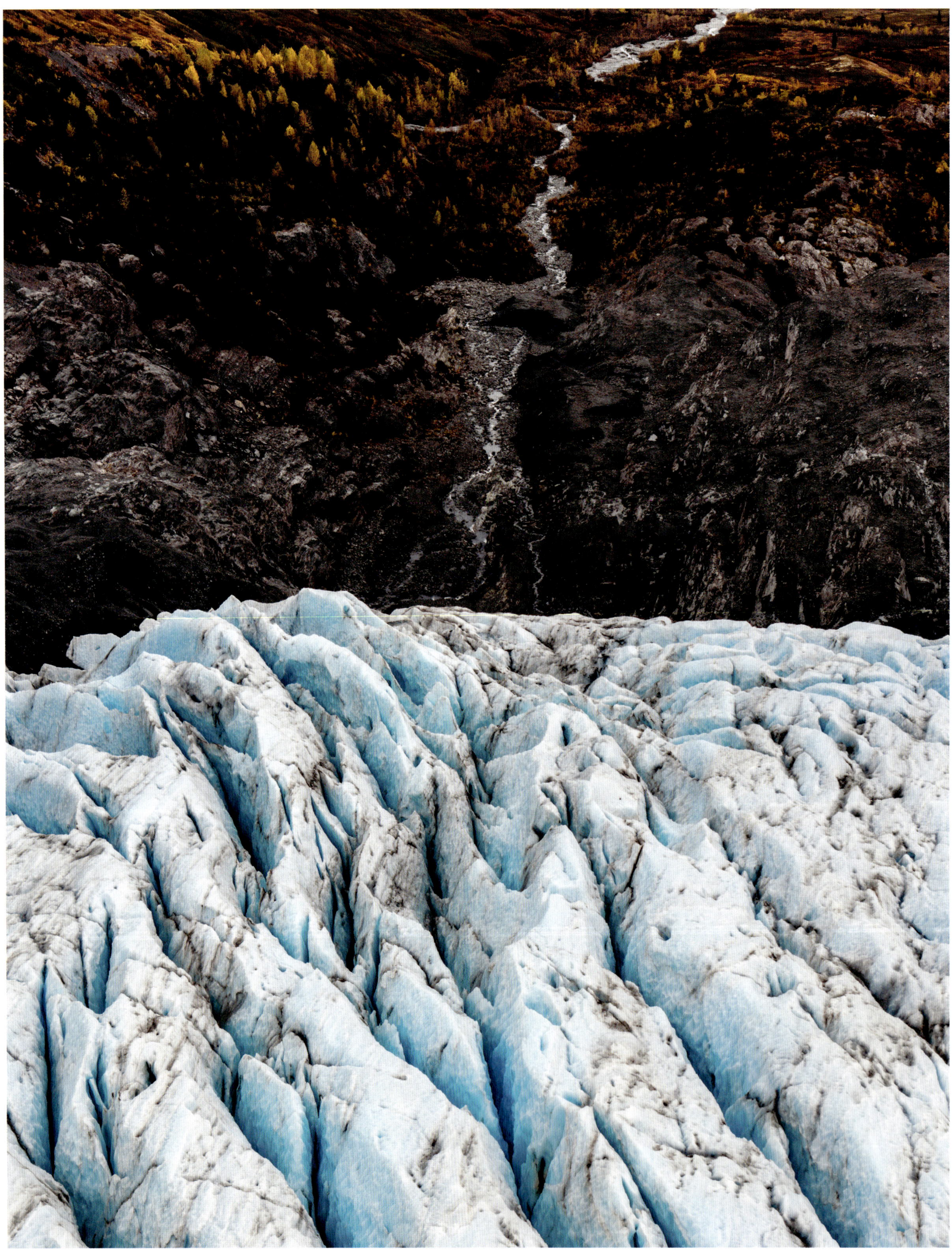

Above and opposite: Worthington Glacier, Thompson Pass

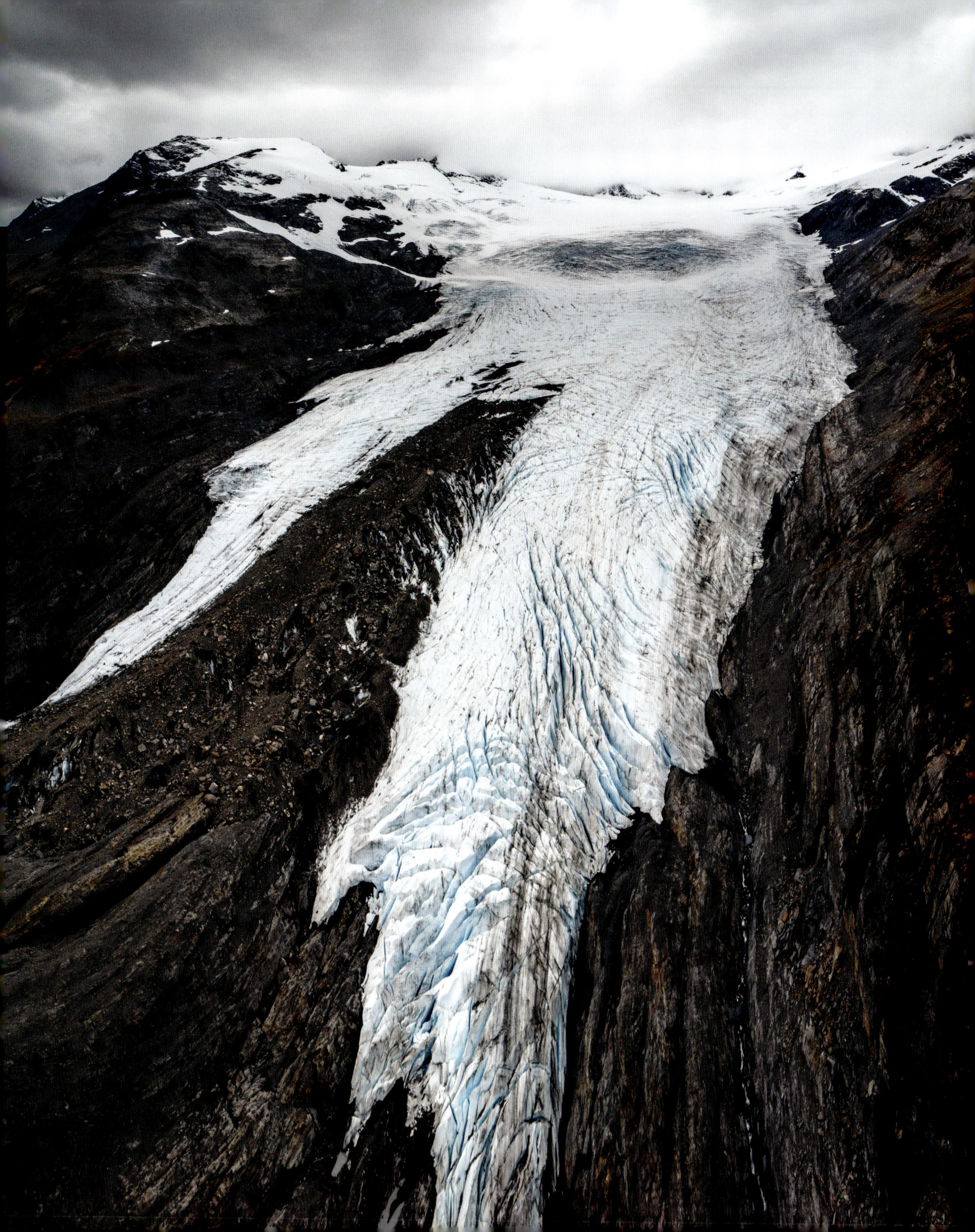

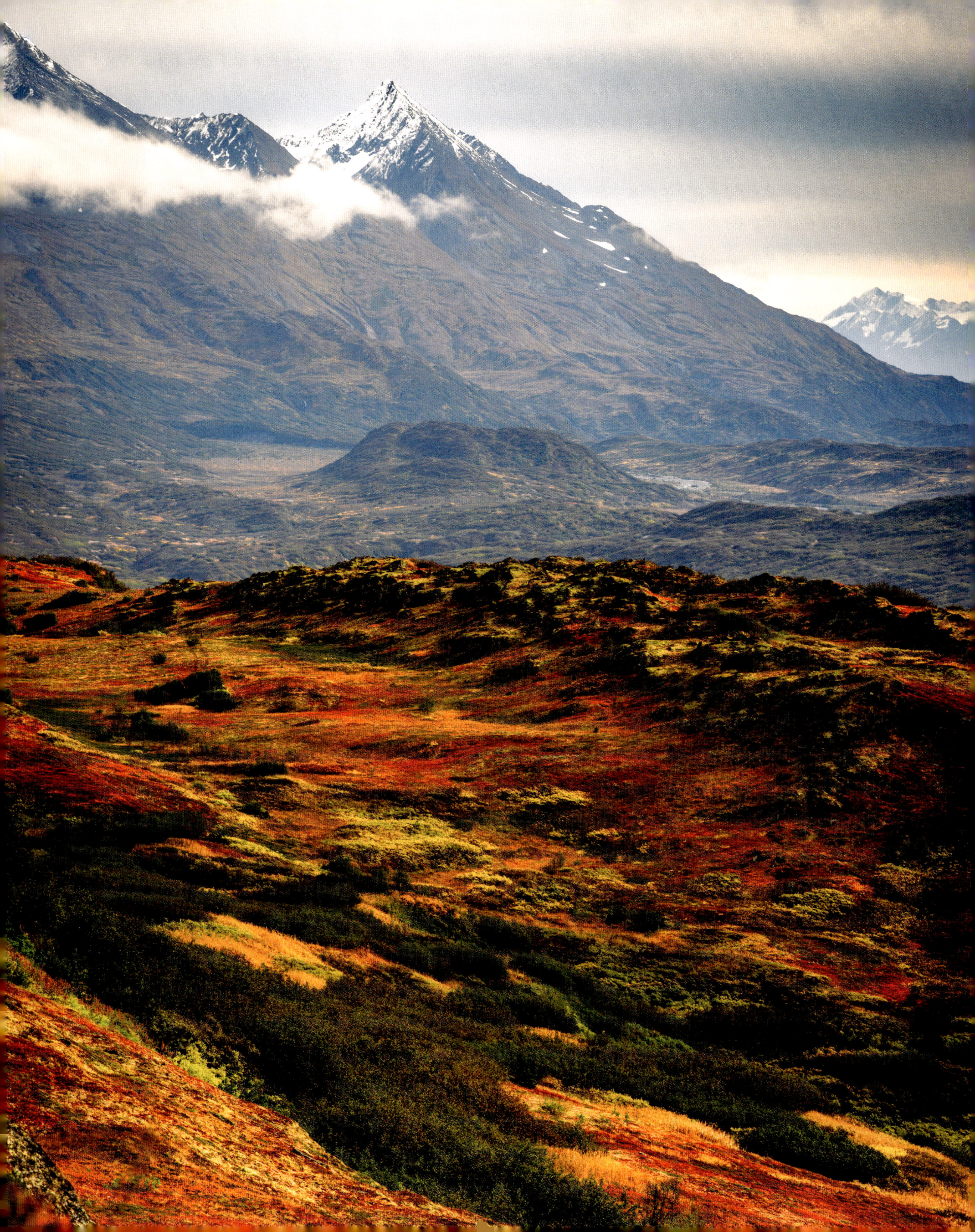

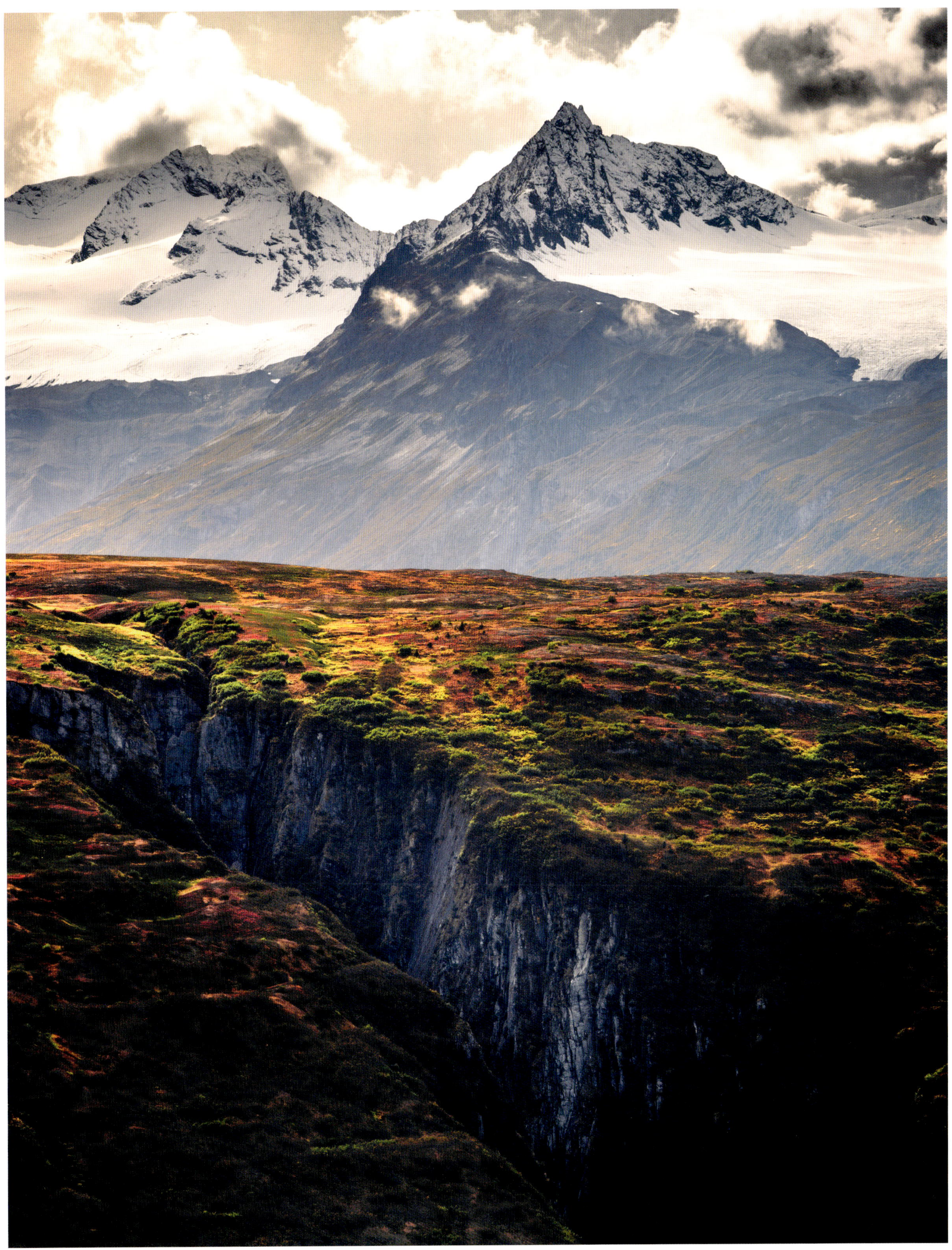

Above and opposite: Thompson Pass, Chugach Mountains

KATMAI NATIONAL PARK & PRESERVE

Watching a grizzly bear catch salmon mid-leap at Brooks Falls is one of the most iconic wildlife experiences in North America. But Katmai is more than bears—it's a wild land of smoldering volcanoes, vast tundra, alpine lakes, and the haunting beauty of the Valley of Ten Thousand Smokes. Remote and raw, Katmai is a true frontier of wilderness and wonder.

Region: Pacific

State: Alaska

Coordinates: 58°30'00.0"N 155°00'00.0"W

Focal features: A dramatic blend of active volcanoes, vast wilderness, and dense brown bear populations centered around Brooks River and Naknek Lake

Formation attributes: Created after the 1912 eruption of Novarupta, one of the largest volcanic eruptions in recorded history, which formed the Valley of Ten Thousand Smokes—a 40-square-mile (103.6km²) ash flow.

Fun fact: Katmai is home to the highest concentration of brown bears anywhere in the world—sometimes over a hundred in the Brooks Camp area alone during peak salmon runs.

Best time to visit: Late June to September, with July offering peak bear-viewing at Brooks Falls and September featuring stunning fall colors and more active, foraging bears.

How to access: Katmai can be reached by plane from Anchorage or King Salmon (no roads lead to the park), and floatplanes and boats provide access to Brooks Camp, the primary visitor area. Backcountry access typically requires guided tours or bush pilot services. Note that there are no roads, gas stations, or amenities outside Brooks Camp, so plan thoroughly and prepare for remote travel.

Things to consider: Bear safety is essential. Follow all park guidelines, use designated viewing platforms, and carry bear spray if hiking. Weather is often unpredictable, so pack warm layers, waterproof gear, and sturdy footwear.

RECOMMENDED TRAILS:

Brooks Falls Trail: *1.2-mile (1.9km) round trip; 100 feet (30m) elevation gain; easy.* Walk through boreal forest to one of the world's best bear-viewing platforms.

Valley of Ten Thousand Smokes Trail: *3.4-mile (5.5km) round trip; 1,000 feet (305m) elevation gain; moderate.* Descend into the ash-filled valley and explore the surreal volcanic landscape.

Dumpling Mountain Trail: *9-mile (14.5km) round trip; 2,600 feet (792m) elevation gain; strenuous.* Offers sweeping views of Naknek Lake, Brooks Camp, and the surrounding mountains.

Tips for taking a great photo

- Use a telephoto lens (300mm or higher) for bear photography from a safe distance.
- Early morning and late afternoon provide the best light, especially at Brooks Falls.
- A fast shutter speed (1/1000 or faster) is key to freeze action during salmon jumps and bear catches.
- Bring a dry bag and weatherproof gear; rain is frequent, and conditions can change quickly.

Opposite: A bear along the shore of Naknek Lake in Katmai National Park

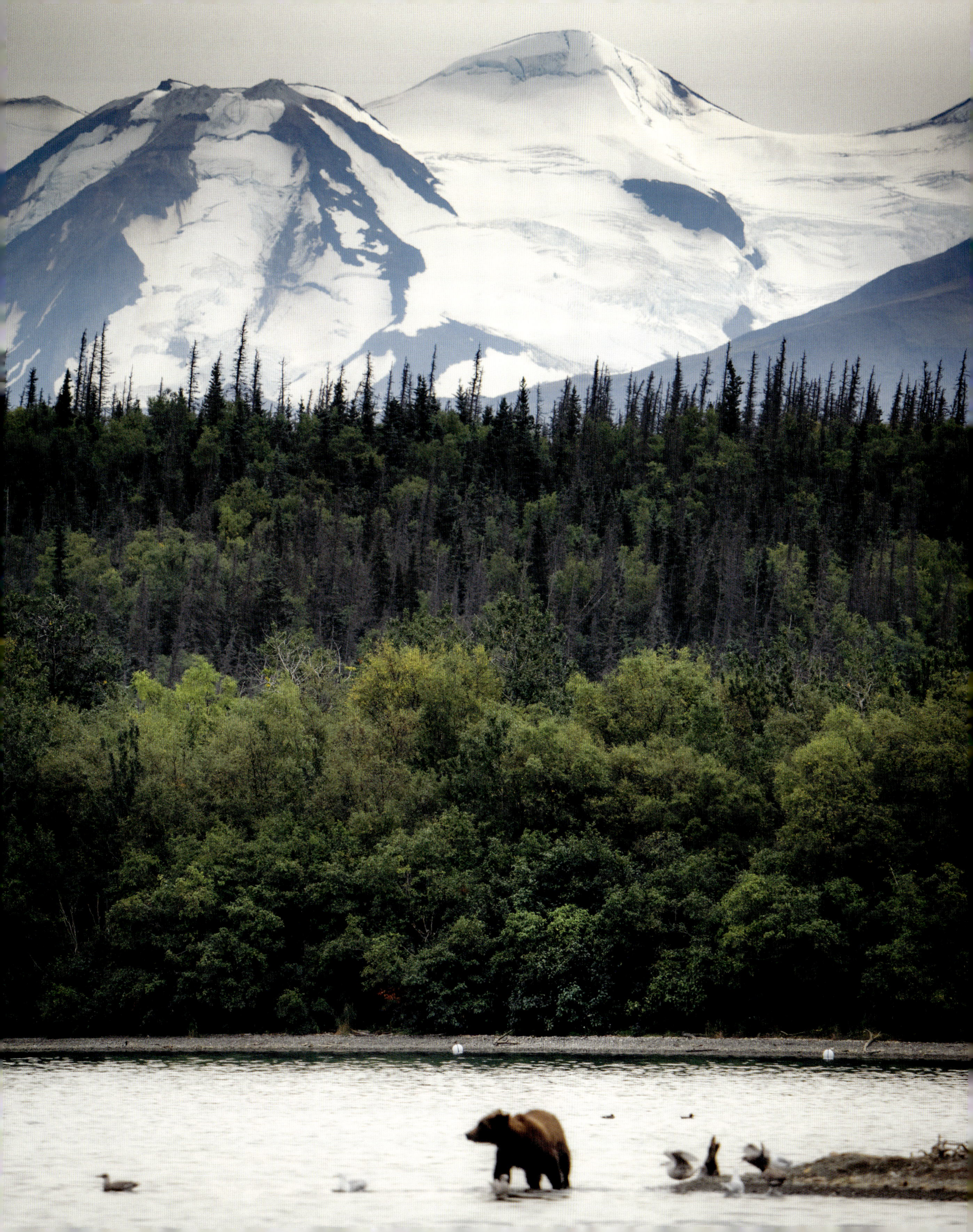

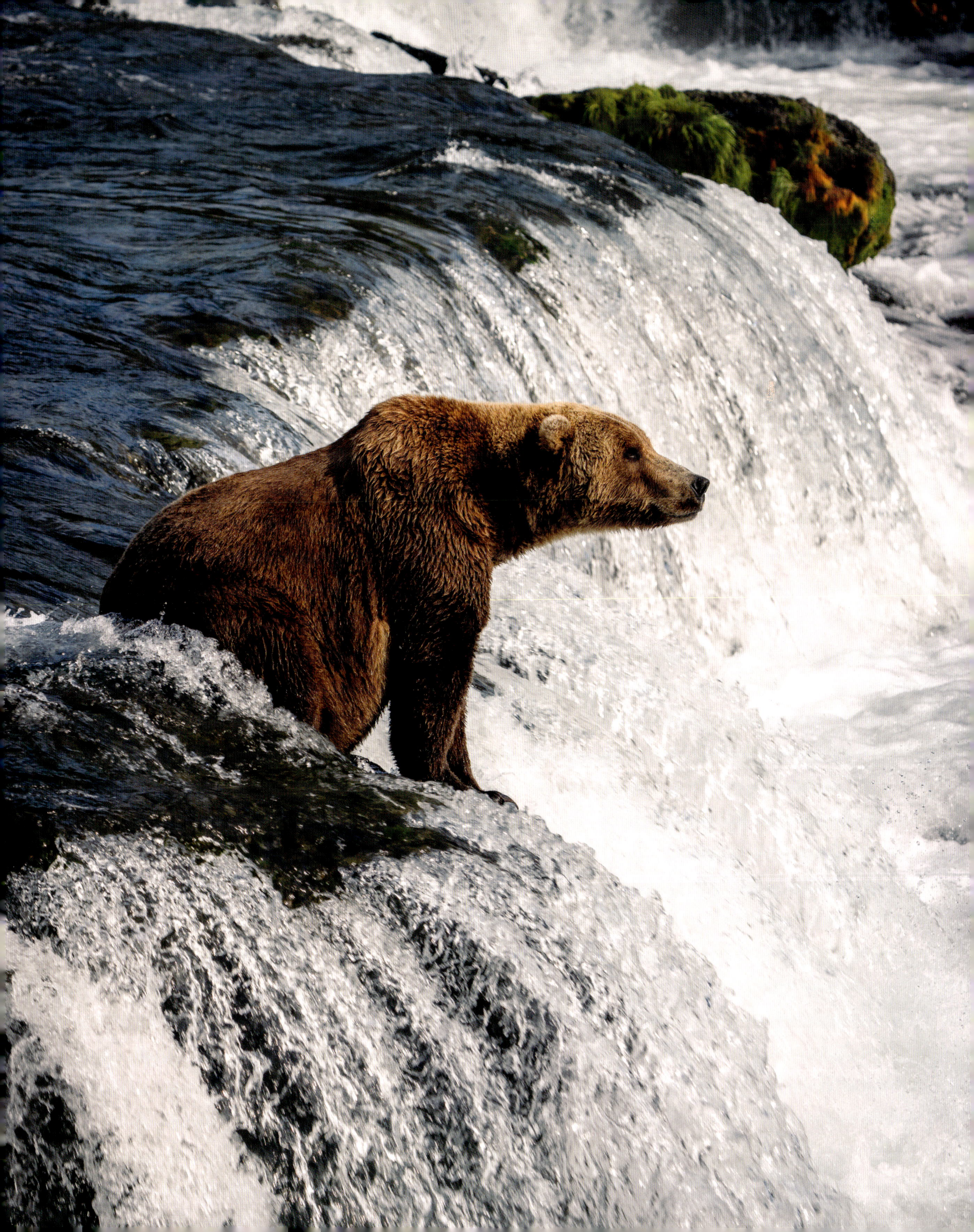

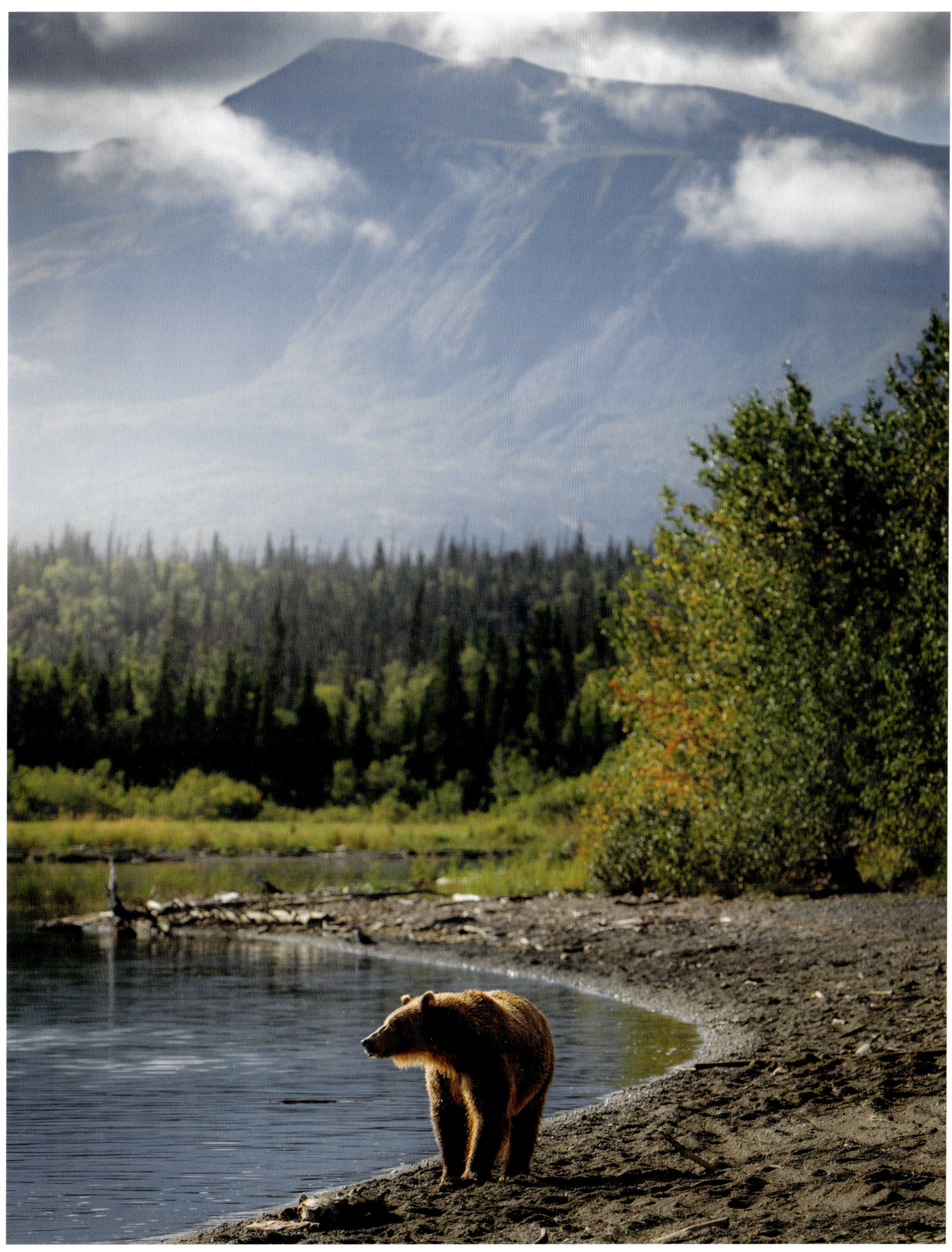

Above: A grizzly along the water in Katmai National Park | Opposite: A grizzly sitting on Brooks Falls | Pages 44–45: Bruin Bay, Cook Inlet

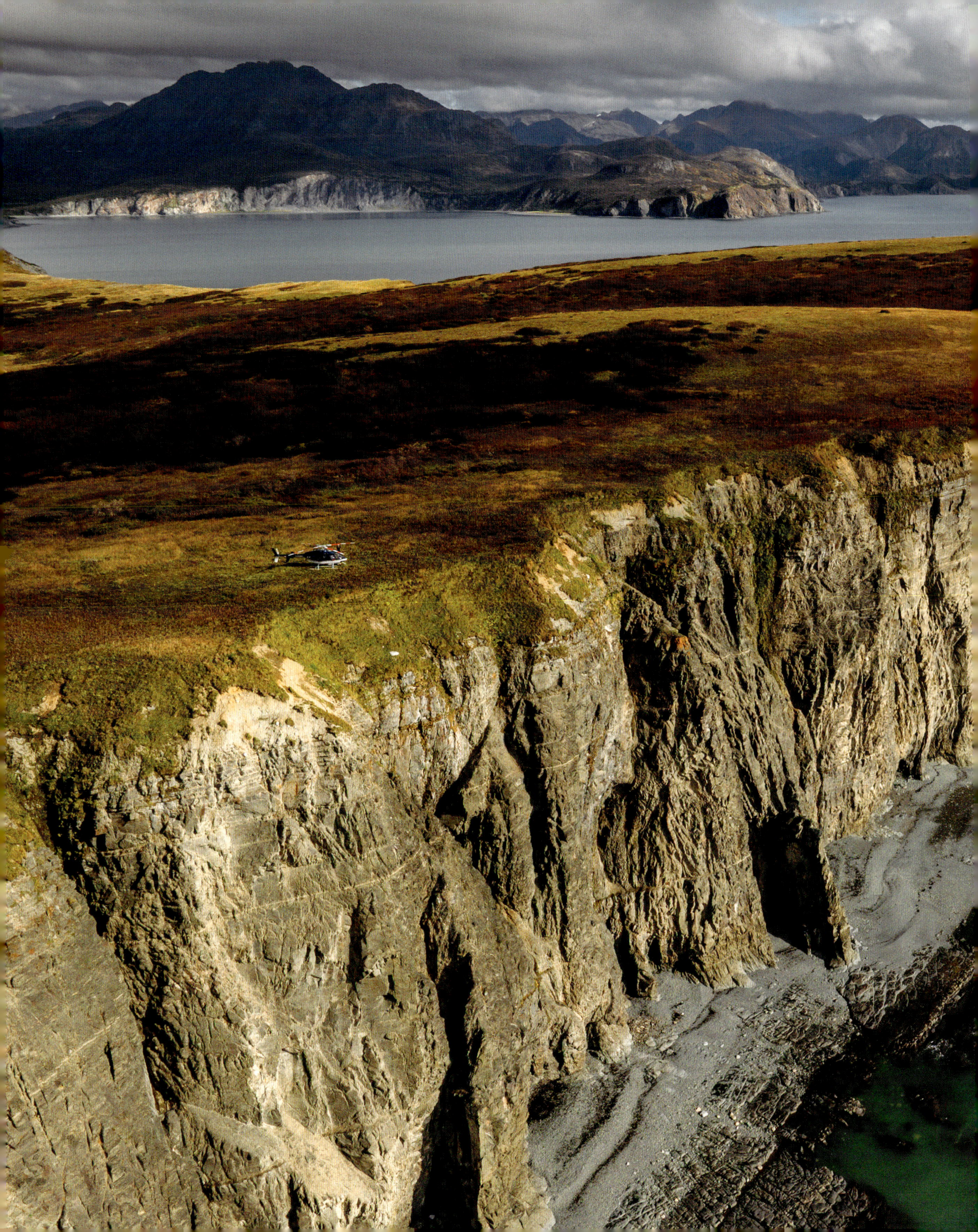

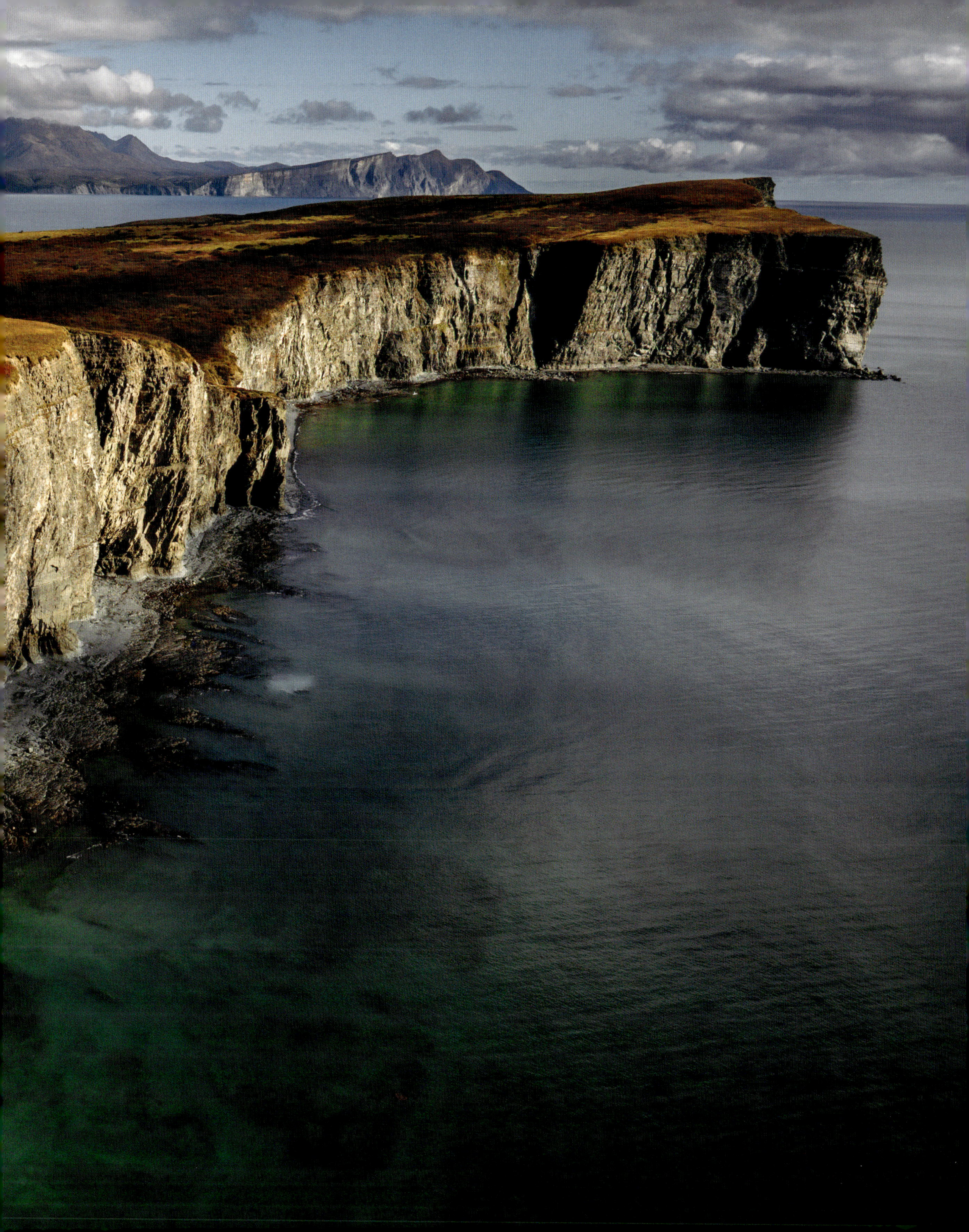

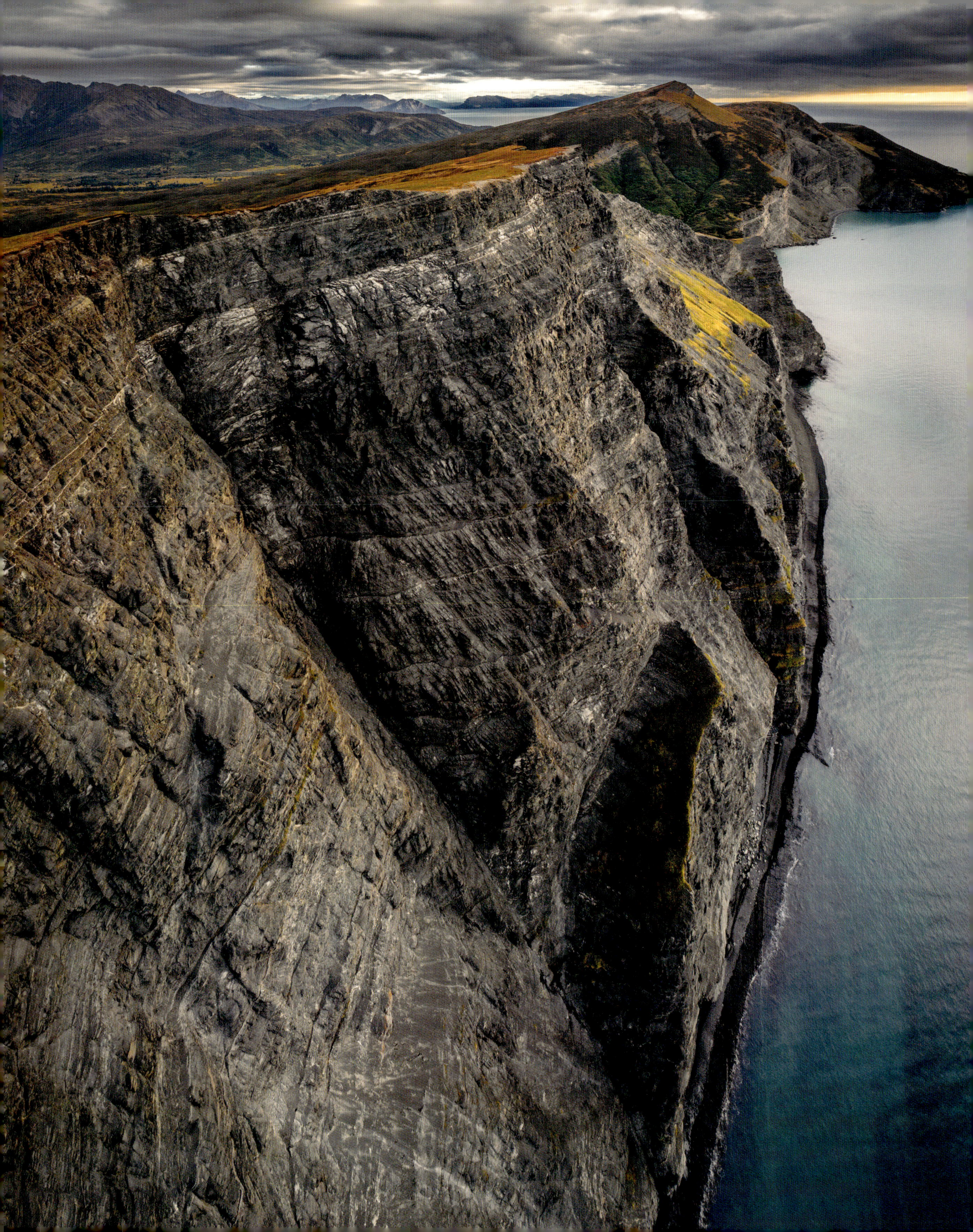

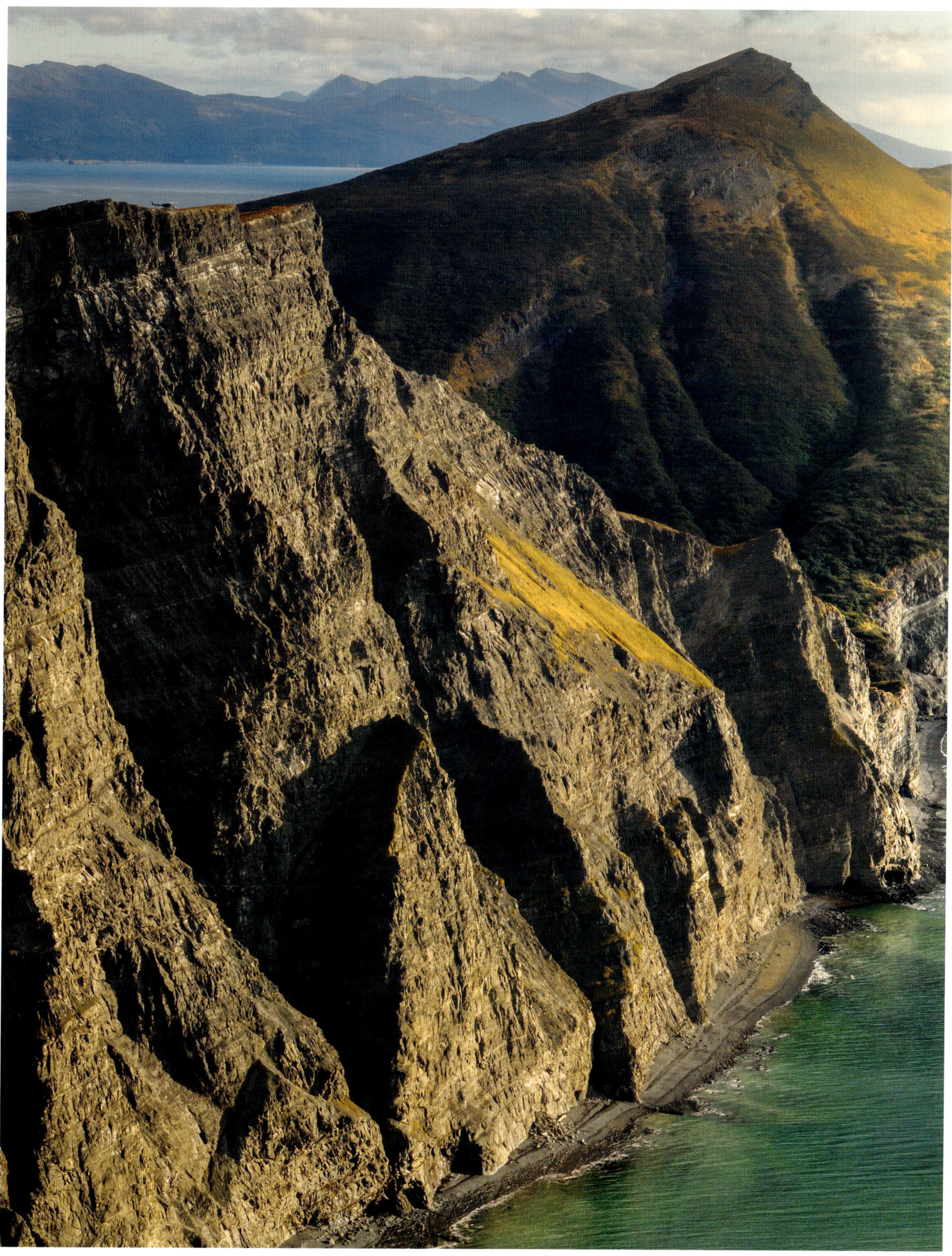

Above and opposite: Fortification Bluff, Step Mountain, Kamishak Bay, Cook Inlet

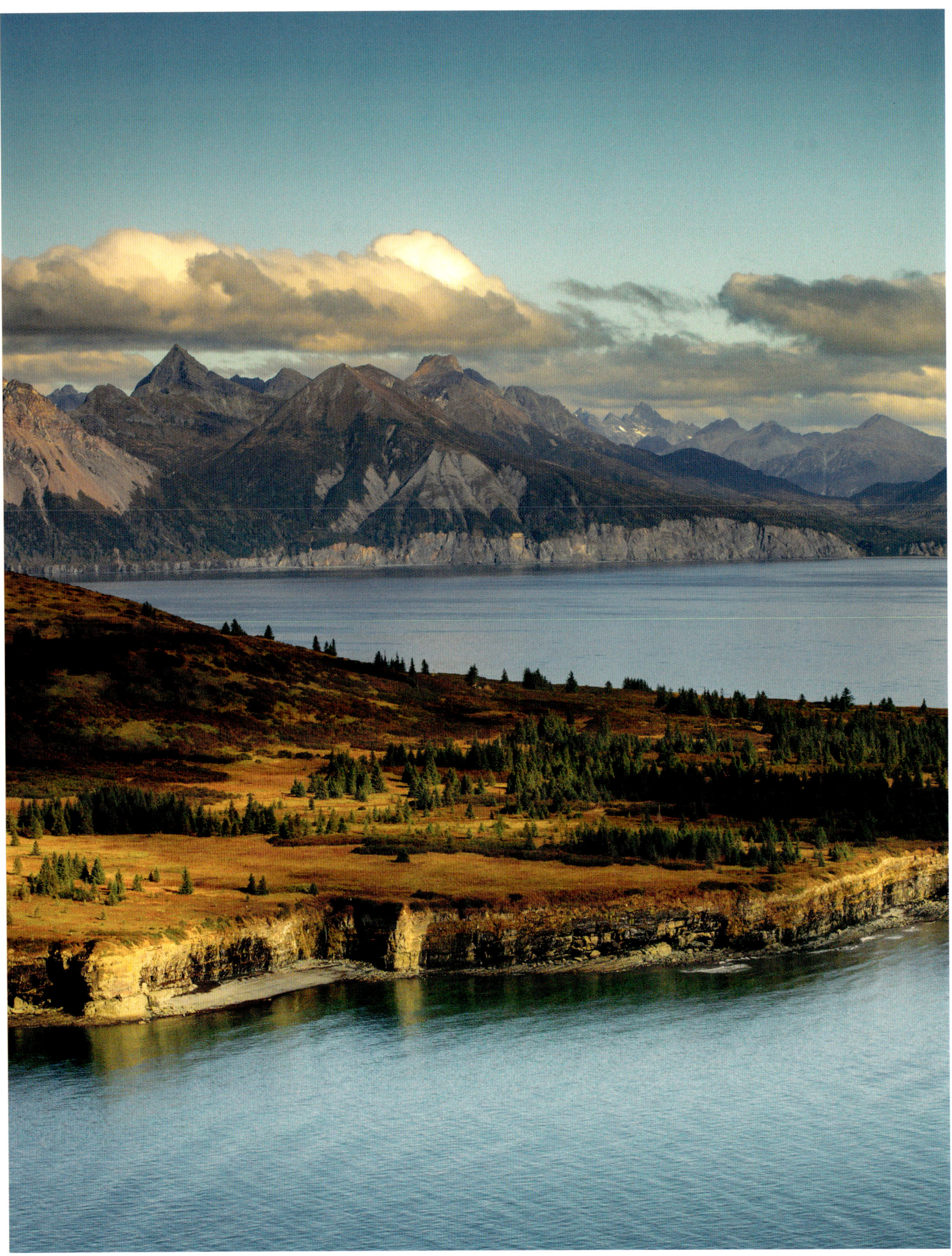

Above and opposite: Lake Clark National Park

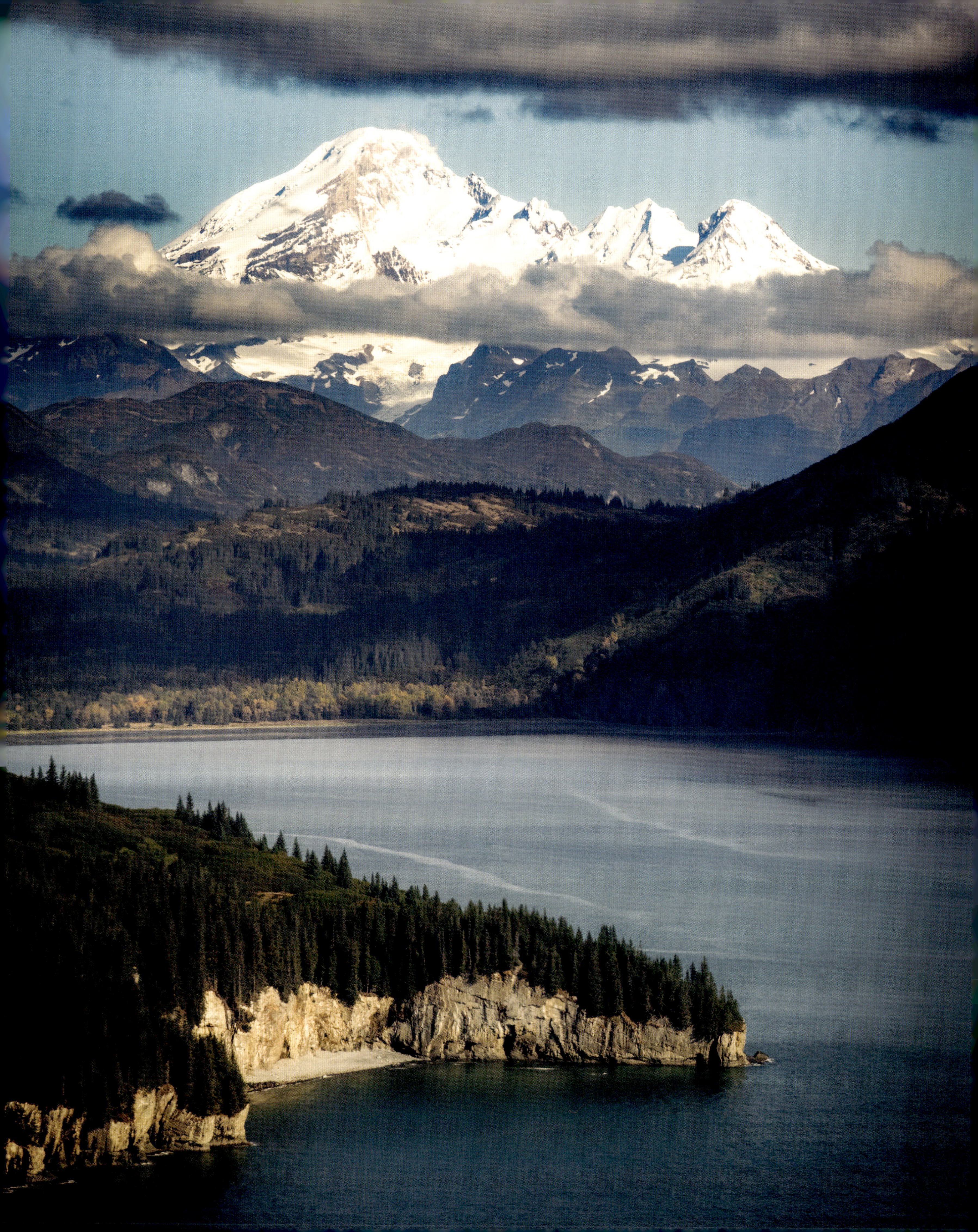

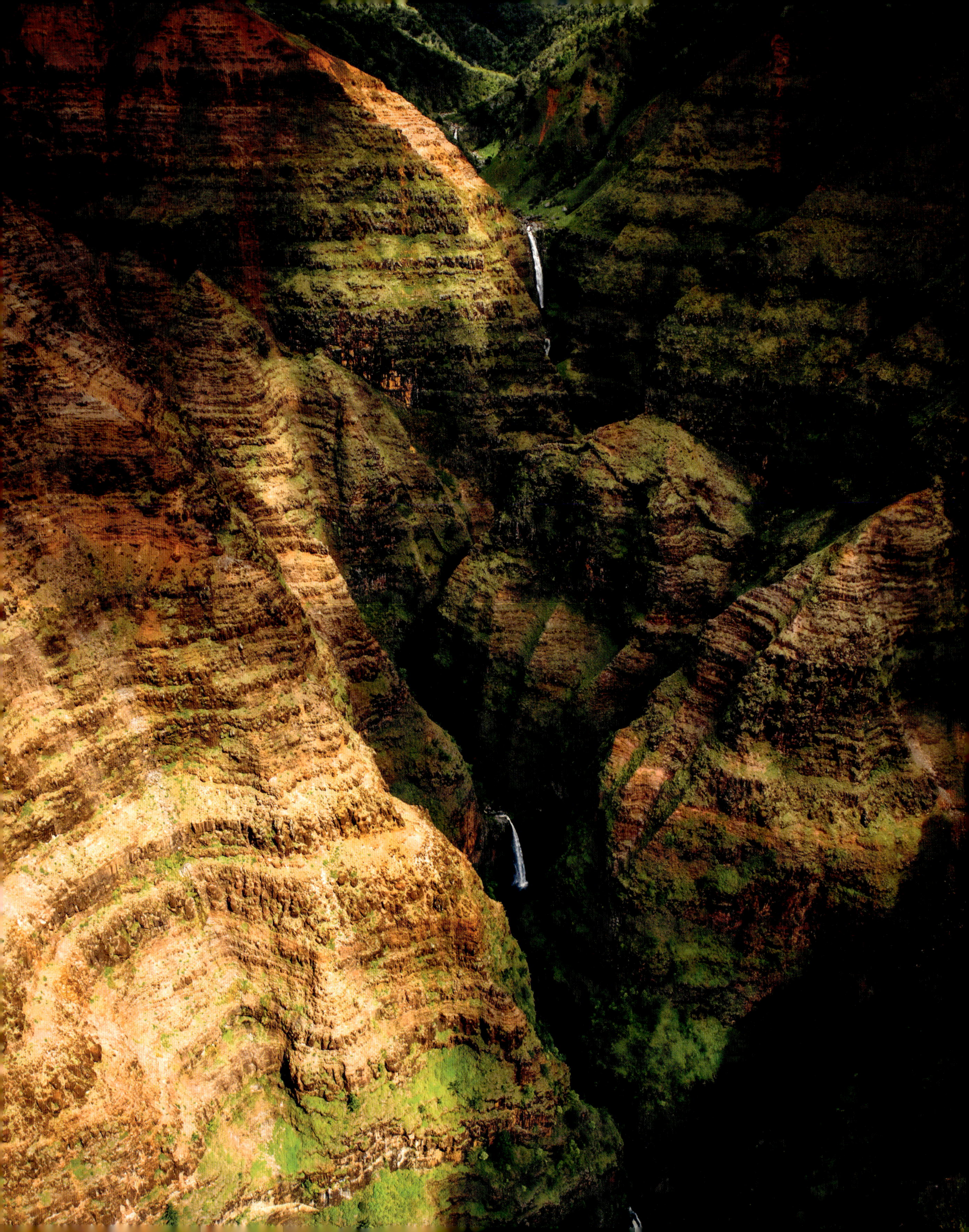

HAWAI'I

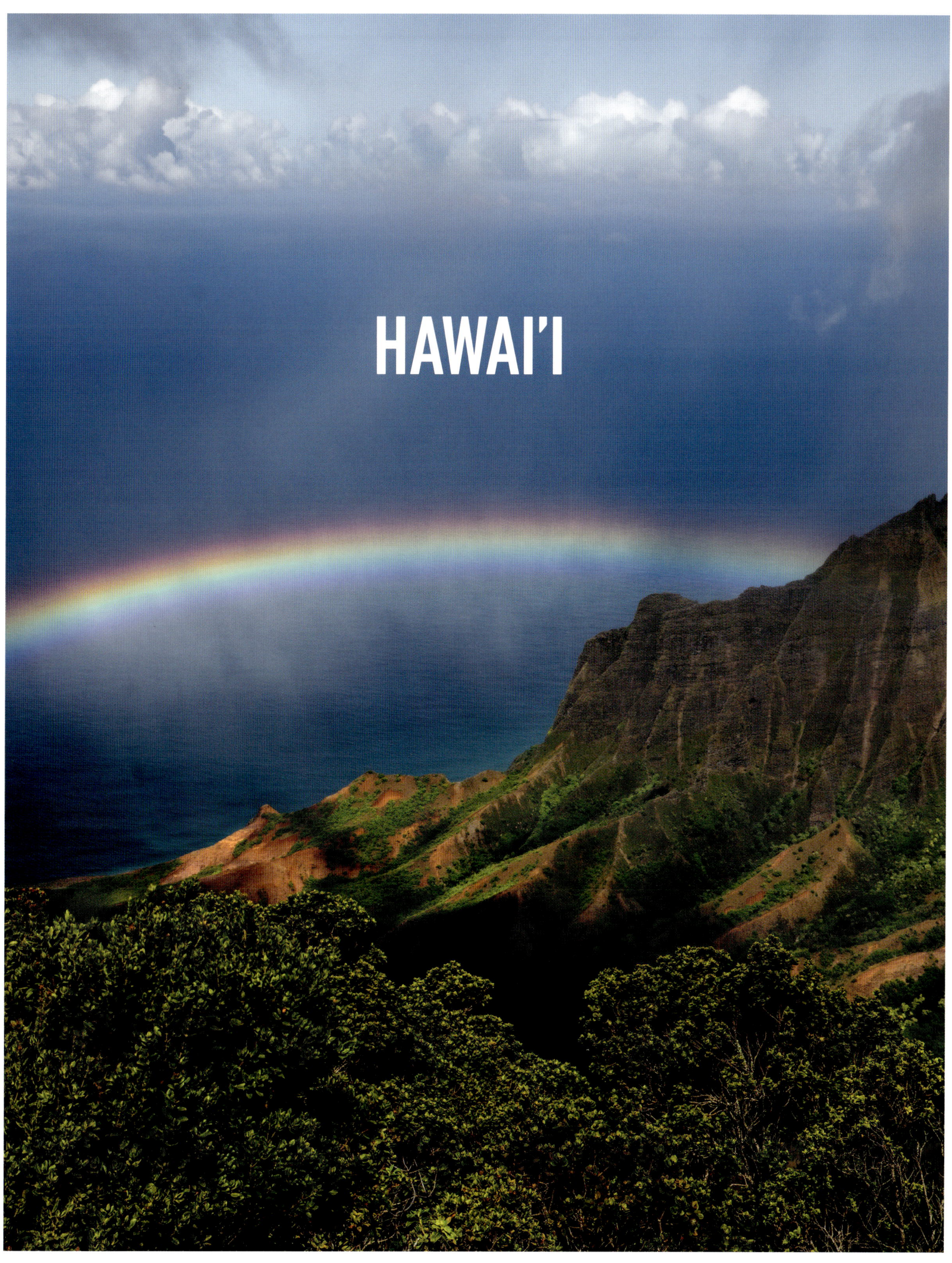

KAUAʻI

When you explore Kauaʻi, you'll feel as though you're wandering through *Jurassic Park* (parts of it were filmed here!), with its jagged cliffs, emerald valleys carved by waterfalls, and untouched beaches. Known as the Garden Isle, Kauaʻi offers a raw, verdant beauty that feels both ancient and alive, a showcase of natural grandeur and biodiversity. Whether you're hiking along the Nā Pali Coast or watching the sunrise over Waimea Canyon, the island's landscapes are unforgettable.

Region: Pacific

State: Hawaiʻi

Coordinates: 22°05'18.7"N 159°29'46.4"W

Focal features: Towering sea cliffs, lush rainforests, and deep canyons

Formation attributes: Formed by volcanic activity over five million years ago, Kauaʻi is the oldest of the main Hawaiian Islands, giving it time to erode into some of the most iconic topography in the Pacific.

Fun fact: Mount Waiʻaleʻale near the center of the island is one of the wettest places on Earth, receiving over 33 feet (10m) of rain annually.

Best time to visit: April to June and September to November for ideal weather, fewer crowds, and vibrant landscapes. Winter brings heavier rain but also lush greenery and dramatic surf.

How to access: Fly into Lihue Airport (LIH), then explore the island by car. Many iconic sites are accessible by road, while others require hiking or helicopter access due to the island's rugged terrain.

Things to consider: Weather in Kauaʻi can change quickly, especially in mountainous areas. Pack layers, rain protection, and proper footwear. Respect local customs and natural areas—many sacred sites and fragile ecosystems are present throughout the island.

RECOMMENDED TRAILS:

Waimea Canyon Trail (to Waipoʻo Falls): *3-mile (4.8km) round trip; 1,100 feet (335m) elevation gain; moderate.* Hike through the "Grand Canyon of the Pacific," with overlooks aplenty and valley views.

Sleeping Giant (Nounou) Trail: *3.2-mile (5.1km) round trip; 1000 feet (305m) elevation gain; moderate.* Hike to panoramic views of the east coast and inland mountain ridges from the summit.

Kalalau Trail (Nā Pali Coast): *19.8-mile (32km) round trip; 6,500 feet (1,981m) elevation gain; strenuous.* Sweeping coastal views, waterfalls, and sea caves. Permits are required for the full hike.

Tips for taking a great photo

- Sunrise at Kapaʻa or Hanalei Bay provides soft, golden light reflecting off the water and mountains.
- For dramatic aerial landscapes, a helicopter tour offers access to remote cliffs, waterfalls, and crater interiors.
- Use a polarizing filter to enhance the blues and greens in water and rainforest scenes.
- Cloud cover often creates moodier lighting inland—perfect for capturing misty mountains and jungle textures.

Page 50: Waimea Canyon State Park, Kauaʻi

Page 51: Kalalau Lookout, Nā Pali Coast, Kauaʻi

Opposite and pages 53–54: Nā Pali Coast, Kauaʻi

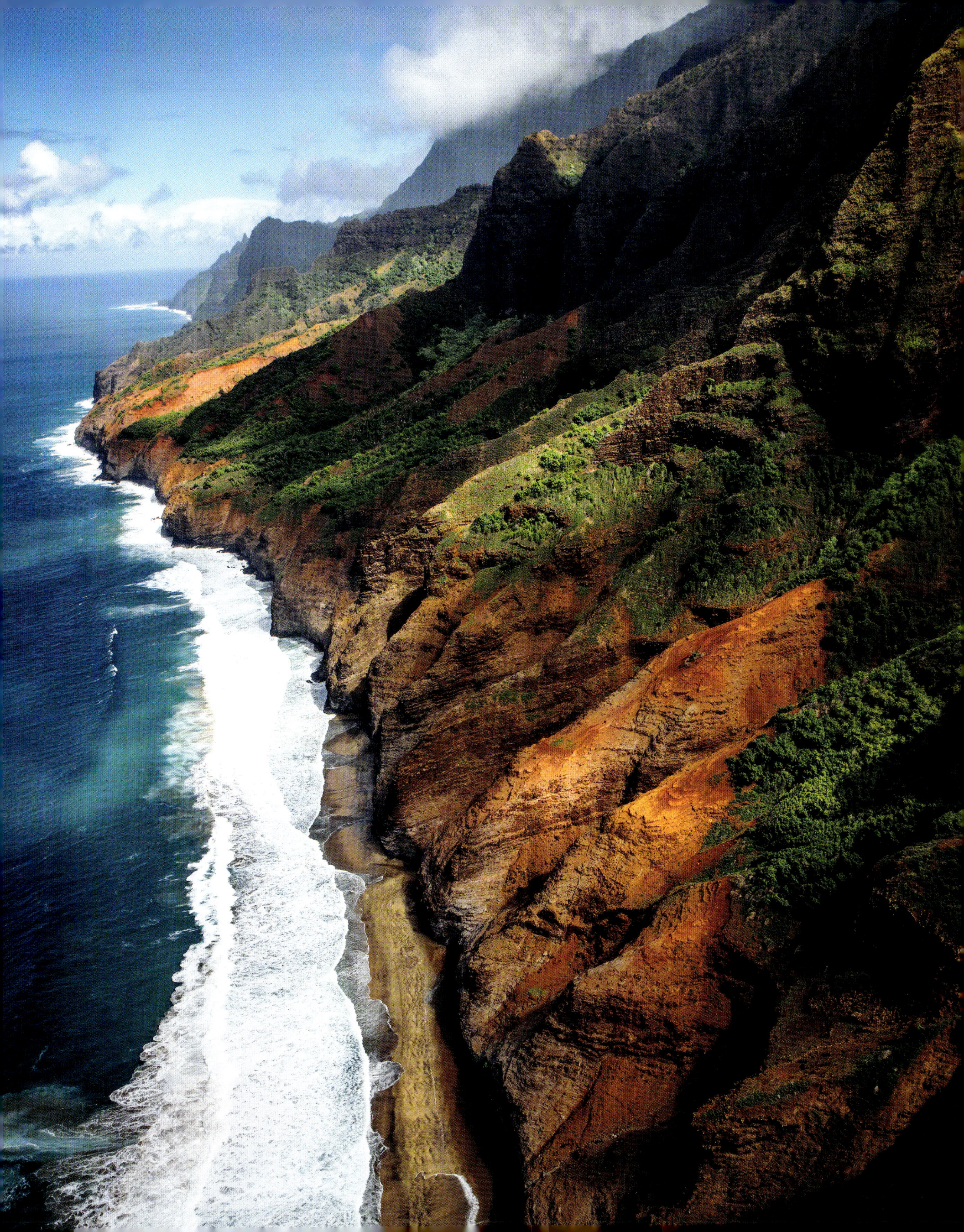

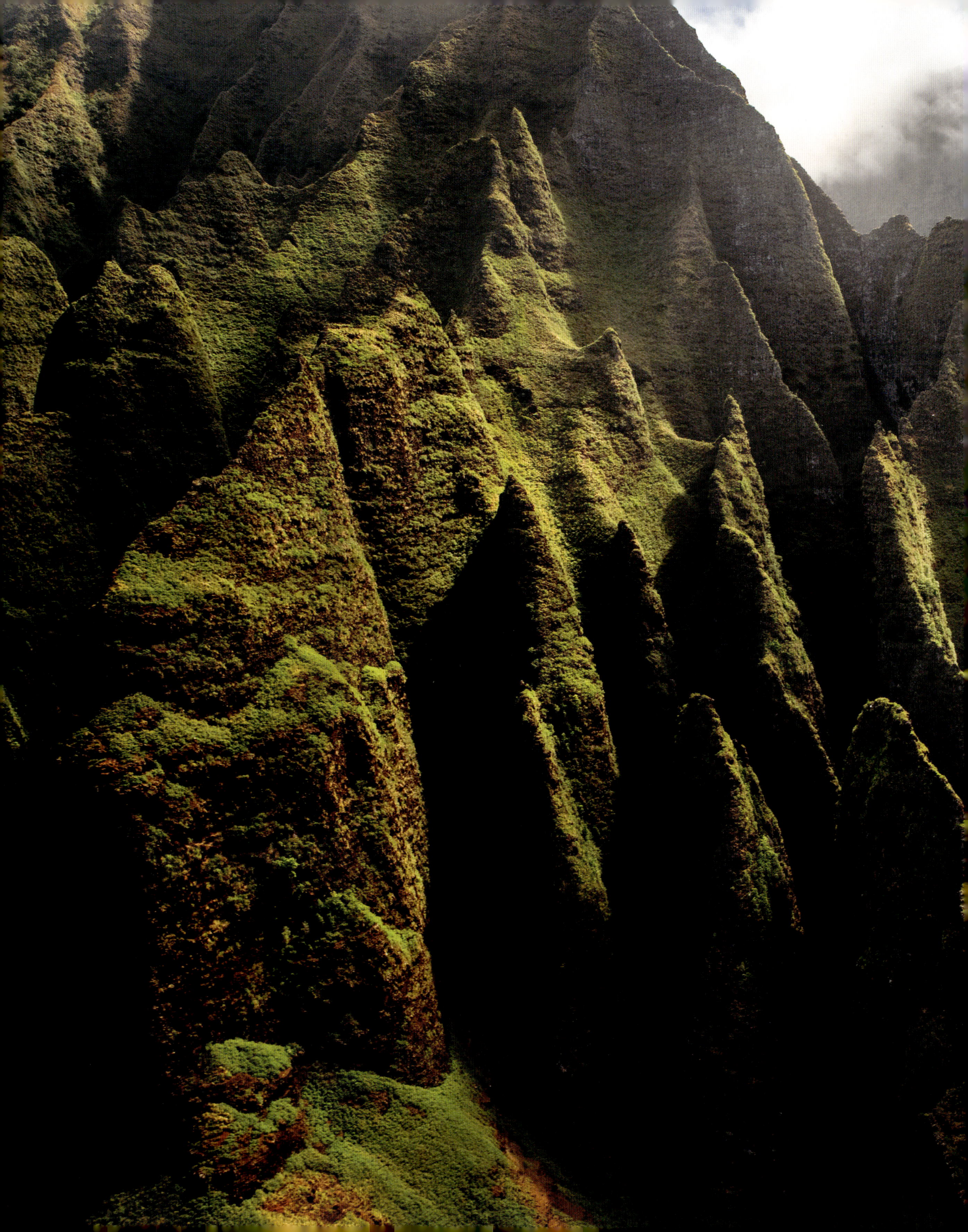

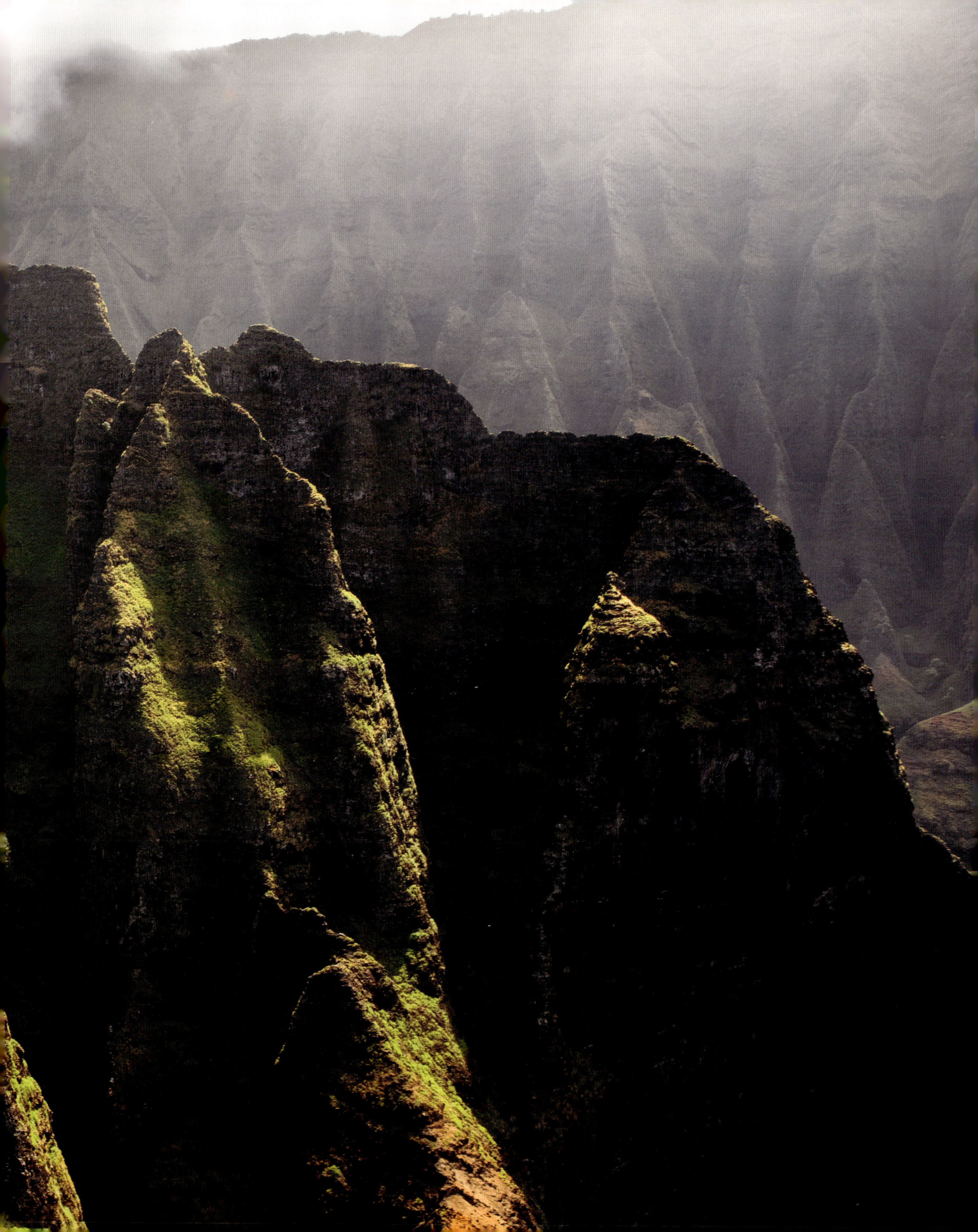

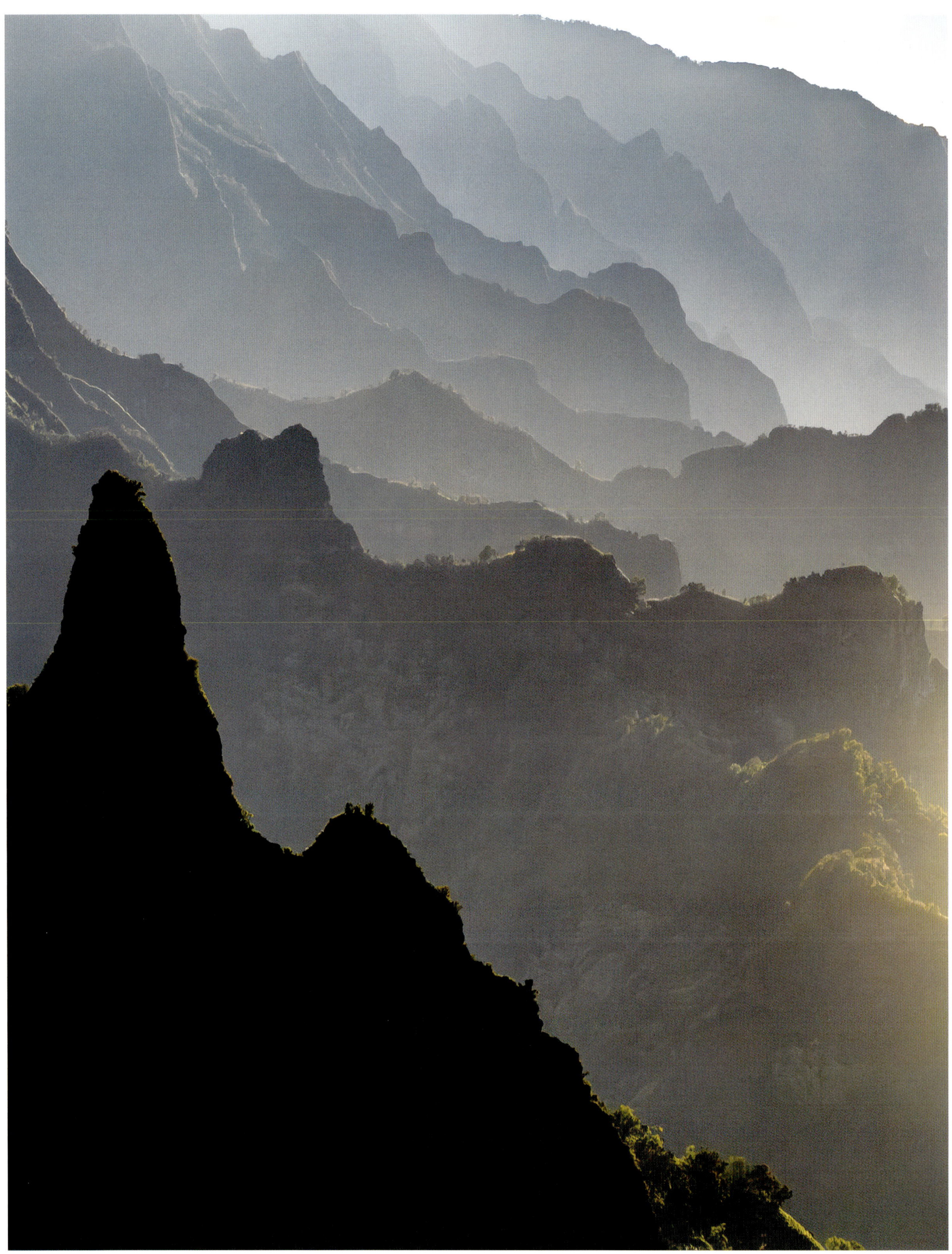

Above and opposite: Nā Pali Coast, Kaua'i

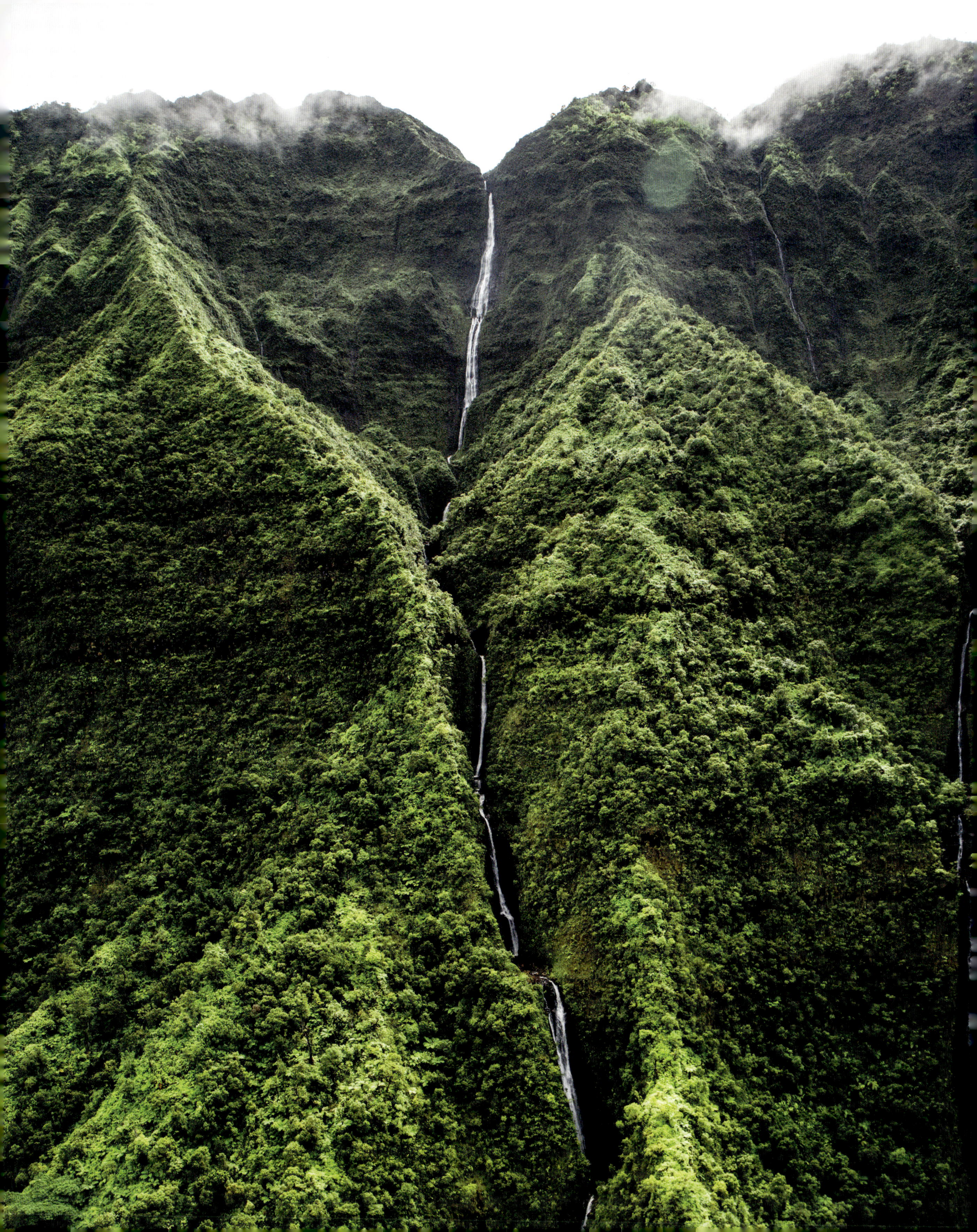

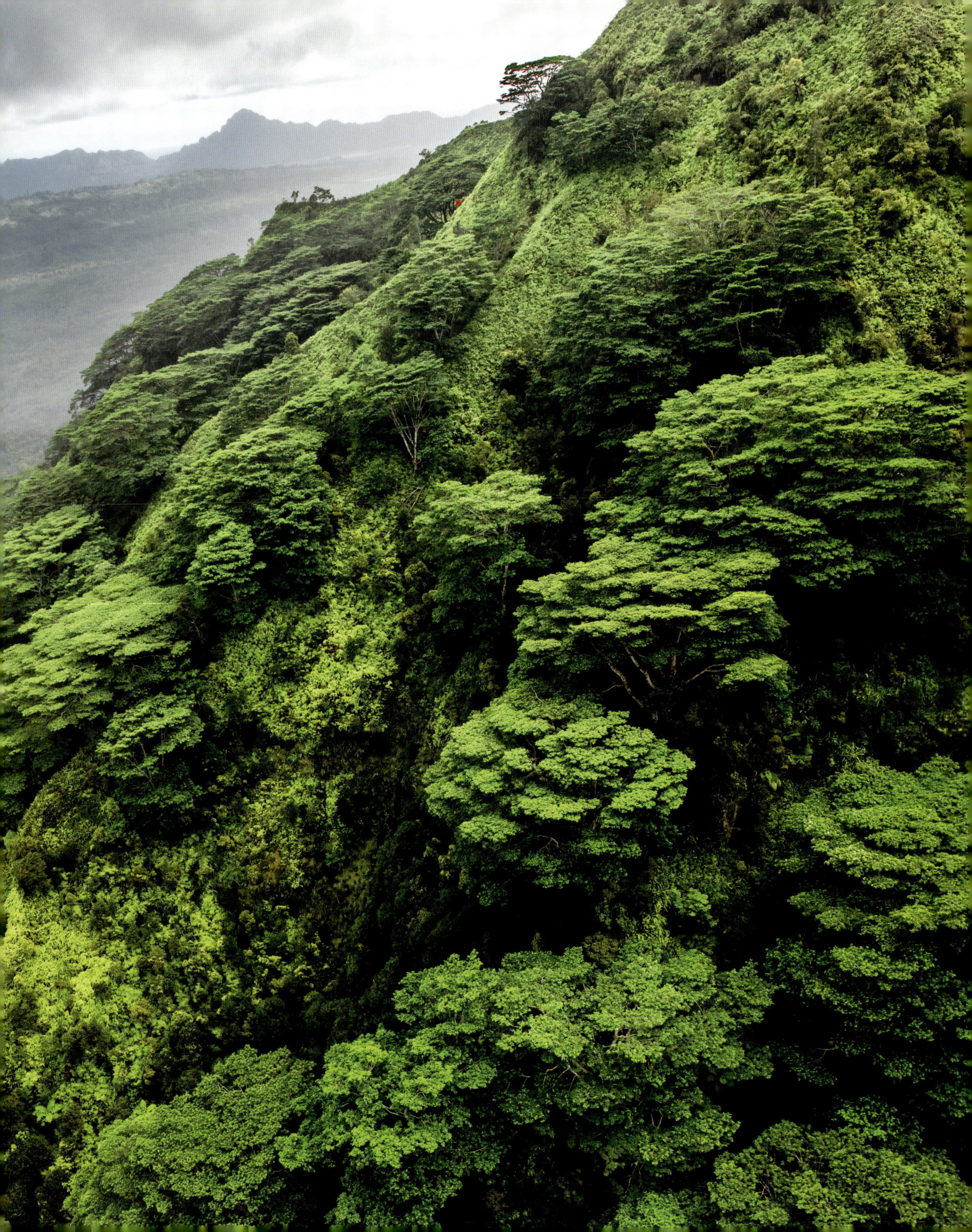

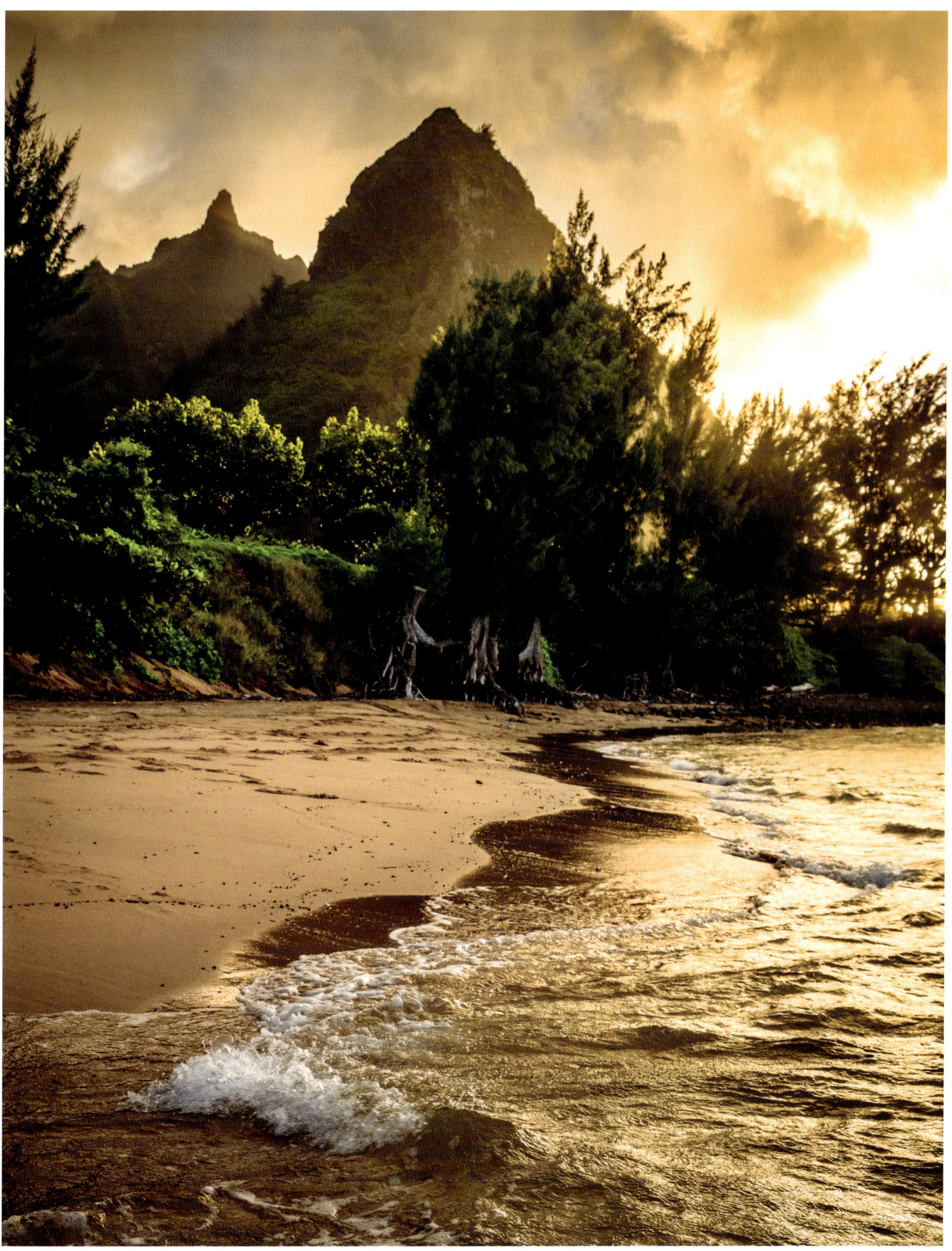

Above: Ke'e Beach, Kaua'i | Opposite: Halele'a Forest Reserve, Kaua'i

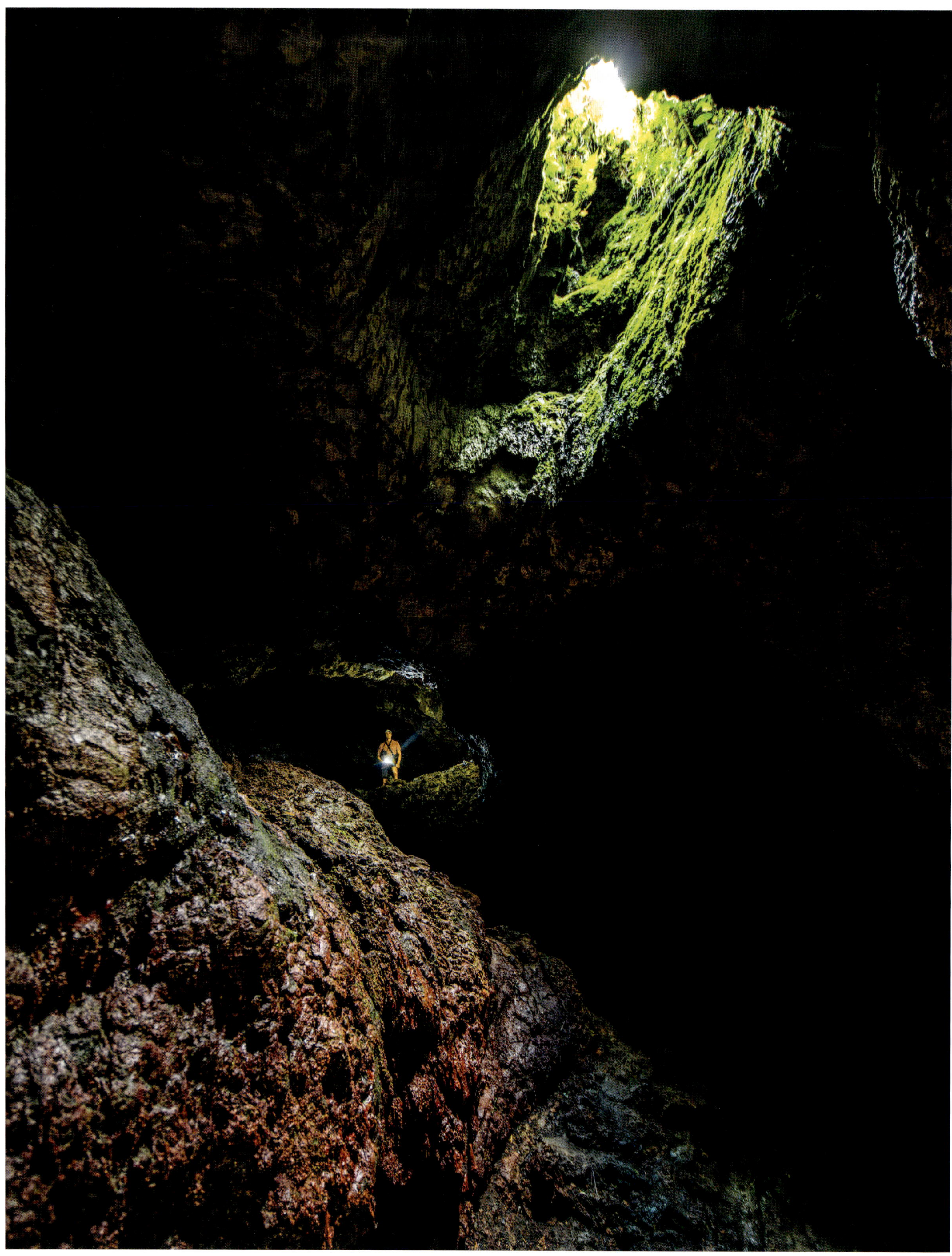

Above: Hana Lava Tube, Maui | Opposite: Banyan tree, Maui

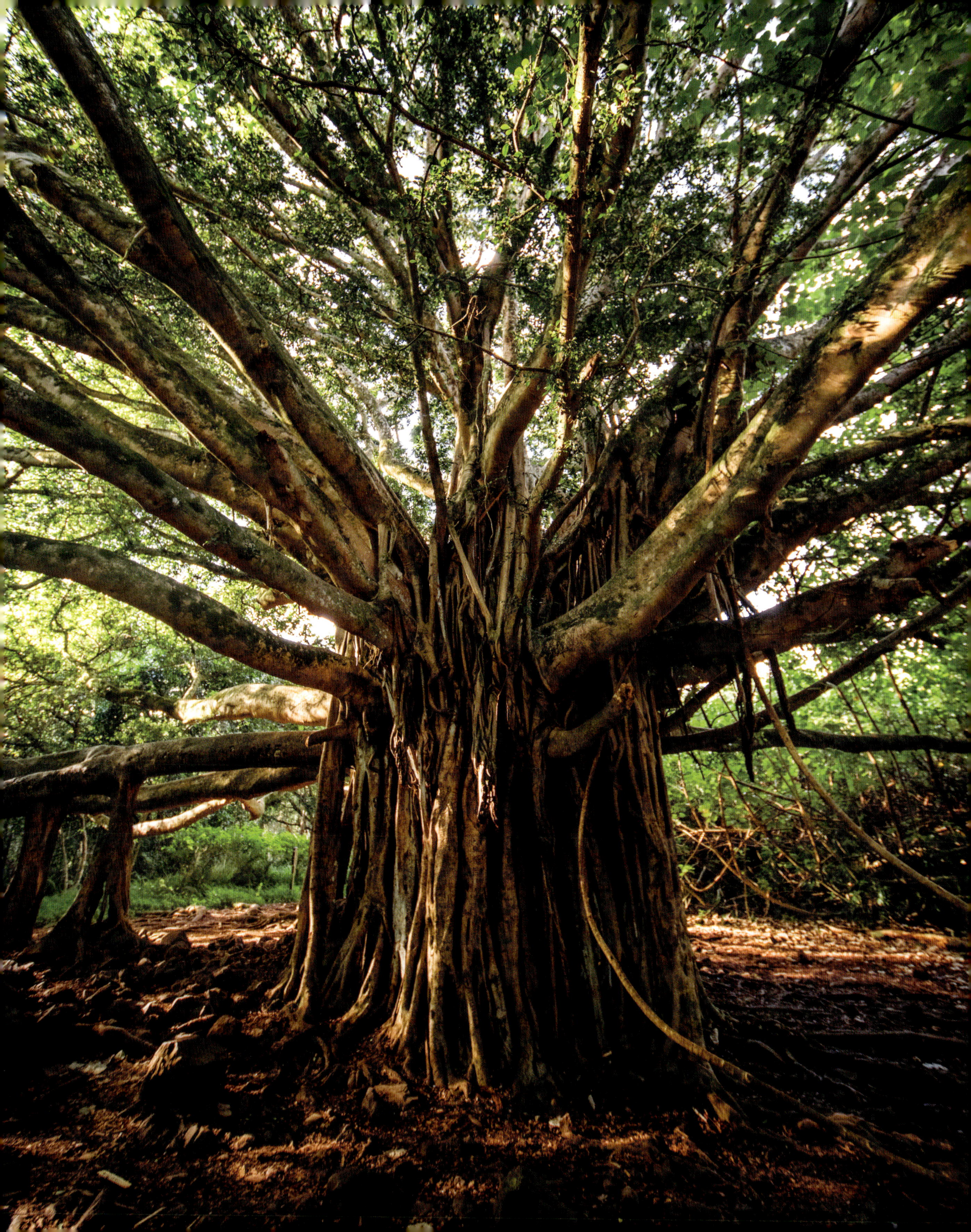

WEST

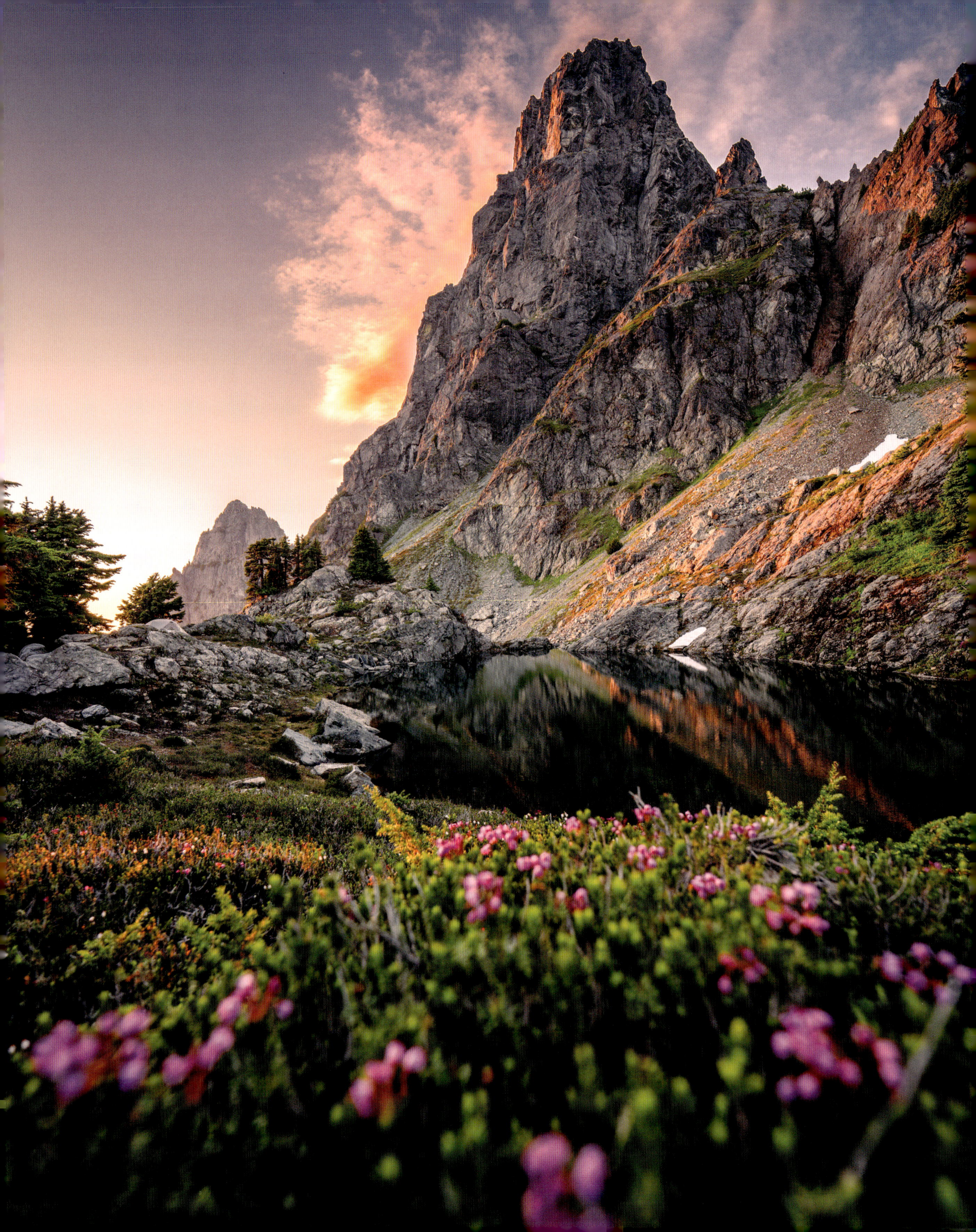

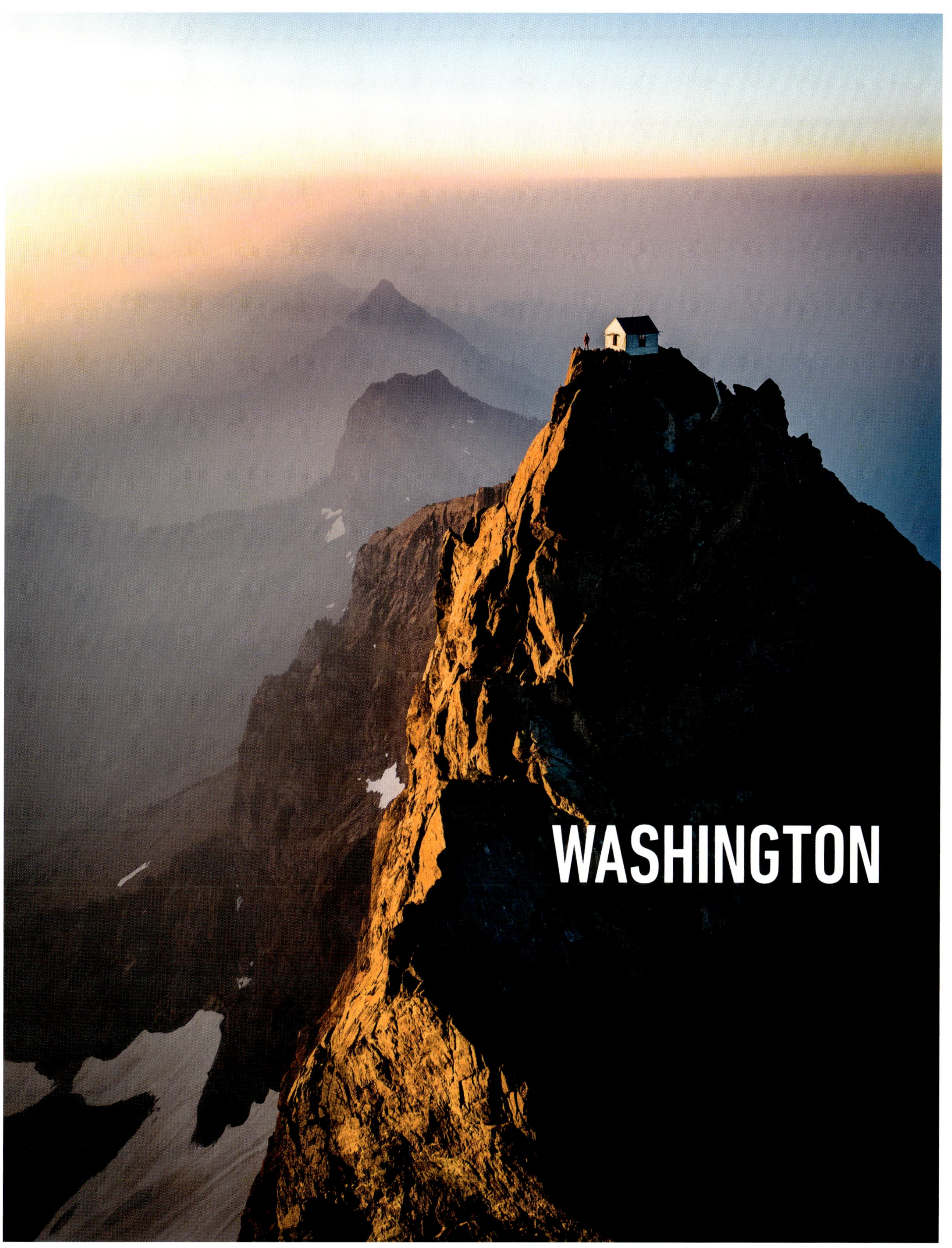

WASHINGTON

NORTH CASCADES

The North Cascades are a remote wilderness relatively untrammeled by development. Most of the area is accessible only by backpacking. The first time I reached Sahale Arm, I was stunned by the endless layers of jagged peaks stretching toward the horizon. The autumn golden larches made the entire landscape glow, contrasting beautifully with the deep-blue alpine lakes below. On another trip to Cascade Pass, I sat in silence as a herd of mountain goats wandered by, seemingly unbothered by my presence. The North Cascades offer a level of solitude and grandeur that's hard to find elsewhere, making every adventure unforgettable.

Region: Pacific Northwest

State: Washington

Coordinates: 48°42'00.0"N 121°12'00.0"W

Focal features: North Cascades National Park, rugged peaks like Mount Baker and Eldorado Peak, glaciers, and deep valleys

Formation attributes: The North Cascades contain more than three hundred glaciers—the most of any US national park outside of Alaska. Jagged peaks, some exceeding 9,000 feet (2,743m), define the landscape, with valleys carved by glacial action.

Fun fact: The North Cascades are often called the "American Alps" due to their dramatic, craggy peaks and extensive glacial coverage.

Best time to visit: July to September for hiking and backpacking, when the snow has melted from most trails. Late September to early October features stunning golden larch trees.

How to access: The main access road to the national park is North Cascades Highway (SR 20), which provides stunning views and connects to popular trailheads.

Things to consider: Much of the park is designated wilderness with no road access, requiring backcountry permits for overnight stays. Be prepared for unpredictable weather; rain and even snow can occur year-round, especially at higher elevations. Many areas of the park are remote, so bring plenty of food, water, and emergency supplies.

RECOMMENDED TRAILS:

Rainy Lake Trail: *2-mile (3.2km) round trip; minimal elevation gain; easy.* A short, paved trail leading to a gorgeous alpine lake surrounded by towering peaks, perfect for families and casual hikers.

Maple Pass Loop: *7.2-mile (11.6km) loop; about 2,100 feet (640m) elevation gain; moderate.* One of the most scenic hikes in the North Cascades, offering breathtaking ridgeline views, wildflowers in the summer, and golden larches in the fall.

Cascade Pass and Sahale Arm: *12 miles (19.3km) round trip; about 4,000 feet (1,219m) elevation gain; strenuous.* A challenging but rewarding hike that climbs to Cascade Pass before continuing to Sahale Glacier, where hikers are treated to panoramic views and a chance to see mountain goats.

Tips for taking a great photo

- Early morning offers the best lighting and fewer crowds. Sunset from high-elevation viewpoints can also be spectacular.
- Blue-green alpine lakes like Diablo Lake and Ross Lake are best captured on clear days when the water is calm to reflect the mountains.
- Bring a zoom lens to capture details of the park's glaciers from viewpoints like Sahale Arm.
- Late September to early October is prime time for golden larches and other fall colors along trails like Maple Pass, Wing Lake, and Cutthroat Pass.

Page 64: White Chuck Mountain, North Cascades

Page 65: Three Fingers Lookout, Central Cascades

Opposite: Chain Lakes Loop, Mount Baker, North Cascades

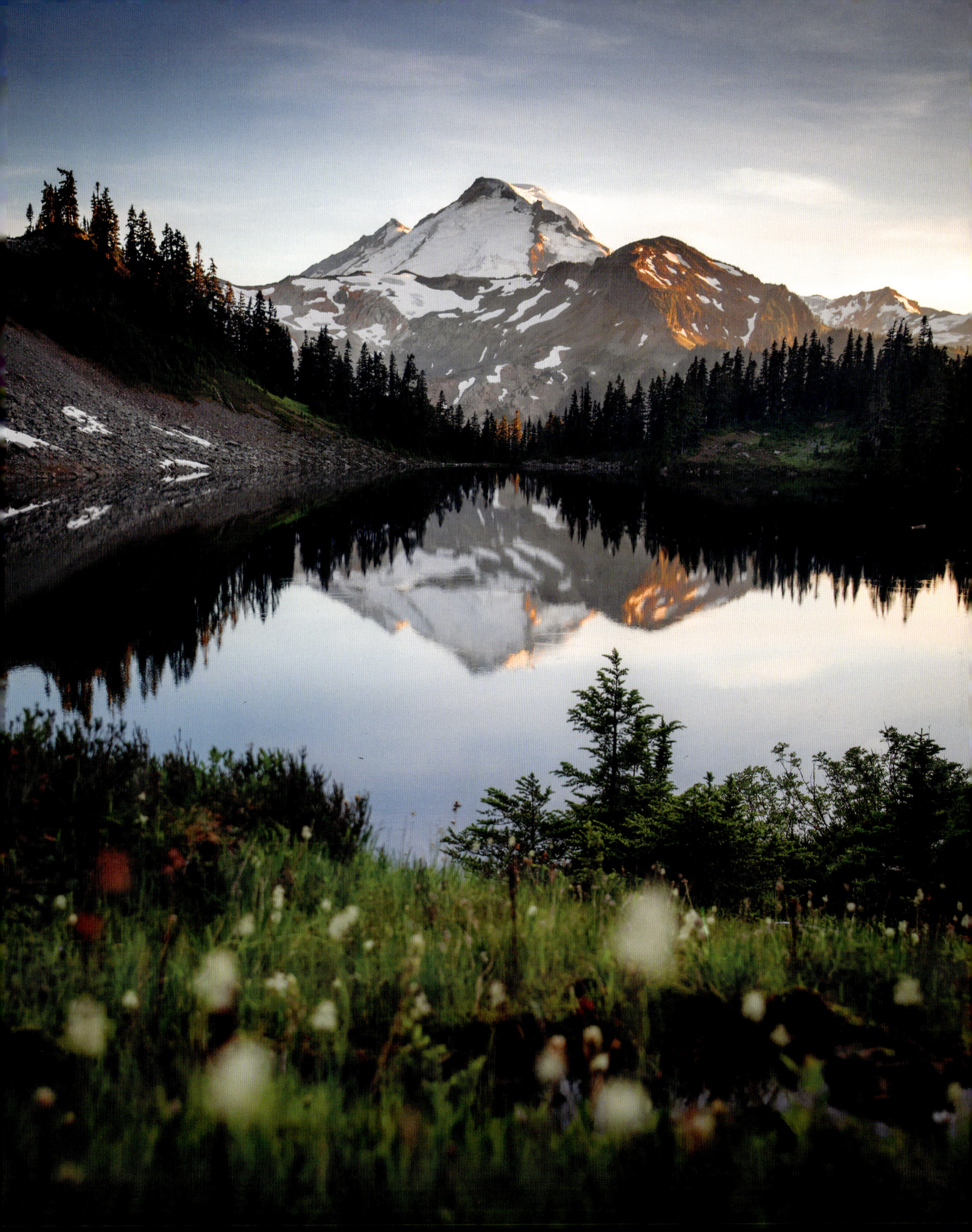

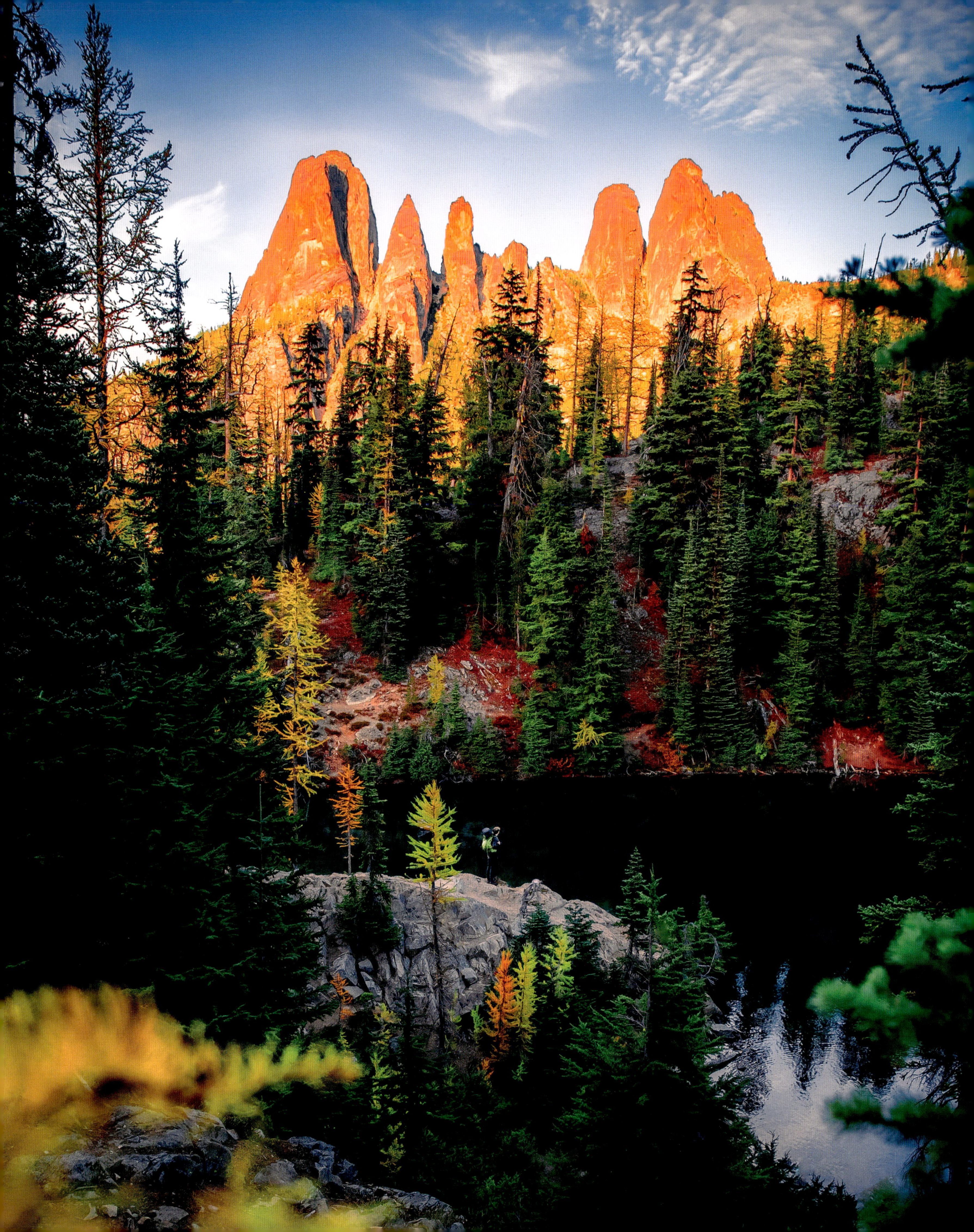

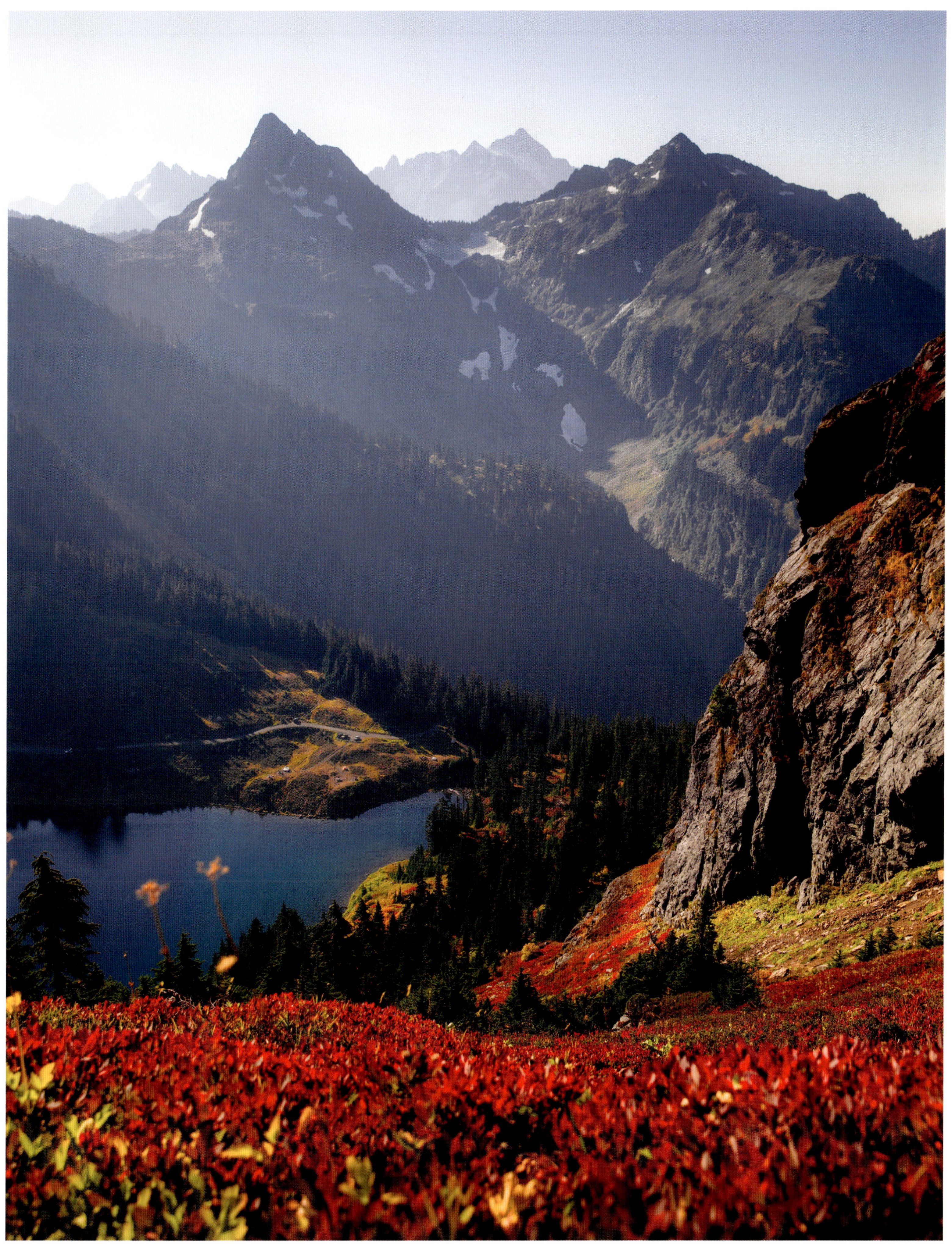

Above: Winchester Mountain Lookout, Twin Lakes, North Cascades | Opposite: Blue Lake, North Cascades

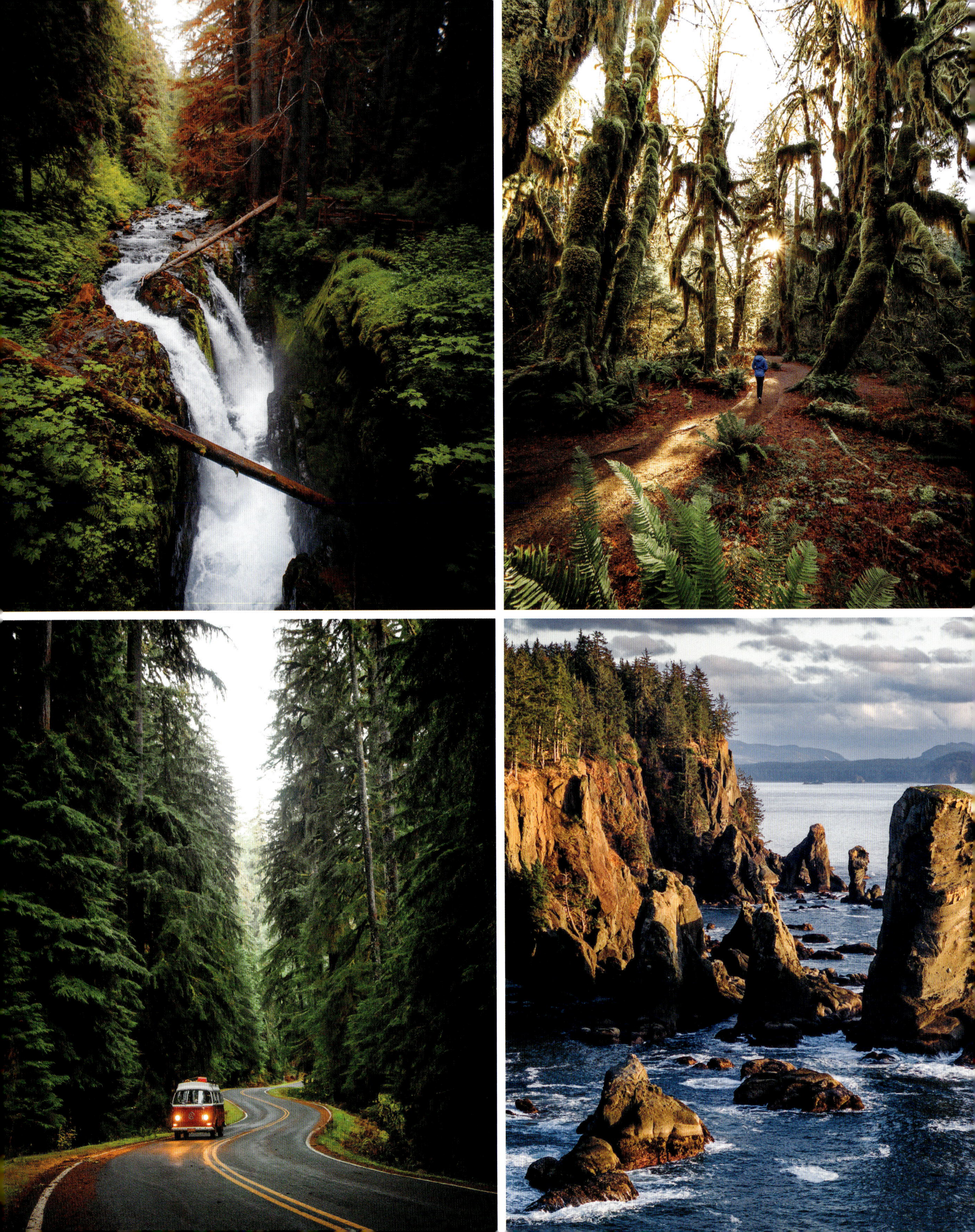

OLYMPIC NATIONAL PARK

Standing in the Hoh Rainforest feels like stepping into another world—lush, green, and impossibly quiet, except for occasional drops of rain on the leaves. Paired with watching the sun set over Ruby Beach, the sea stacks silhouetted against the sky, visiting Olympic National Park is an unforgettable experience. The park's diverse landscape makes it feel like multiple parks in one, each with its own unique beauty.

Region: Pacific Northwest

State: Washington

Coordinates: 47°48′07.6″N 123°36′15.8″W

Focal feature: The diverse landscape, which includes mountains, rainforests, and coastline

Formation attributes: Covers nearly 1 million acres, with Mount Olympus standing as the highest peak at 7,980 feet (2,432m).

Fun fact: Olympic National Park is home to one of the few temperate rainforests in the world, the Hoh Rainforest, which receives up to 14 feet (4.3m) of rain per year!

Best time to visit: July to September for the best weather, but winter can be a magical time for storm-watching along the coast.

How to access: The park has multiple entrances, with the main access point via US Highway 101. There is no road that fully crosses the park, so traveling between different areas takes time. Many locations, such as Hurricane Ridge, can get crowded in peak season—arriving early is recommended.

Things to consider: Be prepared for rapidly changing weather and layer up!

RECOMMENDED TRAILS:

Hoh River Trail to Five Mile Island: *10.6-mile (17km) round trip; minimal elevation gain; easy.* A stunning walk through towering moss-covered trees, with lush ferns and possible elk sightings. Shorter loops are available for those who prefer a brief stroll.

Hurricane Hill Trail: *3.2-mile (5.1km) round trip; about 700 feet (213m) elevation gain; moderate.* A relatively short but rewarding hike with panoramic views of the Olympic Mountains, the Strait of Juan de Fuca, and, on clear days, even Canada.

High Divide Loop / Seven Lakes Basin: *19-mile (30.6km) round trip; about 4,500 feet (1,371m) elevation gain; strenuous, multiday hike.* A breathtaking alpine hike featuring crystal-clear lakes, stunning ridgeline views, and a chance to see wildlife such as mountain goats and black bears.

Tips for taking a great photo

- Just after sunrise and just before sunset are the best times of day for softer lighting in the rainforest; sunset or sunrise is an ideal time for mountain views.
- For the best rainforest shots, use a polarizing filter to reduce glare and enhance the vibrant greens.
- Visit the coast at low tide for tide-pool shots, or during storm season for dramatic waves.
- For mountain views, position the sun behind you, and use a wide-angle lens for expansive shots.

Clockwise from top left: Sol Duc Falls; Hall of Mosses, Hoh Rainforest; Fuca Pillar, Washington Coast; driving through Olympic National Park

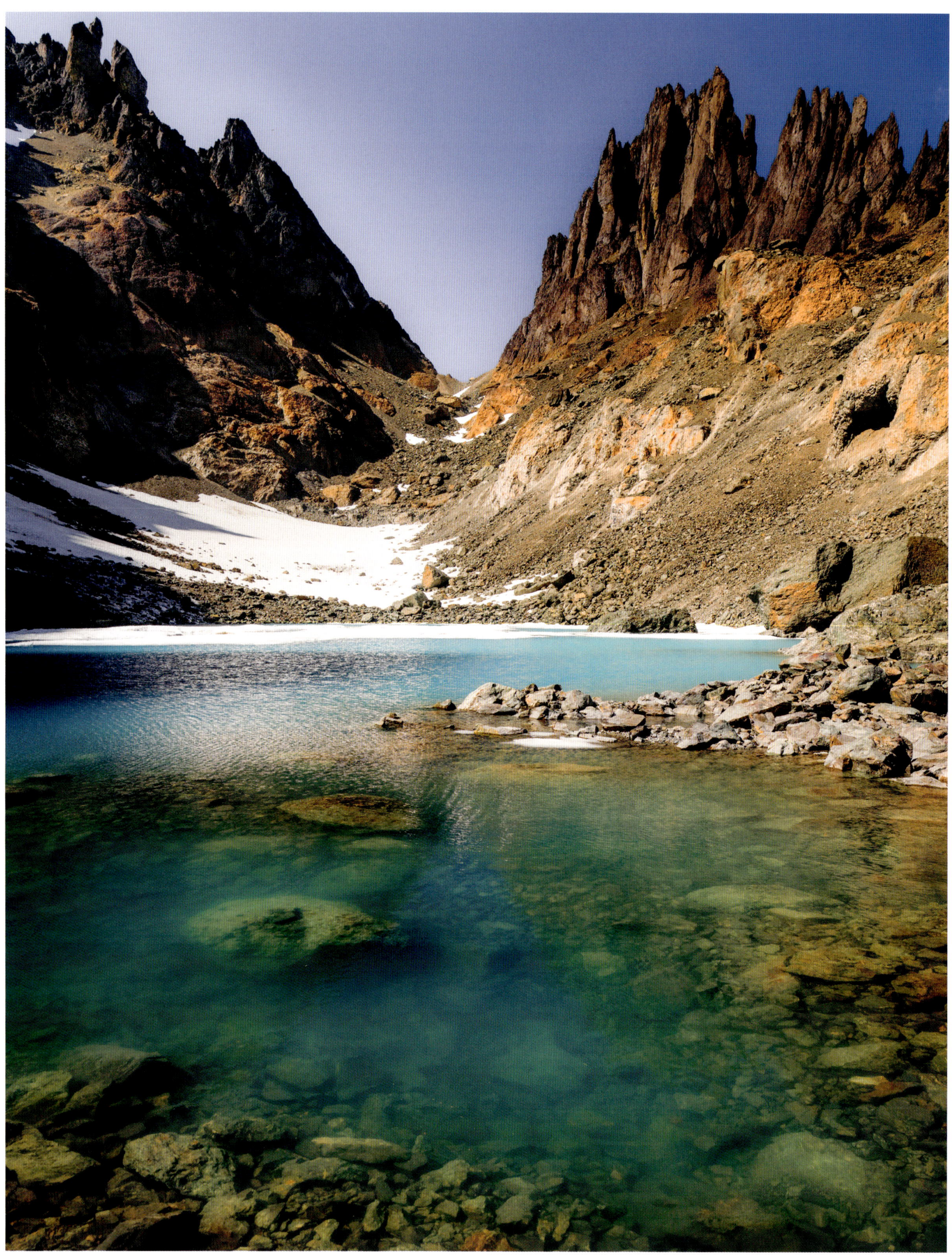

Above and opposite: Royal Basin, Olympic National Park

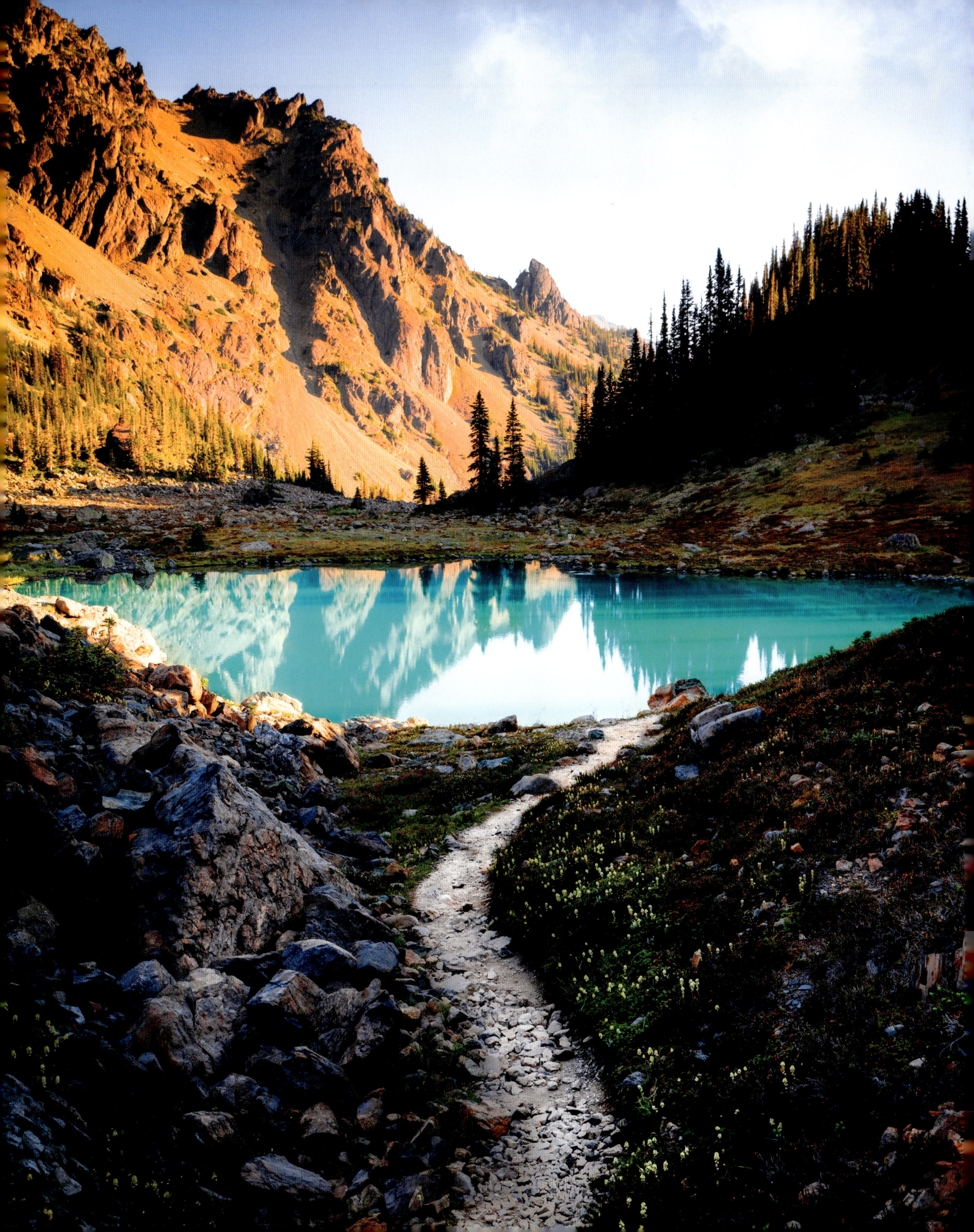

CENTRAL CASCADES

The Alpine Lakes Wilderness in the Central Cascades provides unforgettable hikes. One of my favorite trails, Tank Lakes, starts in a dense forest before opening up to sweeping mountain views. The first sight of the deep-blue water framed by rugged peaks was breathtaking. With the crisp alpine air, the sound of distant waterfalls, and the reflection of the mountains in the lake, it felt like stepping into a postcard. Later in the season, the golden hues of larches near Lake Ingalls give the landscape a surreal feel, with their bright colors contrasting against the dark granite peaks. Every trail in the Alpine Lakes Wilderness offers something unique, making it one of the most rewarding areas to explore in the Central Cascades.

Region: Pacific Northwest

State: Washington

Coordinates: 47°30'00.0"N 121°00'00.0"W

Focal feature: The Enchantments within the Alpine Lakes Wilderness

Formation attributes: The Cascades are a volcanic mountain range stretching from British Columbia to Northern California. The Central Cascades in Washington are known for their jagged peaks, deep valleys, lush forests, and glacier-fed lakes.

Fun fact: The Enchantments, one of the most famous alpine areas in the Central Cascades, is home to a population of mountain goats often spotted along the trails.

Best time to visit: July to October for hiking and backpacking, as snow lingers at higher elevations well into summer. Fall brings stunning larch trees in places like Lake Ingalls and Lake Valhalla.

How to access: US Highway 2 and Interstate 90 are the main routes to access the Central Cascades.

Things to consider: Many popular trailheads, such as those in the Alpine Lakes Wilderness, require a permit, and parking can fill up early. If visiting the Enchantments, an advance lottery system is required for overnight camping due to high demand. Weather can change quickly, so bring layers and rain gear, even in the summer.

RECOMMENDED TRAILS:

Franklin Falls Trail: *2-mile (3.2km) round trip; about 400 feet (122m) elevation gain; easy.* A short but rewarding hike leading to a picturesque waterfall, accessible year-round.

Lake Serene and Bridal Veil Falls Trail: *8.2-mile (13.2km) round trip; about 2,000 feet (610m) elevation gain; moderate.* A stunning hike through old-growth forest, leading to a pristine alpine lake, with an optional side trip to Bridal Veil Falls.

The Enchantments Thru Hike: *18 miles (29km); about 4,500 feet (1,372m) elevation gain; strenuous, full-day or multiday hike.* A breathtaking trek through granite basins, turquoise lakes, and high mountain passes, often regarded as one of the most scenic hikes in Washington.

Tips for taking a great photo

- Just after sunrise and just before sunset is the best time of day for soft lighting and fewer crowds.
- Use a tripod and a slow shutter speed to create a silky effect on waterfalls like Franklin Falls and Bridal Veil Falls.
- Calm mornings provide the best reflections in alpine lakes like Colchuck and Tank Lakes.
- The golden larches in late September and early October make for stunning photography—look for them in the Enchantments and near Lake Ingalls.

Opposite: From the summit of Del Campo Peak, Central Cascades

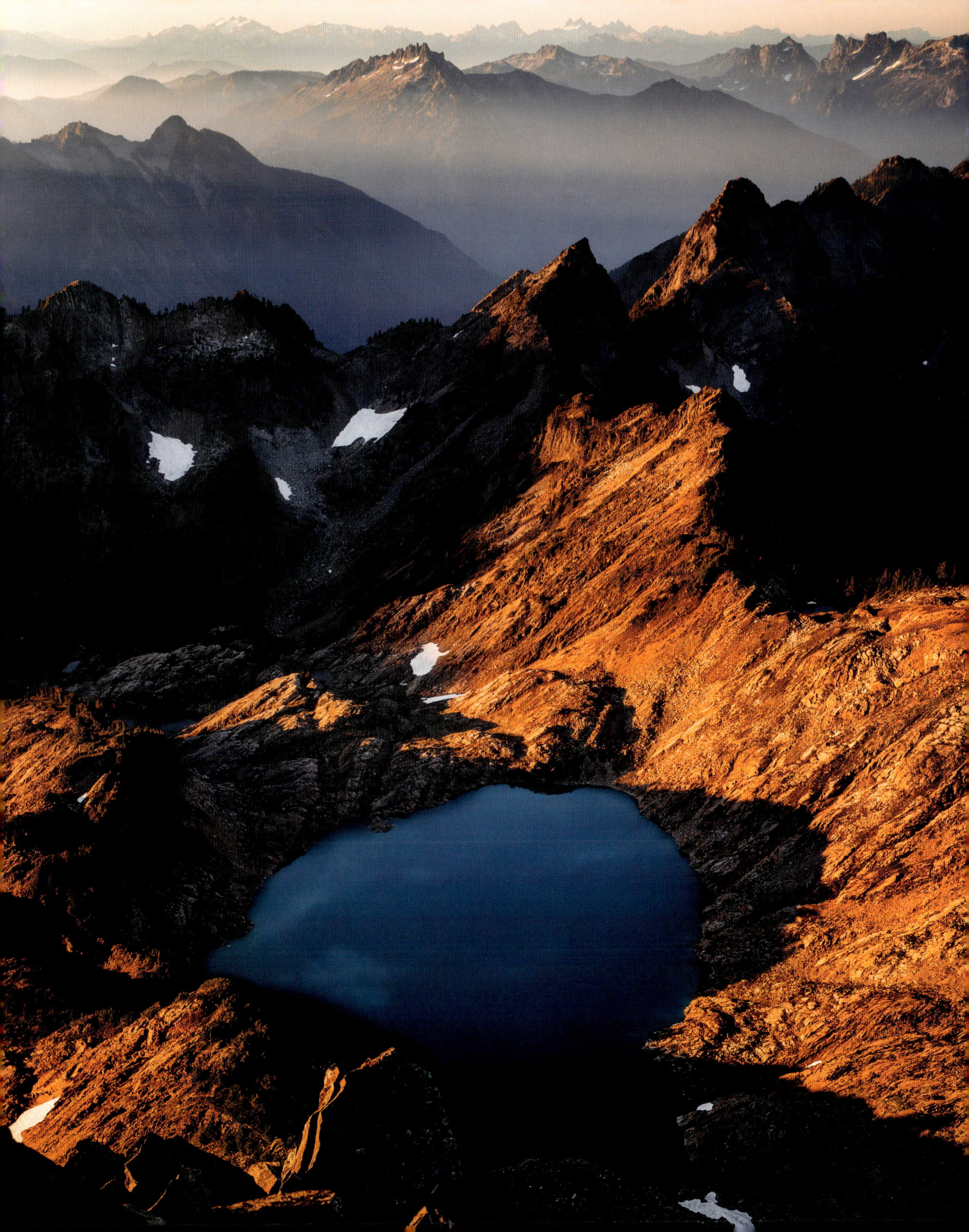

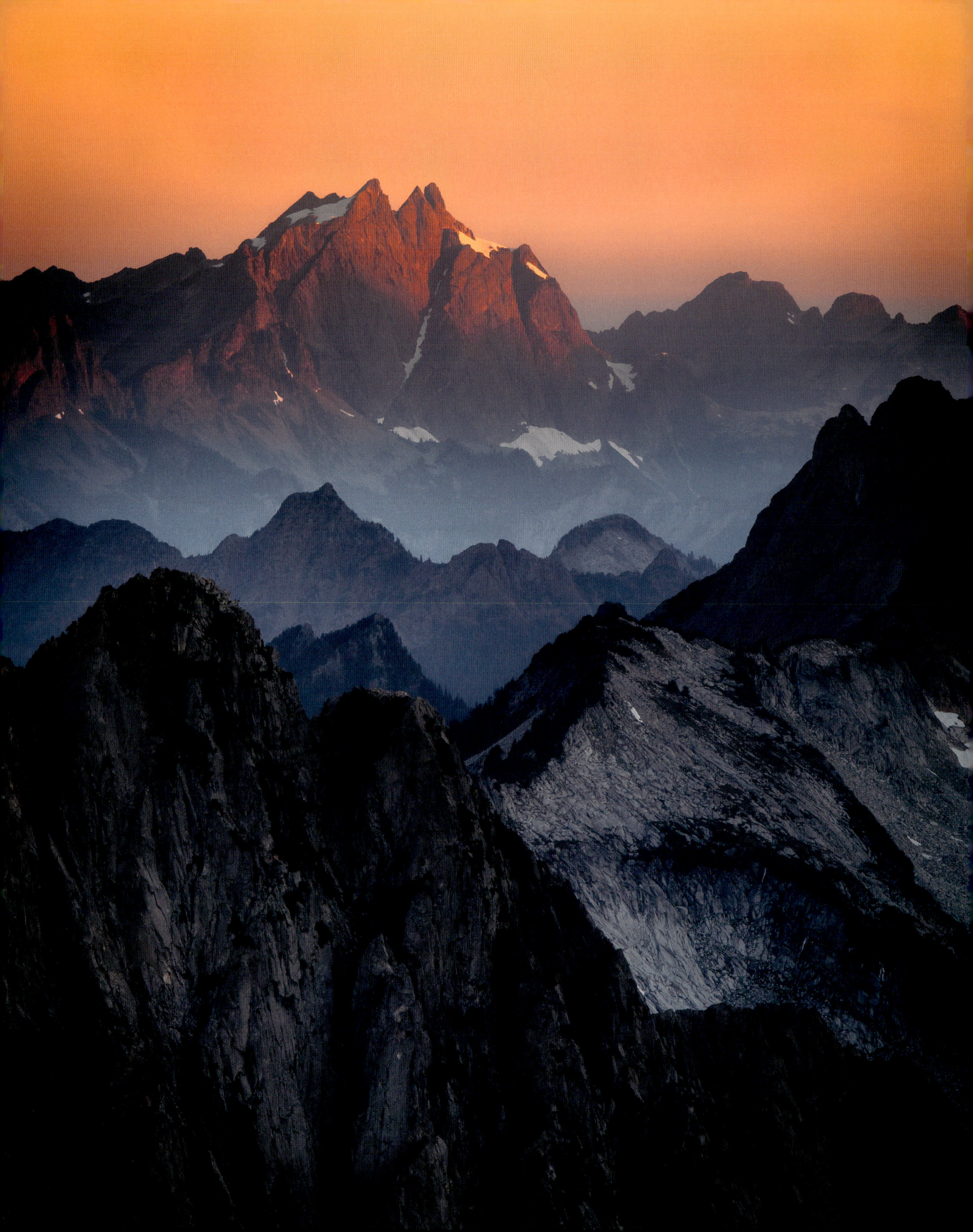

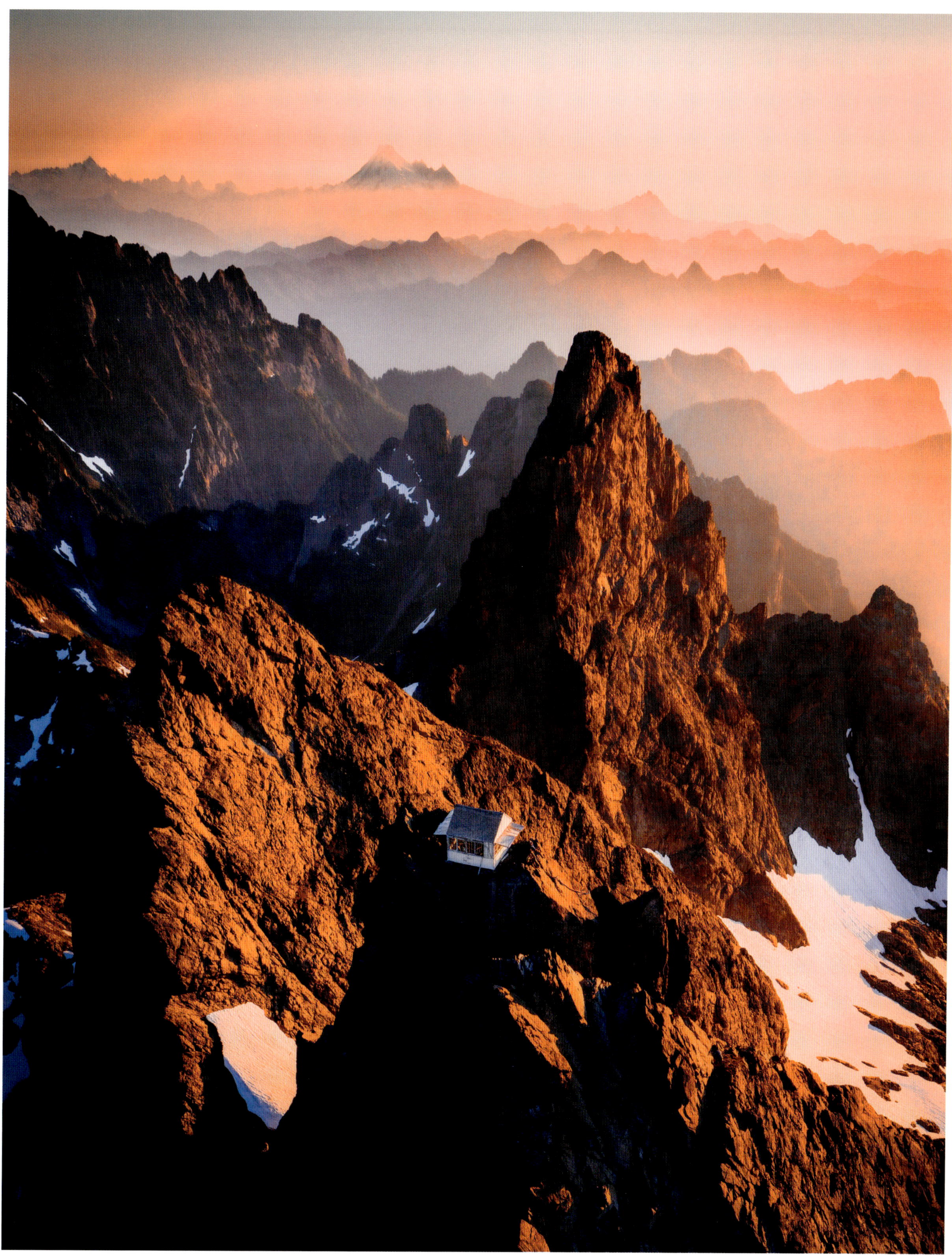

Above: Three Fingers Lookout, Central Cascades | Opposite: Looking toward Three Fingers from Del Campo Peak, Central Cascades

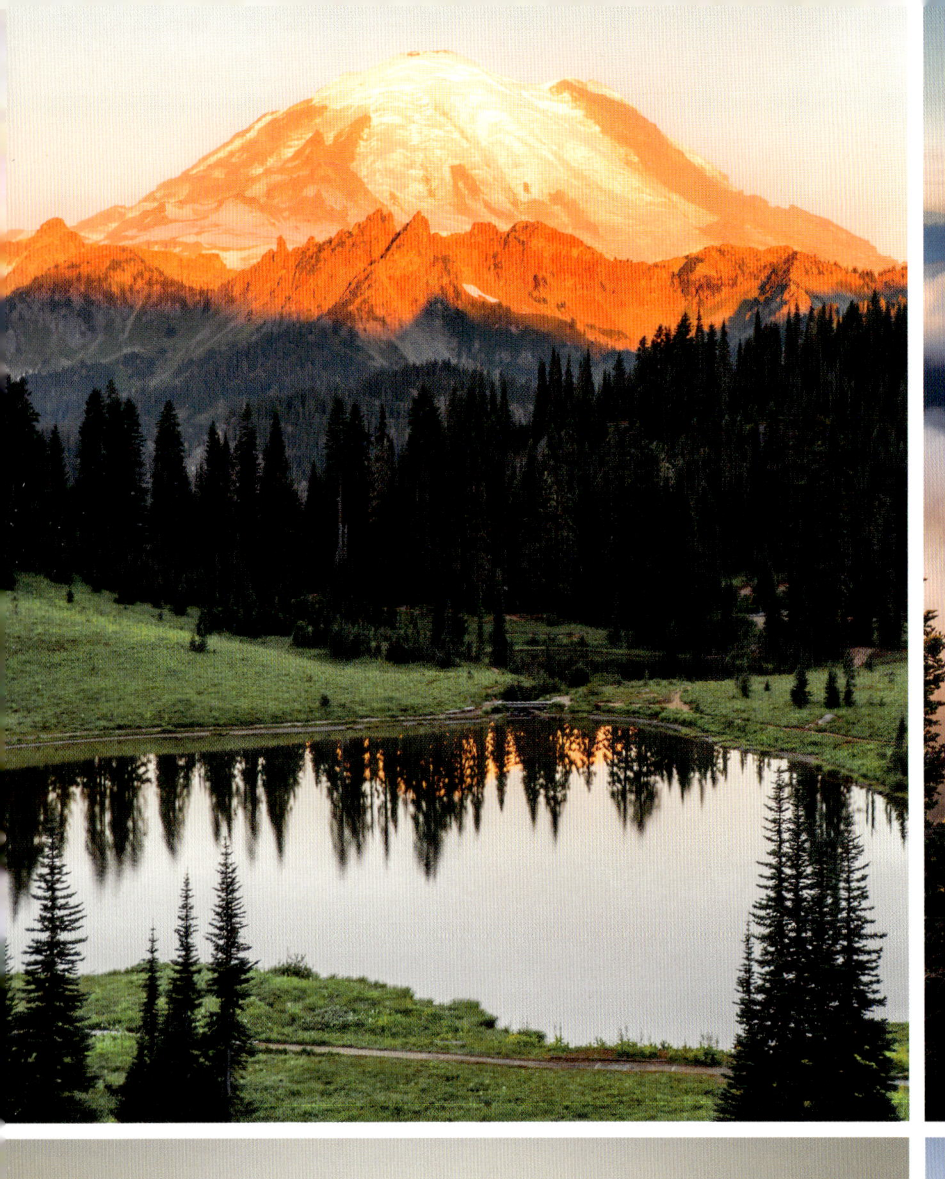
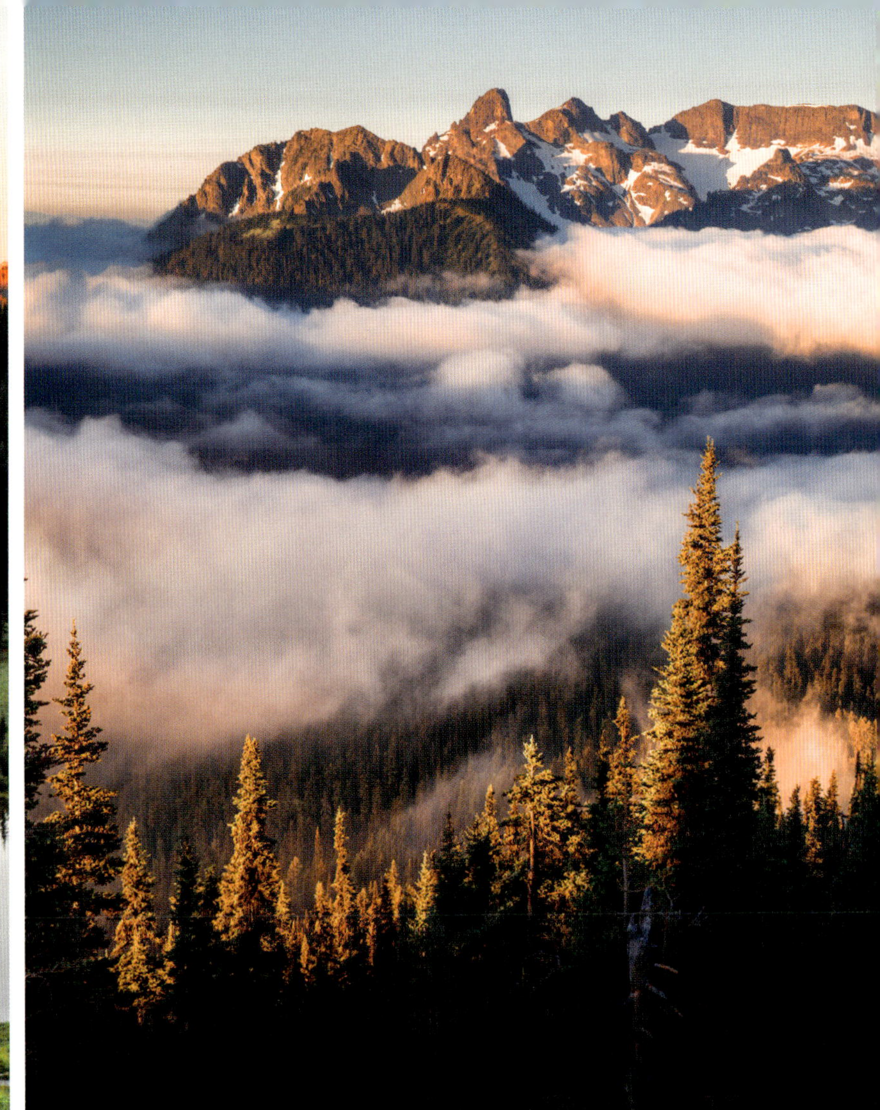
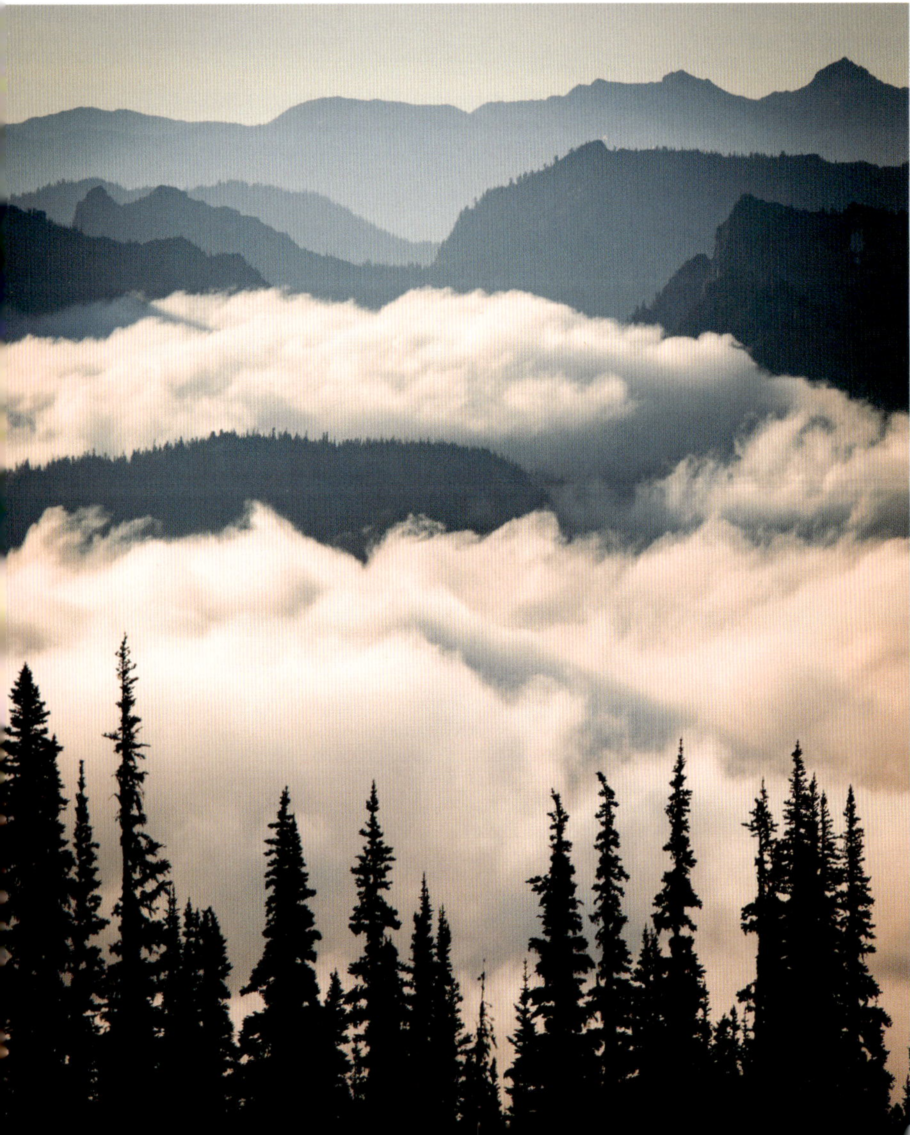
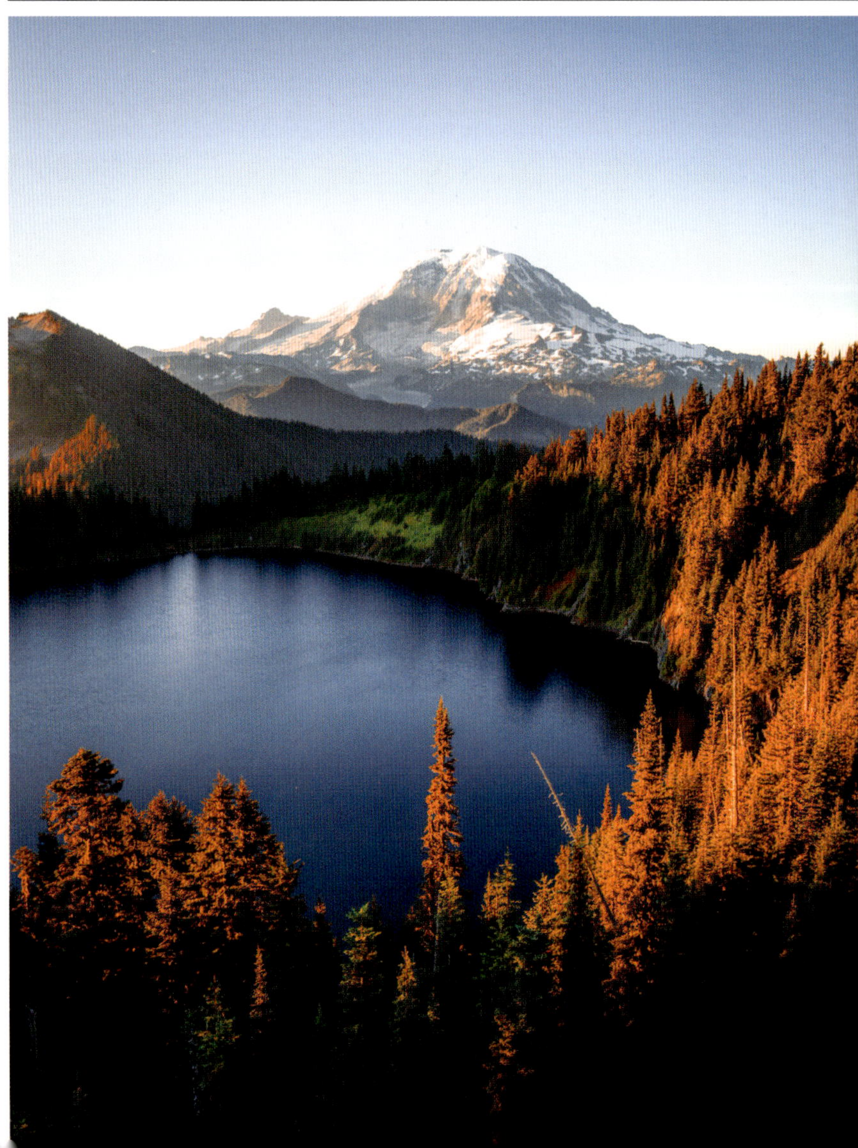

MOUNT RAINIER NATIONAL PARK

Watching the first light of dawn hit Mount Rainier from the Sunrise area of the park was one of the most breathtaking moments I've ever experienced. The entire peak glowed in hues of pink and orange, while the meadows below shimmered with dew-covered wildflowers. The Skyline Trail hike in the summer was like walking through a dream. Marmots whistled in the distance, and I could hear the faint rumble of glaciers shifting high above. Mount Rainier's presence is both humbling and awe-inspiring, a true gem of the Pacific Northwest.

Region: Pacific Northwest

State: Washington

Coordinates: 46°51'08.3"N 121°45'37.1"W

Focal feature: Mount Rainier (aka Tahoma), the highest peak in the Cascade Range

Formation attributes: Mount Rainier stands at 14,410 feet (4,392m) tall and has twenty-five major glaciers—the largest glacial system in the contiguous United States.

Interesting fact: Mount Rainier is an active stratovolcano and is considered one of the most dangerous volcanoes in the world due to its massive glacier system, which may contribute to powerful mudflows, or lahars, in the event of an eruption.

Best time to visit: July to September, when wildflowers bloom in the meadows and most of the snow at lower elevations has melted.

How to access: The park has multiple entrances, the most popular being the Nisqually Entrance in the southwest via SR 706. Summer is the busiest season, and entry lines can be long, so arrive early to secure parking, especially at the Paradise and Sunrise entrances.

Things to consider: A park entrance fee is required, and permits are necessary for backcountry camping and climbing. I recommend shooting sunrise here; it gets very busy in the summer, but the crowds are a lot smaller in the morning.

RECOMMENDED TRAILS:

Nisqually Vista Trail: *1.2-mile (1.9km) loop; minimal elevation gain; easy.* A short, paved loop with breathtaking views of Mount Rainier and its glaciers, especially stunning during wildflower season.

Skyline Trail Loop: *5.5-mile (8.9km) round trip; about 1,700 feet (518m) elevation gain; moderate.* One of the most famous trails in the park, leading to Myrtle Falls, panoramic views of Mount Rainier, and the chance to spot marmots and mountain goats.

Wonderland Trail: *93-mile (150km) loop; about 22,000 feet (6,705m) elevation gain; strenuous, multiday hike.* A bucket-list trek that completely encircles Mount Rainier, passing through alpine meadows, old-growth forests, and glacial rivers.

Tips for taking a great photo

- Early morning is the best time of day for clear views, as clouds often build around the peak by midday.
- July and August offer peak wildflower shots in places like Paradise and Sunrise. Use a macro lens for close-ups.
- Reflection Lakes at sunrise provides an incredible mirrored image of the mountain. Sunrise at Sunrise Visitor Center offers golden alpenglow on the peak.
- For glacier photography, a telephoto lens helps capture the details of crevasses and icefalls from a distance.

Opposite: Mount Rainier National Park

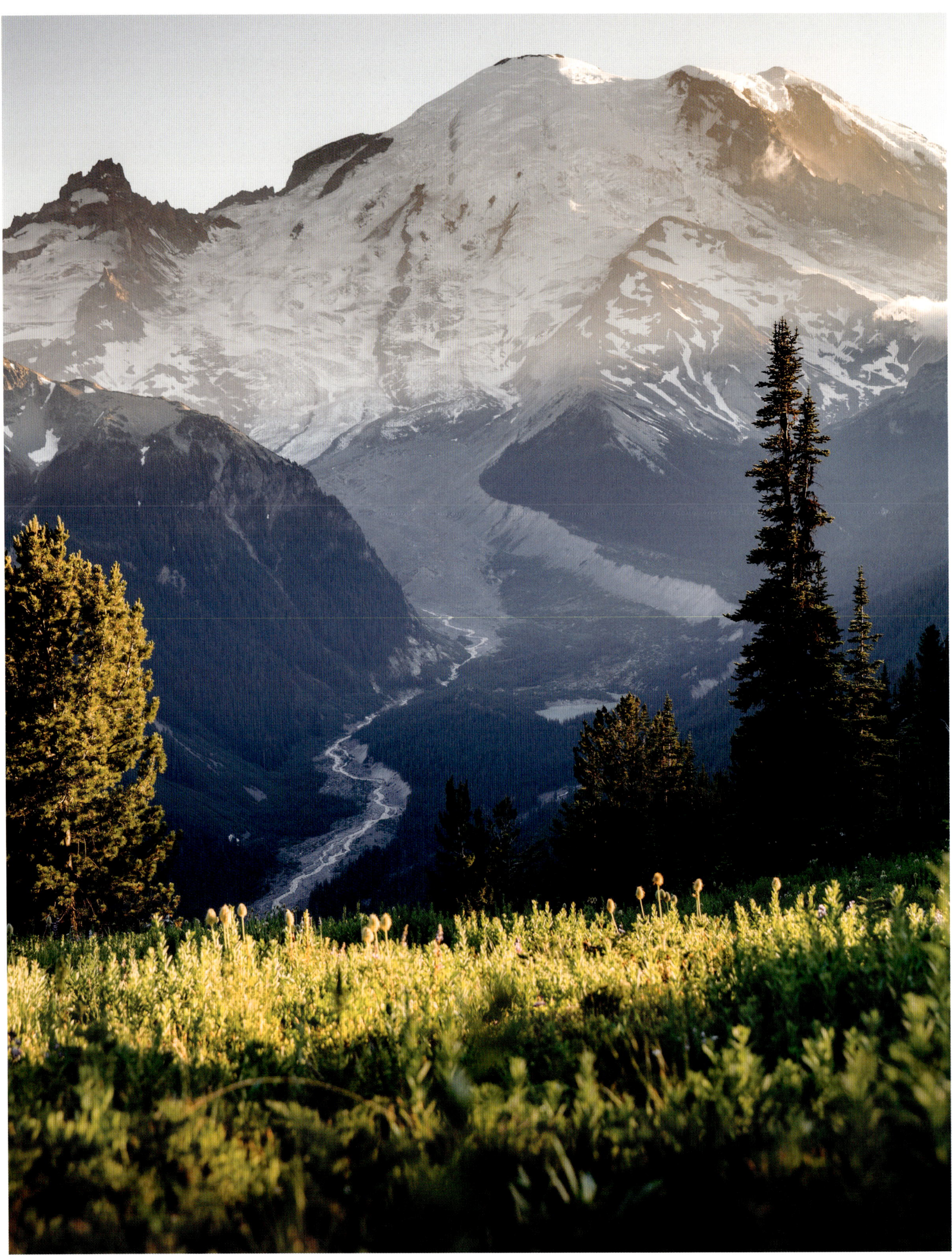

Above: Mount Rainier | Opposite: Another peak in Mount Rainier National Park

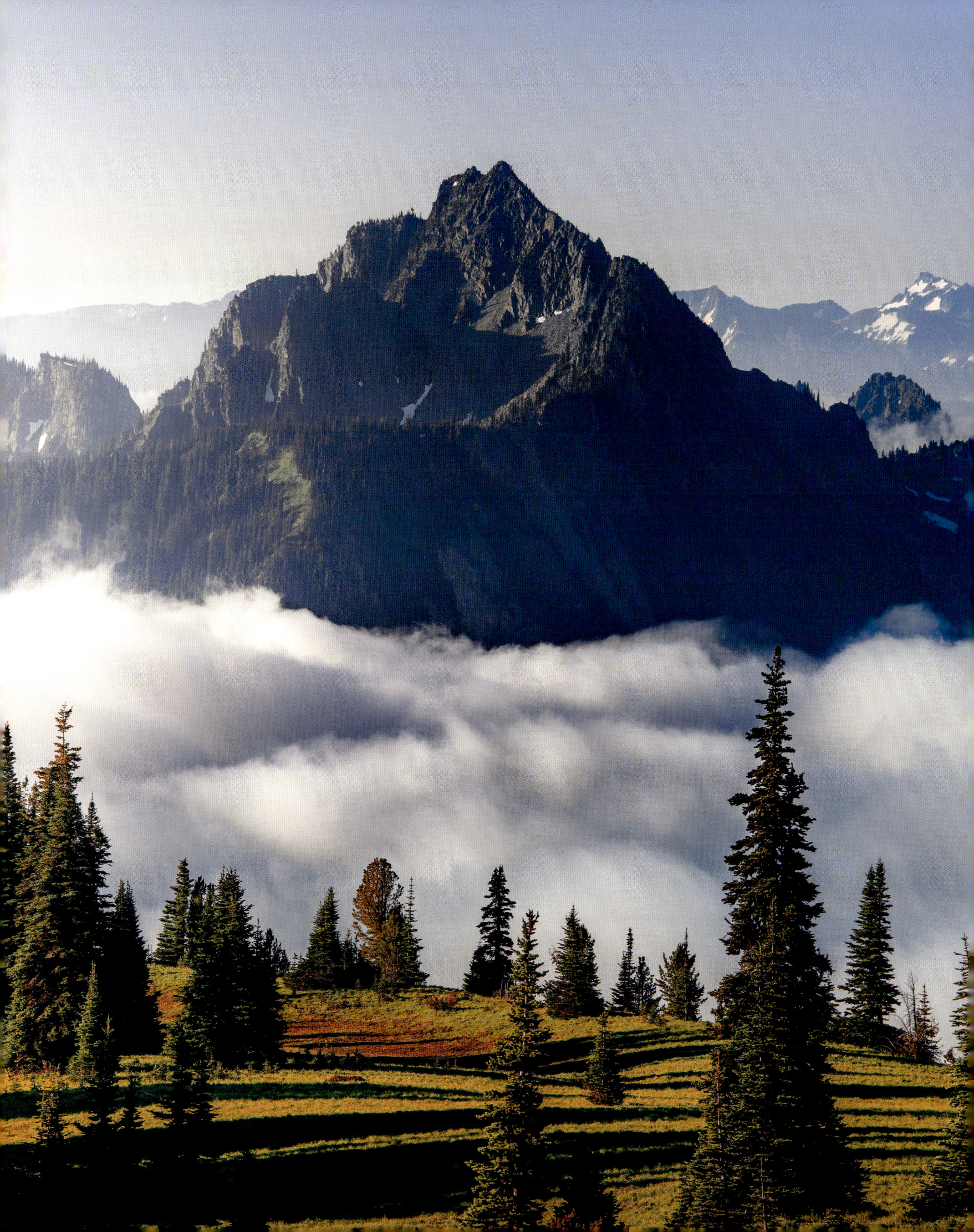

SOUTH CASCADES

At the edge of Mount St. Helens's crater, I couldn't help but feel incredibly humbled. The ground beneath me was still covered in ash, and steam vents in the distance reminded me that the volcano is very much alive. As you hike through the blast zone, it feels like you're walking through history—seeing the aftermath of massive trees toppled like matchsticks, yet also spotting vibrant wildflowers pushing through the volcanic soil, a testament to nature's resilience. The South Cascades, in which Mount St. Helens sits, with their mix of active volcanism, deep forests, and high-alpine peaks, are a reminder of the wild forces that shaped the Pacific Northwest.

Region: Pacific Northwest

State: Washington

Coordinates: 46°12'00.0"N 122°12'00.0"W

Focal features: Mount St. Helens and Mount Adams in the Gifford Pinchot National Forest and Mount Adams Wilderness

Formation attributes: Mount St. Helens stands at 8,363 feet (2,549m) after its 1980 eruption, which removed the upper 1,300 feet (396m) of the peak. The surrounding South Cascades feature a mix of volcanic peaks, deep forests, and high-alpine meadows.

Fun fact: The 1980 eruption of Mount St. Helens was the most economically destructive volcanic event in US history, and its blast zone is still a fascinating landscape of regrowth and recovery.

Best time to visit: Late June to October for the best access to trails and viewpoints. Wildflowers peak in July, and fall colors are vibrant in late September.

How to access: Mount St. Helens is best accessed via SR 504 (the west side) for visitor centers and viewpoints, or FR 83 and 99 (the east side) for closer access to the blast zone and trails. Other areas of the South Cascades, like Mount Adams and Goat Rocks Wilderness, can be reached via forest roads off US Highway 12 and SR 14.

Things to consider: Weather can change quickly, so bring layers, especially if hiking at higher elevations. Some areas require permits for access, like Mount St. Helens, which requires a permit to hike to the summit. Some roads and trails are closed in winter due to snow, so be sure to check road access ahead of time.

Opposite: Mount St. Helens

RECOMMENDED TRAILS:

Windy Ridge Viewpoint Trail: *0.5-mile (0.8km) round trip; minimal elevation gain; easy.* A short but dramatic walk up a staircase to a panoramic view of Mount St. Helens and Spirit Lake, with its thousands of floating logs still visible from the 1980 eruption.

Lava Canyon Trail: *5-mile (8km) round trip; about 1,600 feet (488m) elevation gain; moderate.* A stunning hike along waterfalls, lava-carved rock formations, and suspension bridges, showcasing the volcanic power of Mount St. Helens.

Mount St. Helens Summit Climb (via Monitor Ridge): *10-mile (16.1km) round trip, about 4,500 feet (1,372m) elevation gain; strenuous.* A challenging ascent that takes hikers through volcanic ash, lava fields, and boulder scrambles to the rim of the crater, offering an unforgettable view into the heart of the volcano. A permit is required.

Tips for taking a great photo

- After sunrise and before sunset are the best times of day for softer lighting and dramatic shadows on the crater and blast zone.
- Capture the contrast of the varying volcanic landscapes, from barren lava fields to forest and wildflower regrowth.
- Mid-to-late July is the best time to photograph wildflowers with brilliant displays of lupine and paintbrush in the Mount St. Helens blast zone.
- Bring a wide-angle lens for summit shots of the crater and for panoramic mountain vistas, including Mount Rainier, Mount Adams, and Mount Hood in the distance.

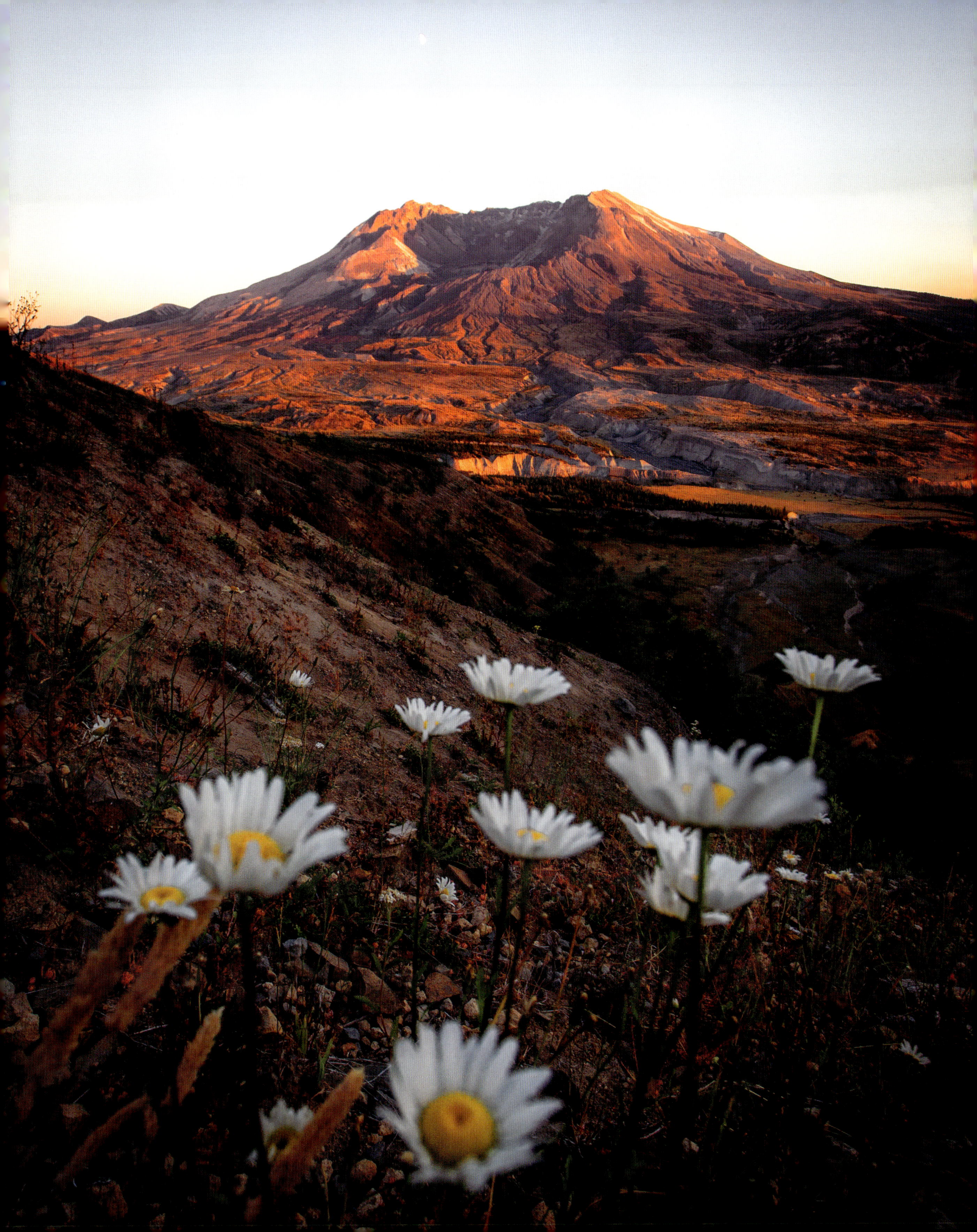

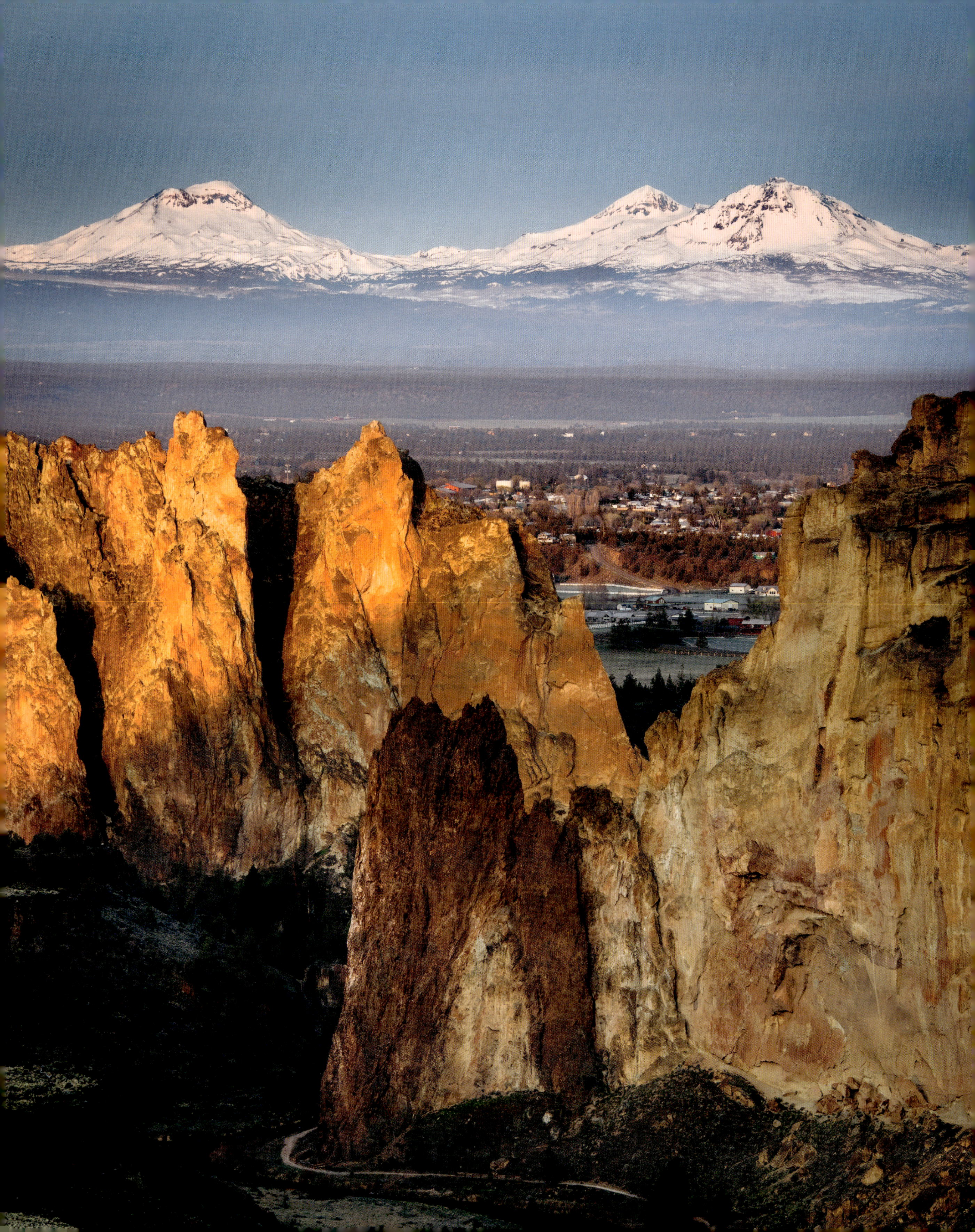

OREGON

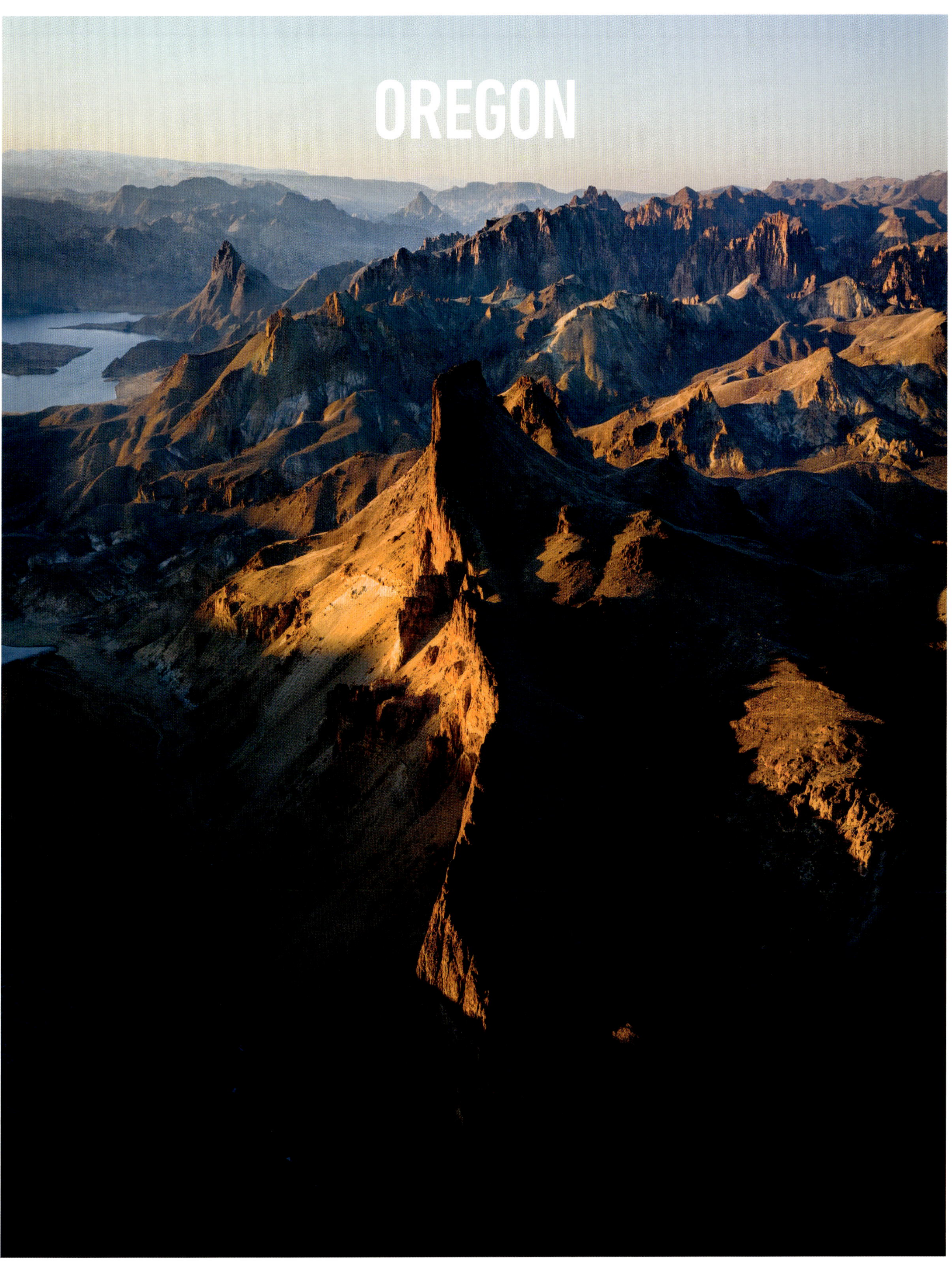

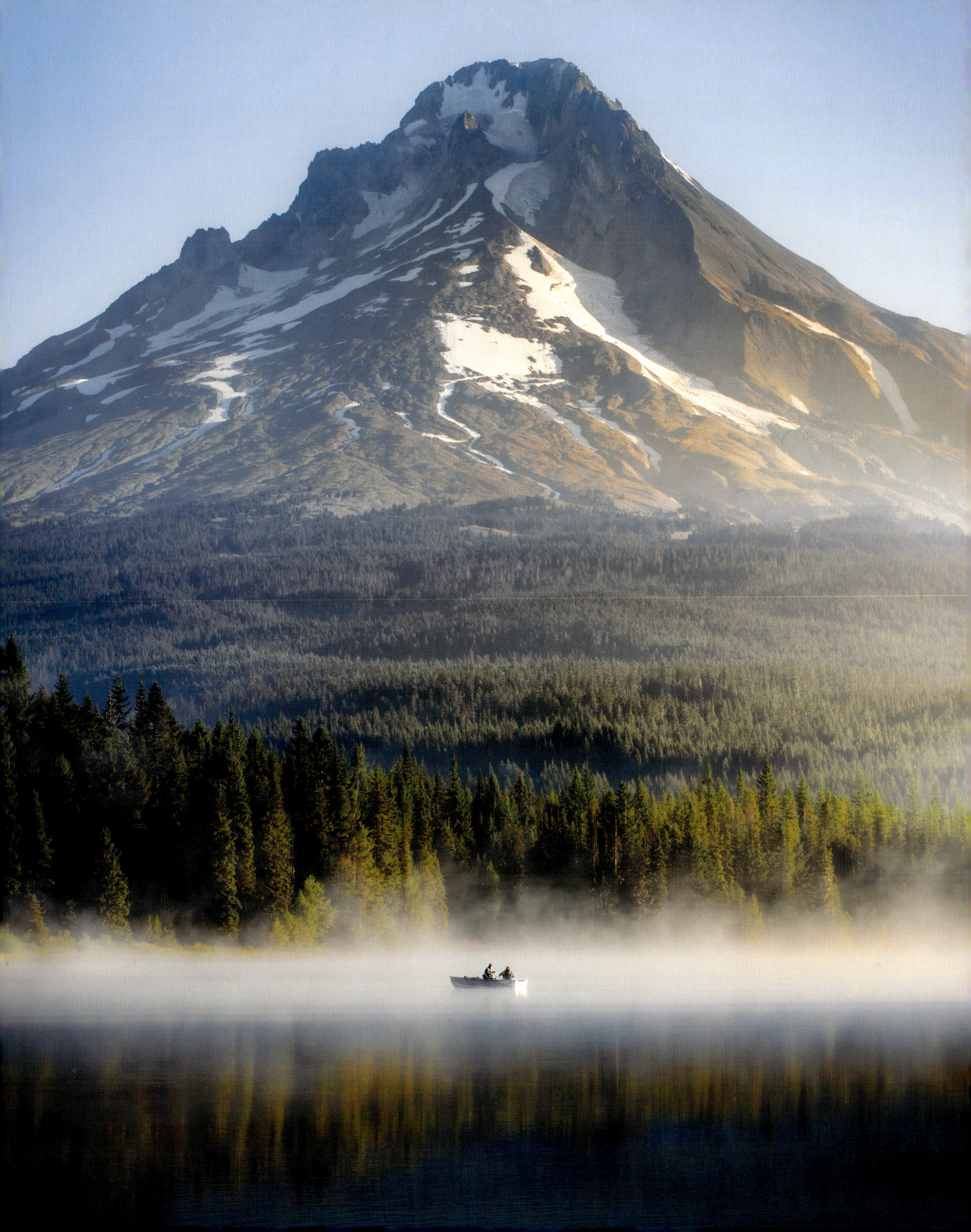

MOUNT HOOD NATIONAL FOREST

The peak glowed pink and orange as the first light of the day hit Mount Hood and the sky slowly brightened. From where I stood at Trillium Lake, it was an unforgettable moment. Later in the day, I hiked through the alpine meadows along the Timberline Trail, with wildflowers blooming in every direction and panoramic views stretching to the Cascade Range. In winter, snowshoeing near Timberline Lodge is a completely different but equally magical experience, with the mountain looming overhead and the landscape blanketed in pristine snow. Whether exploring in summer or winter, Mount Hood always offers something breathtaking.

Region: Pacific Northwest

State: Oregon

Coordinates: 45°22'25.0"N 121°41'45.6"W

Focal feature: Mount Hood, Oregon's tallest peak and a dormant stratovolcano, in Mount Hood National Forest

Formation attributes: Standing at 11,245 feet (3,427m), Mount Hood is the highest point in Oregon and features twelve named glaciers and permanent snowfields.

Fun fact: Mount Hood is home to the only year-round ski resort in North America, with Timberline Lodge offering skiing even in the summer months.

Best time to visit: July to September for hiking and wildflowers; December to April for skiing and snow sports. Fall is excellent for fewer crowds and beautiful foliage.

How to access: Mount Hood is easily accessible via US Highway 26 from Portland (about a ninety-minute drive). The Mount Hood Scenic Byway loops around the mountain, offering stunning views and access to trailheads, lakes, and ski resorts. Be prepared for snow-covered roads in the winter and check conditions before heading up.

Things to consider: Weather can change rapidly on the mountain—bring layers, even in the summer. Snow lingers at higher elevations well into July. Some areas, like Timberline Lodge and Trillium Lake, can get very busy, so visiting early or on weekdays is best.

RECOMMENDED TRAILS:

Trillium Lake Loop: *1.9-mile (3km) loop; minimal elevation gain; easy.* A scenic stroll around a reflective lake with postcard-perfect views of Mount Hood, especially fantastic at sunrise and sunset.

Tamanawas Falls Trail: *3.6-mile (5.8km) round trip; about 600 feet (183m) elevation gain; moderate.* A beautiful hike through a lush forest, leading to a powerful 100-foot (30m) waterfall that cascades over a basalt cliff.

Timberline Trail: *40-mile (64km) loop; about 11,000 feet (3,353m) elevation gain; strenuous, multiday hike.* A classic Oregon backpacking route that circumnavigates Mount Hood, crossing glaciers, alpine meadows, and wildflower-filled valleys.

Tips for taking a great photo

- Sunrise is the best time of day for alpenglow on the peak, sunset for golden reflections on Trillium Lake.
- Visit Trillium Lake or Mirror Lake on a calm day to capture Mount Hood mirrored in the water.
- Use a wide-angle lens to showcase the mountain's scale and surrounding wildflower meadows.
- For a classic Mount Hood winter scene, frame Timberline Lodge in the snow with the mountain towering above.

Page 84: Three Sisters as seen from Smith Rock State Park

Page 85: Mountains near Owyhee Lake

Opposite: Mount Hood reflected in Trillium Lake

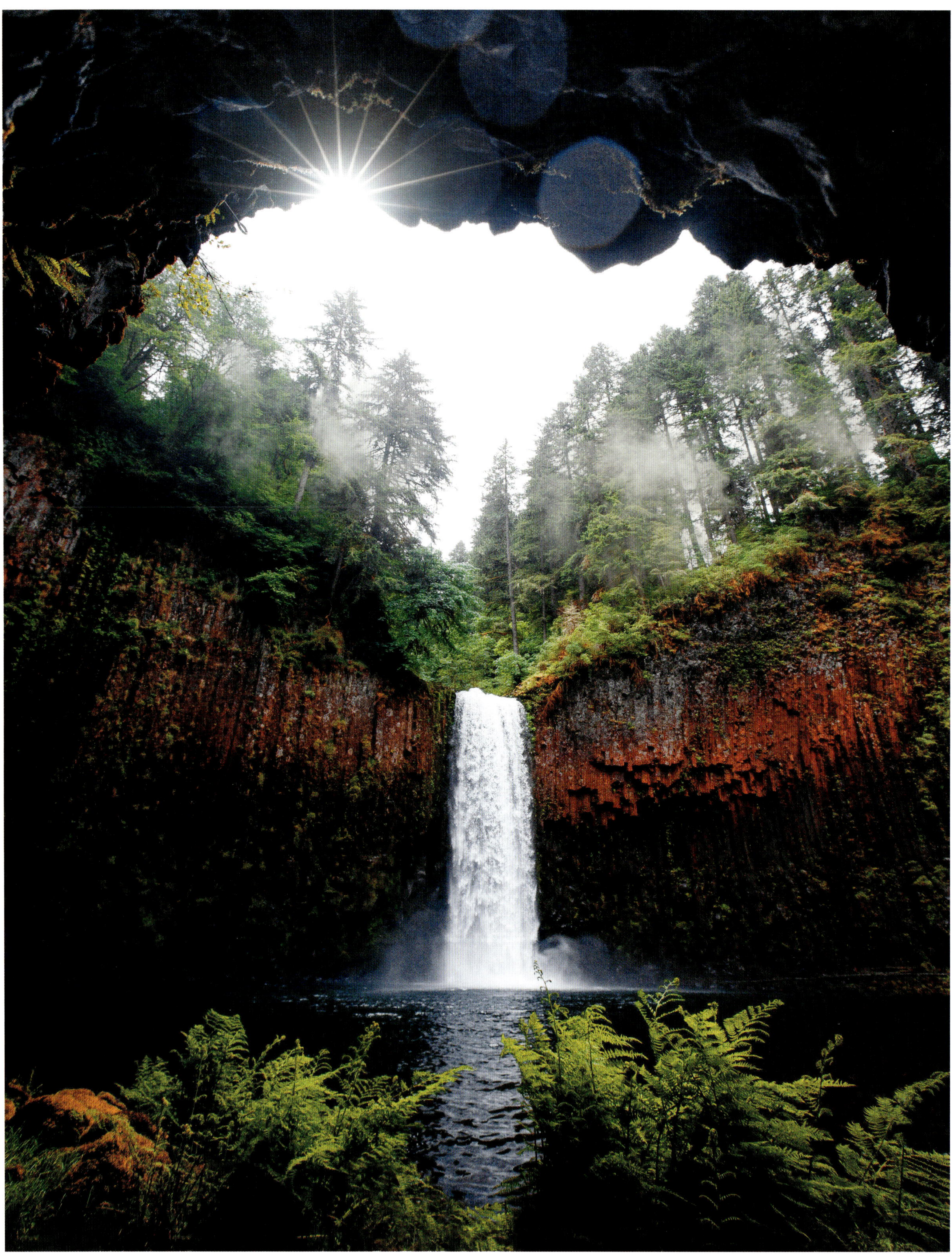

Above: Abiqua Falls | Opposite: Silver Falls

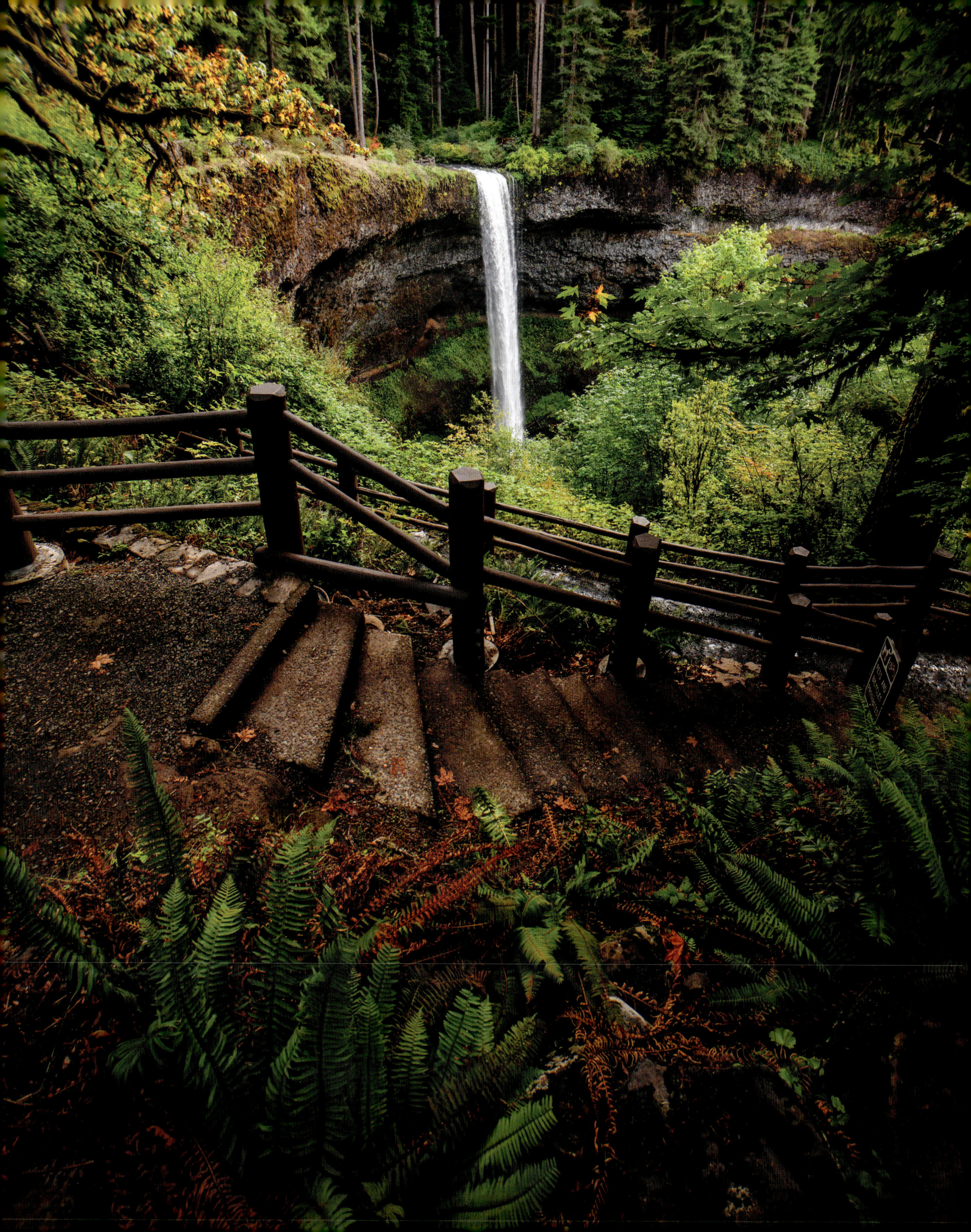

OREGON COAST

Entering the Samuel H. Boardman State Scenic Corridor on the Oregon Coast is like stepping into a hidden world of rugged cliffs, secluded beaches, and towering sea stacks. Every turn along its trails reveals another breathtaking vista—arches carved by the ocean, dense coastal forests opening to dramatic drop-offs, and waves crashing against the rocks far below. One of the most awe-inspiring spots I visited was Natural Bridges, where the Pacific Ocean surges through rocky openings framed by lush greenery. As the sun dipped toward the horizon, the golden light illuminated the mist rising from the waves, making the entire coastline glow. I felt like I'd discovered one of the most wild and untouched places left in the world.

Region: Pacific Northwest

State: Oregon

Coordinates: 44°00'00.0"N 124°00'00.0"W

Focal features: State parks, scenic areas, and the Siuslaw National Forest

Formation attributes: The coastline features dramatic rock formations, rugged cliffs, sea stacks, vast and windswept sandy beaches, old-growth forests, and towering dunes, all shaped by the relentless force of the Pacific Ocean.

Fun fact: The entire Oregon Coast is public land, thanks to the 1967 Oregon Beach Bill, which ensures that all 363 miles (584km) of coastline remain open for public access.

Best time to visit: June to September for the best summer weather, though spring and fall offer fewer crowds. Winter is ideal for storm-watching, as massive waves crash against the cliffs.

How to access: US Highway 101 runs the entire length of the Oregon Coast, offering easy access to beaches, scenic viewpoints, and charming coastal towns. Some areas, like Sand Lake and the Oregon Dunes, allow for off-road vehicles, while others, like Ecola State Park, are best explored on foot.

Things to consider: The Oregon Coast is known for its unpredictable weather, so be prepared for mist, wind, and sudden rain, even in summer. Tides play a big role in accessibility to beaches and tide pools, so check tide charts before visiting.

RECOMMENDED TRAILS:

Natural Bridges Viewpoint Trail: *0.6-mile (1km) round trip; slight elevation gain; easy*. A short walk to one of the most popular viewpoints on the Oregon Coast, offering breathtaking views of the ocean and dramatic cliffs.

Hug Point Trail: *0.7-mile (1.km) round trip; about 50 feet (15m) elevation gain; moderate*. A scenic coastal walk past tide pools, caves, and an old wagon road carved into the rock, accessible only at low tide.

South Neahkahnie Mountain Trail: *3.4-mile (5.5km) round trip; about 1,100 feet (335m) elevation gain; strenuous*. A steep but rewarding hike to a panoramic viewpoint overlooking Manzanita Beach and the Pacific Ocean.

Tips for taking a great photo

- Sunrise is the best time of day for soft lighting on the sea stacks, sunset for dramatic silhouettes and golden reflections on the water.
- Visit during low tide for the best access to tide pools. Look for colorful sea stars and anemones.
- Winter storms create powerful crashes at places like Thor's Well and Shore Acres State Park. Check the calendar for king tides, which produce the best waves.
- Use a tripod and a slow shutter speed for long exposures to capture the movement of waves around sea stacks and rock formations.

Opposite: Samuel H. Boardman State Scenic Corridor, Oregon Coast

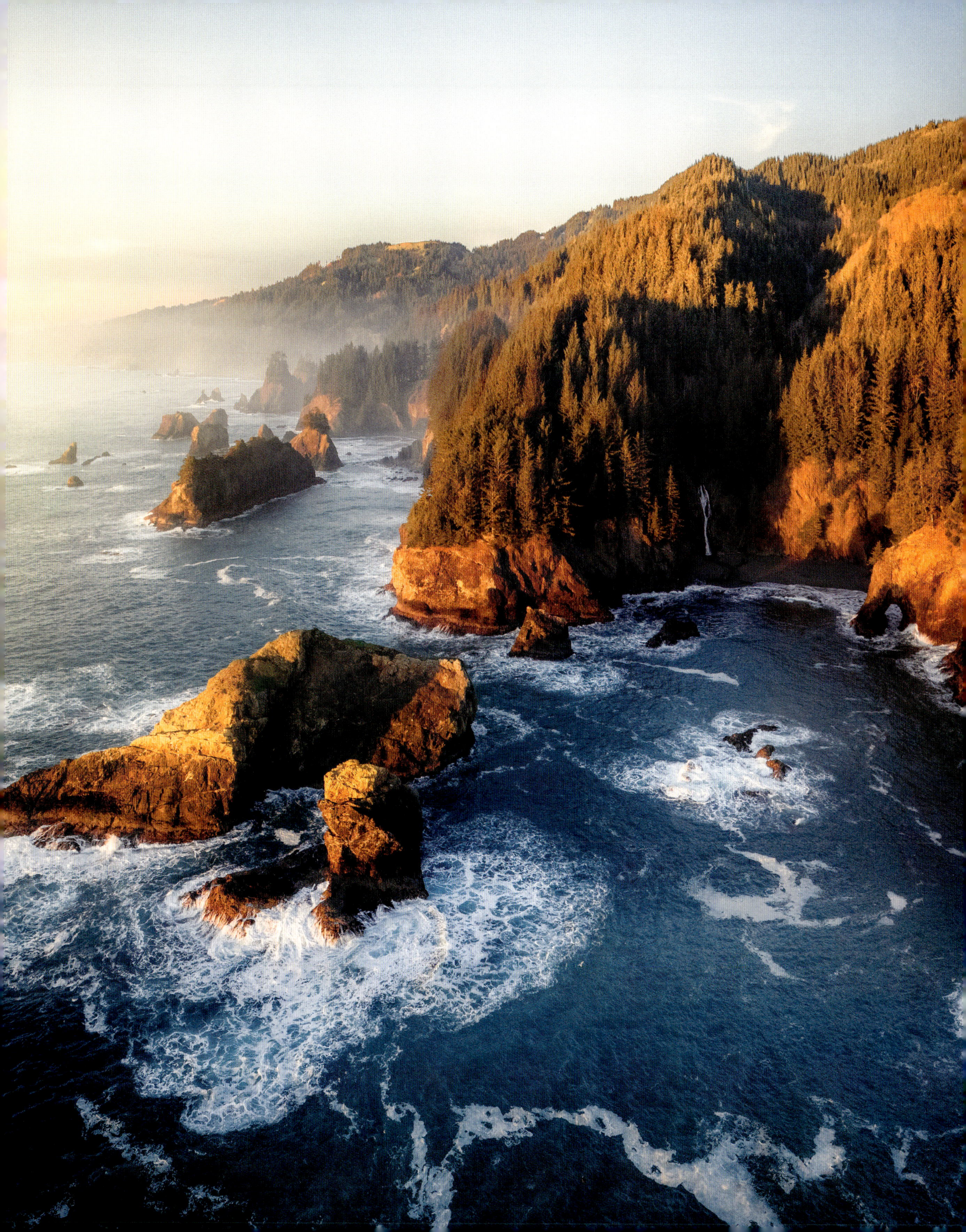

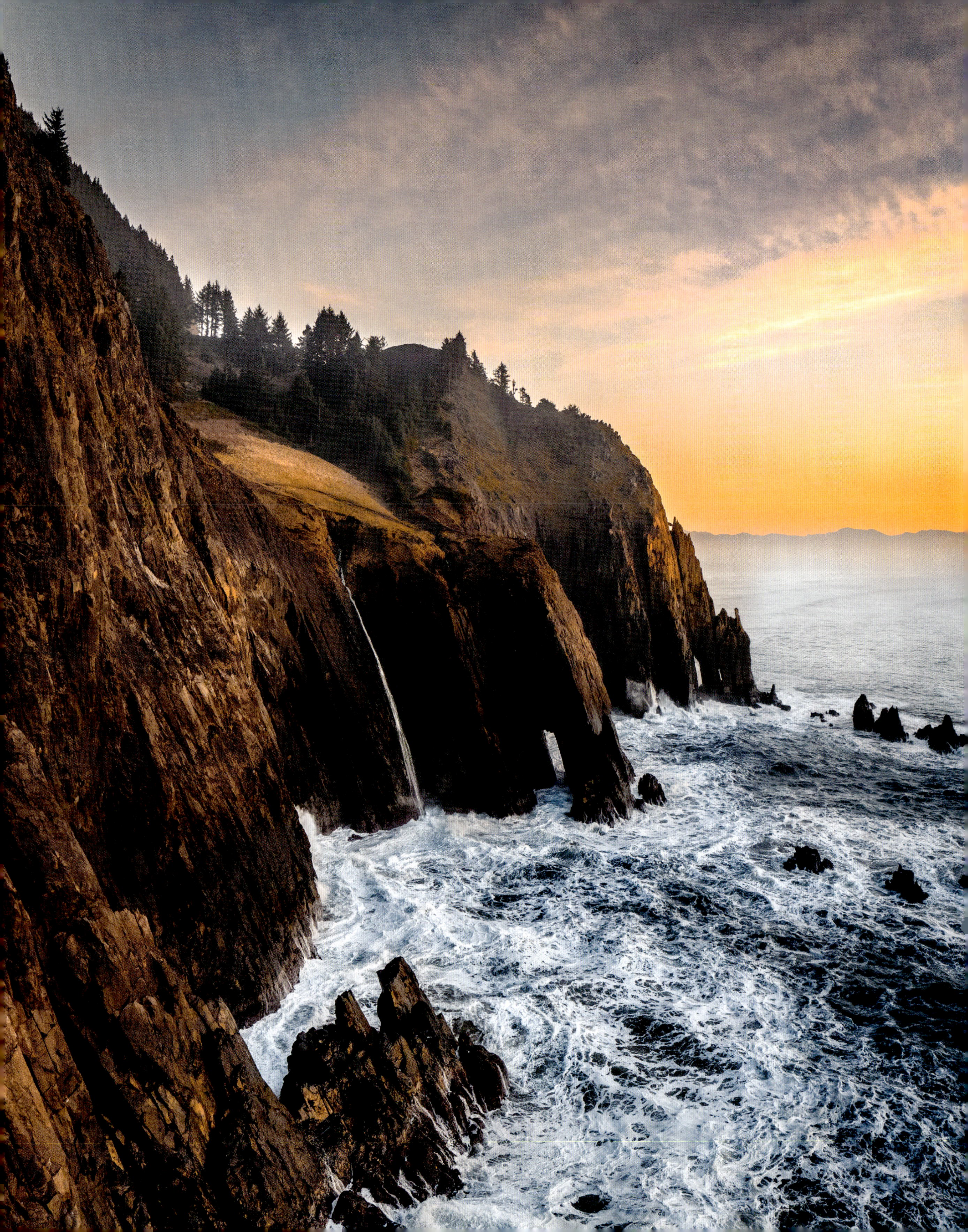

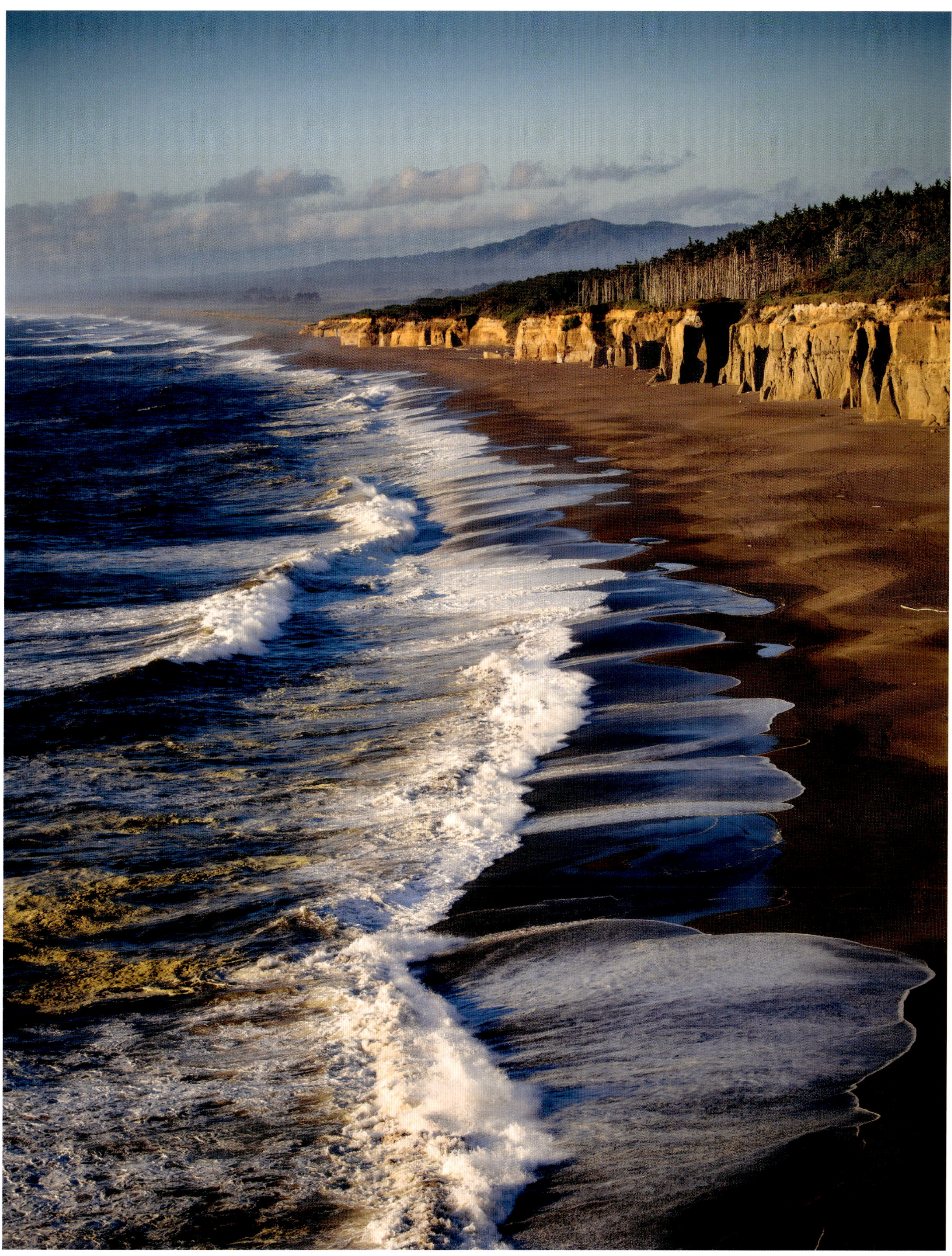

Above: Blacklock Cliffs | Opposite: Near Elk Flats Rock viewpoint

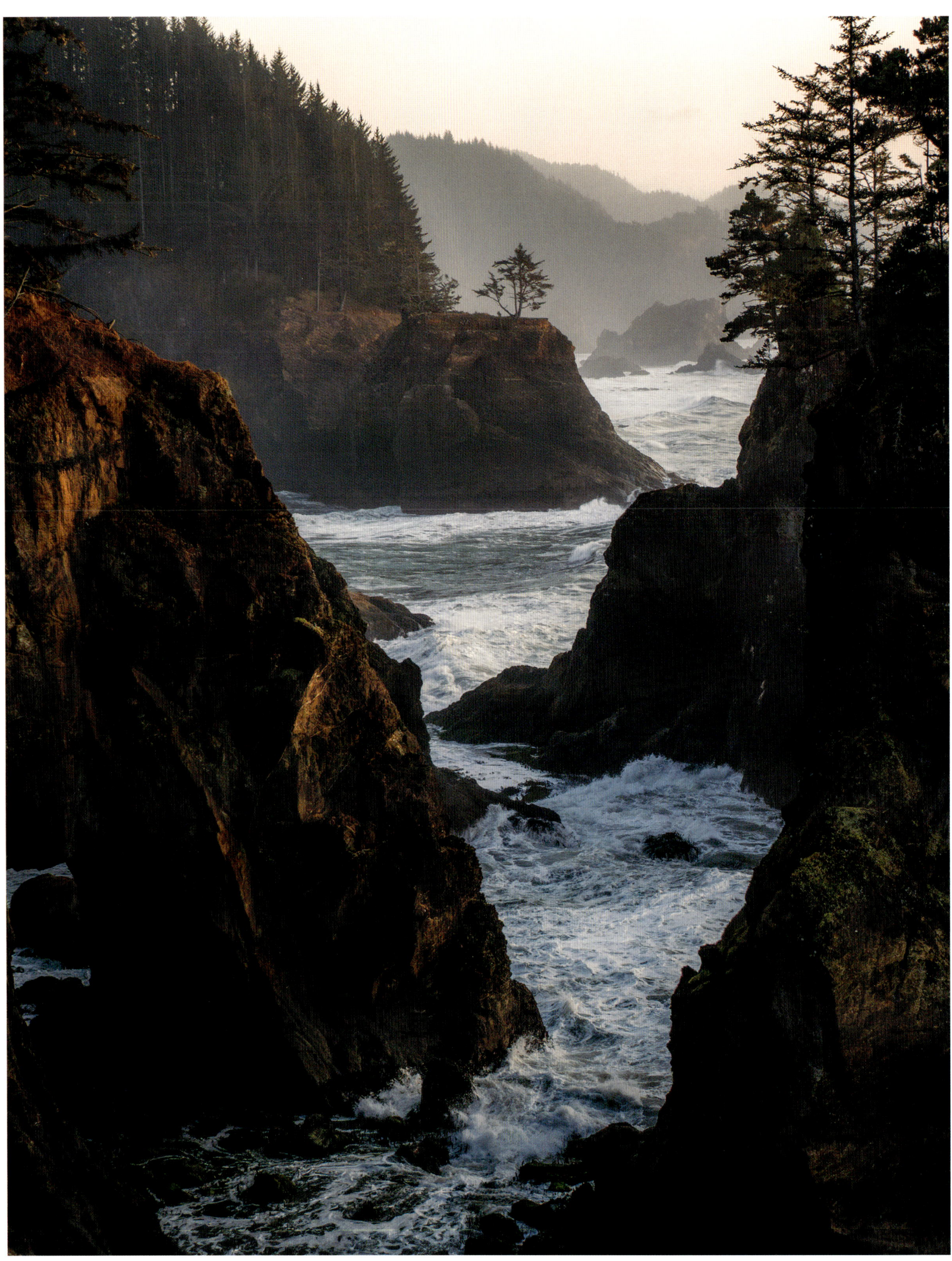

Above: Natural Bridge, Samuel H. Boardman State Scenic Corridor | Opposite: Oregon Coast

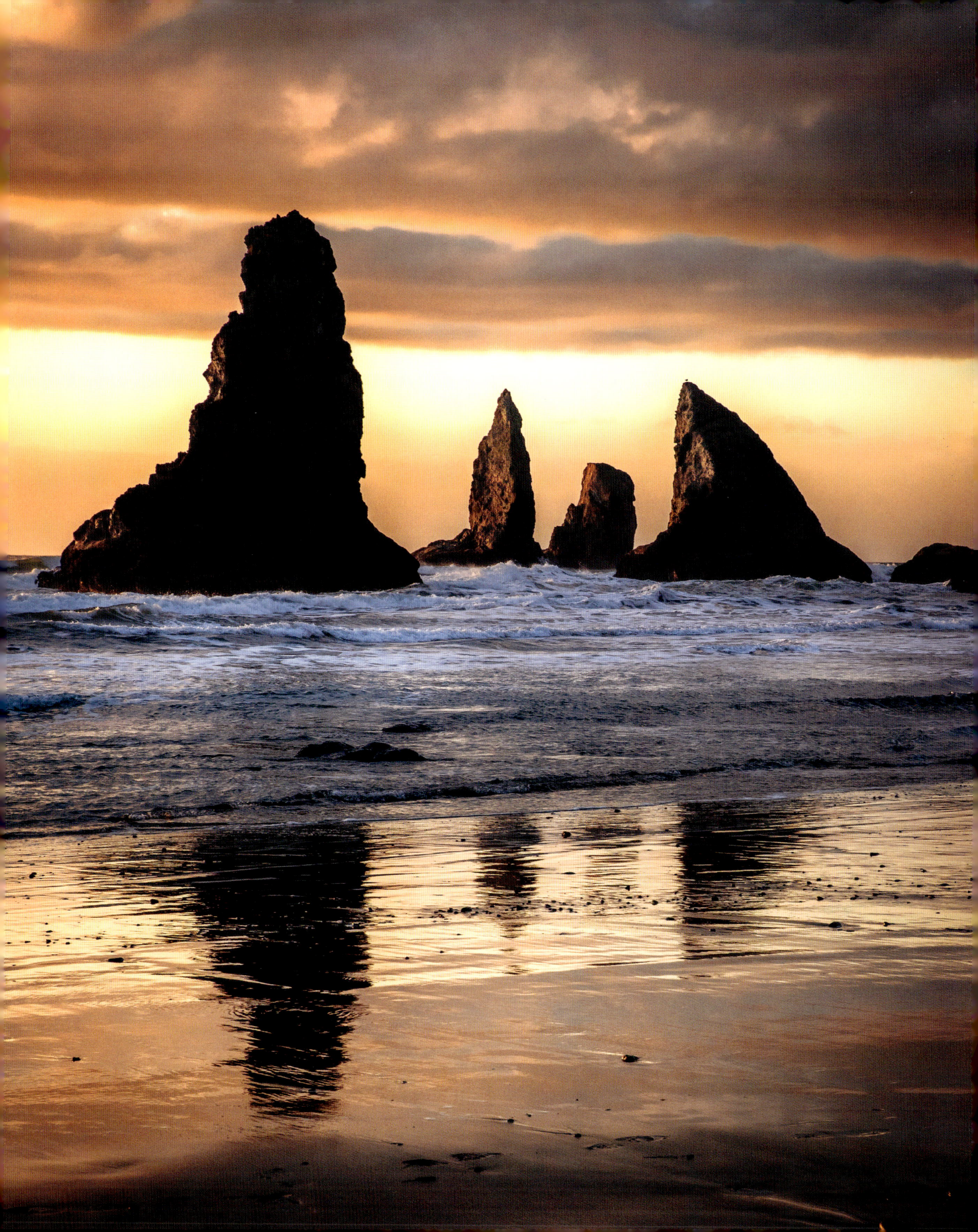

CASCADE LAKES SCENIC BYWAY

The Cascade Lakes Scenic Byway offers jaw-dropping view after view—every turn highlighting another alpine lake, towering peak, or lava flow that makes you want to pull over to take it all in. One of my favorite moments was watching the sunrise at Sparks Lake. The water was so still it looked like glass, perfectly reflecting South Sister as the sky turned shades of pink and gold. Hiking to Green Lakes, I couldn't get over how blue the water was, surrounded by rugged peaks and wildflowers. By the time I made it to Elk Lake, the afternoon heat had me jumping straight in. Floating there, surrounded by the Cascade Range, it hit me: this was one of the most beautiful places I'd ever been.

Region: Pacific Northwest

State: Oregon

Coordinates: 44°01'14.2"N 121°38'41.6"W

Focal feature: Stunning views of the Cascade Range and numerous alpine lakes from a high-elevation scenic drive.

Formation attributes: The byway sits at elevations ranging from 4,000 feet (1,219m) to over 6,000 feet (1,829m) and showcases landscapes shaped by volcanic activity, including lava fields and glacier-carved lakes.

Fun fact: Many of the lakes along the route, including Sparks Lake and Devils Lake, were formed by ancient lava flows that blocked rivers and streams, creating pristine, crystal-clear waters.

Best time to visit: July through September, when the road is fully open and the weather is warm. Fall brings fewer crowds and beautiful golden larch trees.

How to access: The byway starts just outside of Bend, Oregon, and follows Highway 46 through the Deschutes National Forest. There are no gas stations along the route, so fill up beforehand.

Things to consider: This byway is a seasonal road, typically open from late June through October, depending on snow levels. Expect limited cell service and bring plenty of supplies if exploring remote areas. Popular lakes and trailheads can get crowded in summer, so arrive early or visit on weekdays for a quieter experience.

RECOMMENDED TRAILS:

Ray Atkeson Loop: *Varies up to 2 miles (3.2km); about 200 feet (61m) elevation gain; easy.* A short, scenic walk around Sparks Lake, one of the most photographed lakes in Oregon, with stunning reflections of South Sister and Broken Top.

Green Lakes Trail (via Fall Creek): *9-mile (14.5km) round trip; about 1,200 feet (366m) elevation gain; moderate.* One of the most popular hikes in the area, following Fall Creek through a lush forest to the breathtaking Green Lakes basin, nestled beneath South Sister and Broken Top.

Tips for taking a great photo

- Sunrise at Sparks Lake offers the best reflections, while sunset at Elk Lake or Devils Lake creates stunning colors on the water.
- Bring a wide-angle lens to capture the full scope of the lakes reflecting the Cascades in the background.
- Mid-to-late summer brings vibrant wildflower blooms along trails like Green Lakes and Todd Lake.
- The high elevation and lack of light pollution make this a perfect place for astrophotography. Try shooting the Milky Way over Sparks Lake.

Opposite: Views along the Cascade Lakes Scenic Byway featuring Mount Bachelor and Sparks Lake

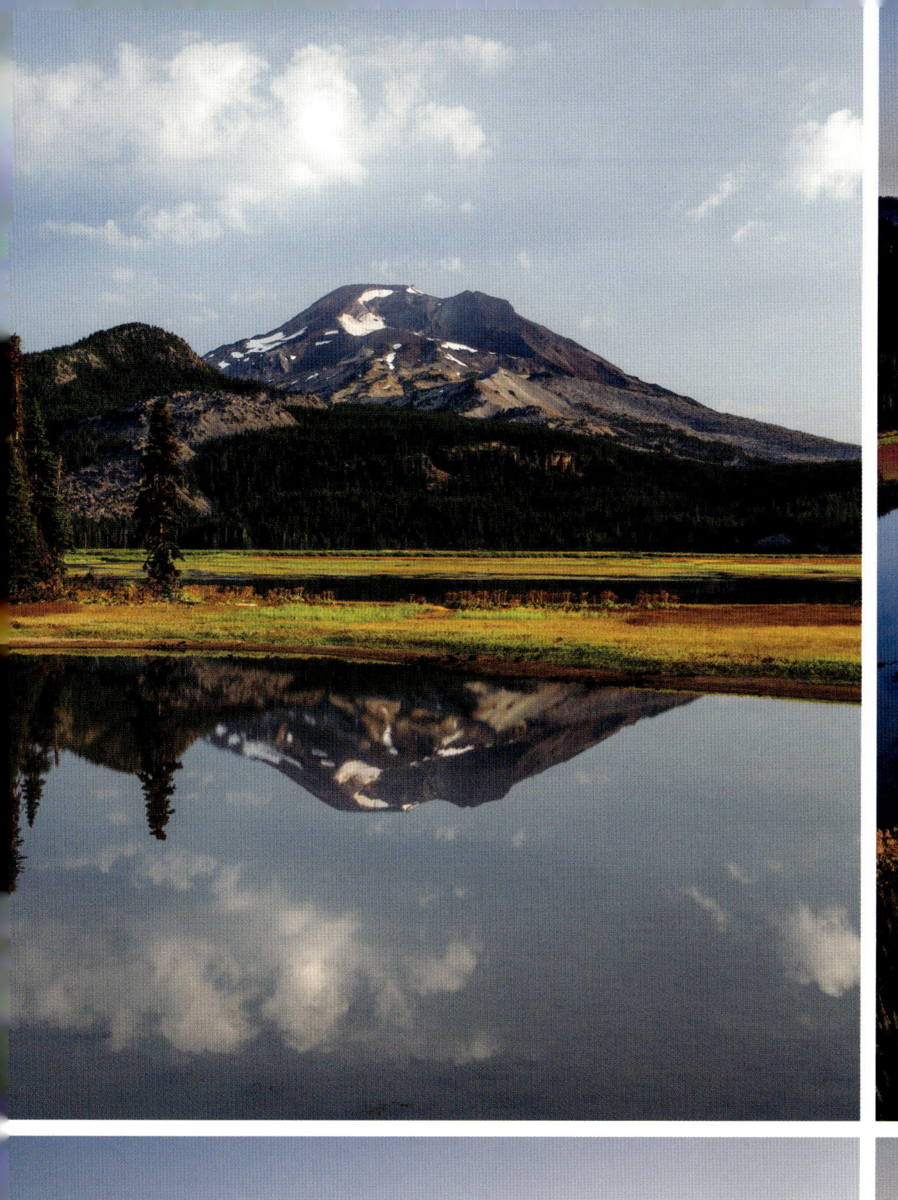
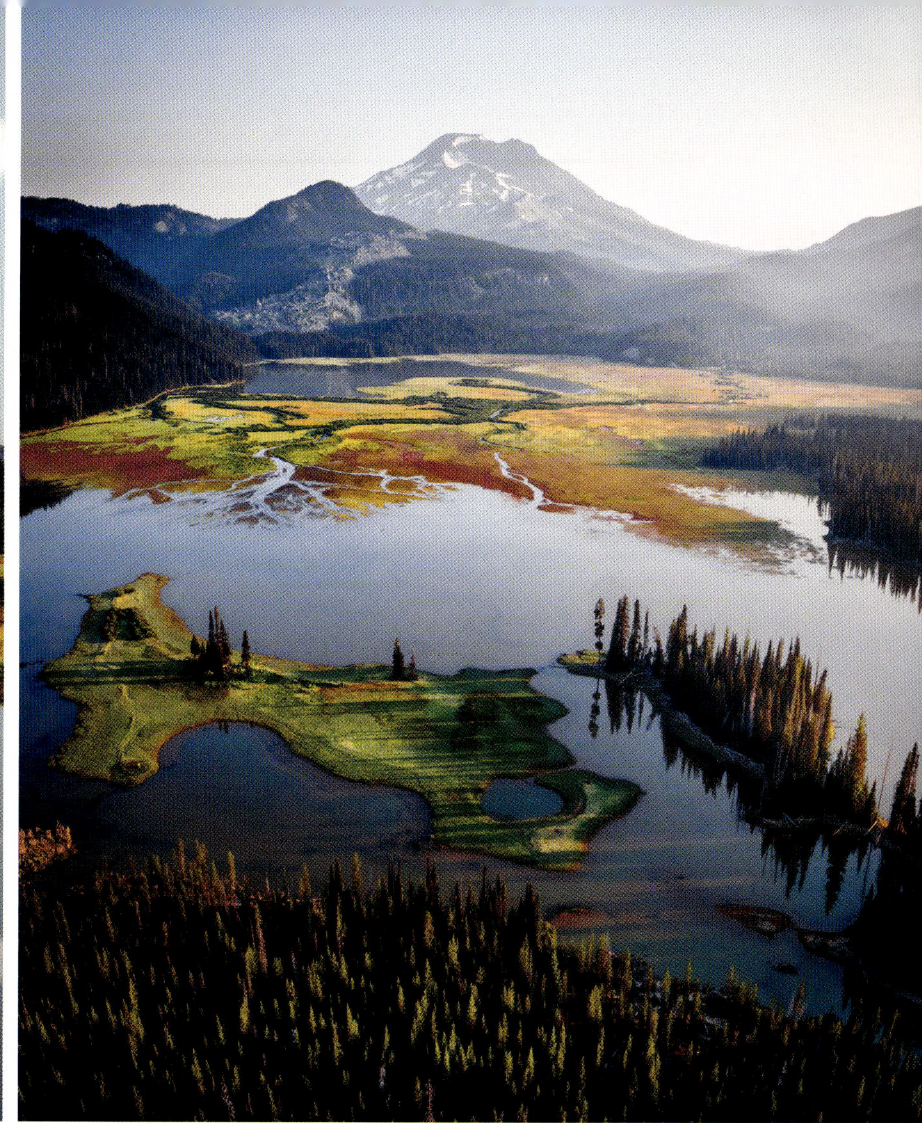
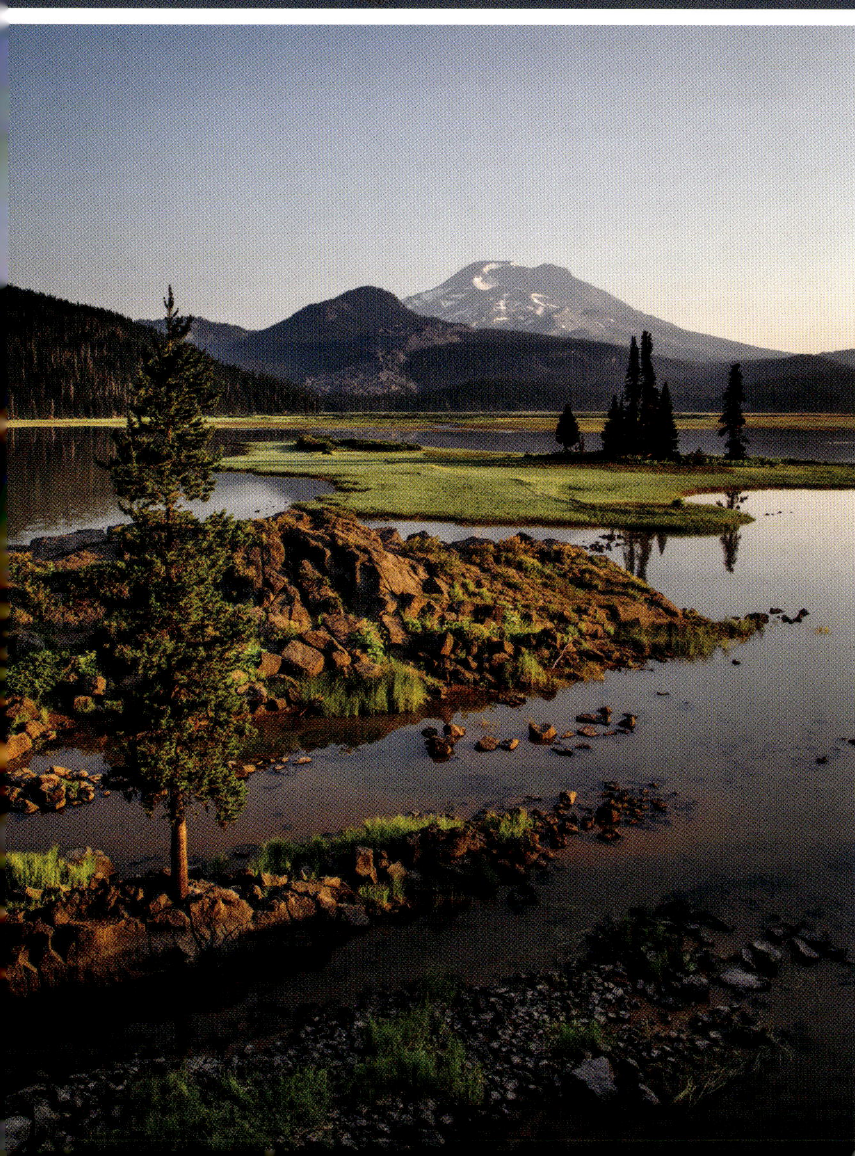
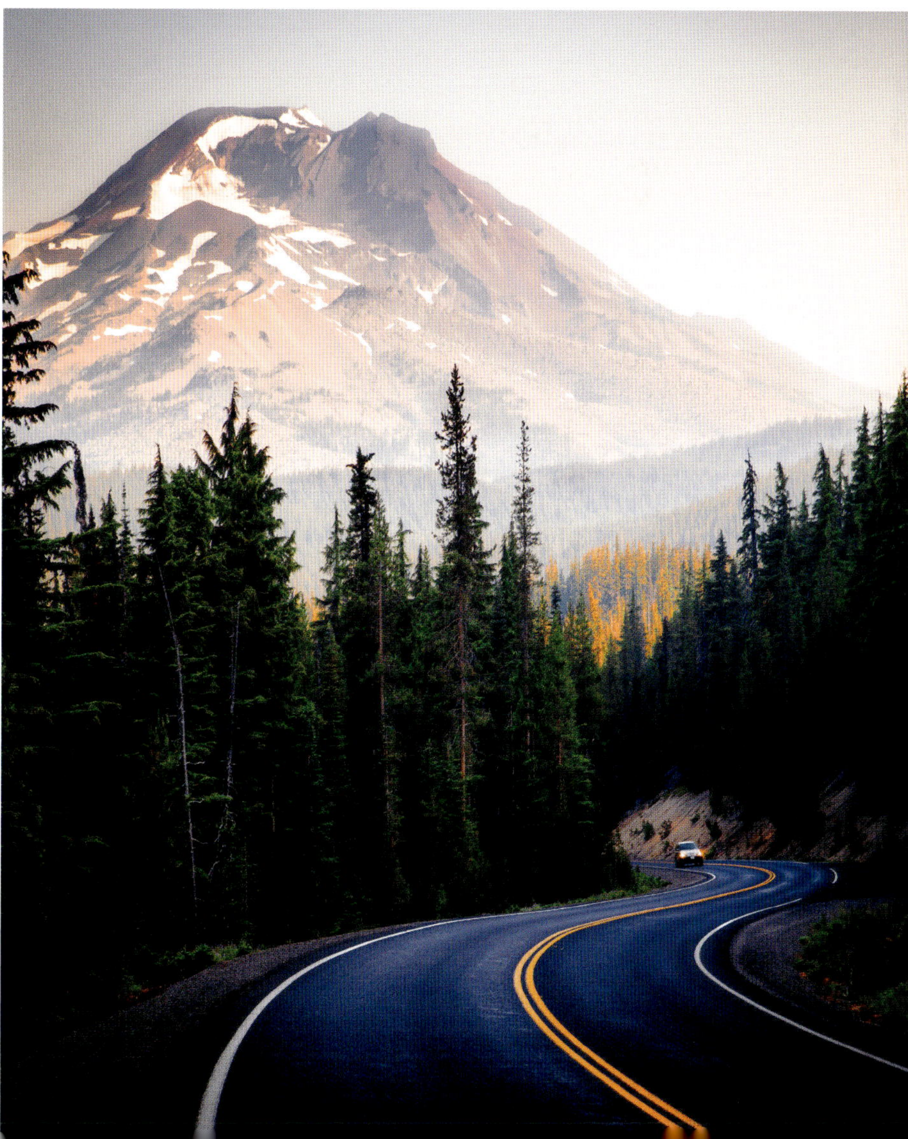

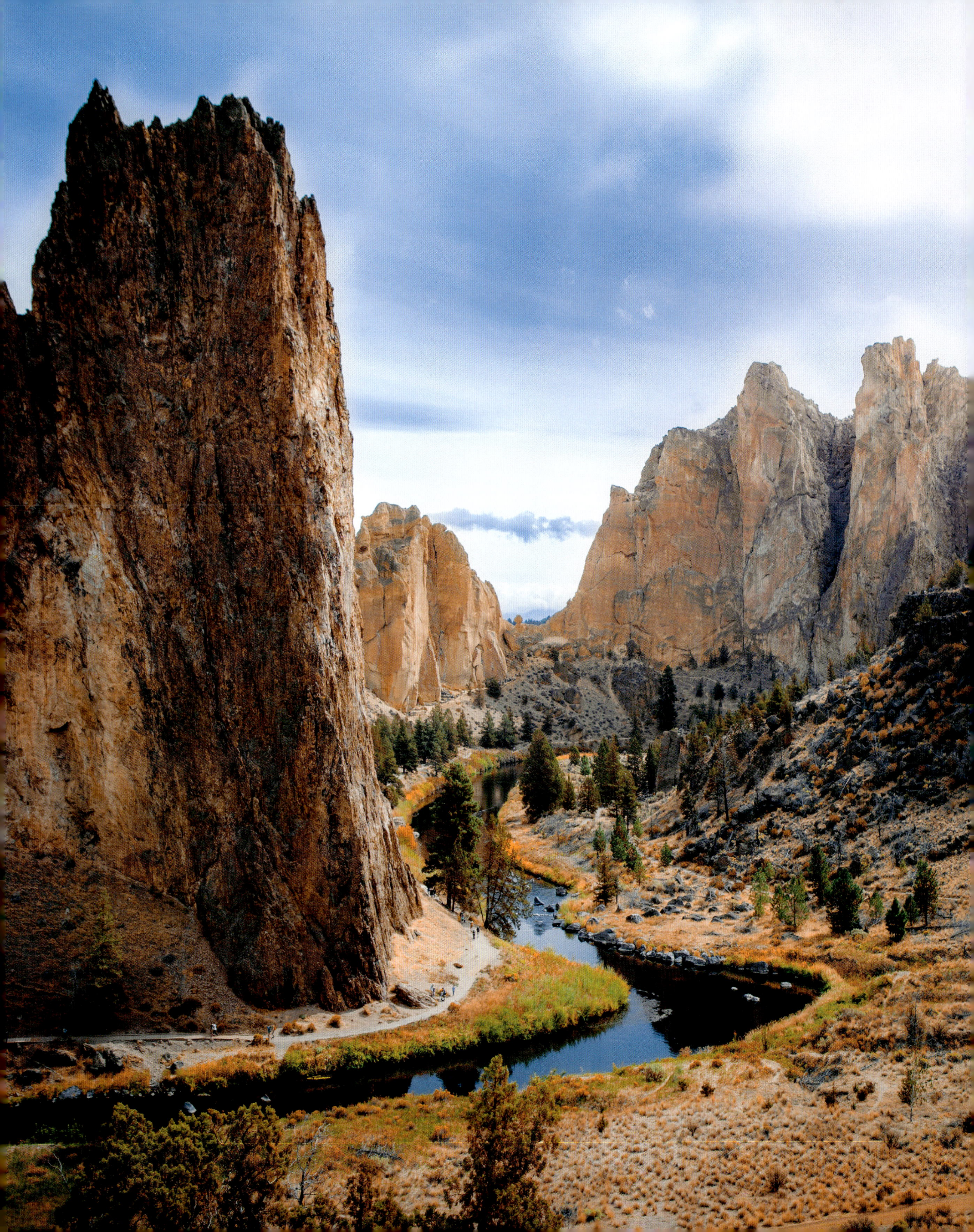

SISTERS & BEND

Bend has a way of making every day feel like an adventure. One of my favorite experiences was hiking up Misery Ridge at Smith Rock. The climb was tough, but the view from the top is absolutely unreal—golden rock spires rising above the winding Crooked River. Walking along the Deschutes River Trail at sunset was another unforgettable moment, with the sky turning pink behind Mount Bachelor while paddleboarders floated downstream. Whether it's grabbing a post-hike beer at one of the local breweries or watching the stars over the lava fields, Bend always leaves me wanting to come back for more.

Region: Pacific Northwest

State: Oregon

Coordinates: 44°03'29.5"N 121°18'55.1"W

Focal feature: A vibrant outdoor town surrounded by mountains, forests, and the Deschutes River, known for its craft beer scene, outdoor recreation, and sunny weather

Formation attributes: Bend sits at an elevation of 3,623 feet (1,104m) on the edge of the Cascade Range and was shaped by ancient volcanic activity. Lava flows, cinder cones, and underground lava tubes are scattered throughout the area.

Fun fact: Bend is home to the last remaining Blockbuster in the world, a nostalgic relic of movie-rental history.

Best time to visit: Spring through fall offers the best hiking and mountain biking, while winter is perfect for skiing and snowshoeing at nearby Mount Bachelor.

How to access: Bend is easily accessible via US Highway 97, about a three-hour drive from Portland. The Redmond Airport (RDM) is just twenty minutes north and offers flights from major cities.

Things to consider: Summers bring crowds—booking accommodations early is a good idea.

RECOMMENDED TRAILS:

Deschutes River Trail: *Varies up to 12 miles (19.3km); minimal elevation gain; easy.* A scenic walk or bike ride along the river, passing waterfalls, lava flows, and pine forests.

Tumalo Falls Trail: *7-mile (11.3km) round trip; about 1,500 feet (457m) elevation gain; moderate.* A must-visit hike leading to a stunning 90-foot (27m) waterfall, with additional trails extending into the Three Sisters Wilderness.

Misery Ridge Trail (Smith Rock State Park): *6.2-mile (10km) round trip; about 1,800 feet (549m) elevation gain; strenuous.* A steep but rewarding climb to panoramic views over the Crooked River and the towering rock formations of Smith Rock.

Tips for taking a great photo

- Sunrise and sunset offer the most dramatic lighting, especially at spots like Tumalo Falls and Smith Rock.
- Capture the unique textures of lava fields at the Newberry National Volcanic Monument.
- The Deschutes River provides perfect opportunities for mirrorlike reflections of Bend's surrounding mountains.
- The dry climate and high elevation make Bend an excellent spot for stargazing and for Milky Way shots.

Opposite: Smith Rock State Park

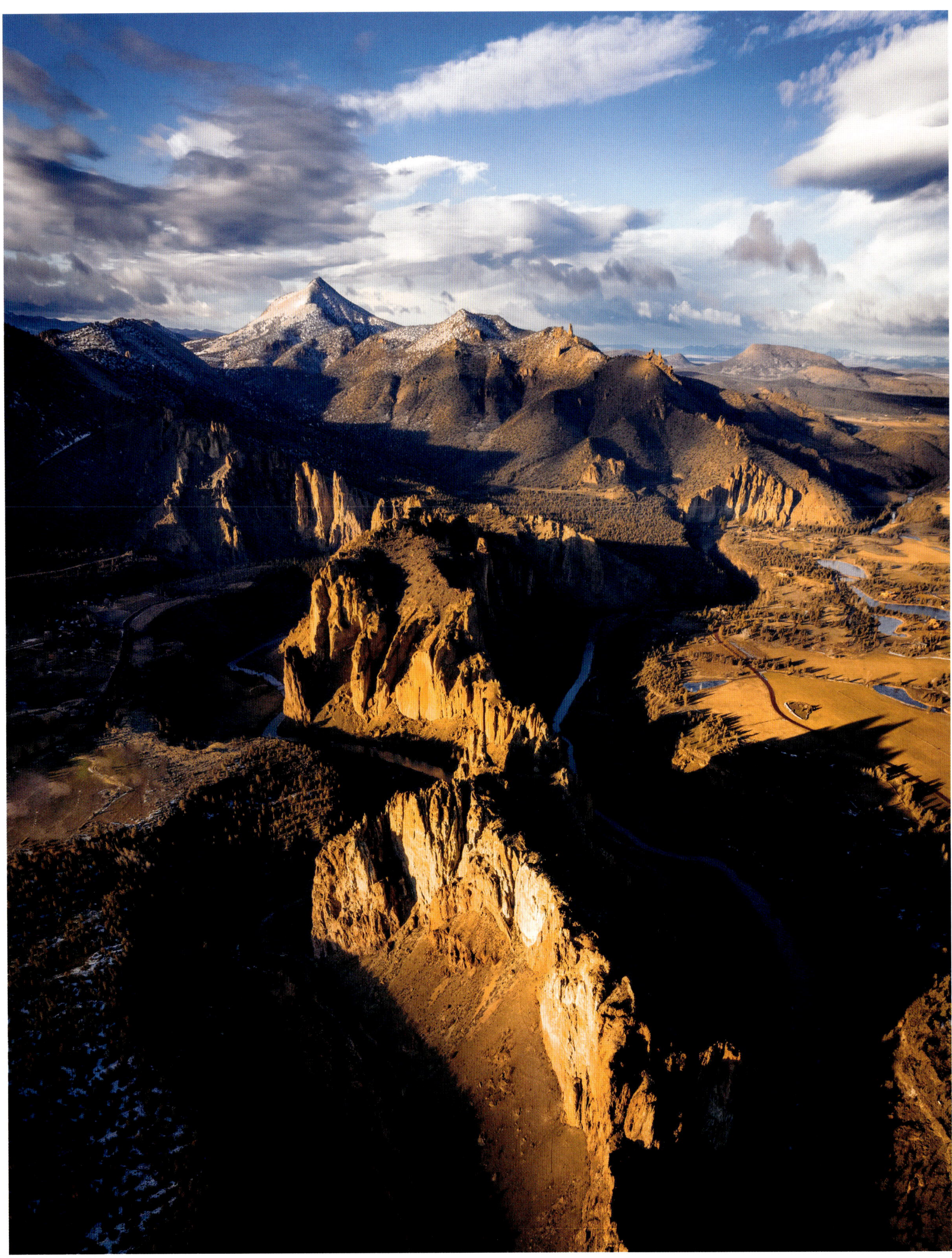

Above: Smith Rock State Park | Opposite: No Name Lake and Broken Top

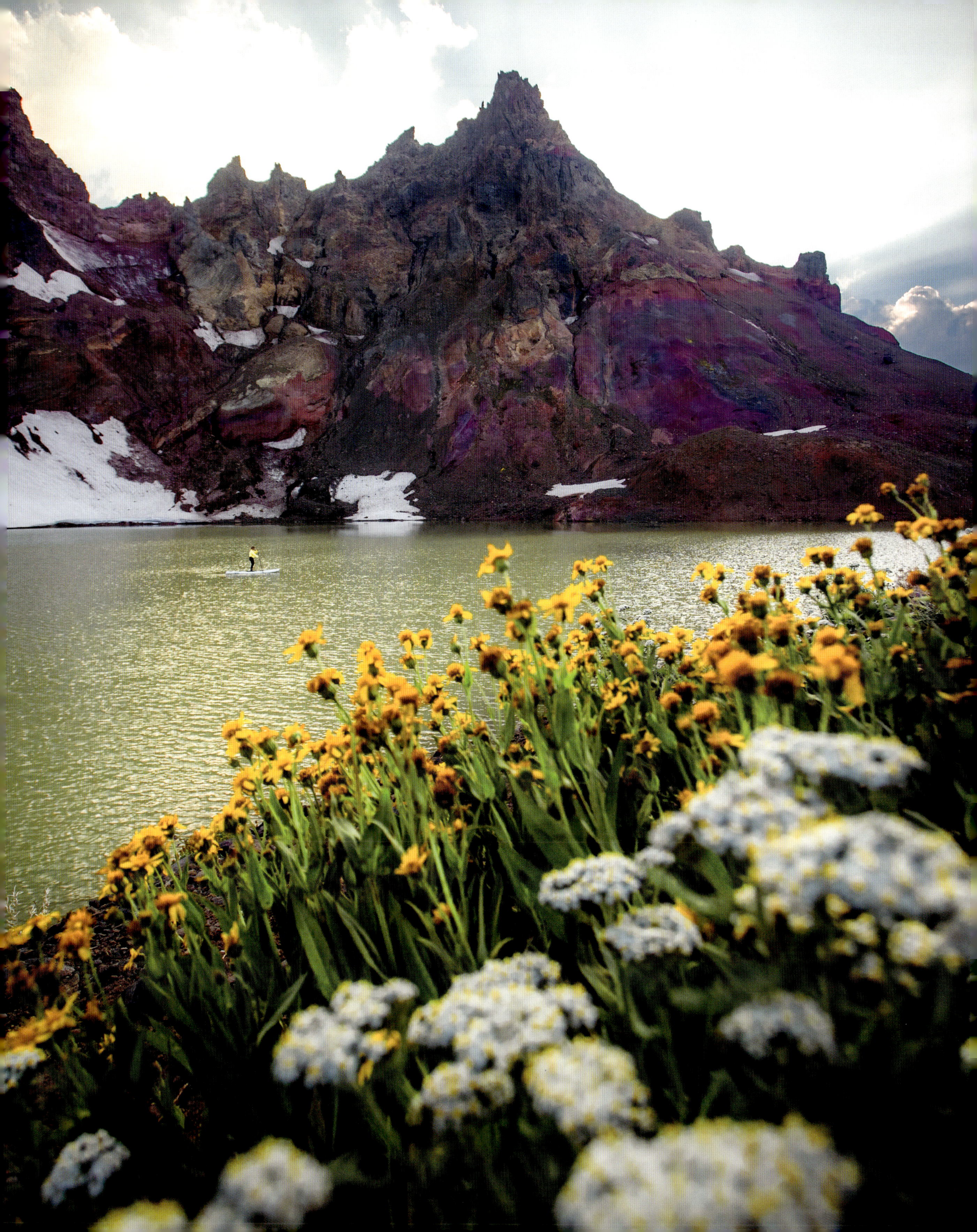

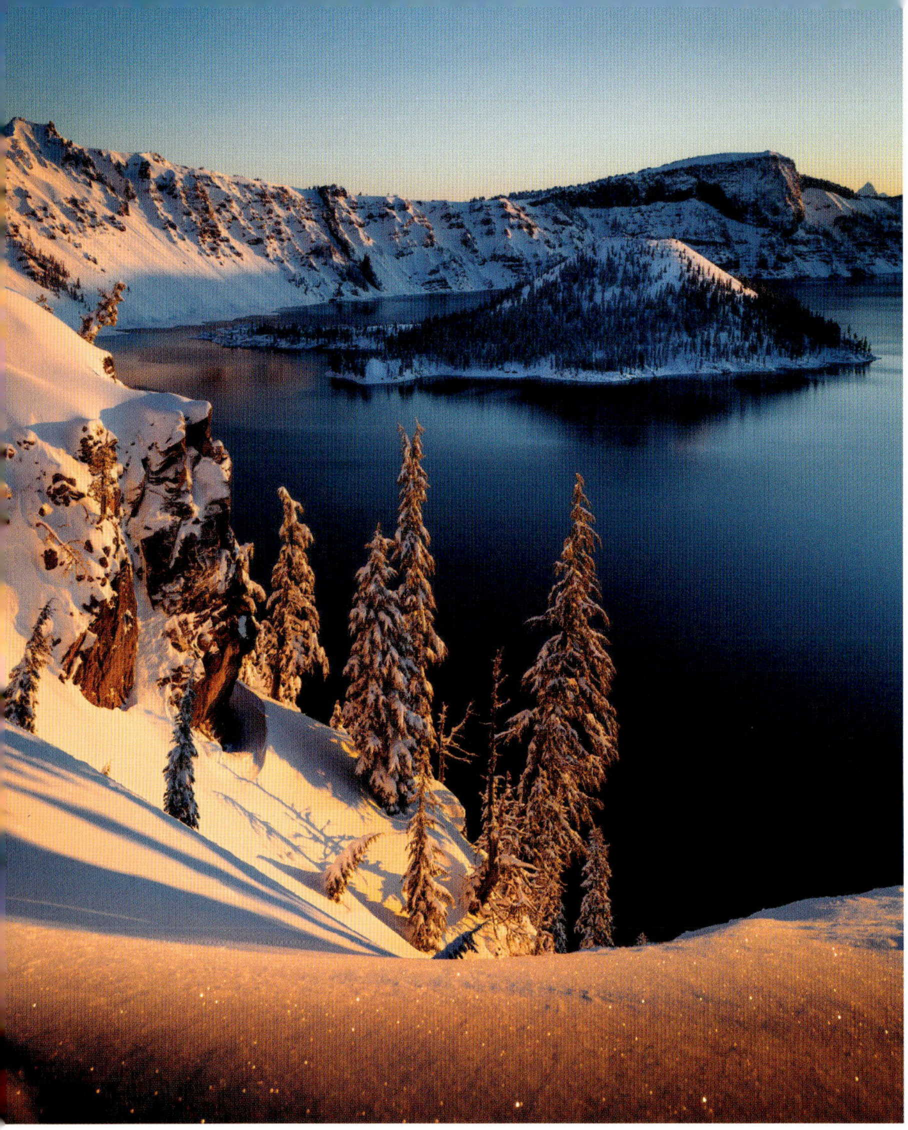

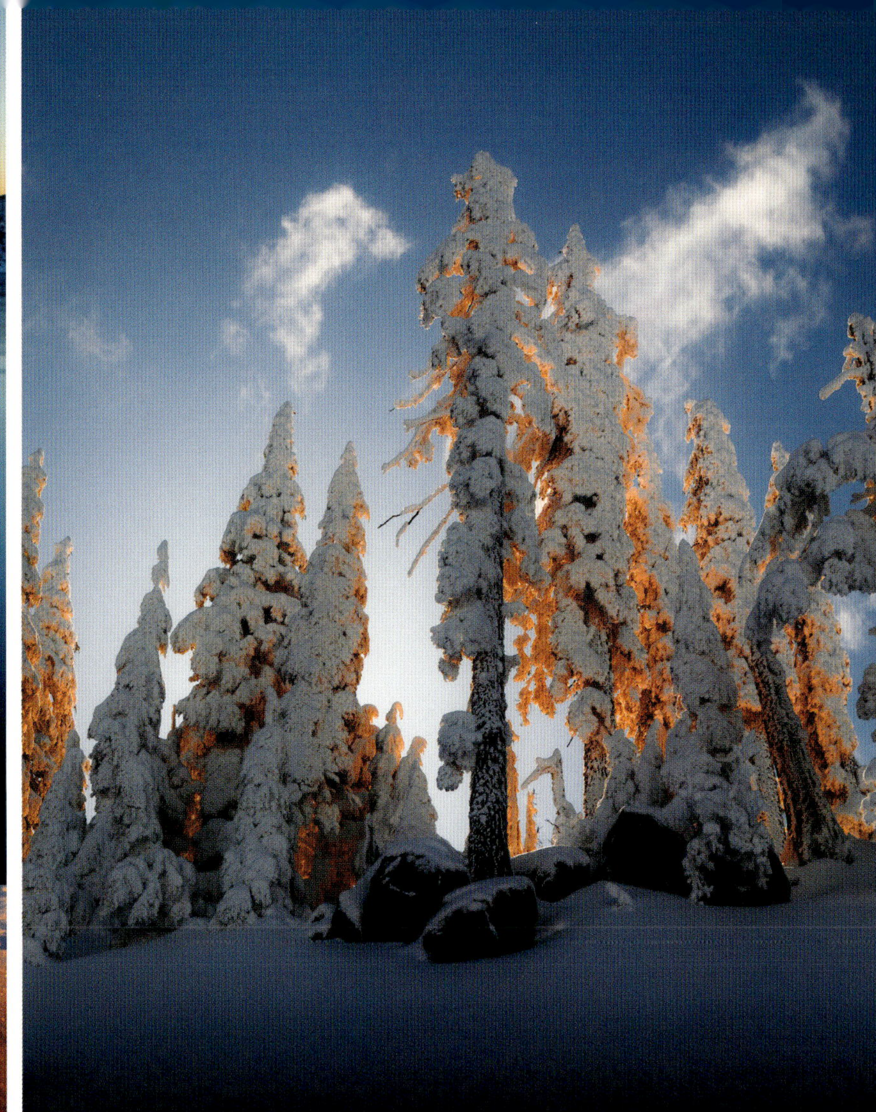

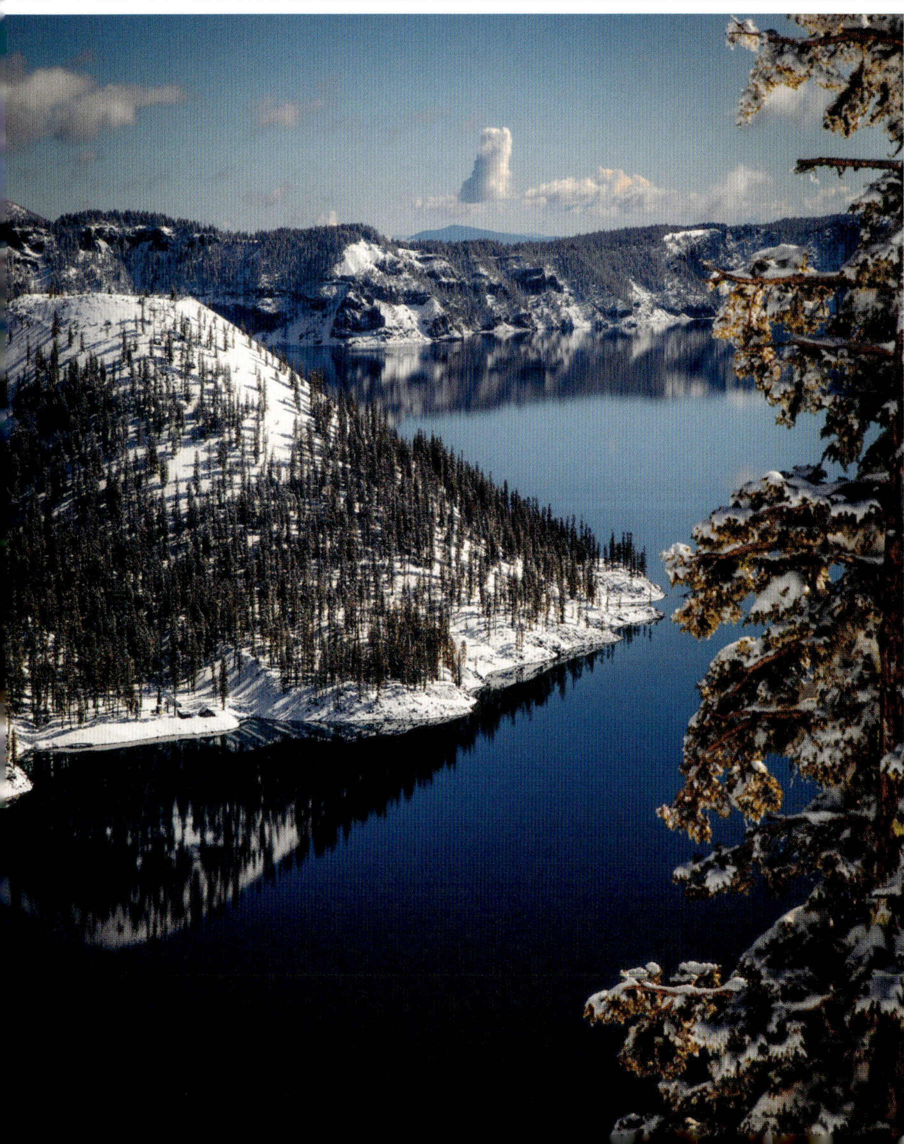

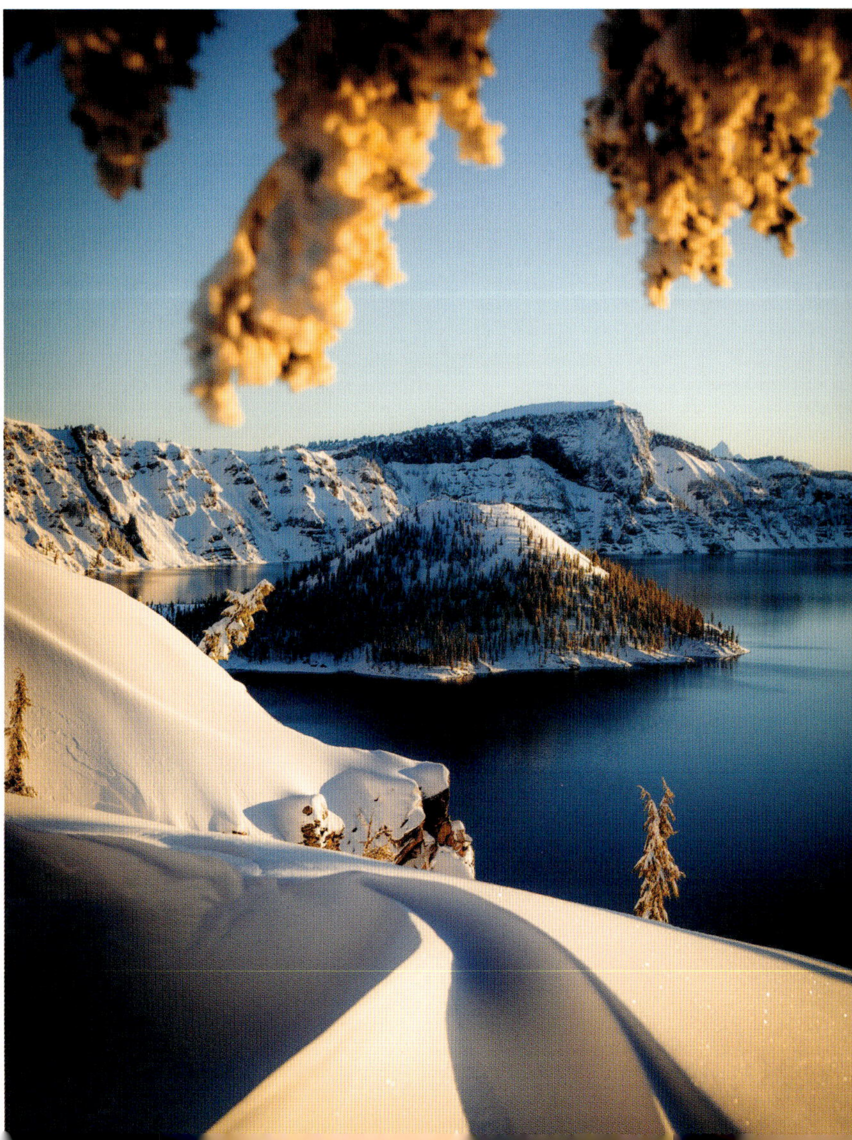

CRATER LAKE NATIONAL PARK

The first time I stood at the rim, I was stunned by the lake's impossibly deep blue color—like a sapphire set into the mountains. The hike up Garfield Peak provides a breathtaking vantage point, with the lake stretching endlessly below, the Cascades in the distance. I hiked down to Cleetwood Cove and dipped my hands into the icy water—another unforgettable moment. So few people get to touch the lake itself, and it felt like a privilege. Crater Lake is completely otherworldly, a reminder of nature's raw power and beauty.

Region: Pacific Northwest

State: Oregon

Coordinates: 42°56′40.6″N 122°06′32.4″W

Focal feature: Crater Lake, a deep volcanic lake formed by the collapse of Mount Mazama

Formation attributes: Crater Lake is 1,943 feet (592m) deep, making it the deepest lake in the US and the ninth deepest in the world. It was formed over 7,700 years ago when Mount Mazama erupted and collapsed, creating a massive caldera that later filled with rain and snowmelt.

Fun fact: Because it has no rivers or streams flowing in or out, Crater Lake is one of the purest and clearest lakes in the world, with visibility reaching up to 139 feet (42m) below the surface of the water. It's known for its intense blue color and stunning caldera views.

Best time to visit: July to September for full access to Rim Drive, hiking trails, and boat tours; November to April for solitude, snowshoeing, and cross-country skiing.

How to access: Crater Lake is located in southern Oregon, with the most common access via Highway 62 from Medford (about 90 miles / 145 kilometers away) or Bend (about 100 miles / 160 kilometers away).

Things to consider: The weather can change quickly, and snow lingers well into summer. Bring layers, as mornings and evenings can be chilly even in summer. Some roads and trails may remain closed until July. The park charges an entrance fee, and Rim Drive, which circles the lake, is typically only open from late June to October due to heavy snowfall in the winter.

RECOMMENDED TRAILS:

Sun Notch Trail: *0.8-mile (1.3km) round trip; about 130 feet (40m) elevation gain; easy.* A short walk leading to one of the best viewpoints of Phantom Ship, a small island in Crater Lake resembling a ghostly ship.

Garfield Peak Trail: *3.5-mile (5.6km) round trip; about 1,100 feet (335m) elevation gain; moderate.* A rewarding climb to a panoramic viewpoint overlooking Crater Lake and the surrounding Cascade peaks.

Cleetwood Cove Trail: *2.2-mile (3.5km) round trip; 700 feet (213m) elevation gain; strenuous.* A steep but worthwhile climb for the chance to touch the pristine waters of Crater Lake or to take a boat tour to Wizard Island. The only trail that provides lake access.

Tips for taking a great photo

- Early morning or late afternoon is the best time of day for excellent lighting on the lake and fewer crowds. Sunrise at Watchman Overlook offers incredible colors.
- Calm days provide stunning mirrorlike reflections of the sky and crater walls on the lake's surface.
- Crater Lake is one of the best places for astrophotography due to its remote location and minimal light pollution. Try capturing the Milky Way above the lake on a clear night.
- Bring a wide-angle lens or use the panoramic mode to capture the full scale of the caldera from viewpoints along Rim Drive.

Opposite: Crater Lake National Park

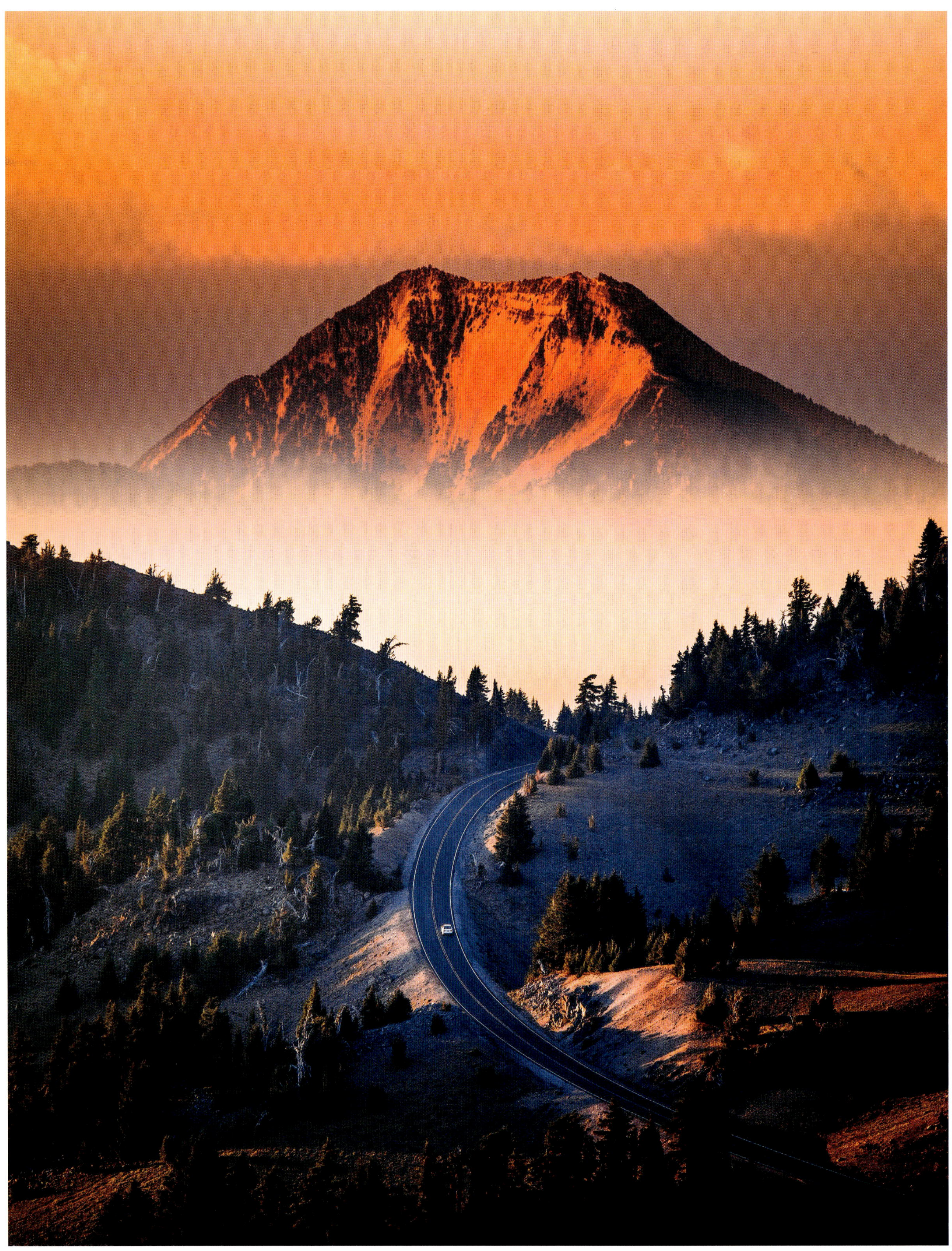

Above: Rim Drive in Crater Lake National Park | Opposite: Wizard Island, Crater Lake

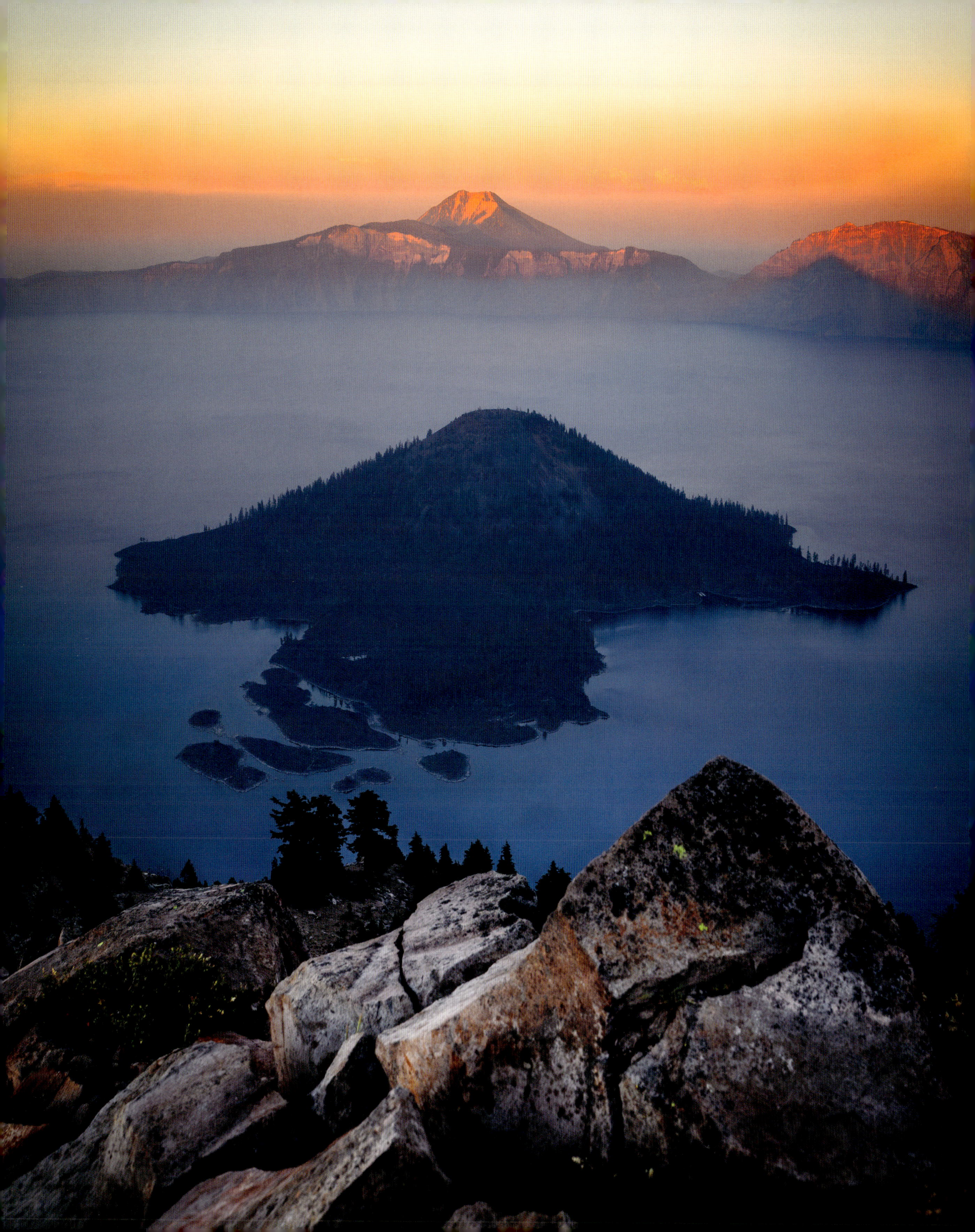

OWYHEE CANYONLANDS

Leslie Gulch transported me to another planet. The towering cliffs, sculpted by millions of years of erosion, glowed in the afternoon sun, and the silence was surreal. Walking through the narrow canyons, I was amazed by the unique formations, some resembling ancient castles. Later, soaking in the natural hot springs along the Owyhee River, surrounded by sheer rock walls and the sound of rushing water, I felt pure solitude and connection with the landscape. Owyhee's remoteness makes it one of Oregon's last true wild places, a must-visit for those willing to venture off the beaten path.

Region: Pacific Northwest

State: Oregon

Coordinates: 43°18'00.0"N 117°12'00.0"W

Focal features: The Owyhee River canyon and the unique rock formations of Leslie Gulch

Formation attributes: Owyhee State Park is part of the larger Owyhee Canyonlands, a vast high-desert region carved by the Owyhee River. The area features towering rhyolite cliffs, deep gorges, and striking rock formations, some over sixteen million years old.

Fun fact: The name "Owyhee" comes from an early nineteenth-century expedition led by Hawaiian trappers, who named the region after their homeland (an older spelling of "Hawaii").

Best time to visit: April to June and September to October offer the best weather, with mild temperatures and blooming desert wildflowers. Summer can be dangerously hot, and winter conditions can make roads impassable.

How to access: Owyhee State Park is in southeastern Oregon, accessible via US Highway 95 and a network of gravel roads. Roads to sites like Leslie Gulch can become impassable after rain due to thick, claylike mud.

Things to consider: The park's remote location means visitors should arrive prepared, with extra water, food, and a full tank of gas. Summer temperatures can be extreme, often exceeding 100°F (38°C), so visiting in the spring or fall is best. Cell service is limited, and roads can be rough—high-clearance or 4WD vehicles are recommended for some areas.

RECOMMENDED TRAILS:

Leslie Gulch Trail: *About 1–4-mile (1.6–6.4km) round trip; minimal elevation gain; easy.* A network of short hikes through towering, honey-colored rock formations, slot canyons, and unique geological features—one of the most scenic areas in Owyhee.

Juniper Gulch Trail: *2.4-mile (3.9km) round trip; about 400 feet (122m) elevation gain; moderate.* A stunning hike through rugged volcanic cliffs, leading to incredible panoramic views and hidden alcoves.

Three Forks Hot Springs Trail: *5.5-mile (8.9km) round trip; about 600 feet (183m) elevation gain; strenuous.* A remote hike leading to natural hot springs along the Owyhee River, requiring river crossings and careful navigation.

Tips for taking a great photo

- Early morning or late afternoon are the best times of day for dramatic lighting on the canyon walls and fewer harsh shadows.
- To photograph rock formations, use a wide-angle lens to capture the scale of Leslie Gulch's towering spires and cliffs.
- Springtime brings a burst of color with desert blooms. Look for vibrant yellow balsamroot and purple lupine.
- The vast, open landscape makes for incredible sunset shots, with the rock formations glowing red and orange in the fading light.

Opposite: Leslie Gulch, Owyhee Canyonlands

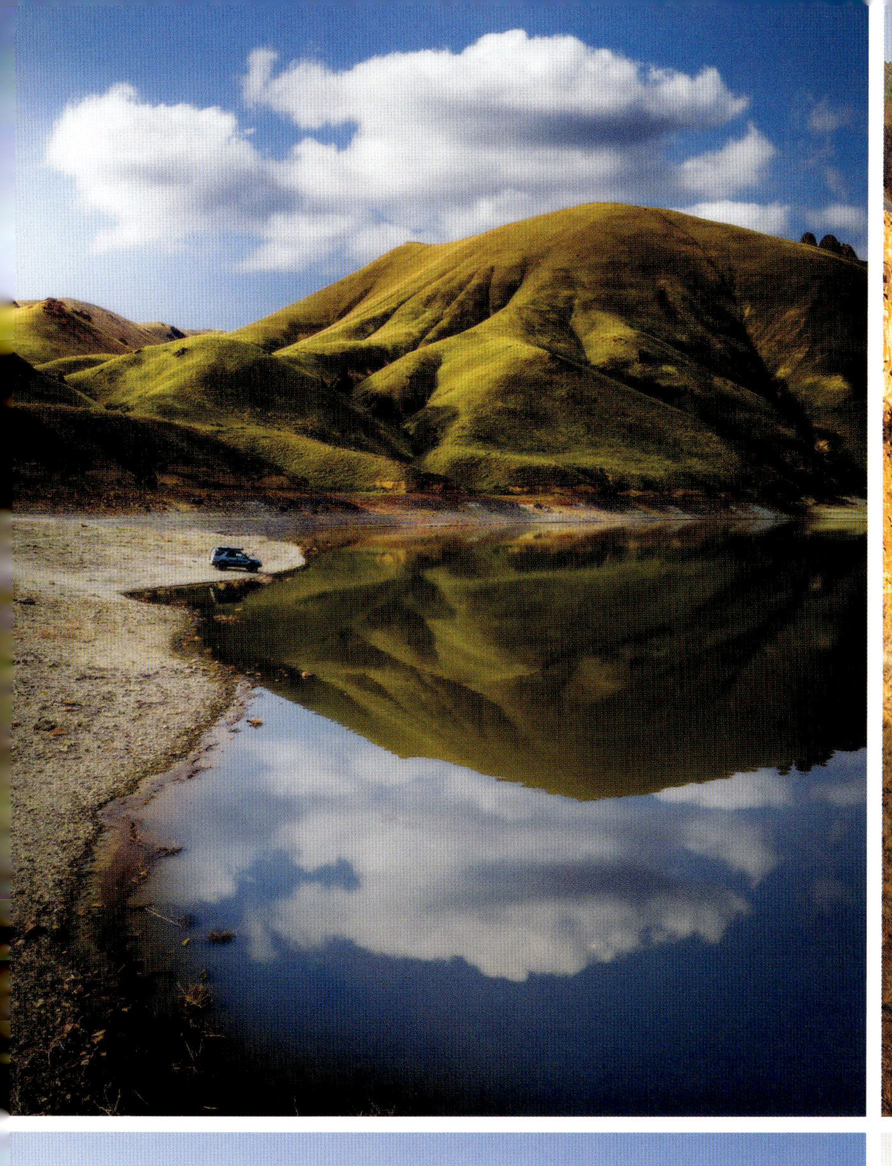
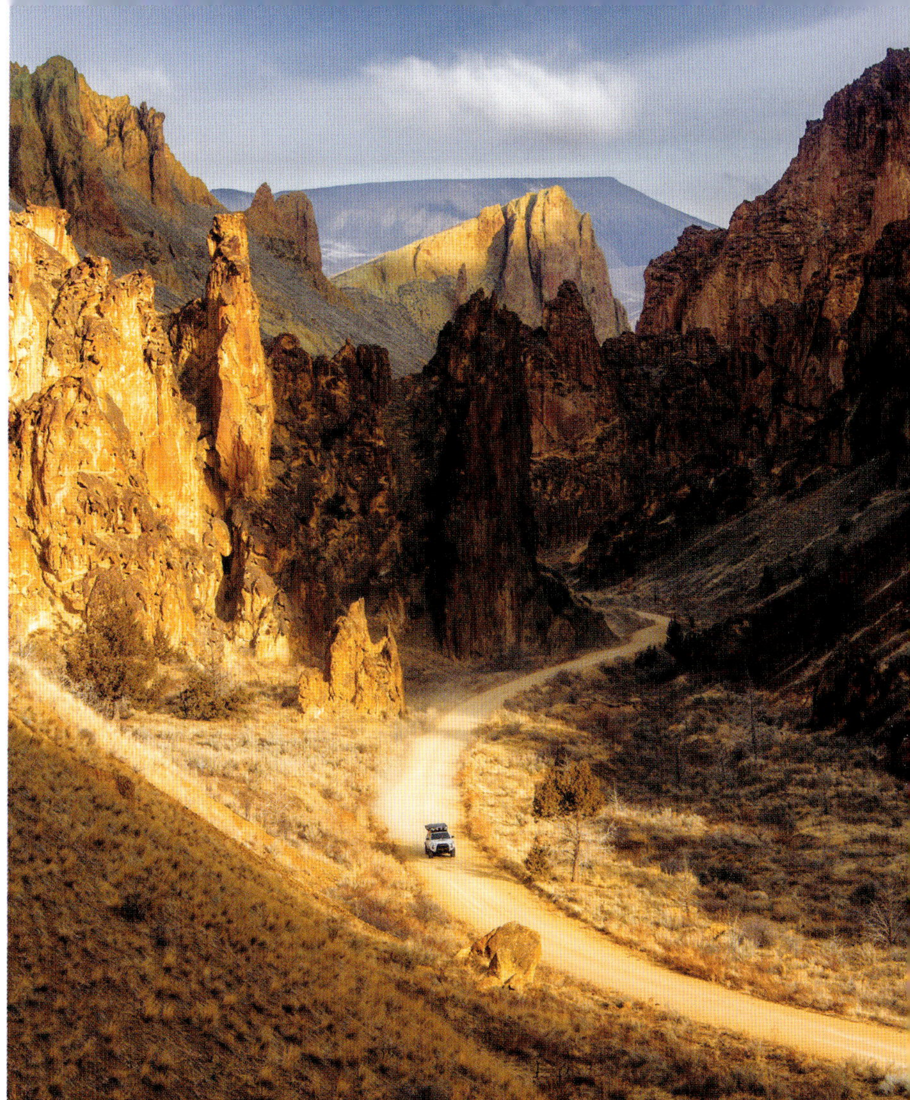
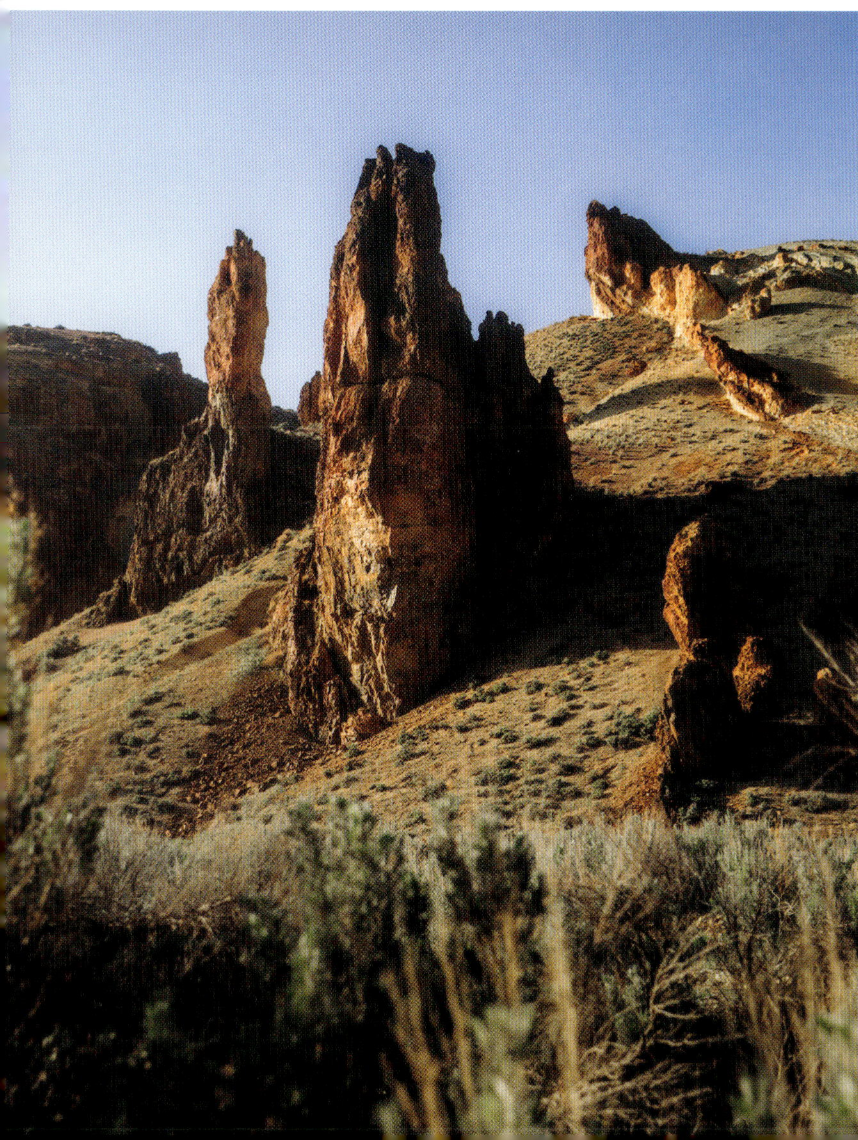
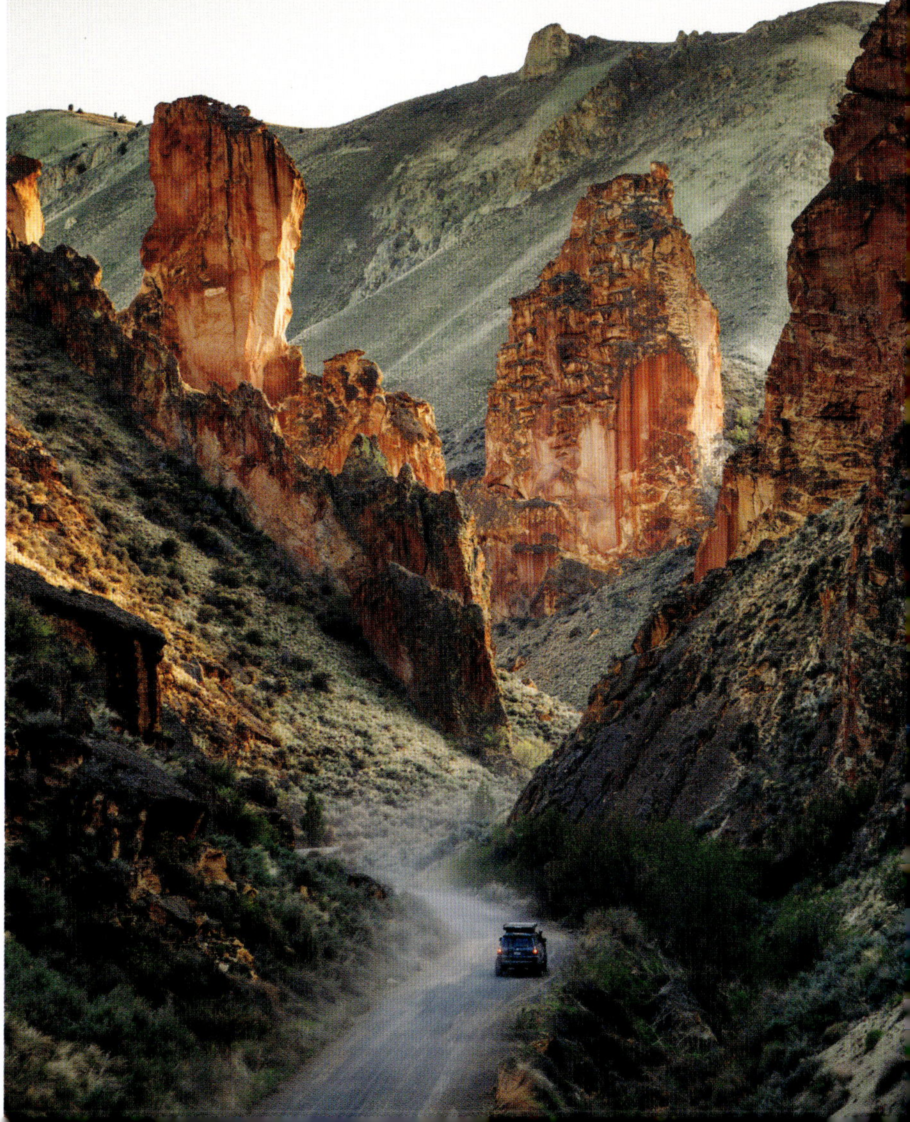

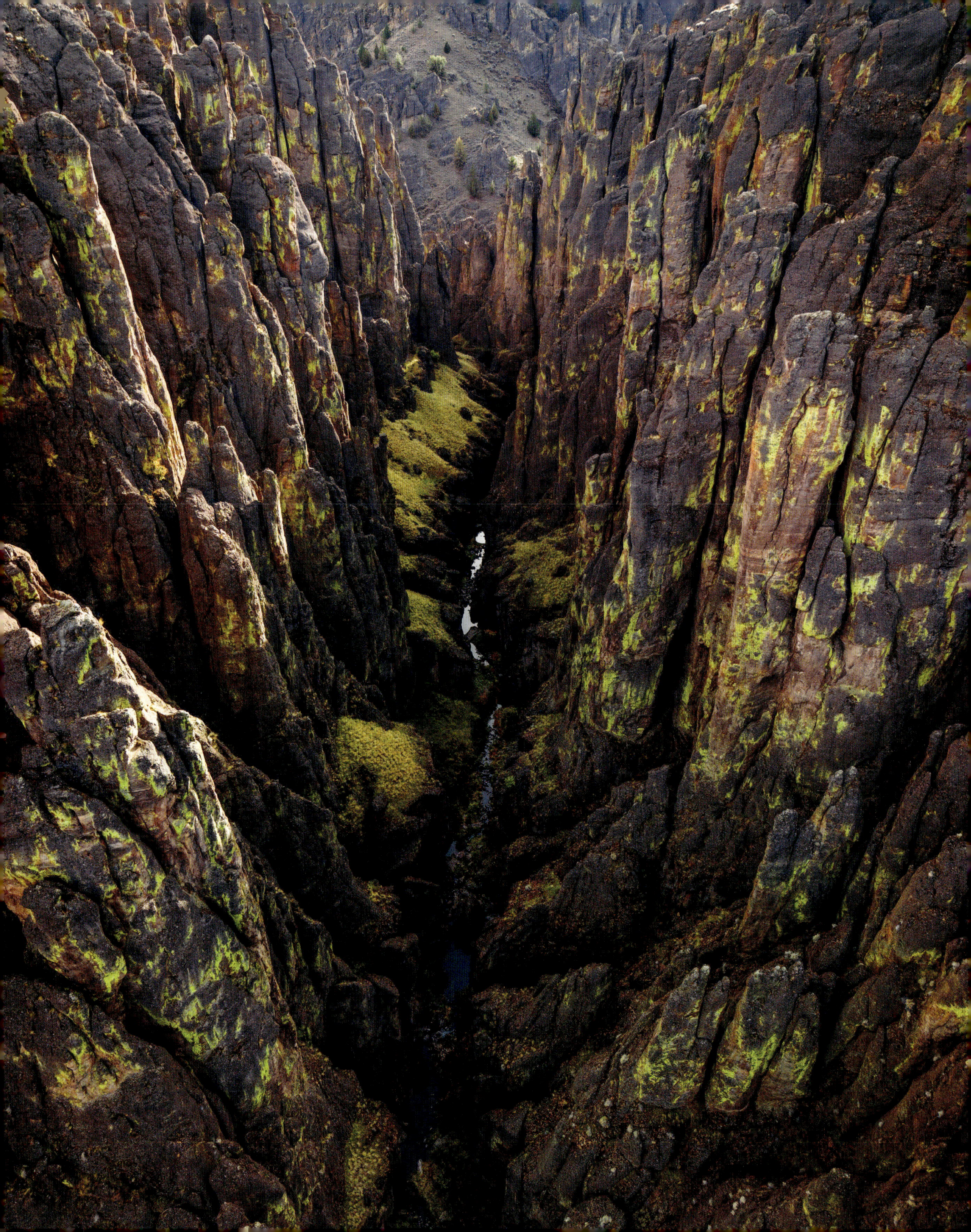

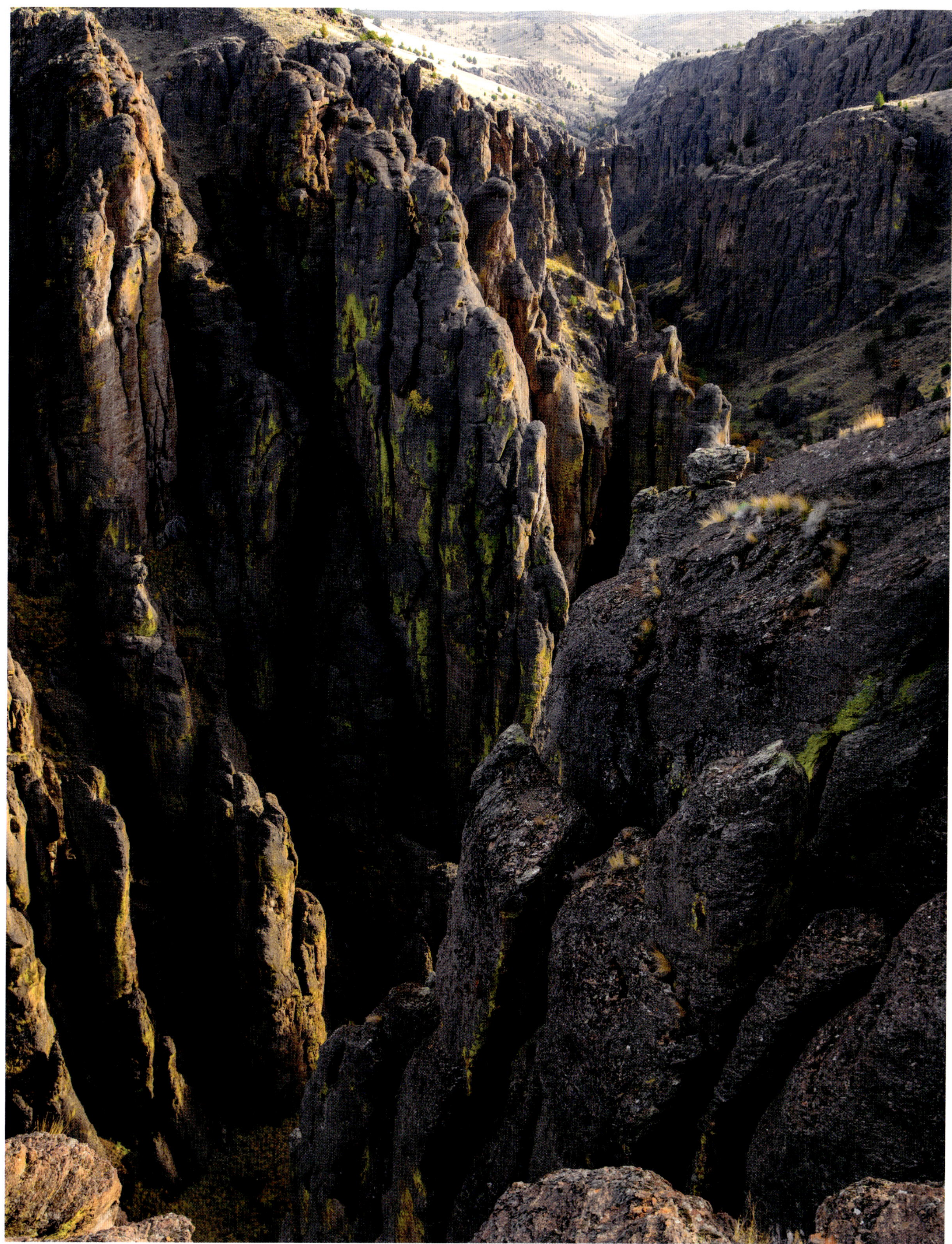

Above and opposite: Owyhee Canyonlands

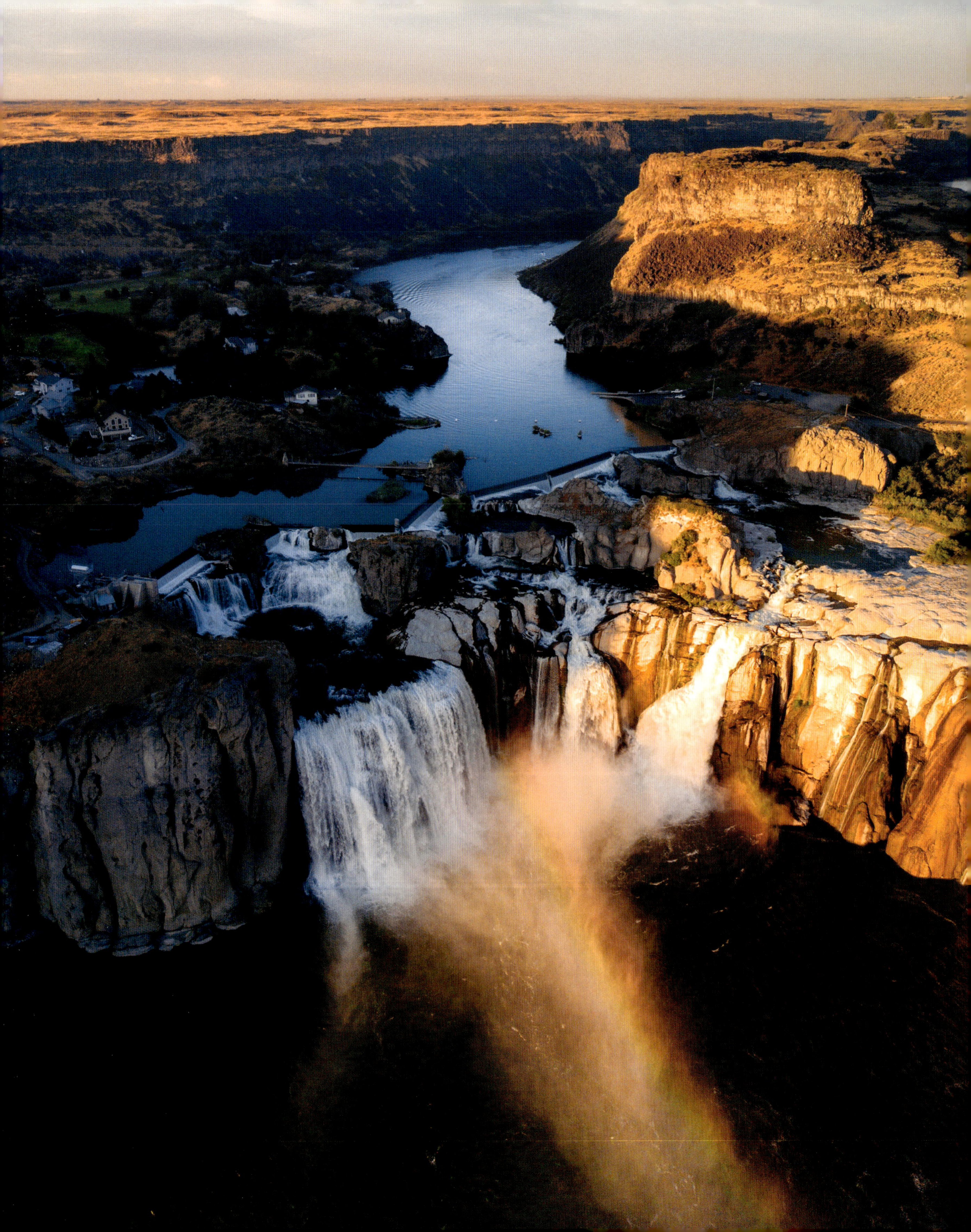

IDAHO

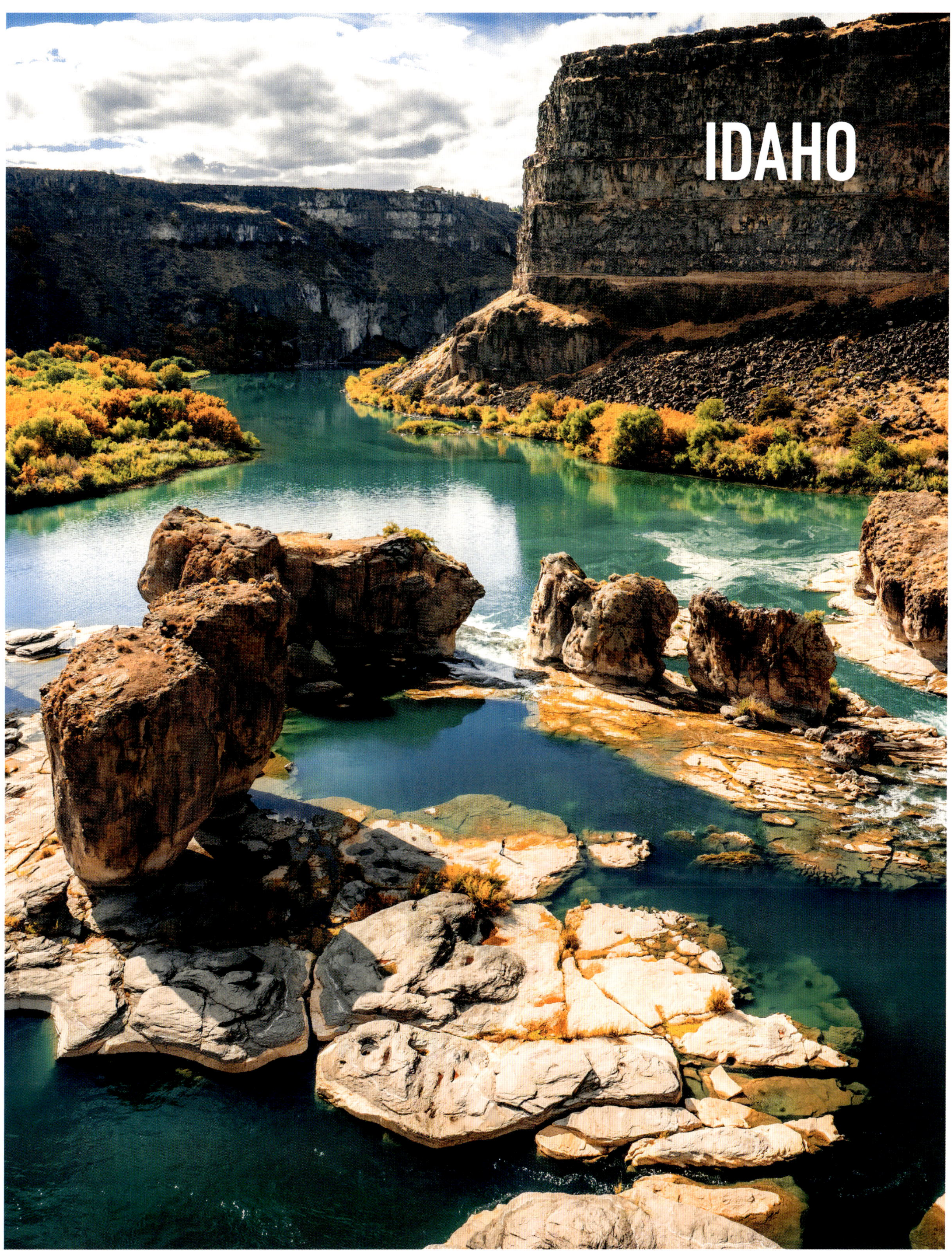

CRATERS OF THE MOON NATIONAL MONUMENT & PRESERVE

Craters of the Moon feels like stepping onto another planet. The ground looks scorched and twisted, frozen in motion from an ancient eruption. From the top of Inferno Cone, you see jagged cinder cones, endless basalt, and pockets of sagebrush clinging to life. The terrain here looks so much like the moon that NASA astronauts trained here in the 1960s to prepare for lunar missions.

Region: Pacific Northwest

State: Idaho

Coordinates: 43°24'58.0"N 113°31'03.4"W

Focal feature: A massive volcanic field filled with lava flows, cinder cones, and caves

Formation attributes: Covering over 750,000 acres, Craters of the Moon was formed by a series of volcanic eruptions between two thousand and fifteen thousand years ago. The park contains some of the best-preserved basalt lava flows in the continental US.

Fun fact: In 1969, the second group of Apollo 14 astronauts studied volcanic geology here to prepare for exploring the moon.

Best time to visit: Spring and fall offer the best weather, as summer can be extremely hot with little shade. Winter turns the park into a unique snow-covered landscape, great for snowshoeing.

How to access: The monument is located off US Highways 20, 26, and 93, between Arco and Carey, Idaho. The 7-mile (11.3km) Loop Road provides easy access to many of the park's key features.

Things to consider: Be prepared for extreme temperatures, limited shade, and rough terrain. Good hiking shoes and plenty of water are essential. There are no services inside the park, so bring all necessary supplies.

RECOMMENDED TRAILS:

Devil's Orchard Trail: *0.5-mile (0.8km) round trip; minimal elevation gain; easy.* A short, paved loop showcasing lava fragments and unique twisted trees adapted to the harsh environment.

Inferno Cone Trail: *0.8-mile (1.3km) round trip; about 140 feet (43m) elevation gain; moderate.* A steep but short climb to the top of a cinder cone with panoramic views of the lava fields and distant mountains.

Caves Trail: *1.6-mile (2.6km) round trip; minimal elevation gain; moderate.* A trail leading to several lava tubes, including Indian Tunnel, which are large enough to walk through. Bring a flashlight and be ready for uneven footing.

Tips for taking a great photo

- Early morning or late evening are the best times of day for dramatic lighting and long shadows over the lava fields.
- Use a macro lens or get close to highlight the rough, detailed surface of the lava.
- Inferno Cone provides one of the best high vantage points for capturing the vast landscape with a wide-angle lens.
- The dark skies make this an excellent spot for astrophotography. Try capturing the Milky Way over the jagged lava formations.

Page 110: Shoshone Falls

Page 111: Pillar Falls, along the Snake River

Opposite: Big Craters, Craters of the Moon National Monument

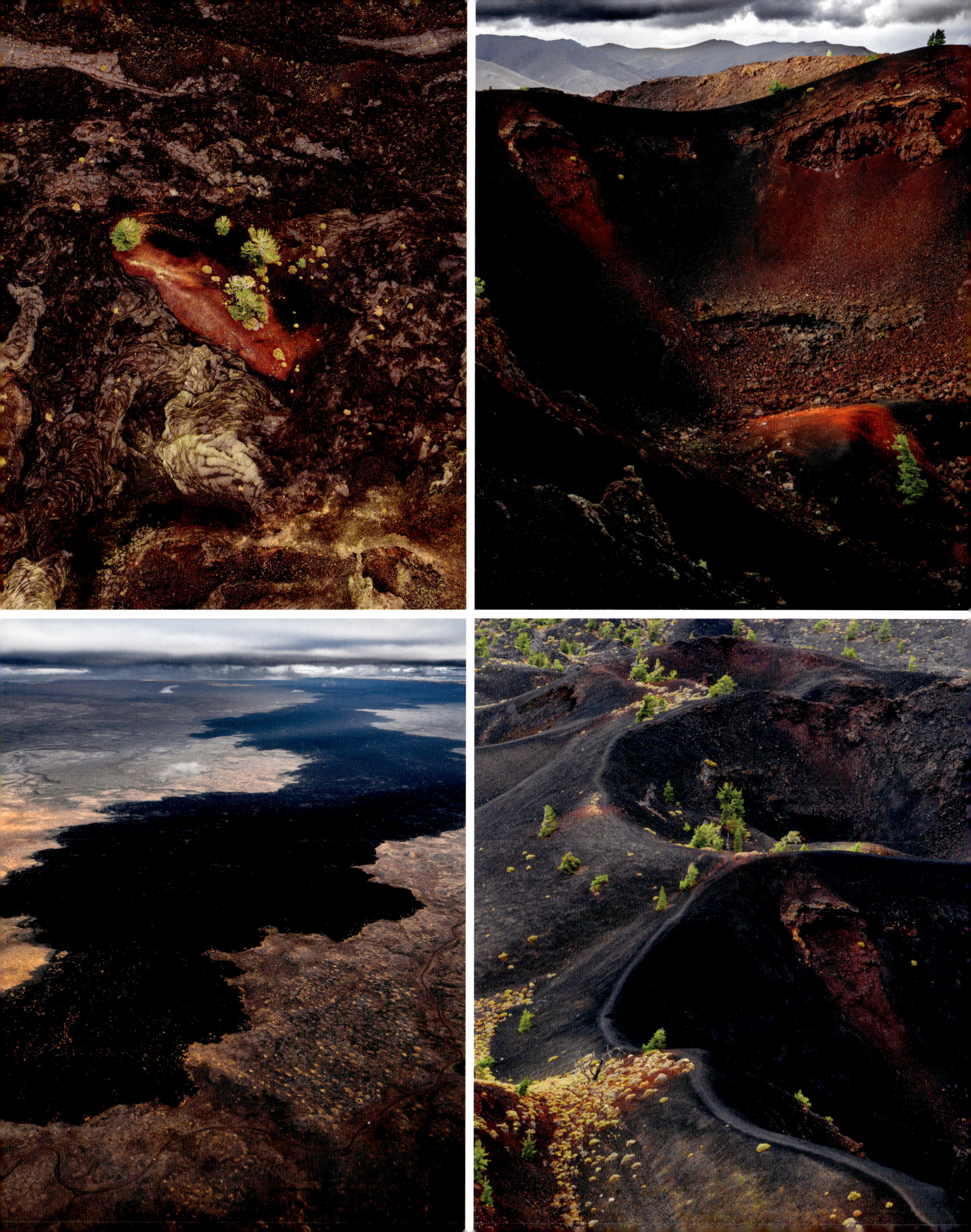

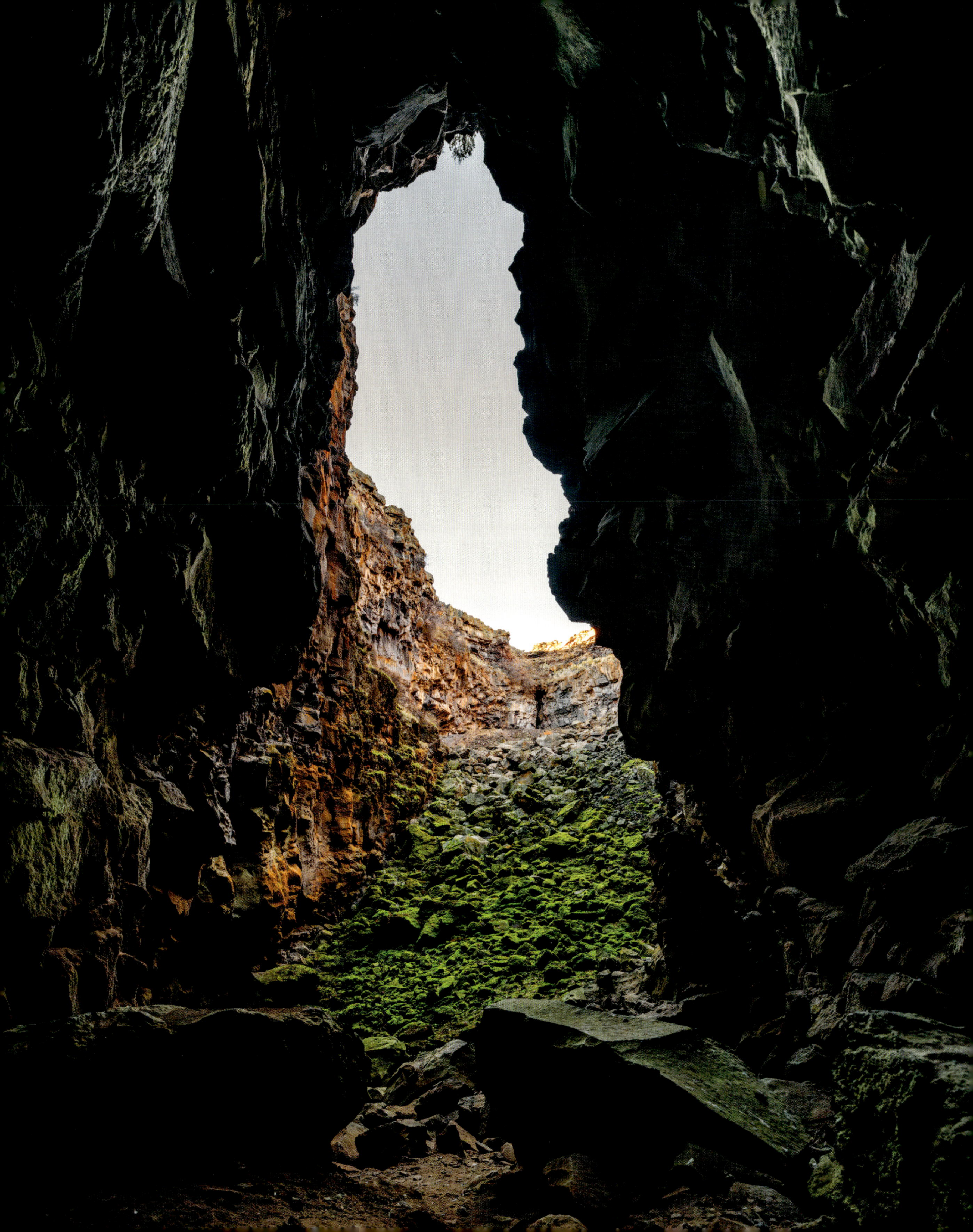

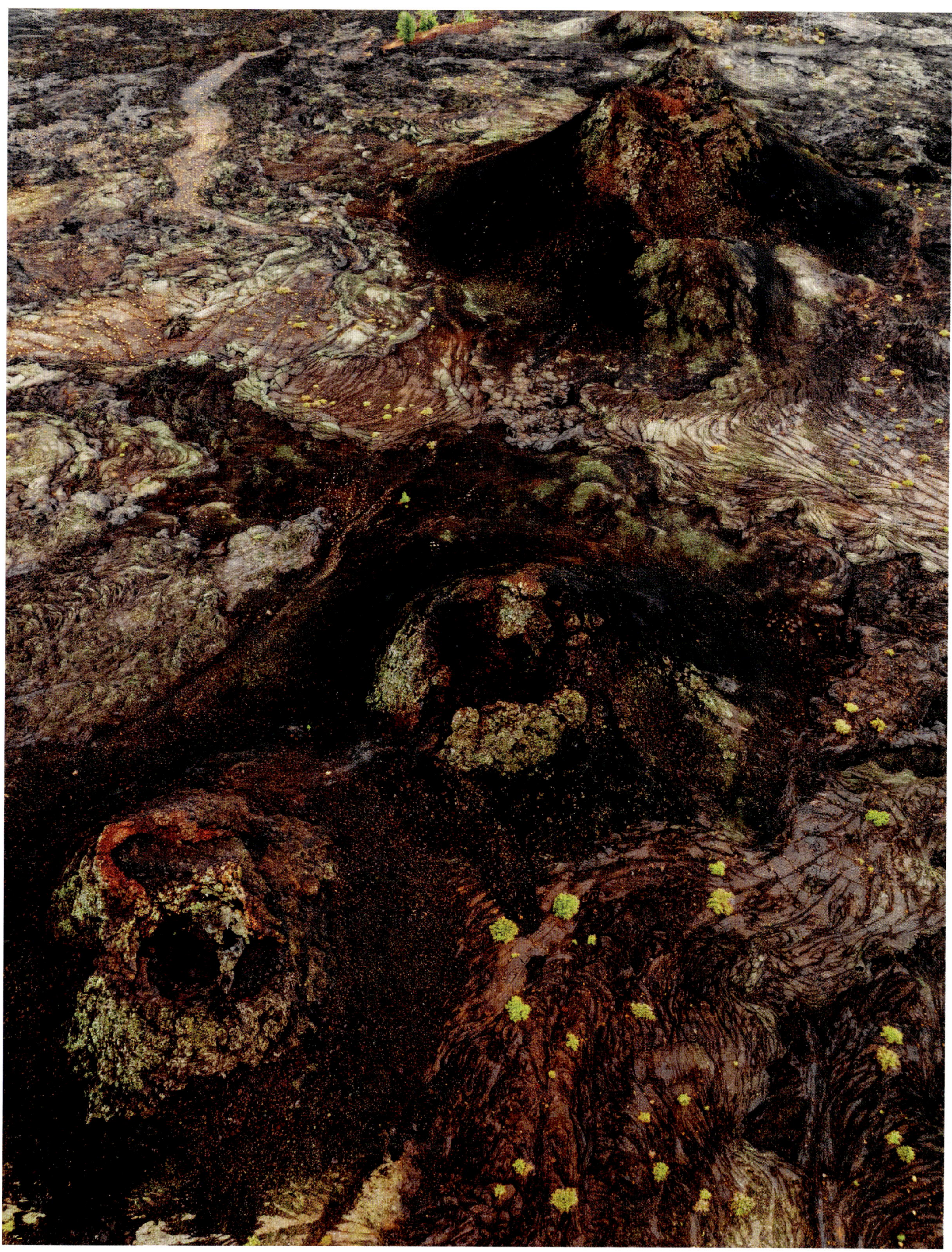

Above: Spatter Cones, Craters of the Moon National Monument | Opposite: King's Bowl, Craters of the Moon National Monument | Pages 116–117: Pillar Falls, Snake River

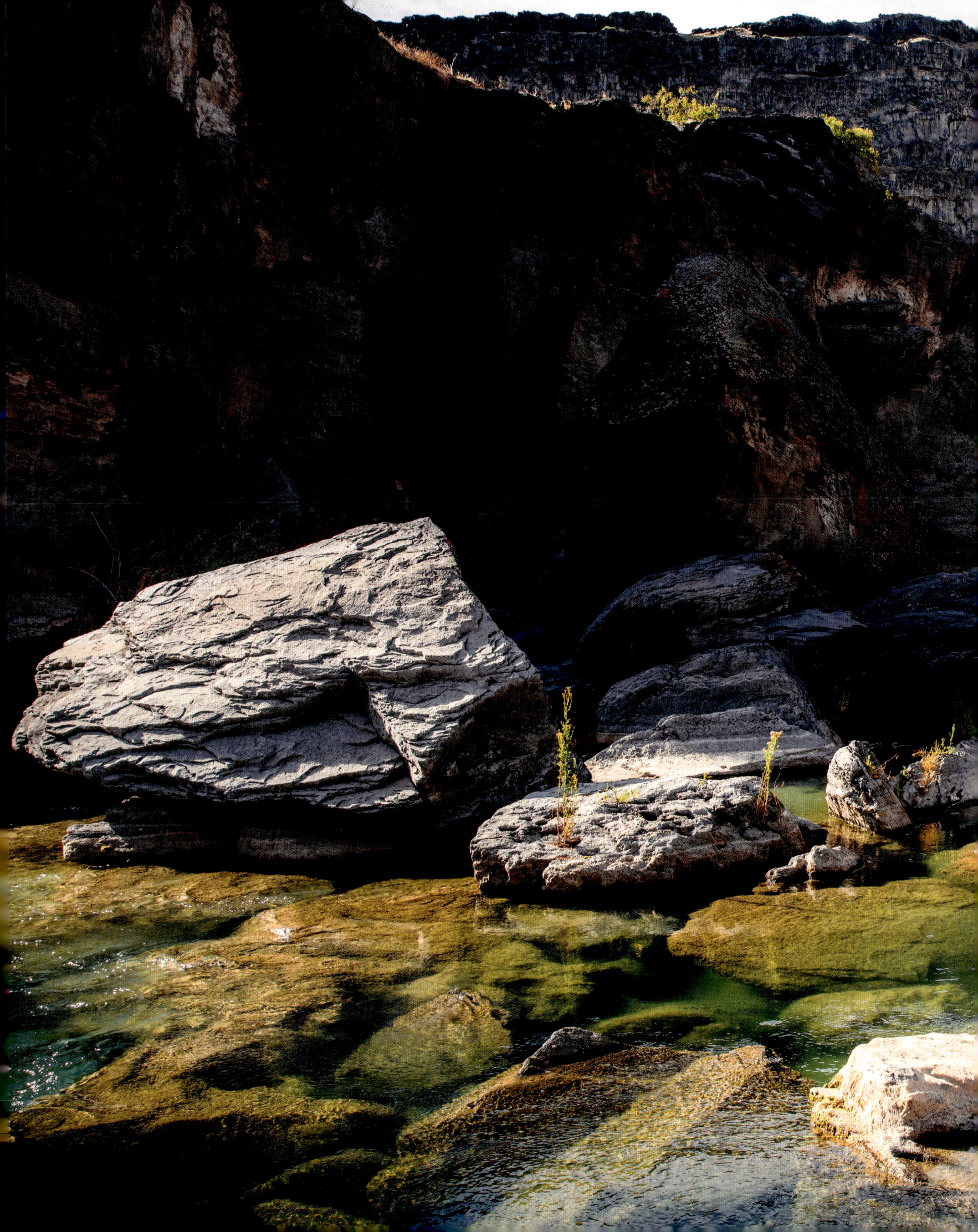

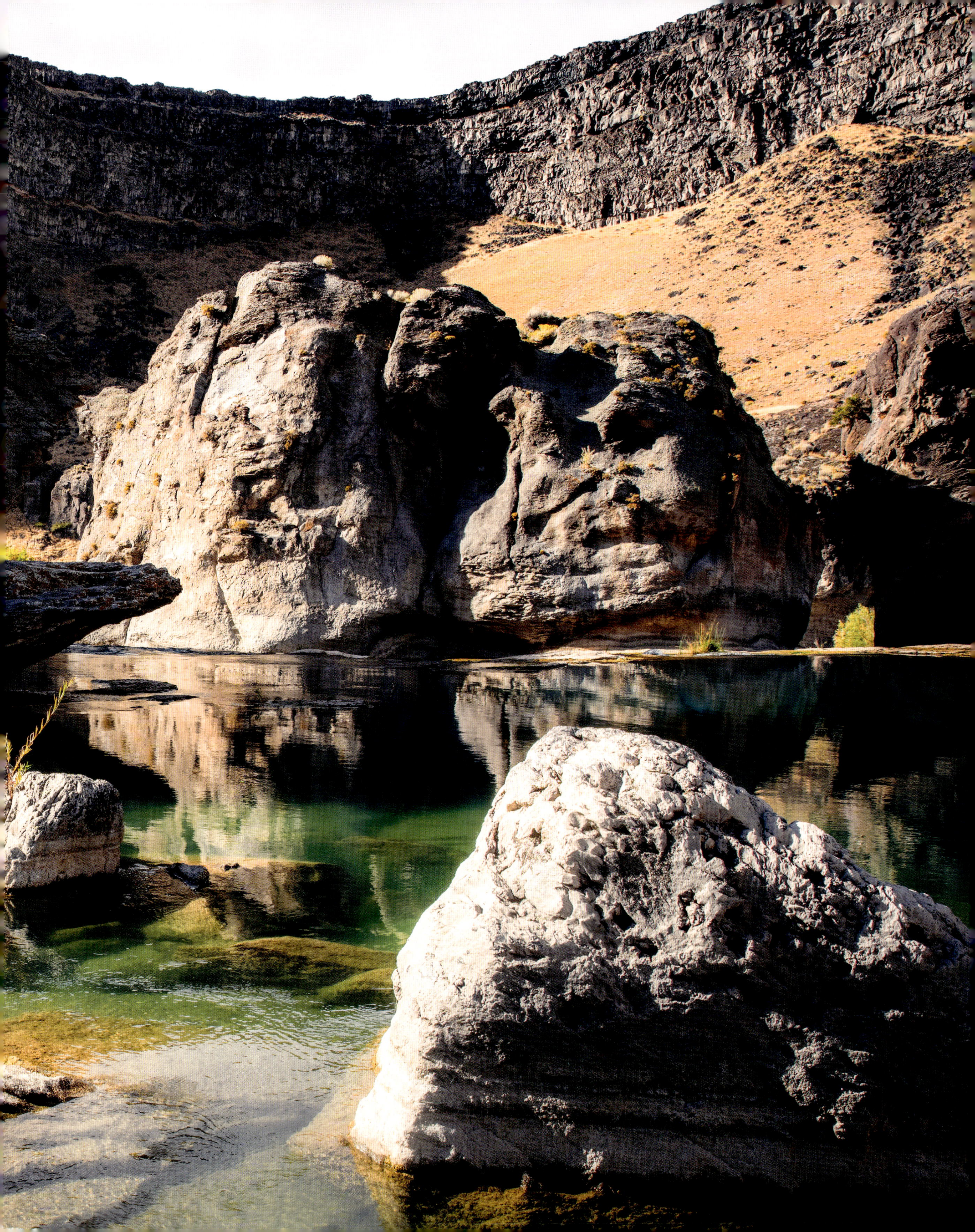

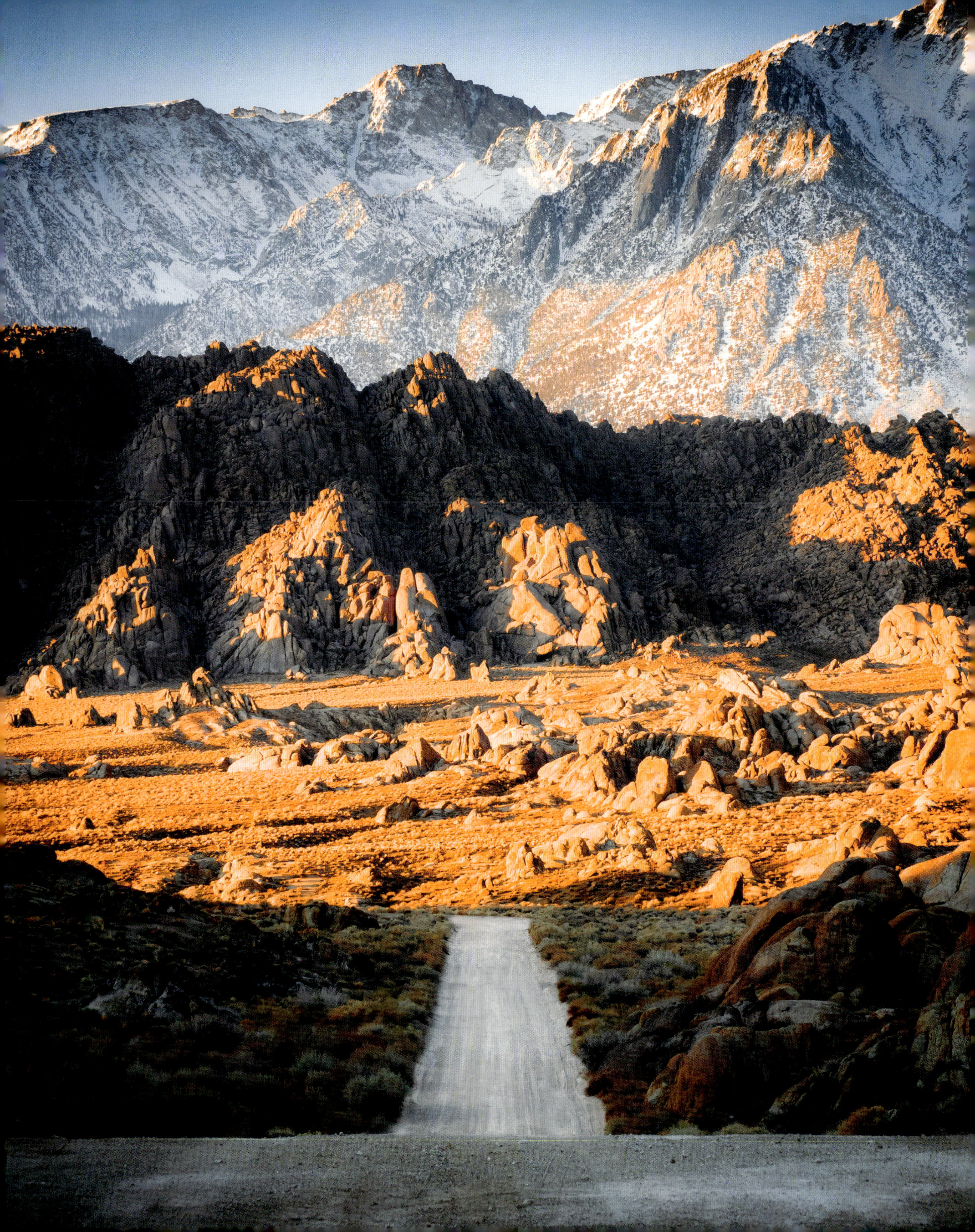

CALIFORNIA

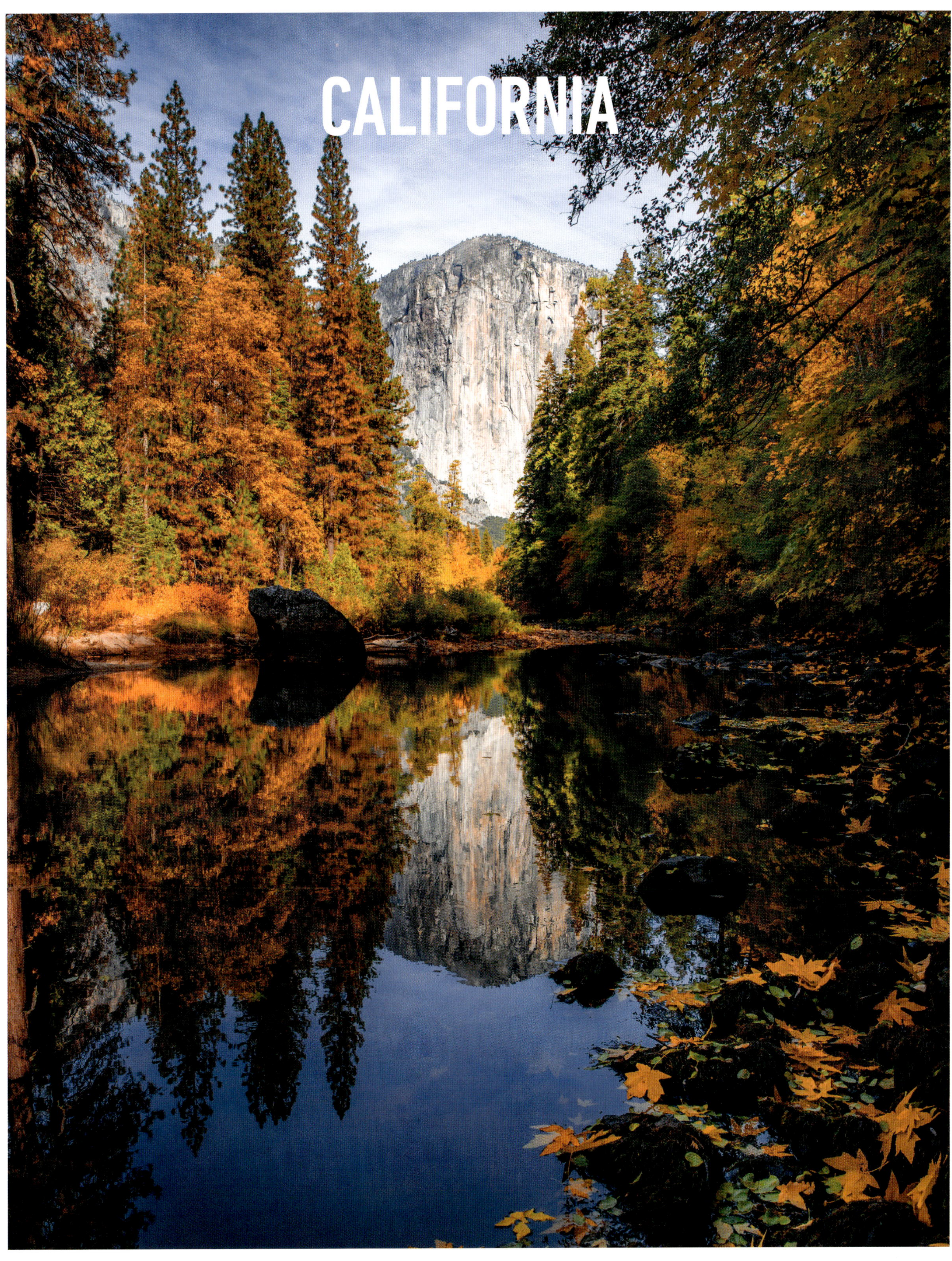

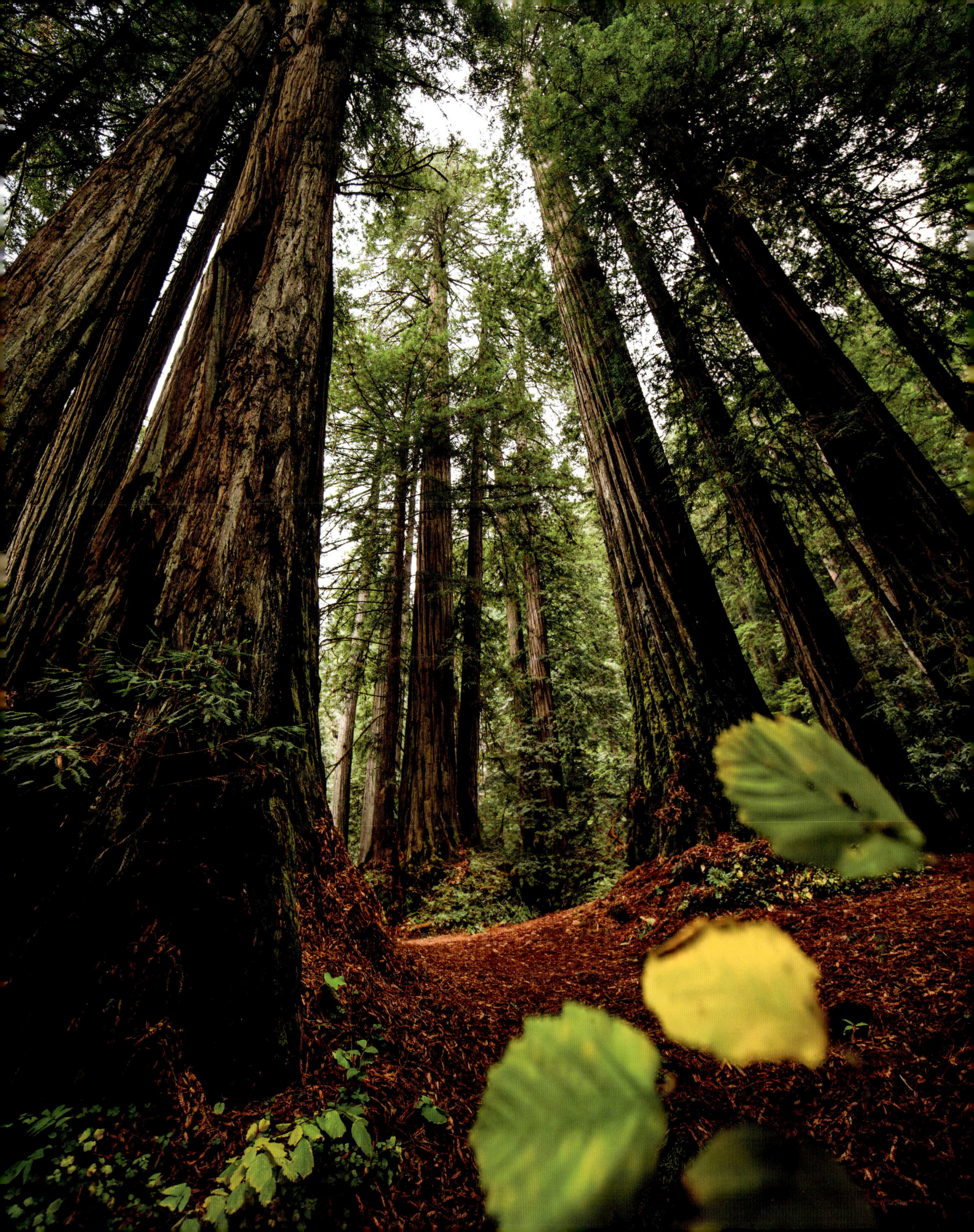

REDWOOD NATIONAL & STATE PARKS

Hiking through Jedediah Smith Redwoods State Park is one of those experiences that just sticks with you. The trees are massive, but what I remember most was how quiet it was—just the sound of my footsteps and the occasional bird in the distance. Walking the Boy Scout Tree Trail, I kept stopping just to take it all in. At one point, I leaned against a fallen redwood and sat there for a while, feeling small in the best way. Later, driving down Howland Hill Road with the windows down, surrounded by towering trees, I couldn't help but smile. It was one of those simple, perfect moments where everything just felt right.

Region: West

State: California

Coordinates: 41°12'47.5"N 124°00'16.6"W

Focal feature: Towering coast redwoods, the tallest trees on Earth

Formation attributes: Coast redwoods can grow over 350 feet (107m) tall and live for more than two thousand years. The park spans over 139,000 acres, protecting these ancient forests, wild rivers, and scenic coastline.

Fun fact: The tallest known tree, Hyperion, is hidden within Redwood National Park and stands at over 379 feet (116m) tall—taller than the Statue of Liberty!

Best time to visit: June to September offers the warmest weather, but spring and fall are great for fewer crowds and lush greenery. Winter brings heavy rains but also fewer visitors and dramatic scenery.

How to access: The park is accessible via US Highway 101. The trees are spread across multiple parks, so plan ahead to accommodate driving times between locations. Be prepared for winding roads and limited cell service.

Things to consider: Redwood National and State Parks protect some of the tallest trees on Earth, stretching along the rugged coastline of Northern California. The park system includes four parks: Redwood National Park, Jedediah Smith Redwoods State Park, Del Norte Coast Redwoods State Park, and Prairie Creek Redwoods State Park. There are no entrance fees for Redwood National Park, but some of the state parks require day-use fees.

RECOMMENDED TRAILS:

Stout Grove Trail: *0.5-mile (0.8km) loop; minimal elevation gain; easy.* A short, peaceful walk through an old-growth redwood grove with towering trees and soft light filtering through the canopy.

Fern Canyon Trail: *1.1-mile (1.8km) loop; minimal elevation gain; moderate.* A stunning hike through a narrow canyon with walls covered in lush, green ferns. This area was used as a filming location for *The Lost World: Jurassic Park*.

Boy Scout Tree Trail: *5.5-mile (8.9km) round trip; about 750 feet (229m) elevation gain; moderate.* A beautiful forest hike leading to an enormous redwood known as the Boy Scout Tree, with quiet groves and moss-covered logs along the way.

Tips for taking a great photo

- Early morning or late afternoon is best for soft, diffused light filtering through the trees.
- Use a wide-angle lens to capture the scale of the trees in the redwood groves and include a person in the shot for perspective.
- A tripod helps in the low light of Fern Canyon, and waterproof boots are a good idea if the creek is flowing.
- Visit the coast during foggy mornings for a dreamy, mystical atmosphere.

Page 118: Alabama Hills

Page 119: Yosemite National Park

Opposite: Redwood National Park

YOSEMITE NATIONAL PARK

I stood on the summit of Half Dome, watching the last rays of sunlight. Earlier that day, I had hiked the Mist Trail, which had been an adventure in itself: I got completely soaked by Vernal Fall's spray. But the view from the top made it all worth it. The power of Yosemite is something you can feel. Whether it's the sheer scale of El Capitan looming overhead, the roar of Yosemite Falls echoing through the valley, or the quiet serenity of the high country, Yosemite plants memories that stay with you long after you leave.

Region: West

State: California

Coordinates: 37°51'54.4"N 119°32'17.9"W

Focal features: Yosemite Falls, El Capitan, Half Dome

Formation attributes: Yosemite Valley was carved by glaciers over millions of years, creating sheer cliffs like El Capitan (3,600 feet / 1,097 meters above the valley floor) and Half Dome (4,737 feet / 1,444 meters above the valley floor). The park spans over 750,000 acres, with elevations ranging from 2,000 feet (610m) to 13,114 feet (3,997m).

Fun fact: Yosemite Falls is one of the tallest waterfalls in North America, dropping a total of 2,425 feet (739m).

Best time to visit: April to June for waterfalls at their peak; July to August for high-elevation hikes; and September to October for fewer crowds. Winter is magical, with snow-covered landscapes and fewer visitors.

How to access: Yosemite can be accessed from several entrances, with the most popular being the Arch Rock Entrance on Highway 140 and the Big Oak Flat Entrance on Highway 120. Parking fills up quickly in Yosemite Valley, so using the park's shuttle system is recommended.

Things to consider: The park is open year-round, but accessibility varies by season; many higher-elevation areas, including Tioga Road and Glacier Point, are closed in winter. Be prepared for crowds in summer months and consider visiting in the spring for waterfalls at their peak flow or in the fall for fewer visitors and crisp mountain air. If visiting in summer, arrive early in the morning or late in the afternoon to avoid crowds.

RECOMMENDED TRAILS:

Bridalveil Fall Trail: *0.5-mile (0.8km) round trip; minimal elevation gain; easy.* A short but stunning walk to the base of one of Yosemite's most famous waterfalls, with misty views.

Vernal and Nevada Falls via Mist Trail: *6.4-mile (10.3km) round trip; about 2,200 feet (610m) elevation gain; moderate.* One of the most iconic hikes in the park, featuring stone staircases alongside roaring waterfalls. Be prepared to get wet!

Half Dome Trail: *14–16-mile (22.5–25.7km) round trip; about 4,800 feet (1,463m) elevation gain; strenuous.* A bucket-list hike featuring the famous cable ascent to the summit. A permit is required, and the climb is not for the faint of heart.

Tips for taking a great photo

- Sunrise at Tunnel View offers an incredible perspective of Yosemite Valley, while sunset at Glacier Point is unforgettable.
- Spring is best for capturing Yosemite's waterfalls at full power. Use a slow shutter speed for a silky effect.
- Mirror Lake in the early morning provides stunning reflections of Half Dome.
- Yosemite's dark skies make it a fantastic place for astrophotography. Try capturing the Milky Way over El Capitan or Glacier Point.

Opposite: El Capitan, Yosemite National Park

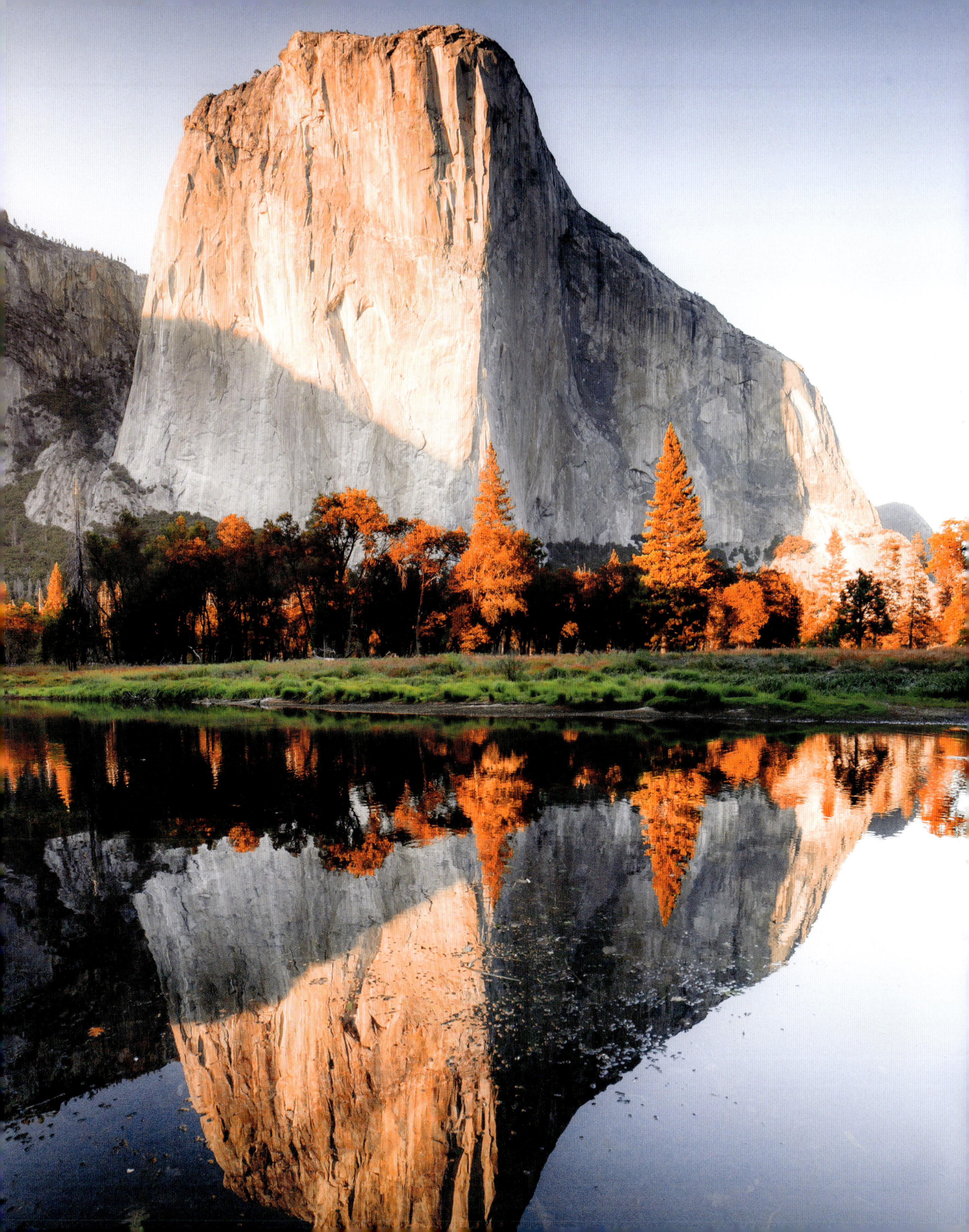

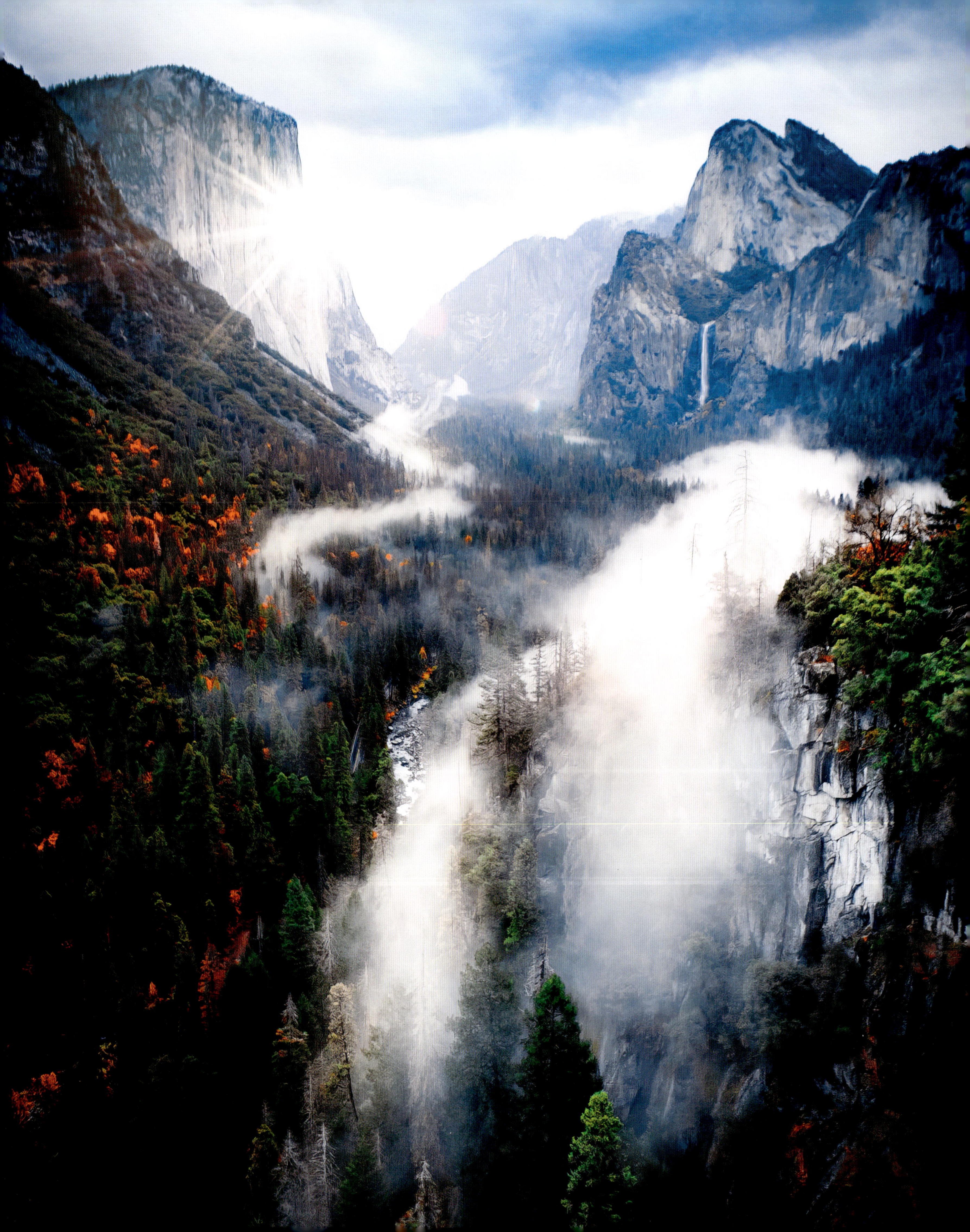

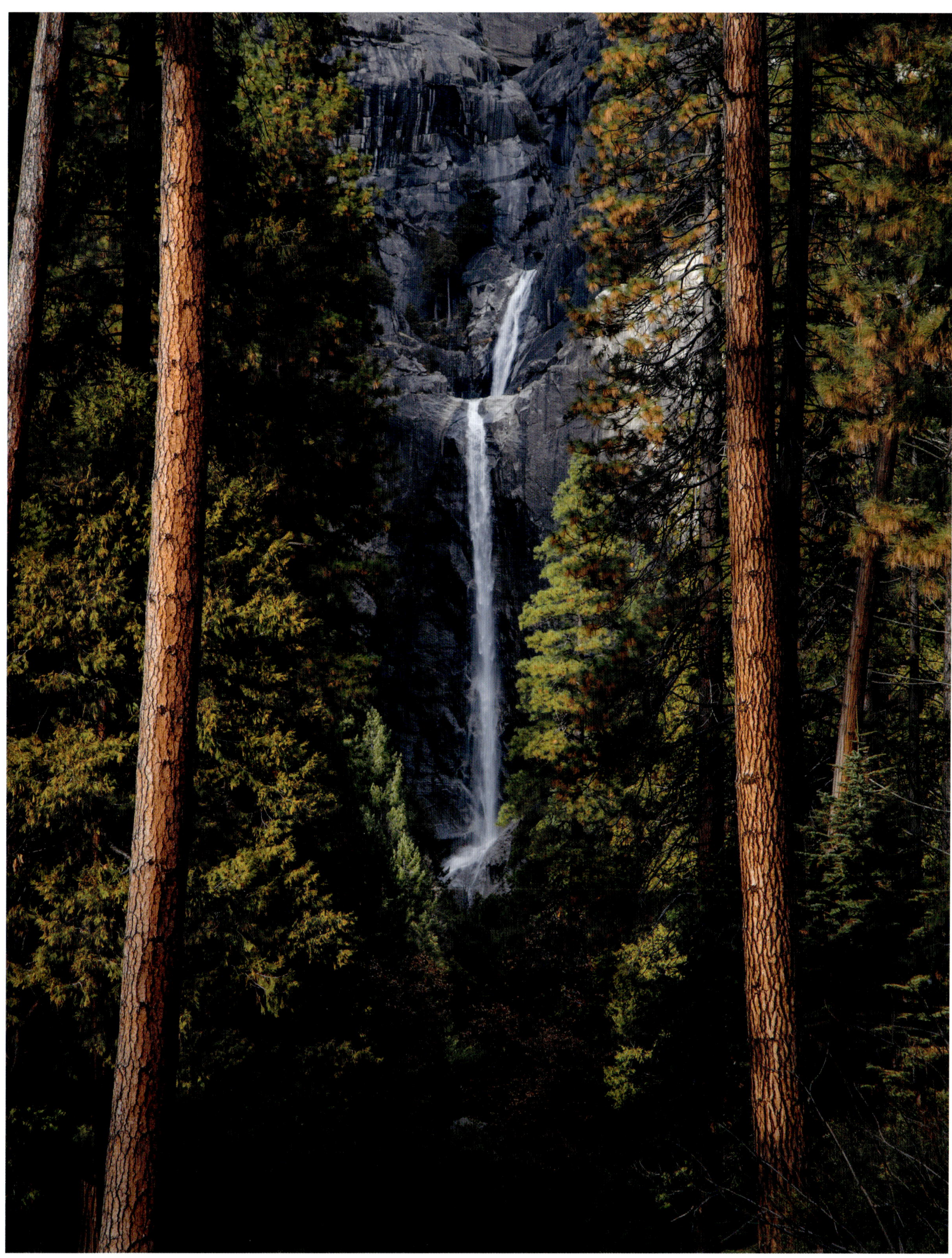

Above: Yosemite Falls, Yosemite National Park | Opposite: Tunnel View, Yosemite National Park

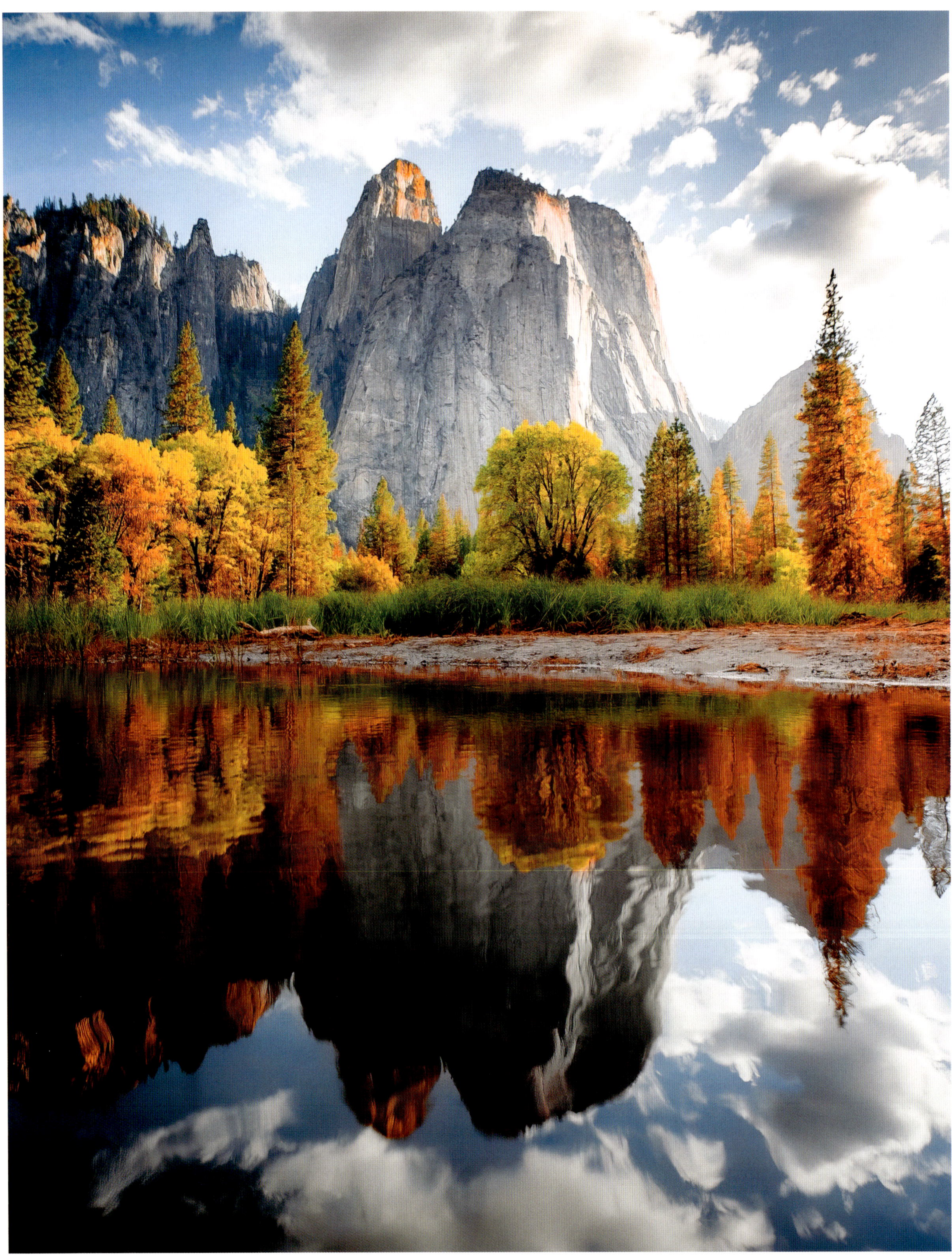

Above: Yosemite Valley | Opposite: View of Half Dome from Glacier Point Drive, Yosemite National Park

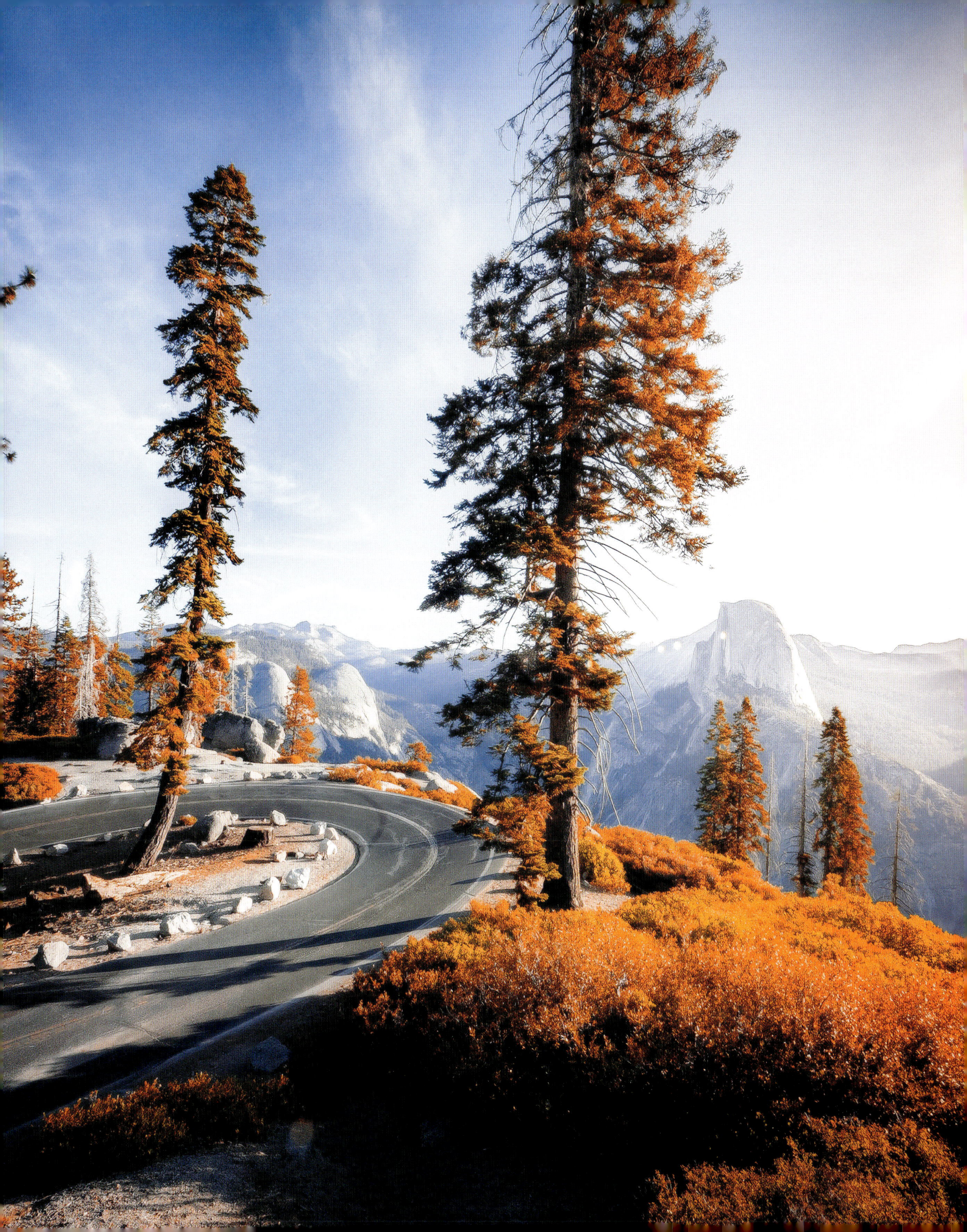

SEQUOIA NATIONAL PARK

As you walk among the giant sequoias, it's hard not to feel small—in the best way possible. Up close, the General Sherman Tree is incredible, its sheer size mind-blowing. Climbing up Moro Rock is another highlight, with steep steps leading to one of the best views I've ever seen. Standing at the top, looking out over the rugged peaks of the Sierra, it's like being on top of the world. Sequoia National Park is a place that sticks in your mind forever.

Region: West

State: California

Coordinates: 36°29'11.0"N 118°33'56.9"W

Focal feature: Giant sequoia trees, including the world's largest tree, General Sherman

Formation attributes: The park protects over 400,000 acres, including the highest peak in the contiguous US: Mount Whitney, at 14,494 feet (4,418m) tall. Giant sequoias grow more than 300 feet (91m) tall and can live for over three thousand years.

Fun fact: The General Sherman Tree is the largest known tree by volume in the world, standing at 275 feet (84m) tall and over 36 feet (11m) in diameter at its base.

Best time to visit: Late spring through early fall offers the best conditions, with summer providing the easiest access to trails and roads. Winter is beautiful but requires preparation for snow and cold temperatures.

How to access: The park is accessible via Highway 198 from the south and Highway 180 from the north. The Generals Highway connects Sequoia and Kings Canyon National Parks but has steep, winding sections. Parking can be limited at popular spots, so arriving early is recommended. Free shuttle services operate in summer.

Things to consider: Sequoia National Park is home to some of the largest trees on Earth, towering above visitors in ancient groves. The park also features deep canyons, high alpine peaks, and underground caves. The elevation varies drastically, so be prepared for changing weather conditions. Snow is common in winter, and some roads may be closed.

RECOMMENDED TRAILS:

Big Trees Trail: *1.2-mile (1.9km) loop; minimal elevation gain; easy.* A short, scenic walk around a lush meadow, surrounded by massive sequoias.

Moro Rock Trail: *0.5-mile (0.8km) round trip; 200 feet (61m) elevation gain; moderate.* A steep climb up stone steps leading to a breathtaking panoramic view of the Sierra Nevada.

Alta Peak Trail: *13.8-mile (22.2km) round trip; about 4,000 feet (1,219m) elevation gain; strenuous.* A tough but rewarding hike to a stunning viewpoint at 11,204 feet (3,415m), offering expansive views of the Great Western Divide.

Tips for taking a great photo

- Early morning or late afternoon is the best time of day for soft light filtering through the trees.
- Use a wide-angle lens to capture the massive scale of the giant sequoias and include a person in the frame for perspective.
- Sunrise and sunset at Moro Rock offer the most dramatic lighting over the mountains.
- Keep an eye out for black bears and deer, especially near meadows and creeks.

Opposite: Towering sequoias in Sequoia National Park

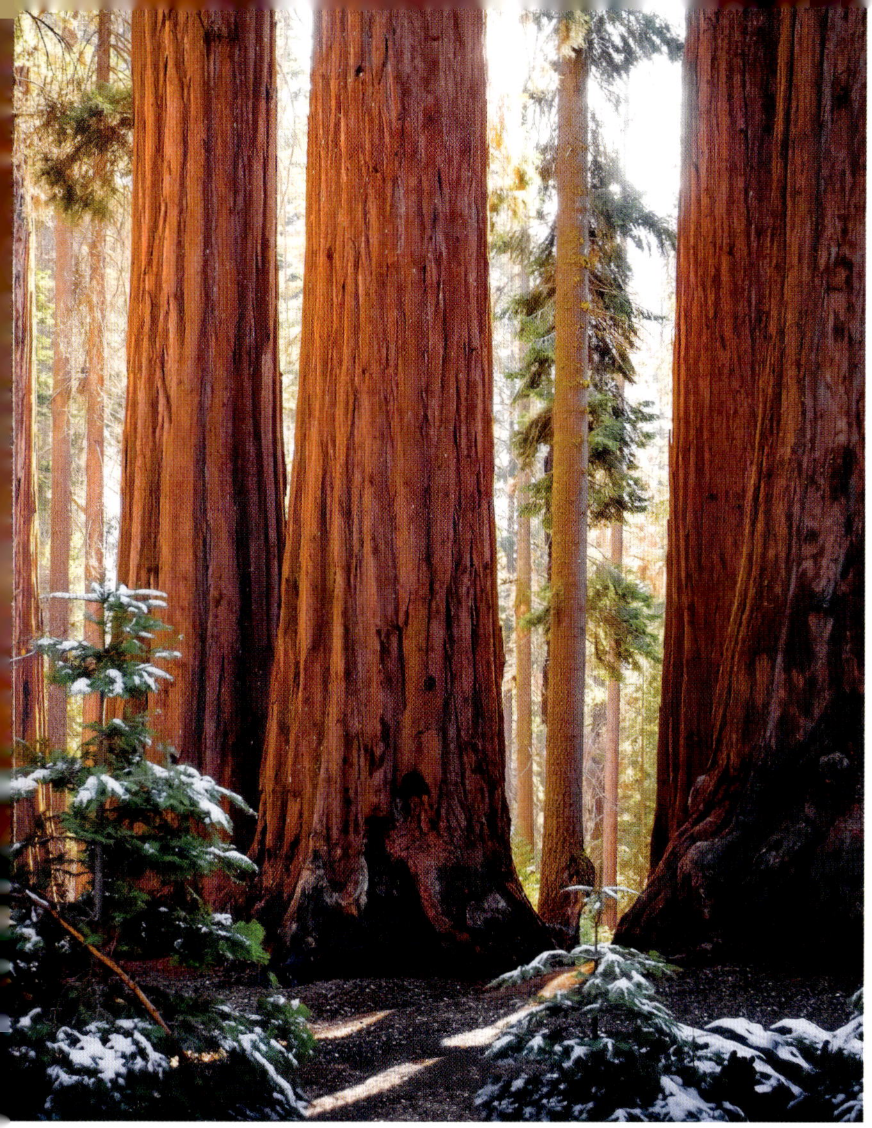

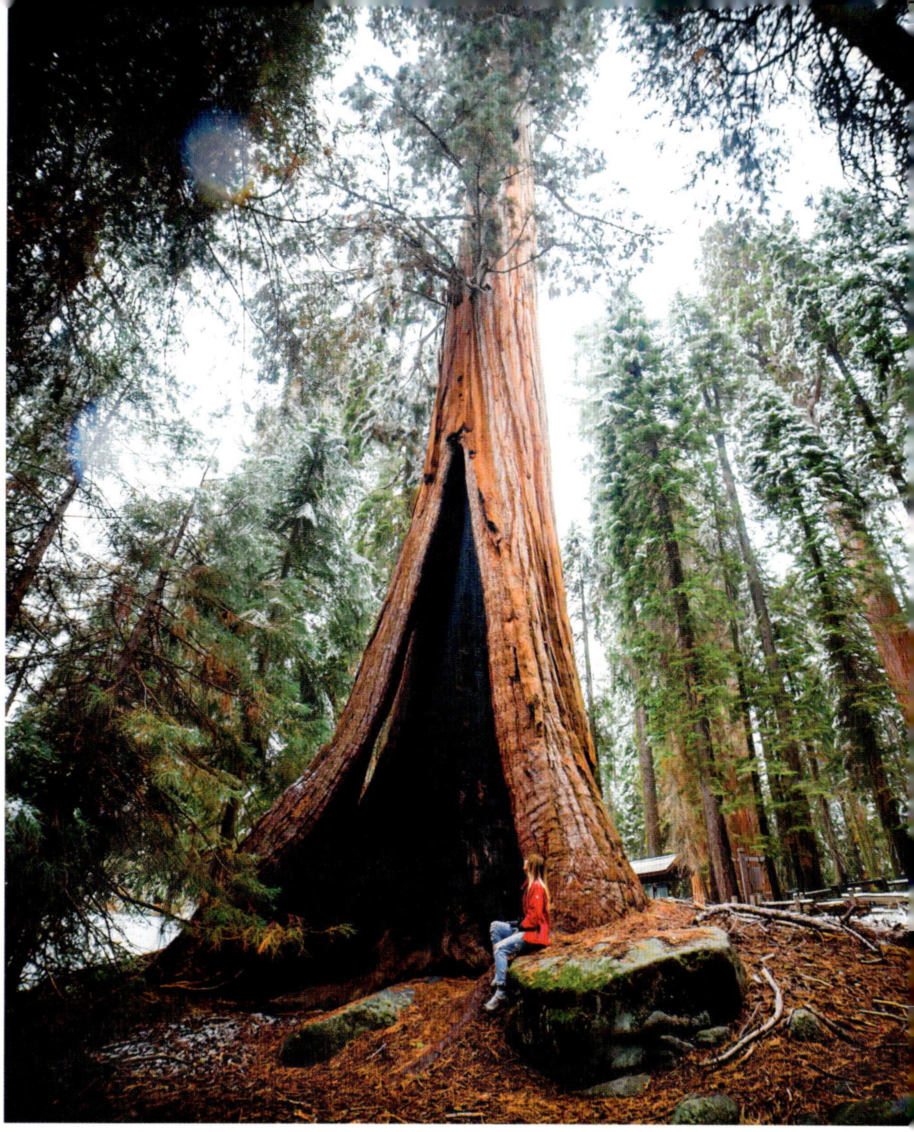

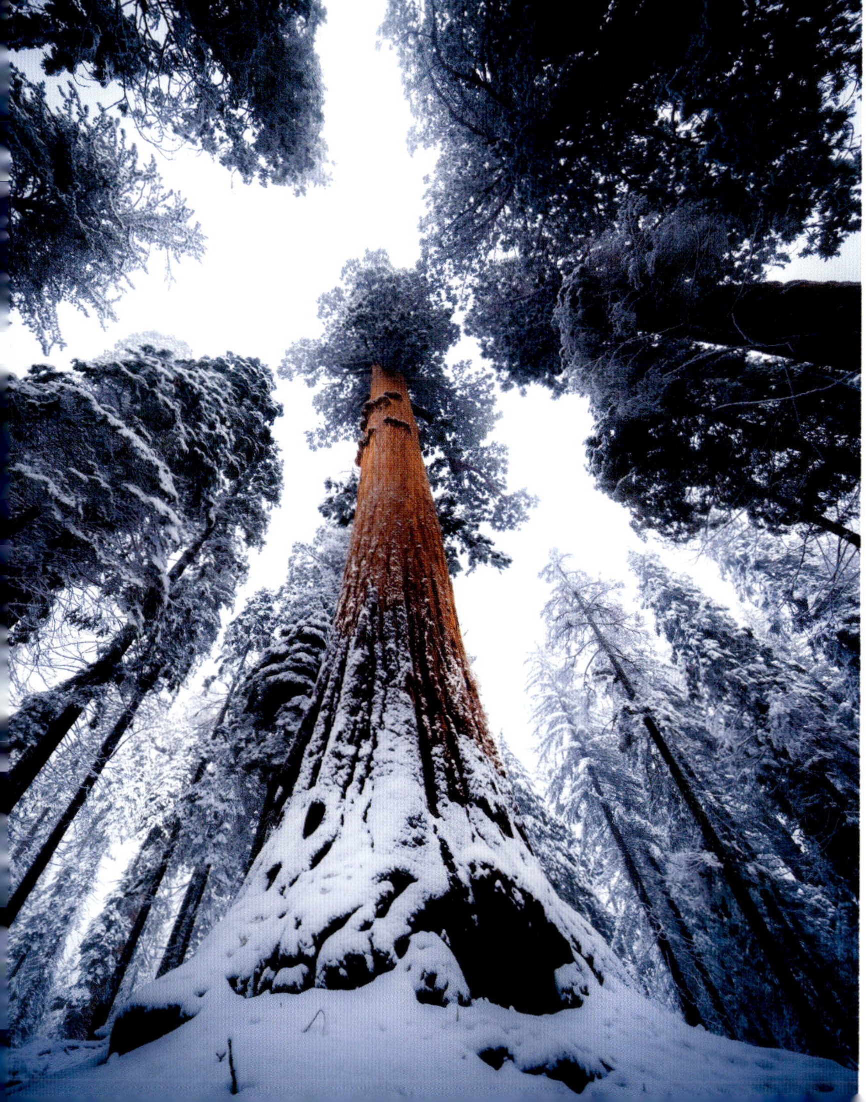

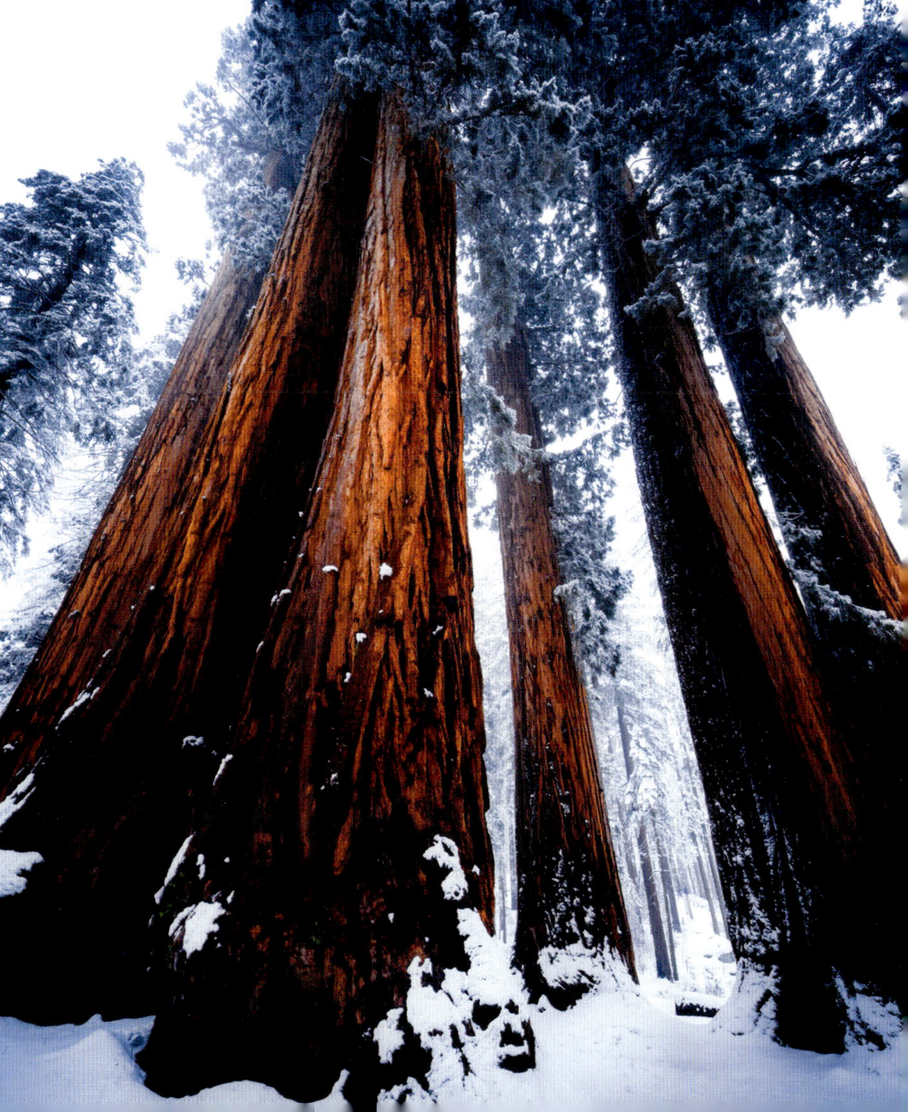

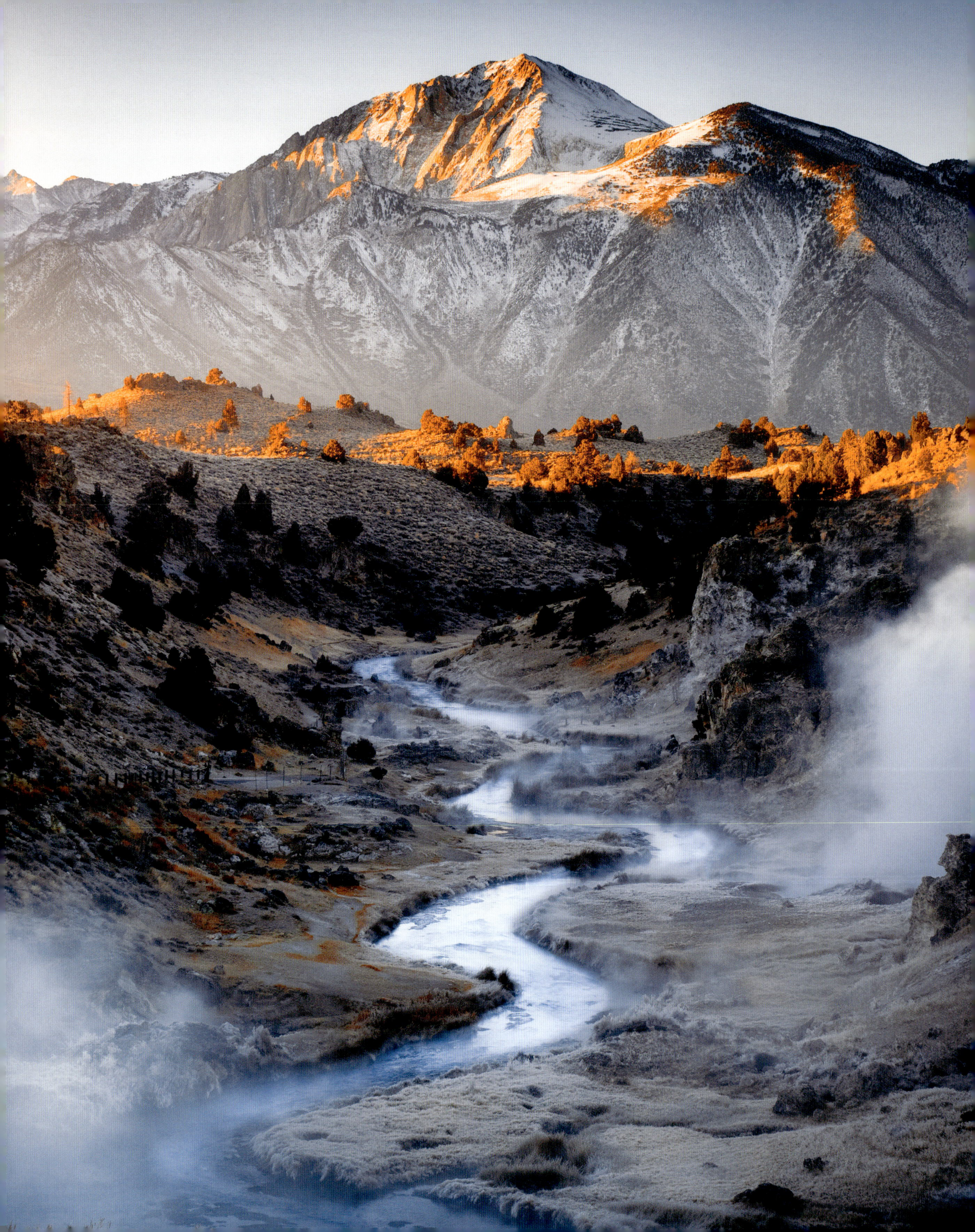

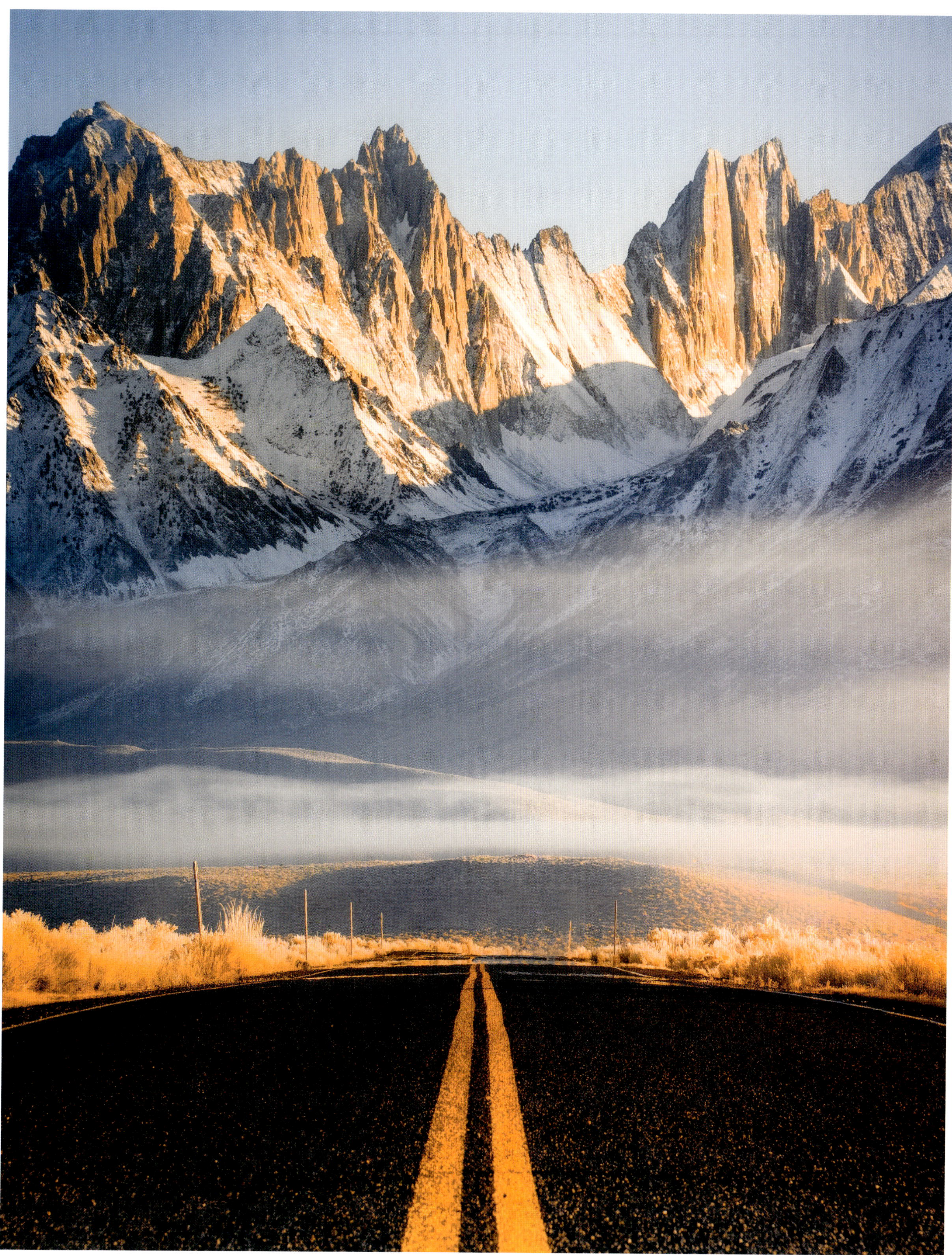

Above: Hot Creek geologic site | Opposite: Near Mammoth Lakes, Sierra Nevada Mountains

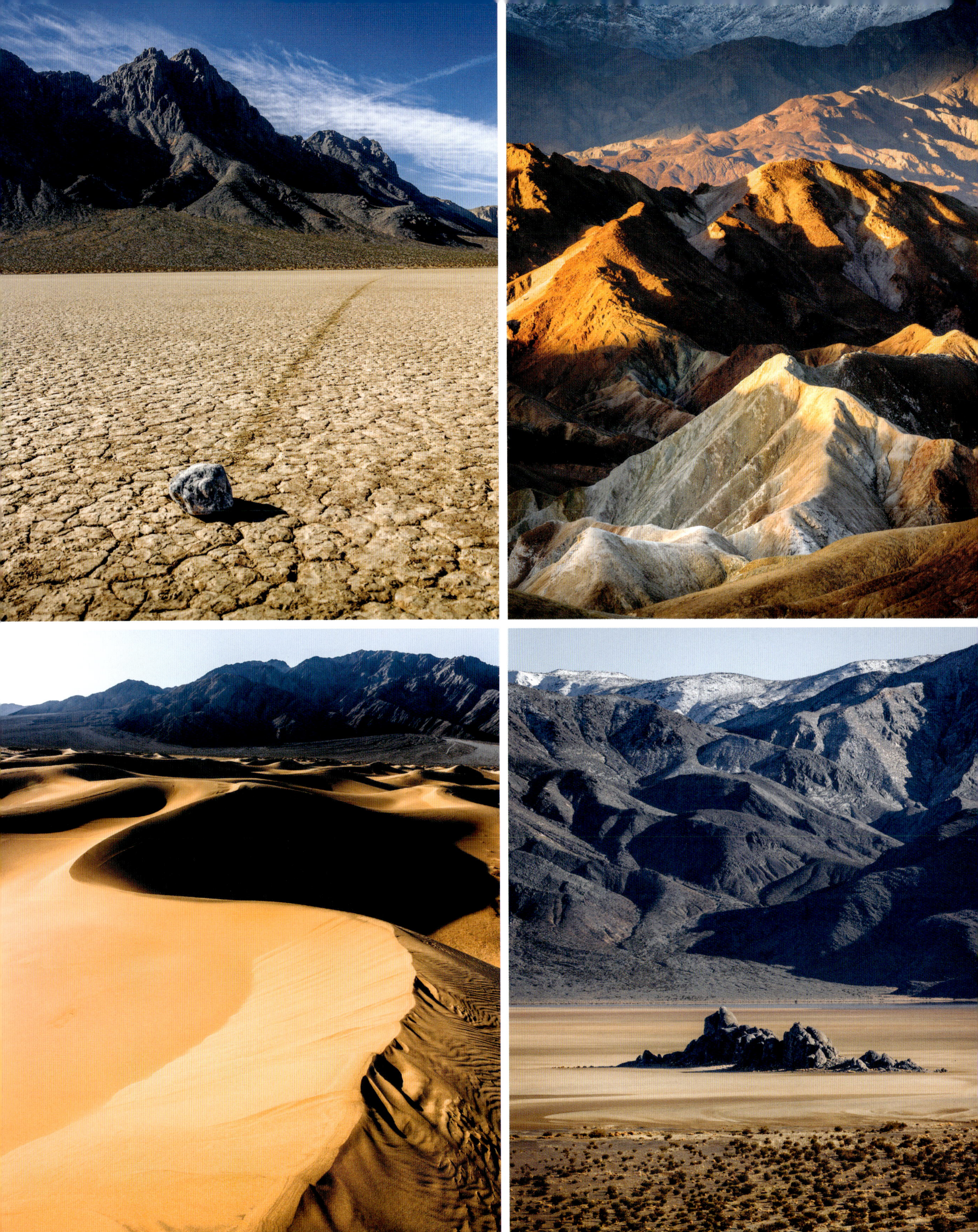

DEATH VALLEY NATIONAL PARK

I stood on Racetrack Playa, finally witnessing the mysterious moving rocks. It's one thing to hear about them, but seeing it in person was unreal. The trails behind the rocks extended hundreds of feet! The hike up the Mesquite Flat Sand Dunes was exhausting, with every step sinking into the sand, but the view from the top made it all worth it. The sheer size of the dunes will blow you away. As the sun set, the dunes glowed and stretched endlessly into the distance. Death Valley is extreme by all means, but it's not a place worth missing.

Region: West

States: California and Nevada

Coordinates: 36°31′56.3″N 116°55′57.0″W

Focal features: Extreme desert landscapes, including Badwater Basin, Mesquite Flat Sand Dunes, and Zabriskie Point

Formation attributes: Death Valley contains the lowest point in North America, Badwater Basin, at 282 feet (86m) below sea level. It also has some of the driest conditions on Earth, with less than two inches (5cm) of rainfall per year. The park covers over 3.4 million acres, making it the largest national park in the lower forty-eight states.

Fun fact: Death Valley holds the record for the highest air temperature ever recorded on Earth: 134°F (57°C) in July 1913.

Best time to visit: November to March offers clear skies, cooler temperatures, and better hiking conditions. March to April brings beautiful wildflower blooms.

How to access: The park is accessible via Highway 190 from the west (California) or via Beatty, Nevada, from the east. There are limited gas stations inside the park, so refueling before entering is essential. Many roads require high-clearance or 4WD vehicles, especially if exploring off the main paved routes.

Things to consider: Summer temperatures can exceed 120°F (49°C), making winter and early spring the best times to visit. Always carry extra water, fuel up before entering the park, and be prepared for limited cell service.

RECOMMENDED TRAILS:

Badwater Basin Salt Flats: *1.9-mile (3km) round trip; minimal elevation gain; easy.* A walk onto the vast salt flats of the lowest point in North America, where the cracked ground creates surreal, otherworldly textures.

Golden Canyon to Red Cathedral: *3-mile (5km) round trip; 600 feet (183m) elevation gain; moderate.* A hike through a narrow, golden-hued canyon that ends at the stunning Red Cathedral rock formation.

Wildrose Peak Trail: *8.4-mile (13.5km) round trip; about 2,200 feet (670m) elevation gain; strenuous.* A high-elevation hike offering some of the best panoramic views of Death Valley and the surrounding mountain ranges.

Tips for taking a great photo

- Sunrise at Zabriskie Point bathes the badlands in golden light, while sunset at Mesquite Flat Sand Dunes creates dramatic shadows.
- For the best cracked salt formations, walk at least a half mile out from the parking area at Badwater Basin.
- Death Valley is an International Dark Sky Park. Visit in the winter to see the clearest night skies and to capture the Milky Way over the dunes.
- A telephoto lens can highlight the intricate ripples of the sand dunes and the rugged landscape of the badlands.

Clockwise from top left: Racetrack Playa, Zabriskie Point, The Grandstand, Mesquite Flat Sand Dunes

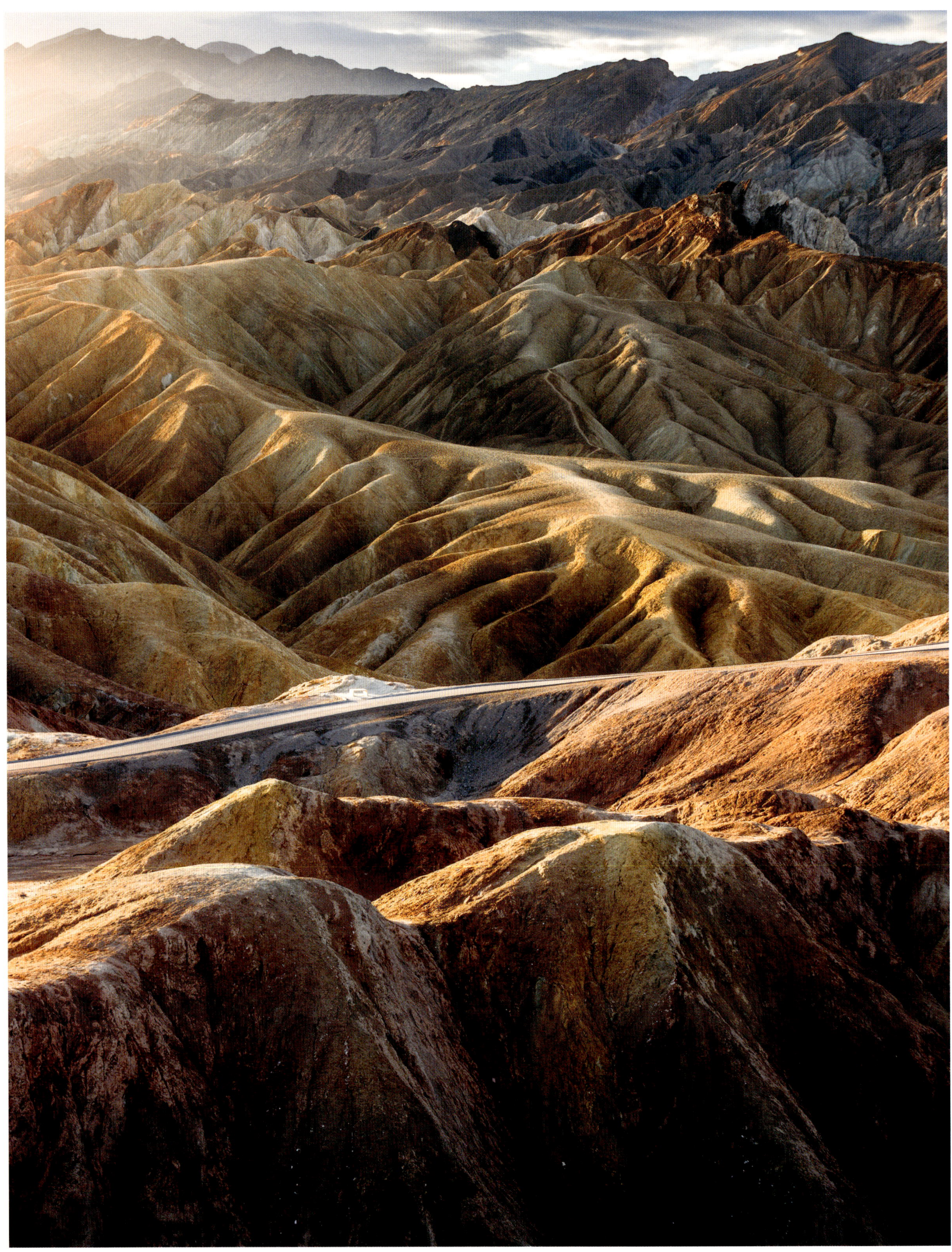

Above and opposite: Zabriskie Point, Death Valley National Park | Pages 136–137: Mesquite Flat Sand Dunes, Death Valley National Park

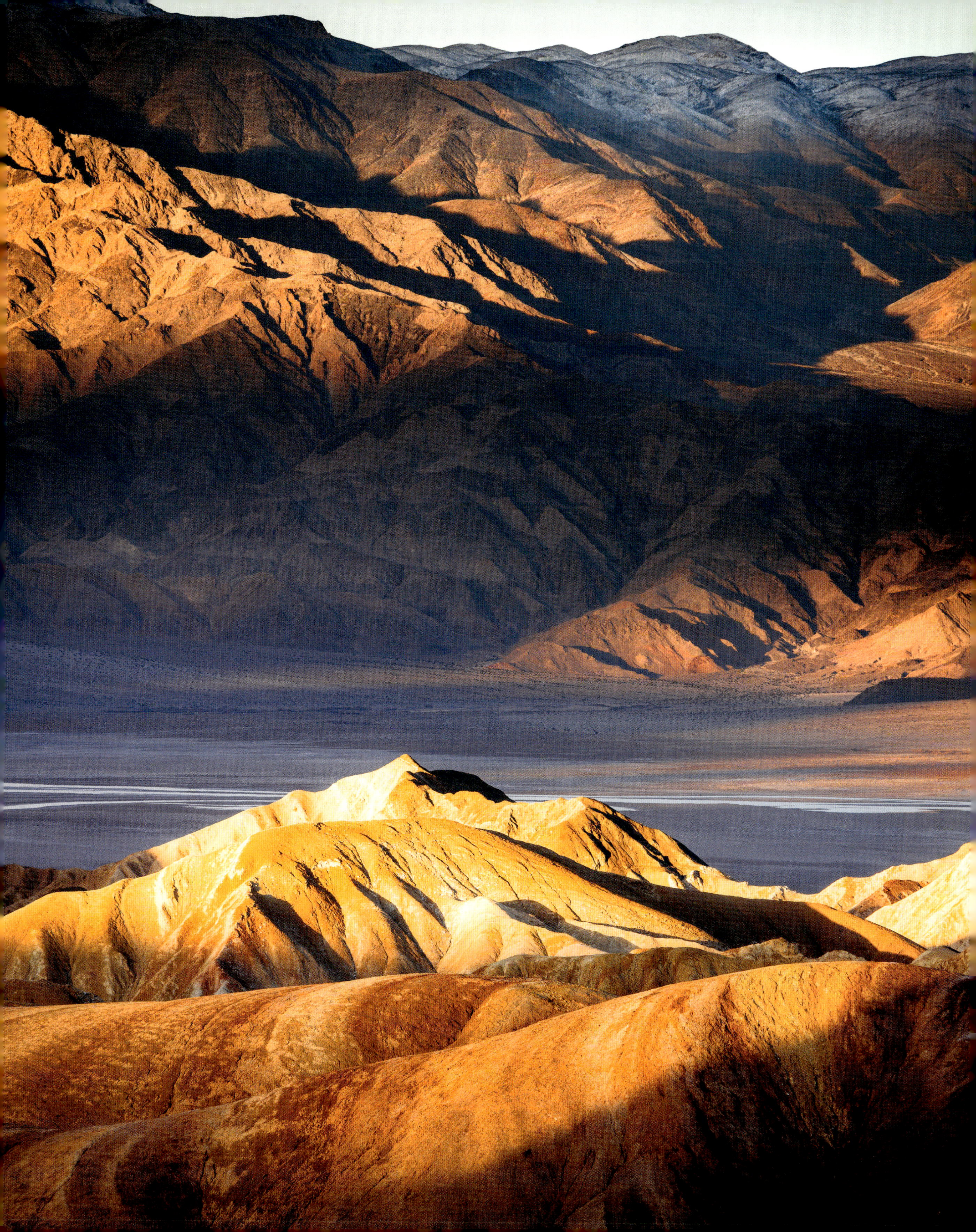

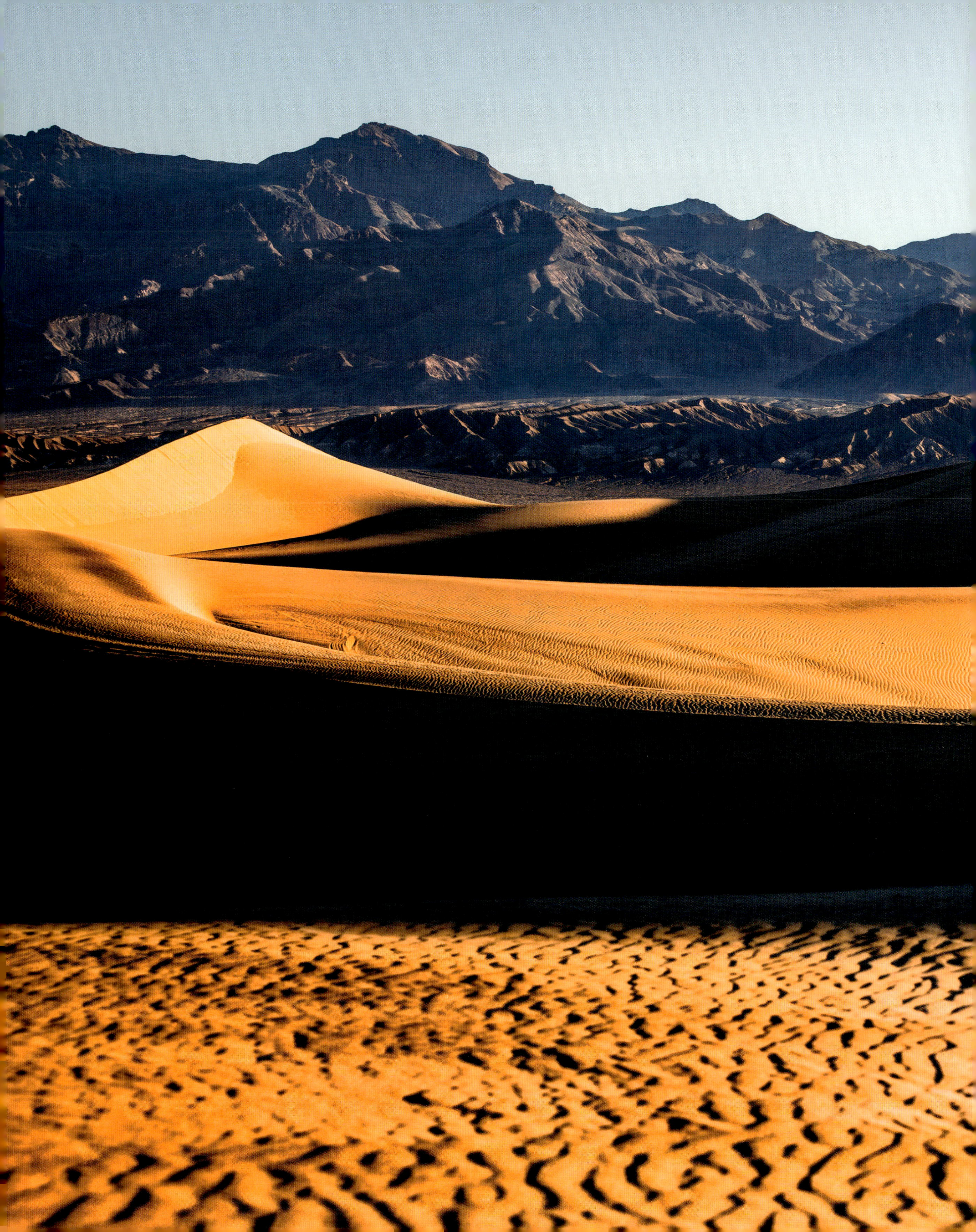

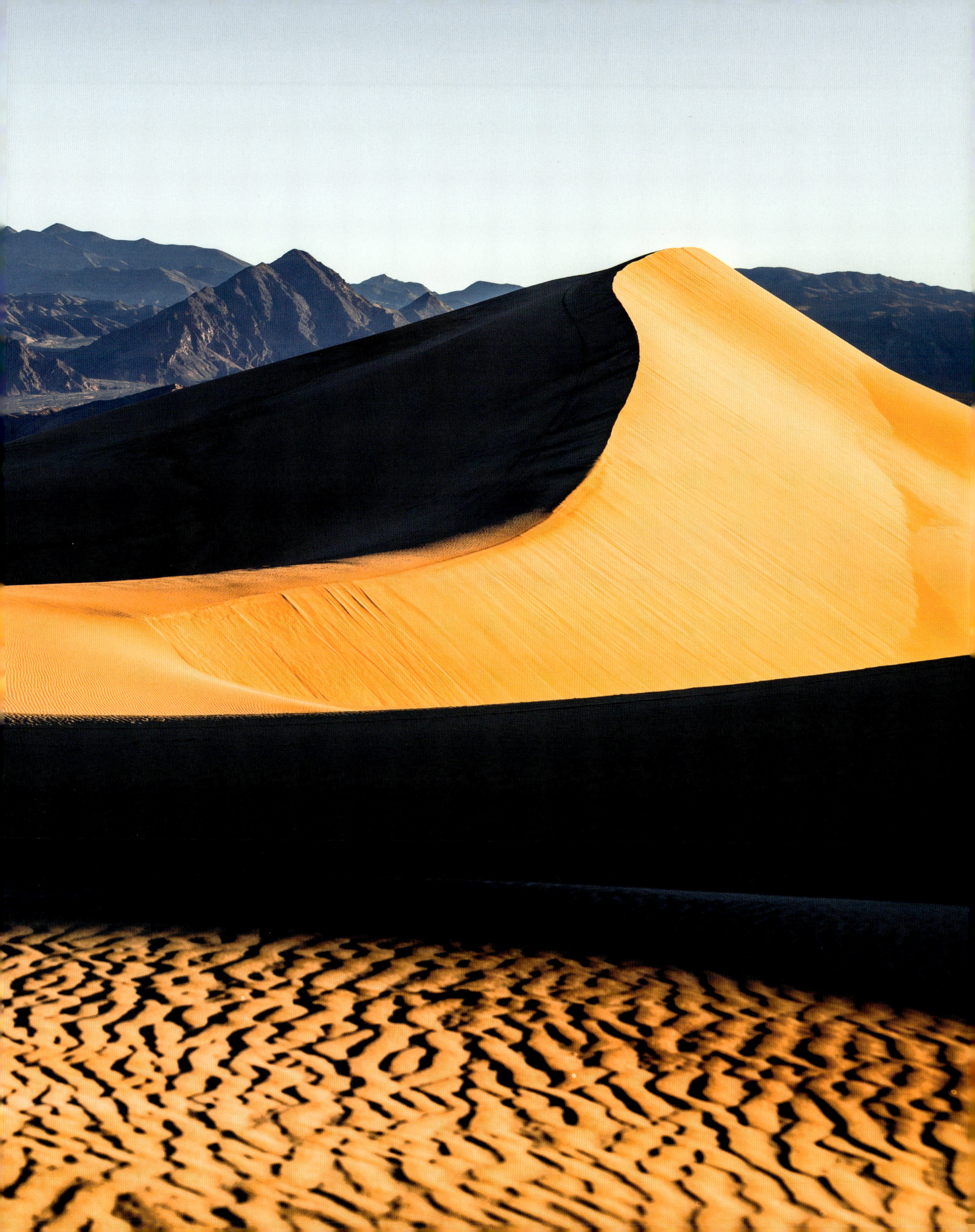

NORTH CENTRAL

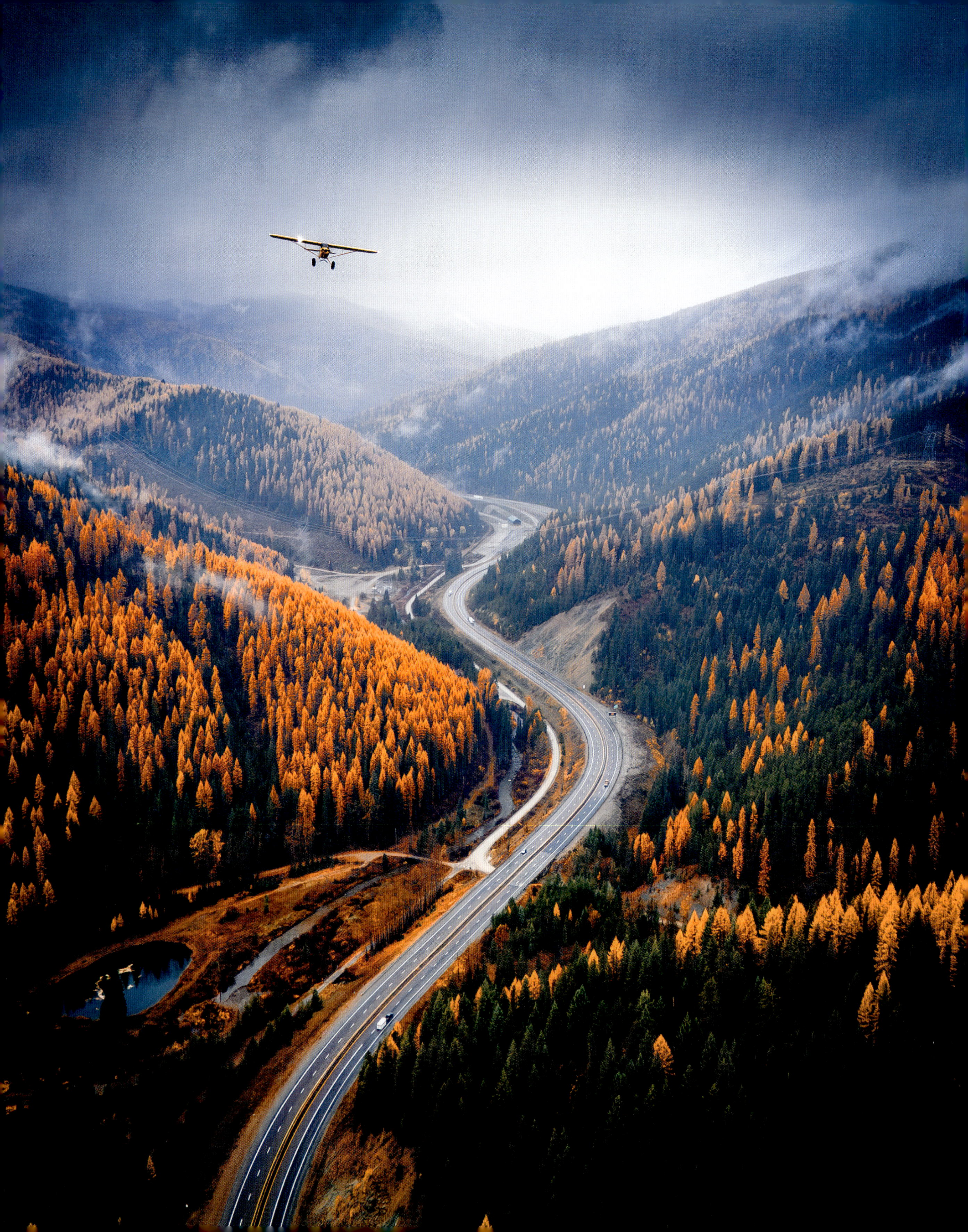

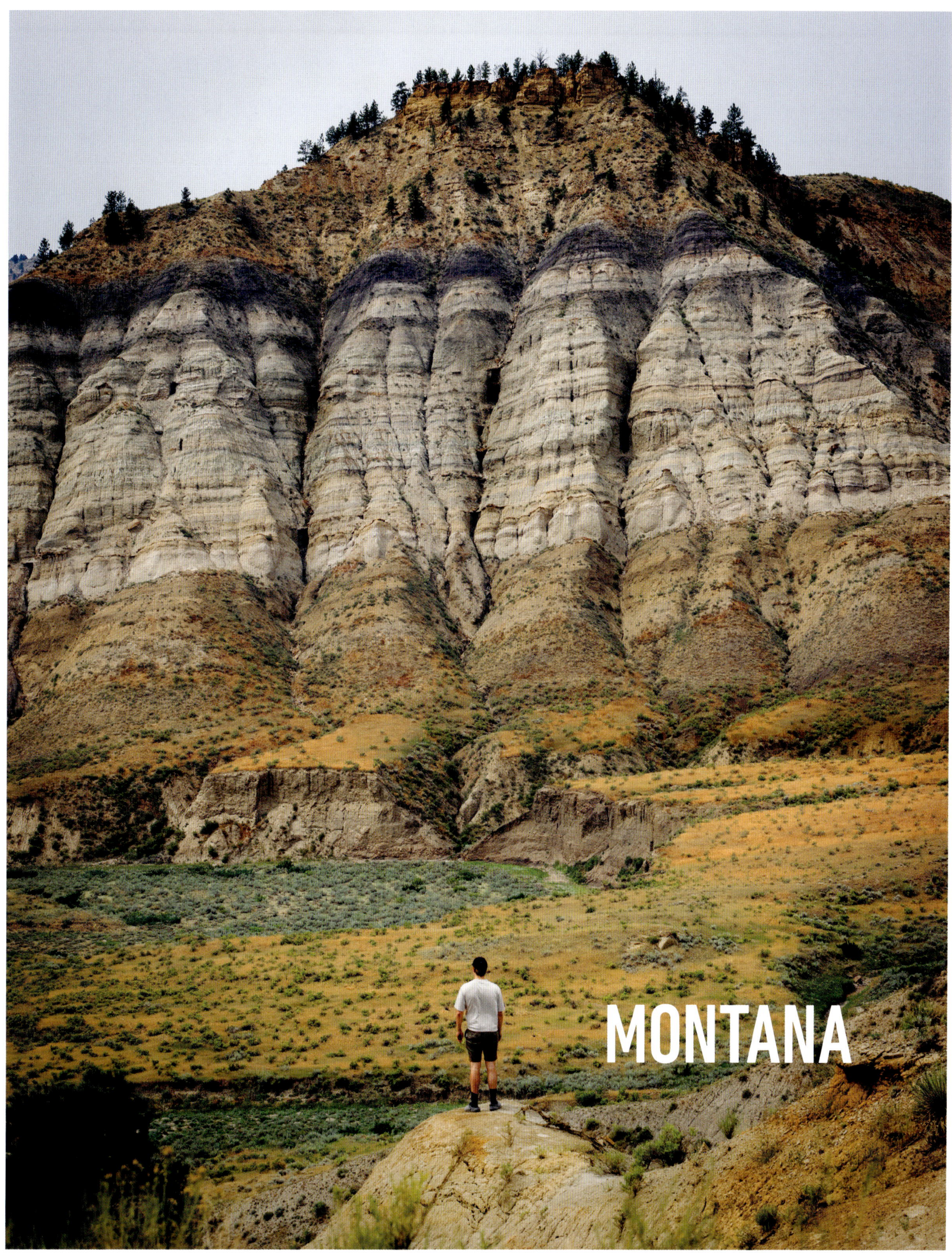
MONTANA

EASTERN MONTANA

Exploring eastern Montana is like uncovering a quiet, endless frontier. Vast plains stretch beneath big, open skies, dotted with badlands, sandstone bluffs, and hidden river valleys. The landscapes feel both ancient and untamed, with fossil beds, dramatic rock formations, and a solitude that makes the land's history and beauty feel personal.

Region: North Central

State: Montana

Coordinates: 47°47'00.0"N 107°28'00.0"W (centered near Fort Peck)

Focal features: A remote and expansive landscape of badlands, prairie grasslands, and Montana's largest reservoir, Fort Peck Lake

Formation attributes: Formed by glacial melt and millions of years of erosion, this landscape includes the ancient Missouri River corridor, fossil-rich sedimentary layers, and one of the most ambitious prairie-restoration projects in the world.

Fun fact: The Fort Peck Dam is one of the largest hydraulically filled earth dams in the US and created a reservoir with more shoreline than the coast of California.

Best time to visit: Late May through October for mild temperatures, blooming wildflowers, and the best access for boating, hiking, and wildlife viewing. Fall brings golden grasses, migrating birds, and stunning sunsets.

How to access: Eastern Montana is best reached by car via US Highway 2 or Highway 200. Small regional airports in Glasgow and Lewistown offer limited flights. Services can be sparse, so come prepared for remote travel.

Things to consider: This region is extremely remote—fuel up and bring extra water, maps, and emergency supplies. Weather can shift quickly; storms roll fast across the plains, and winds can be strong. Cell service is limited in many areas, so download maps ahead of time and carry GPS if hiking or boating.

RECOMMENDED AREAS TO EXPLORE:

Fort Peck Lake and Dam: A massive reservoir offering boating, fishing, scenic drives, and wildlife watching. Visit the Fort Peck Interpretive Center for fossils and regional history.

Upper Missouri River Breaks National Monument: Explore the rugged river bluffs, cottonwood groves, and historic sites along the wild and scenic Missouri River—canoeing or hiking through these breaks offers solitude and incredible views.

American Prairie (Reserve): A groundbreaking conservation project aiming to rewild the prairie with free-roaming bison and native species. Enjoy dispersed camping, wildlife watching, and immersive solitude across over 496,000 acres of protected land.

Tips for taking a great photo

- Golden hour lights up the breaks and badlands with rich color and long shadows—ideal for landscape photography.
- Use a wide-angle lens to capture the scale of the prairie and big skies.
- A telephoto lens is essential for bison, elk, pronghorn, and raptors—especially in the American Prairie.
- Stormy skies and glowing sunsets make dramatic backdrops in this wide-open terrain.

Page 140: Lolo National Forest

Page 141: Near Upper Missouri River Breaks National Monument

Opposite: Fort Peck Lake

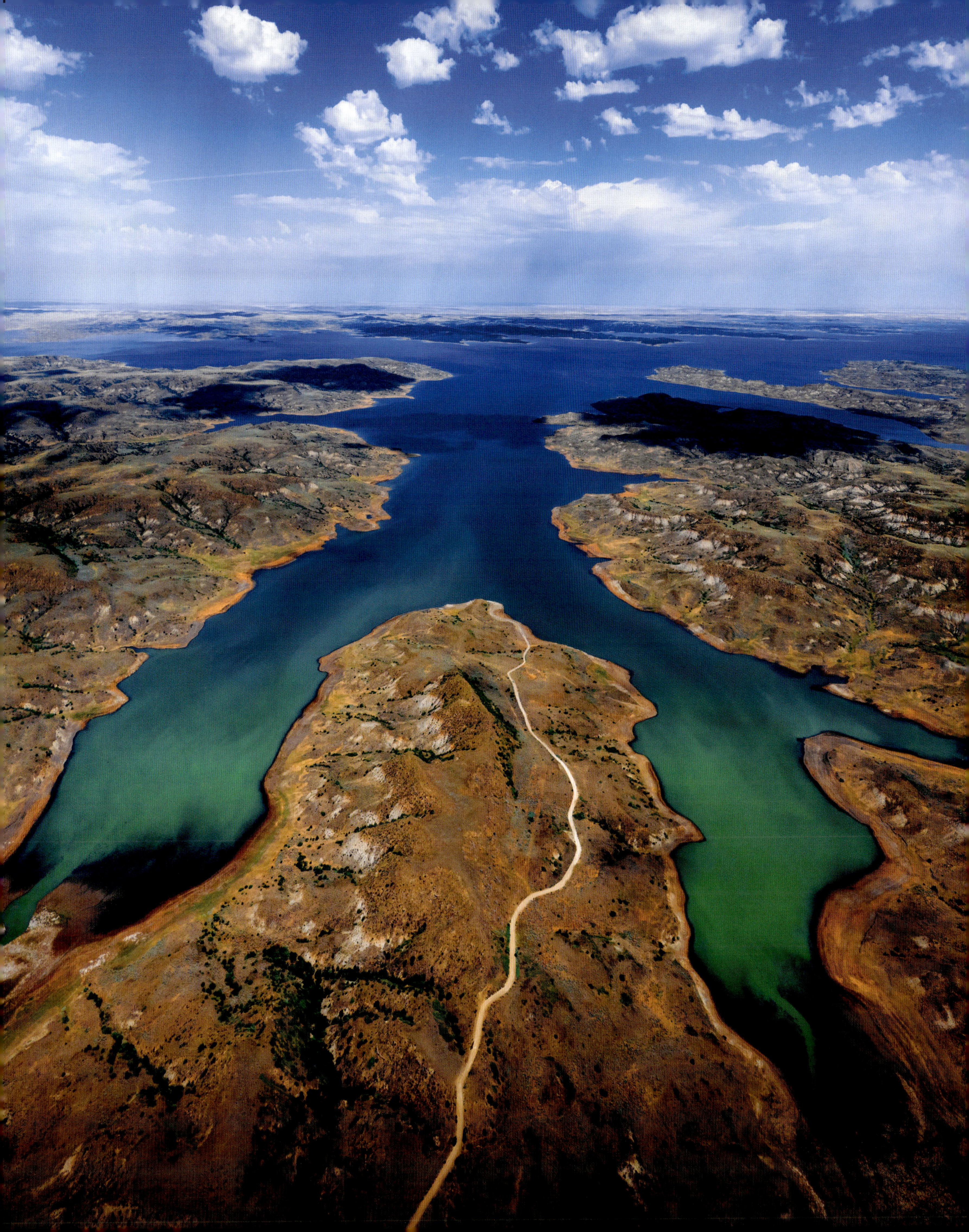

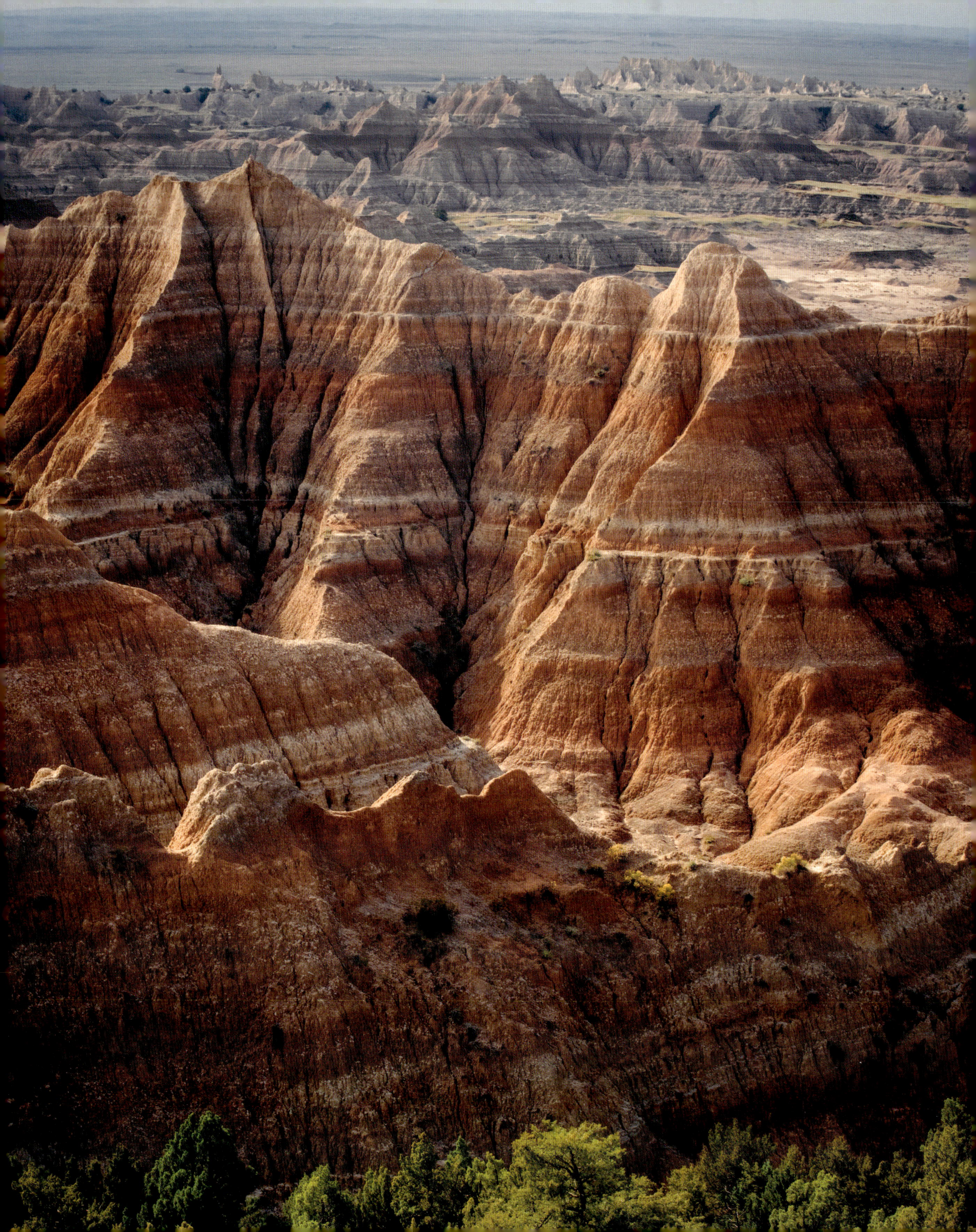

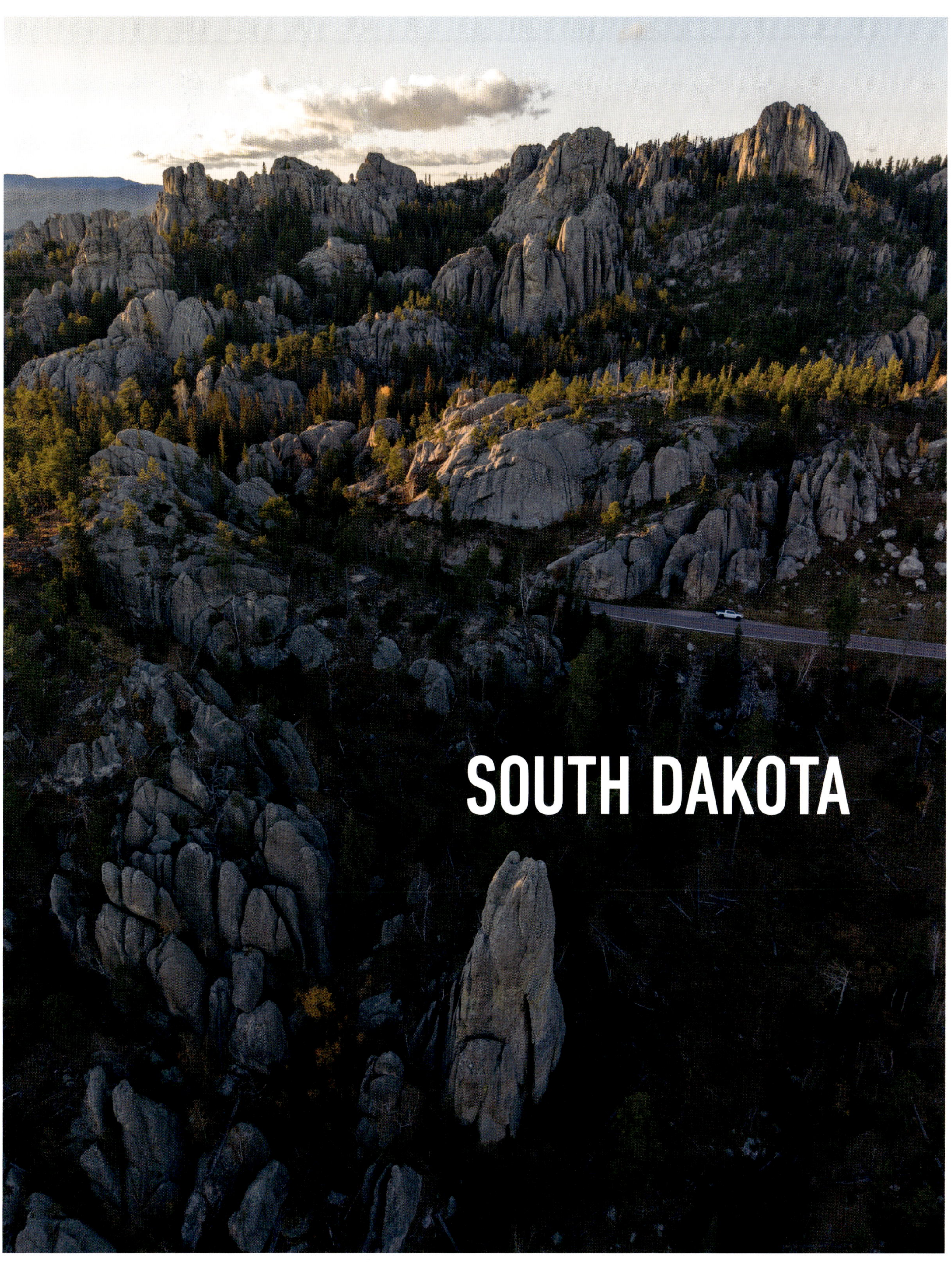

SOUTH DAKOTA

CUSTER STATE PARK

Visiting Custer State Park feels like stepping into a wild, rugged wonderland. Winding roads lead through granite spires, pine forests, and rolling prairies where bison roam freely. You'll see towering rock formations like the Needles, scenic lakes, and wide-open grasslands, all teeming with wildlife and stunning views.

Region: North Central

State: South Dakota

Coordinates: 43°46'30.0"N 103°21'30.0"W

Focal feature: A diverse landscape of granite mountains, rolling prairie, pine forests, and clear lakes—home to iconic wildlife and scenic byways

Formation attributes: Shaped by uplift and erosion of ancient Precambrian granite, the park spans over 71,000 acres and includes the scenic Needles Highway and Sylvan Lake area.

Fun fact: Custer State Park is home to one of the largest publicly owned bison herds in the world, with around 1,400 bison roaming freely throughout the park.

Best time to visit: May through October for warm weather, peak wildlife activity, and access to all scenic drives. Late September through October brings golden aspens and fewer crowds.

How to access: Located along US Highway 16A, about forty minutes south of Rapid City, Custer State Park is easily accessible by car; most major scenic routes (Iron Mountain Road, Needles Highway) are paved but seasonal. Park entry requires a pass available at entrances or online.

Things to consider: Wildlife is abundant, especially bison, pronghorn, and burros. Always keep a safe distance and remain in your vehicle, if needed. Summer afternoons can bring sudden thunderstorms; pack rain gear and sun protection. Scenic drives include narrow tunnels and sharp turns, so be aware that larger vehicles may be restricted.

RECOMMENDED TRAILS & ROUTES:

Sylvan Lake Shore Trail: *1-mile (1.6km) loop; minimal elevation gain; easy.* A picturesque trail around a granite-rimmed alpine lake, perfect for families and casual hikers.

Black Elk Peak Trail (via Sylvan Lake): *7-mile (11.3km) round trip; 1,500 feet (457m) elevation gain; moderate–strenuous.* A hike leading to the highest point in South Dakota with sweeping views from a historic fire lookout.

Sunday Gulch Trail: *3.9-mile (6.3km) loop; 800 feet (244m) elevation gain; moderate.* A unique, rocky trail with metal handrails, creek crossings, and boulder-filled gulches.

Wildlife Loop Road: *18-mile (29km) driving route.* Prime for spotting bison, prairie dogs, and wild burros, especially near dawn or dusk.

Tips for taking a great photo

- Sunrise at Sylvan Lake offers calm reflections and soft alpine light.
- Use a telephoto lens for bison, elk, and burros—keep your distance and photograph from inside your car or a safe pullout.
- Needles Highway features dramatic granite spires, which you can shoot during golden hour to enhance contrast and depth.
- Fall colors and wildlife activity peak in late September, making it one of the best times for photography.

Page 144: Badlands National Park

Page 145: Custer State Park

Opposite: Cathedral Spires, Custer State Park

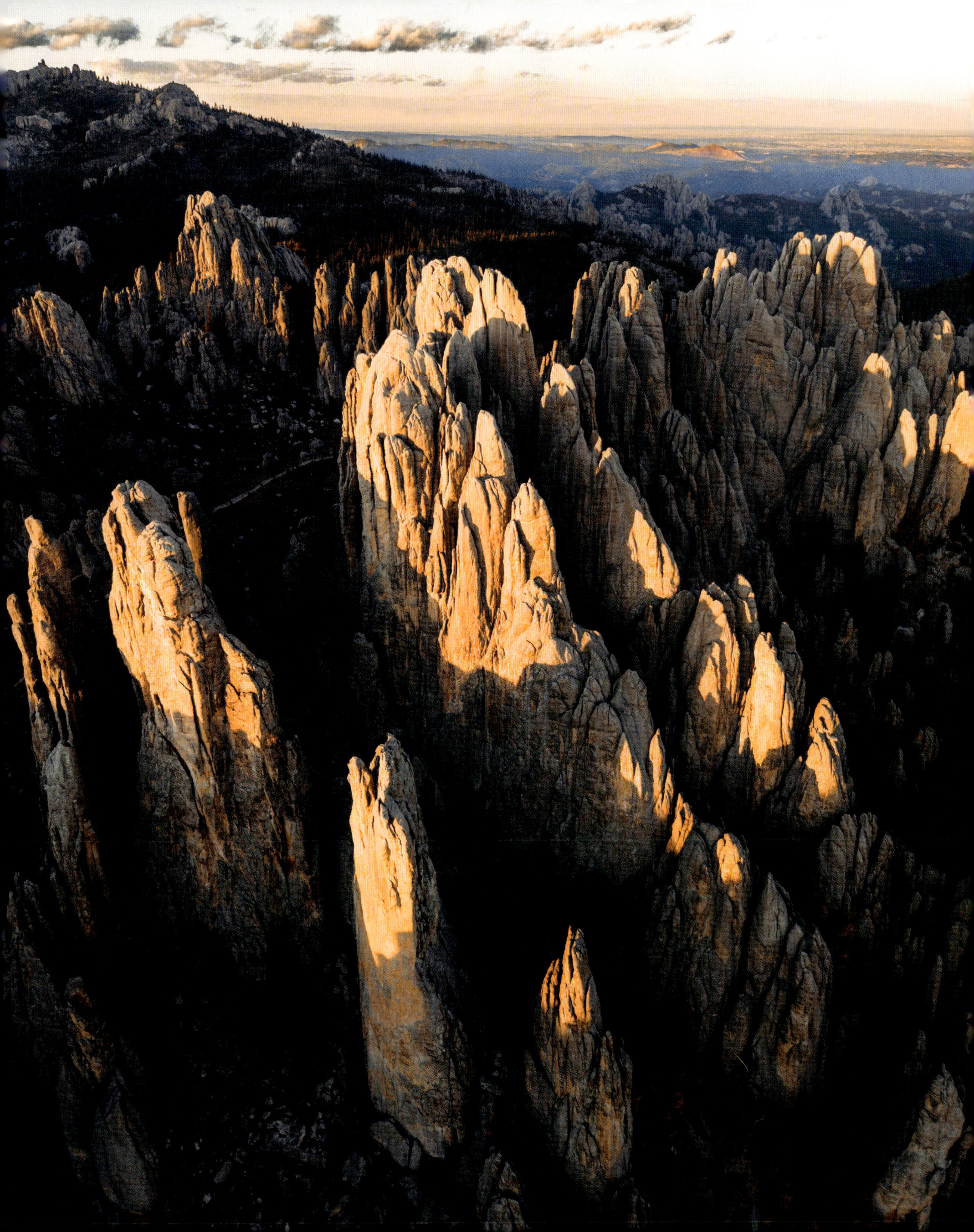

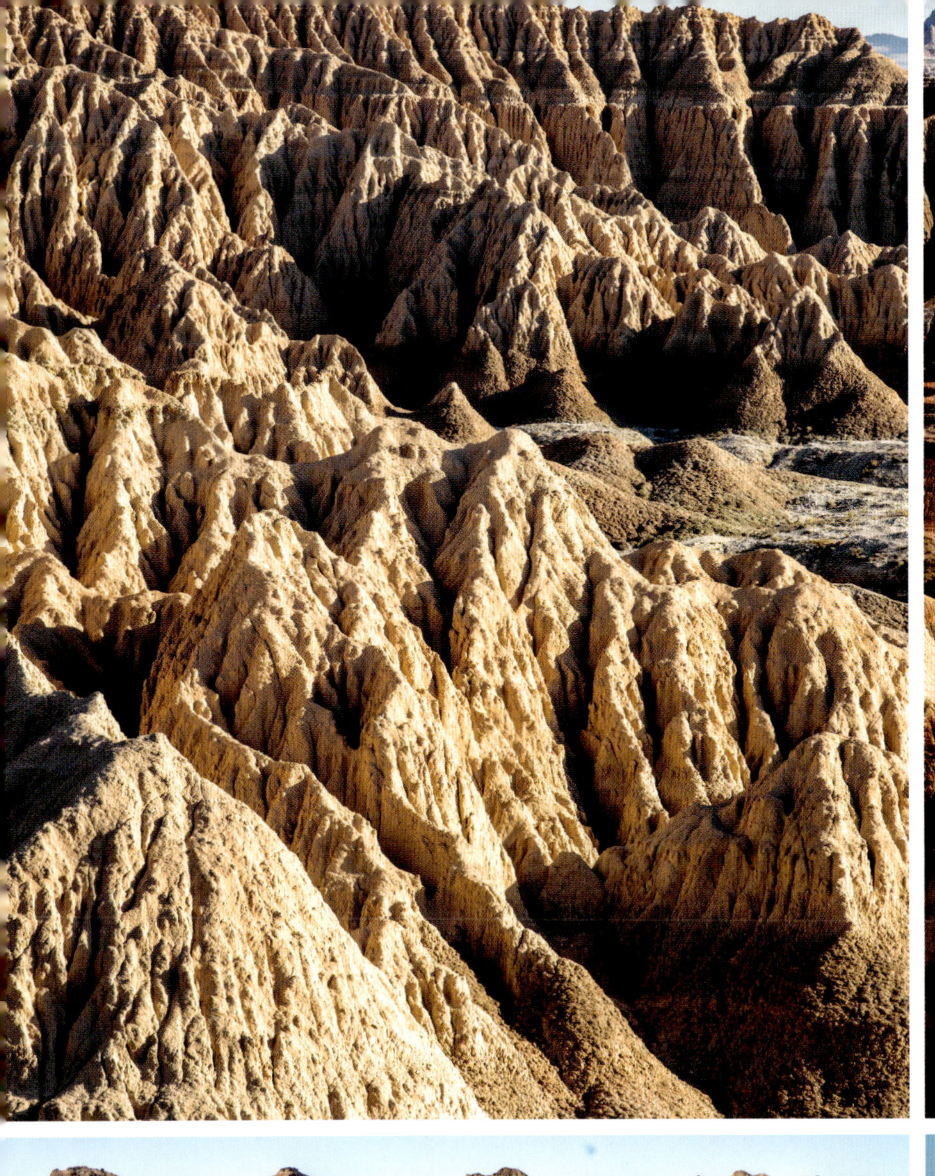
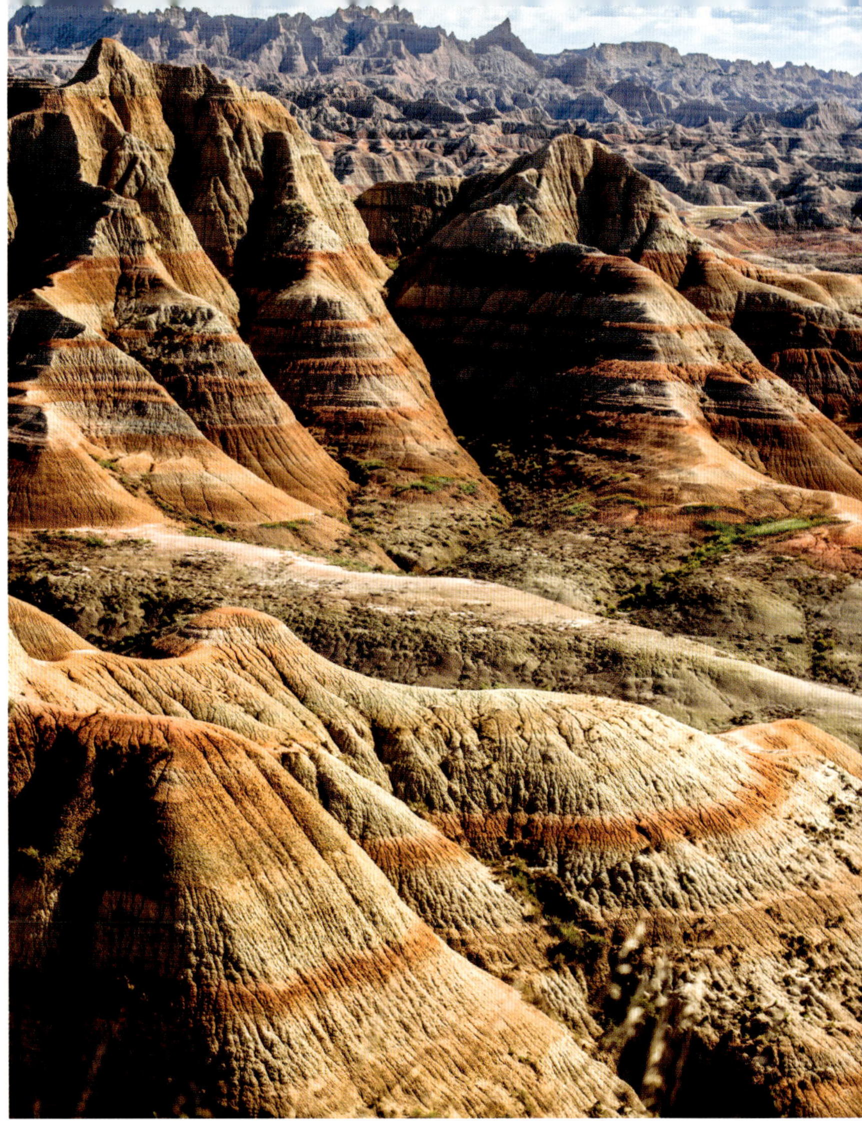
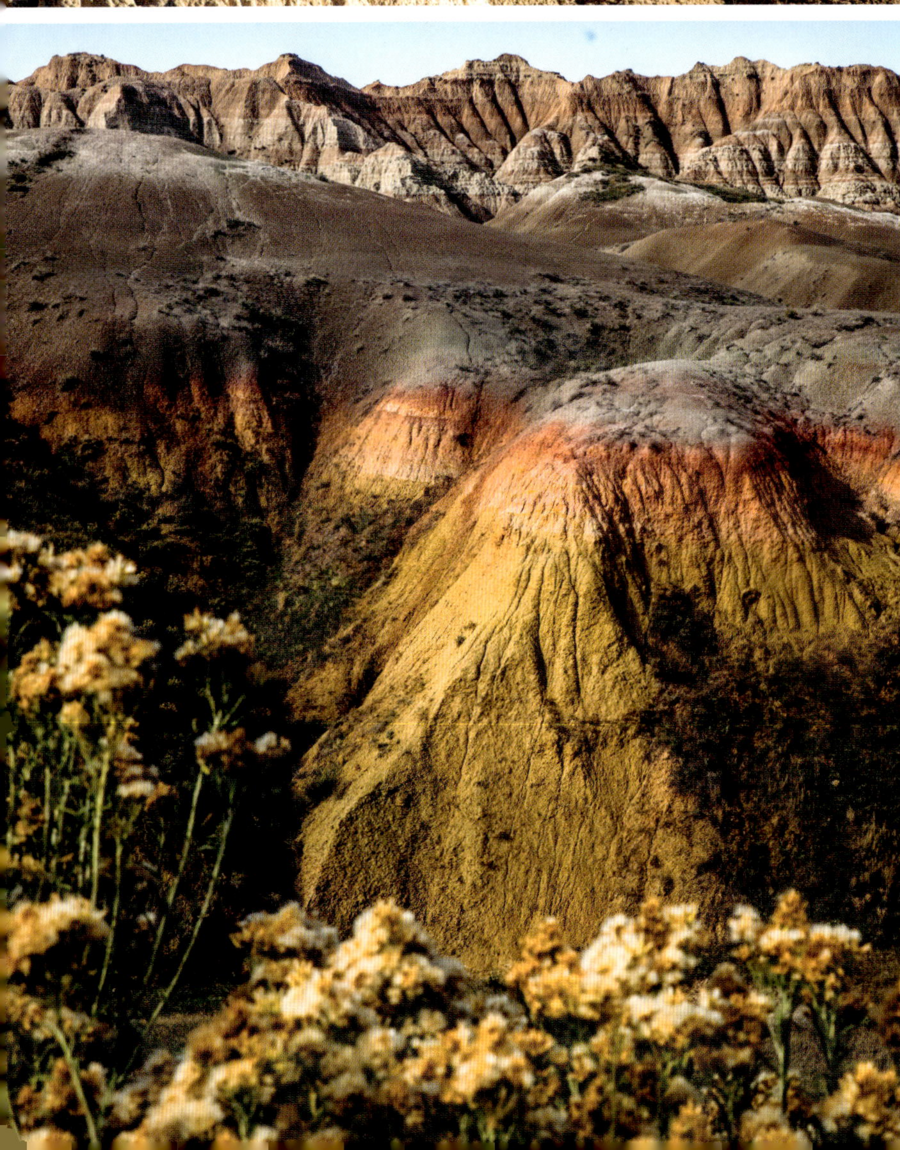
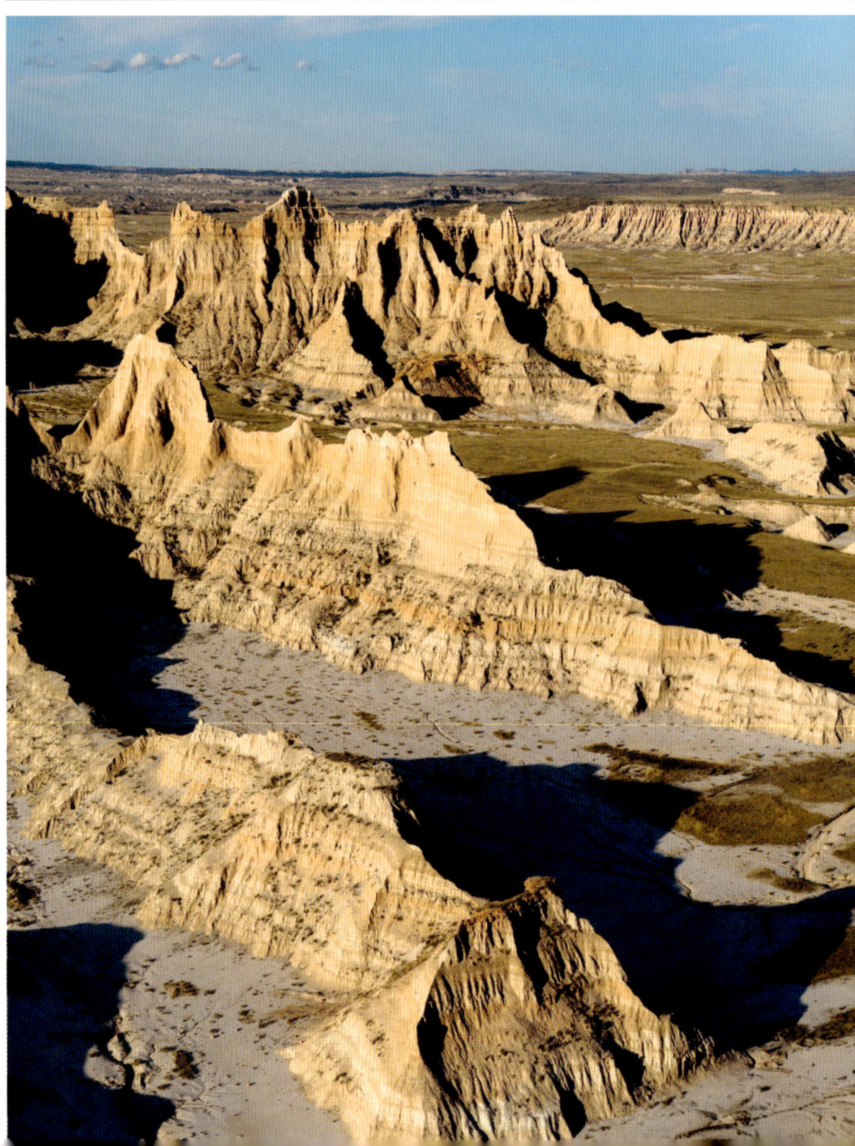

BADLANDS NATIONAL PARK

Stand atop the jagged spires of the Badlands at sunrise, where striped buttes glow gold and crimson and groups of bison roam the grasslands. It's a landscape carved by time and water, revealing seventy-five million years of geologic history in every cliff and fossil-laden ridge.

Region: North Central

State: South Dakota

Coordinates: 43°45'45.0"N 102°00'30.0"W

Focal feature: Dramatic badlands formations—sharp pinnacles, eroded buttes, and colorful sedimentary layers—set against a vast mixed-grass prairie.

Formation attributes: Created by the slow erosion of sedimentary rock deposited over millions of years, exposing some of the richest fossil beds of ancient mammals like saber-toothed cats and rhinos.

Fun fact: Badlands National Park contains one of the world's most complete fossil accumulations from the Oligocene Epoch, roughly thirty-three to twenty-three million years ago.

Best time to visit: Late spring and early fall for mild temperatures, fewer crowds, and ideal lighting for photography. Summer can be hot but provides vibrant prairie blooms and more wildlife sightings.

How to access: Located off Interstate 90 in southwestern South Dakota, the Badlands Loop Road (Highway 240) offers scenic access to overlooks, trailheads, and visitor centers. Nearby Rapid City provides the nearest major airport and services.

Things to consider: The weather is highly variable and temperatures fluctuate rapidly, so bring sun protection, layers, and plenty of water. Rattlesnakes and bison are common—stay alert and keep a safe distance. Prepare for limited cell service, which can be spotty.

RECOMMENDED TRAILS:

Door Trail: *0.8-mile (1.3km) round trip; minimal elevation gain; easy.* A boardwalk hike that leads to a break in the Badlands Wall, with opportunities to explore the formations up close.

Notch Trail: *1.2-mile (1.9km) round trip; 100 feet (30m) elevation gain; moderate.* A short hike through a scenic canyon ending with a dramatic overlook and featuring a log ladder climb.

Castle Trail: *10.3-mile (16.6km) round trip; 300 feet (91m) elevation gain; moderate–strenuous.* The park's longest trail, which winds through eroded formations and open prairie.

Tips for taking a great photo

- Sunrise and sunset cast long shadows and soft light—ideal for capturing texture and color in the rock layers.
- Use a polarizing filter to enhance the contrast between blue skies and warm earth tones.
- A wide-angle lens is perfect for vast panoramic shots; telephoto helps isolate wildlife or distant formations.
- After rain, puddles and soft clay can add reflections and dramatic contrast to your compositions.

Opposite: Badlands National Park

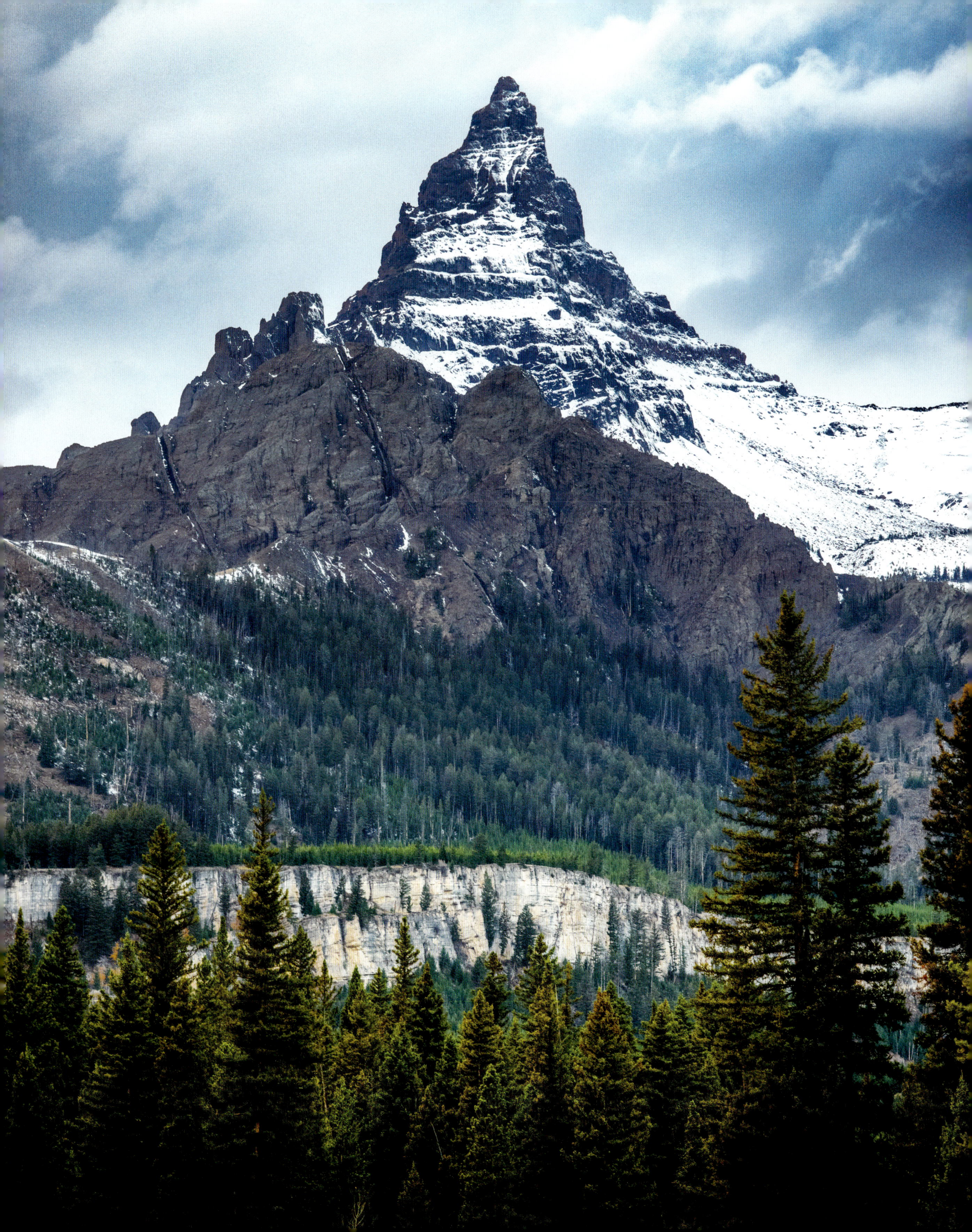

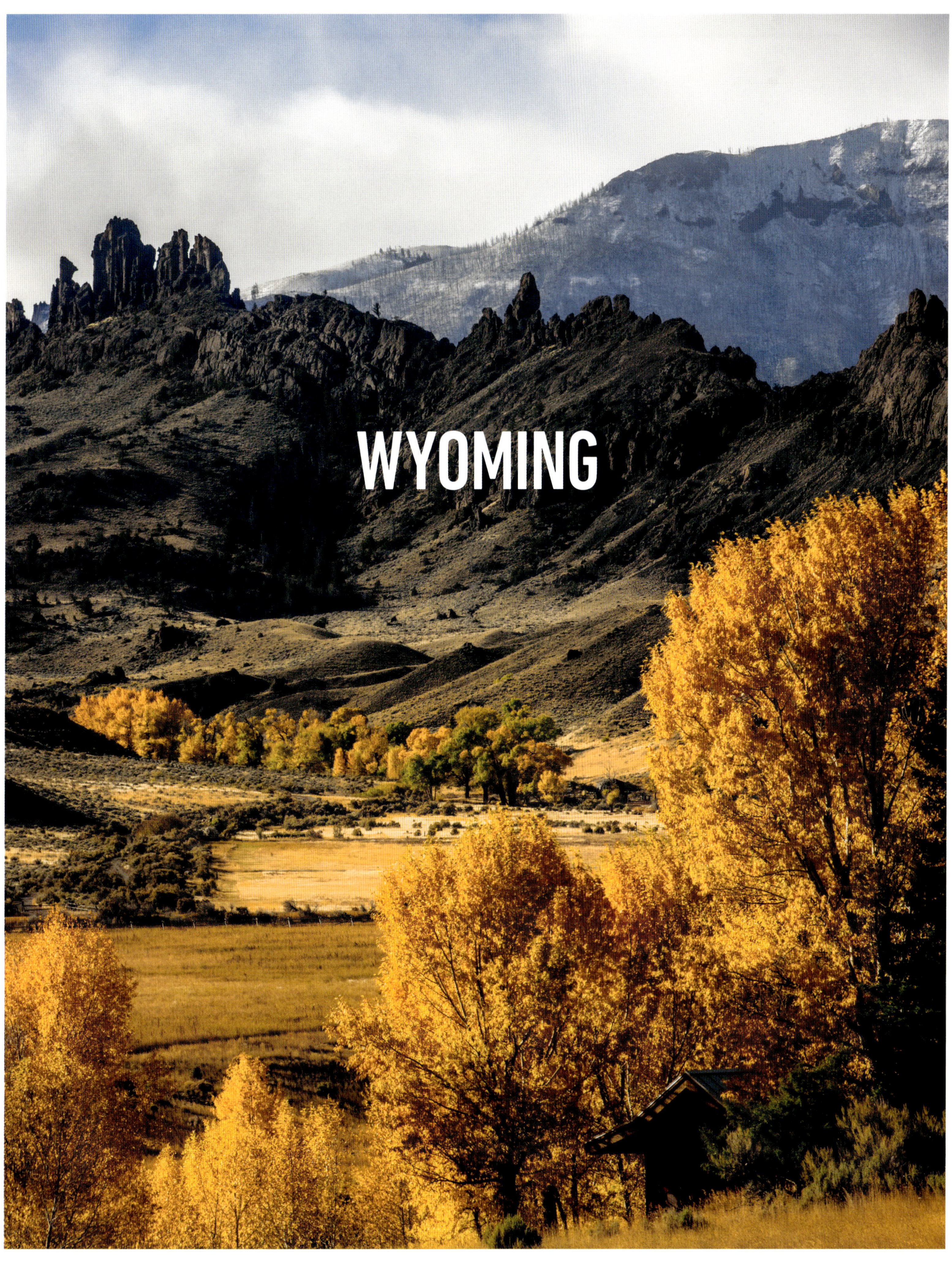

WYOMING

YELLOWSTONE NATIONAL PARK

Yellowstone was on my bucket list for years, and traveling here alone with my camera was a pilgrimage. I caught my first light in Lamar Valley—bison moving through golden fog, steam rising from the ground like the earth was exhaling. I didn't speak all morning, just moved with the light, framing shots and losing track of time. It was quiet, but alive. Each day brought something different—Grand Prismatic Spring's surreal colors, geysers blowing up, and the stillness of Yellowstone Lake at sunset. Being solo let me wait for the perfect shot without distraction. The park didn't feel like a place—it felt like a living thing, wild and unpredictable. I left with my memory cards full.

Region: Rocky Mountains

States: Wyoming, Montana, and Idaho

Coordinates: 44°25'40.8"N 110°35'18.6"W

Focal features: Geysers, hot springs, and abundant wildlife

Formation attributes: Spanning over 2.2 million acres, Yellowstone sits atop a supervolcano, with over ten thousand geothermal features, including half of the world's geysers.

Fun fact: Old Faithful erupts about every ninety minutes, shooting water up to 180 feet (55m) in the air!

Best time to visit: June to September offers the best weather and accessibility, while winter provides a magical, crowd-free experience with steaming geysers amid the snow.

How to access: The park has five entrances, the busiest being the West Entrance near West Yellowstone, Montana. Driving is the best way to explore, but traffic and road closures due to wildlife or weather are common, so plan accordingly.

Things to consider: Weather can be unpredictable; pack for all seasons, even in summer.

RECOMMENDED TRAILS:

Grand Prismatic Overlook Trail: *1.5-mile (2.4km) round trip; about 200 feet (61m) elevation gain; easy.* A short hike leading to a stunning aerial view of the vibrant Grand Prismatic Spring.

Fairy Falls Trail: *4.5-mile (7.2km) round trip; about 170 feet (52m) elevation gain; easy.* A beautiful walk through a lodgepole pine forest to a stunning 200-foot (61m) waterfall, with an optional detour to the Grand Prismatic Overlook.

Dunraven Pass to Mount Washburn: *7-mile (11.3km) round trip; about 1,400 feet (427m) elevation gain; strenuous.* A breathtaking hike to one of the park's highest peaks, offering panoramic views and a chance to see bighorn sheep.

Tips for taking a great photo

- Early morning and late evening offer the best lighting and fewer crowds at popular spots.
- Use a polarizing filter to cut glare and enhance the deep colors of hot springs like the Grand Prismatic and other geothermal features.
- Lamar and Hayden Valleys are prime spots for spotting bison, wolves, and grizzlies. Bring a zoom lens and keep a safe distance.
- Try long exposure shots at waterfalls like Yellowstone Falls for a silky water effect.

Page 150: Pilot Peak

Page 151: Wapiti Valley

Clockwise from top left: Opal Pool, Mammoth Hot Springs, Morning Glory Pool, Tower Fall

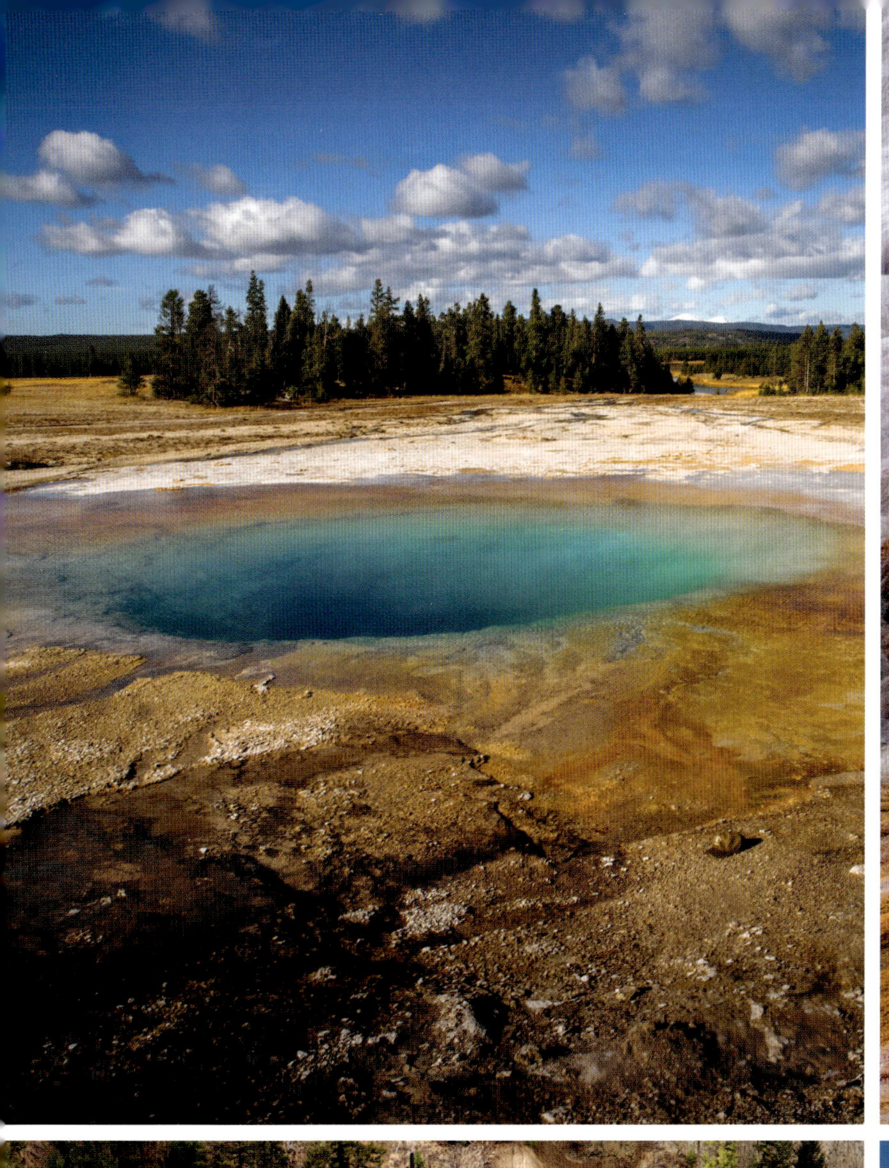
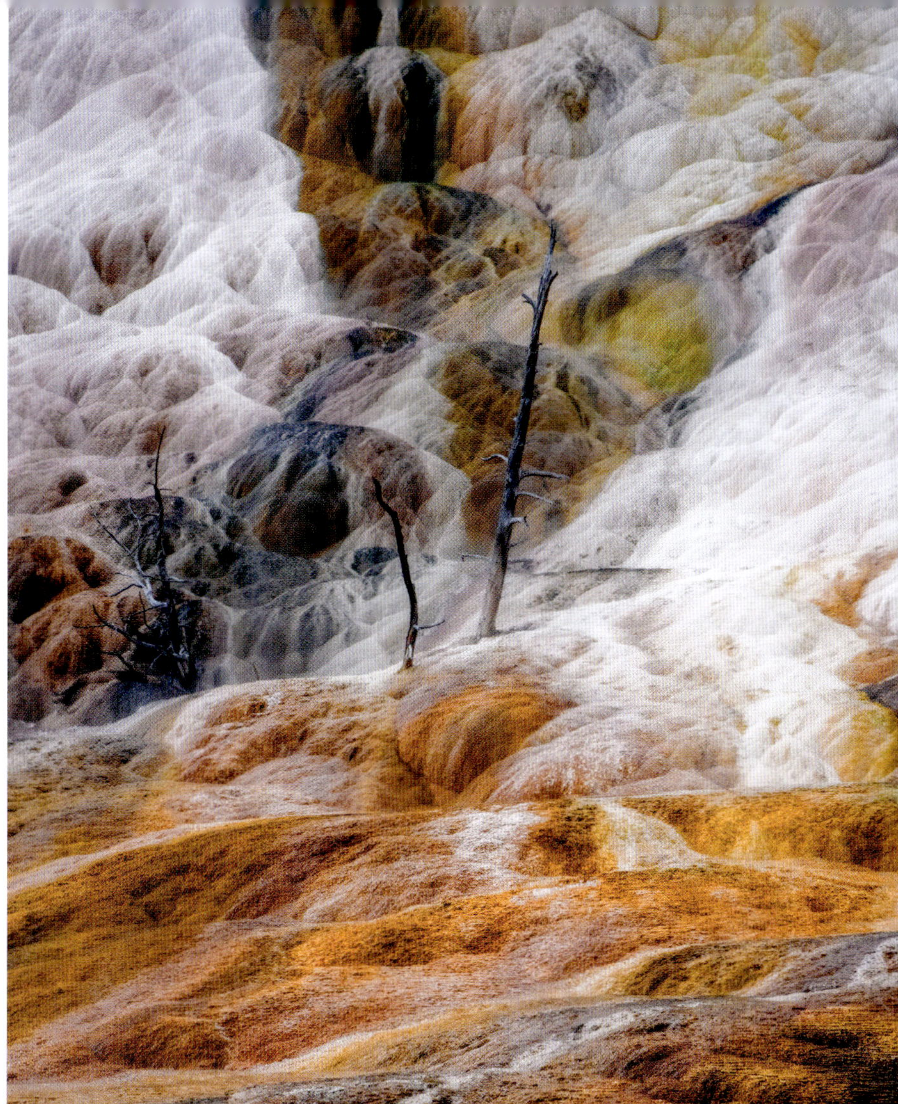
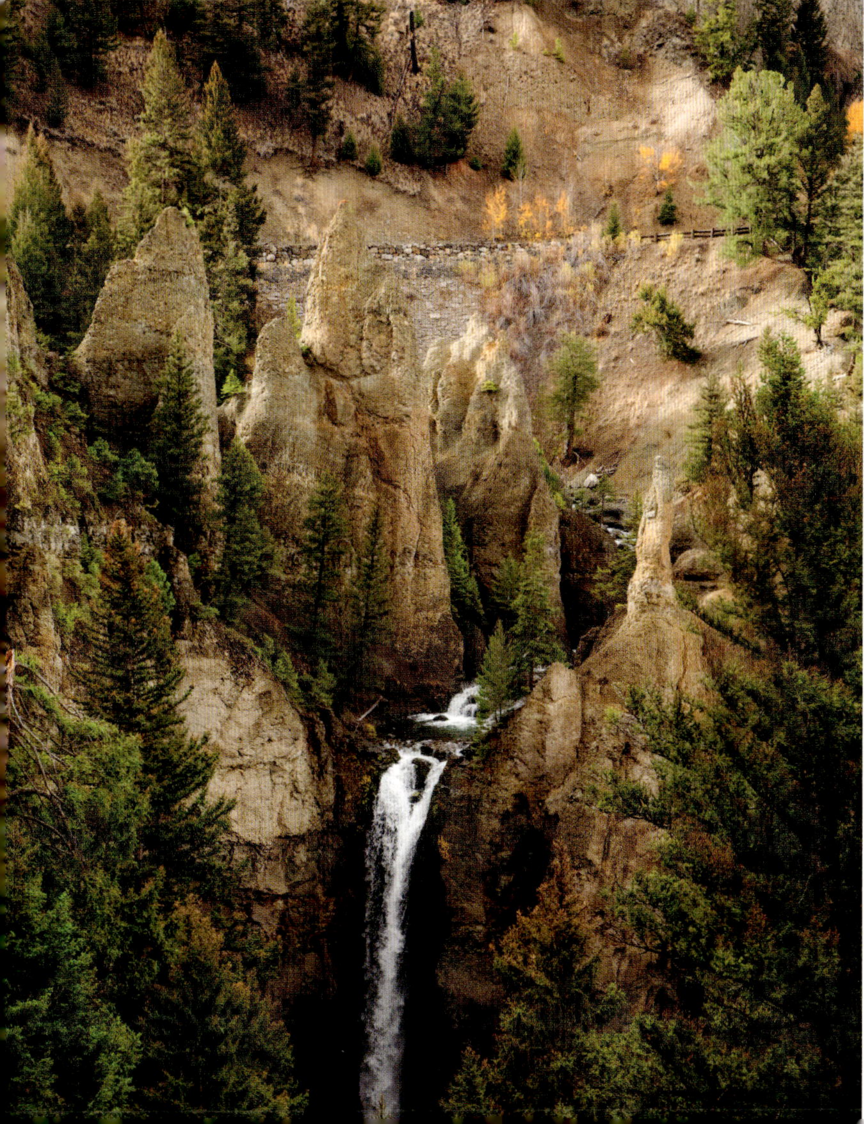
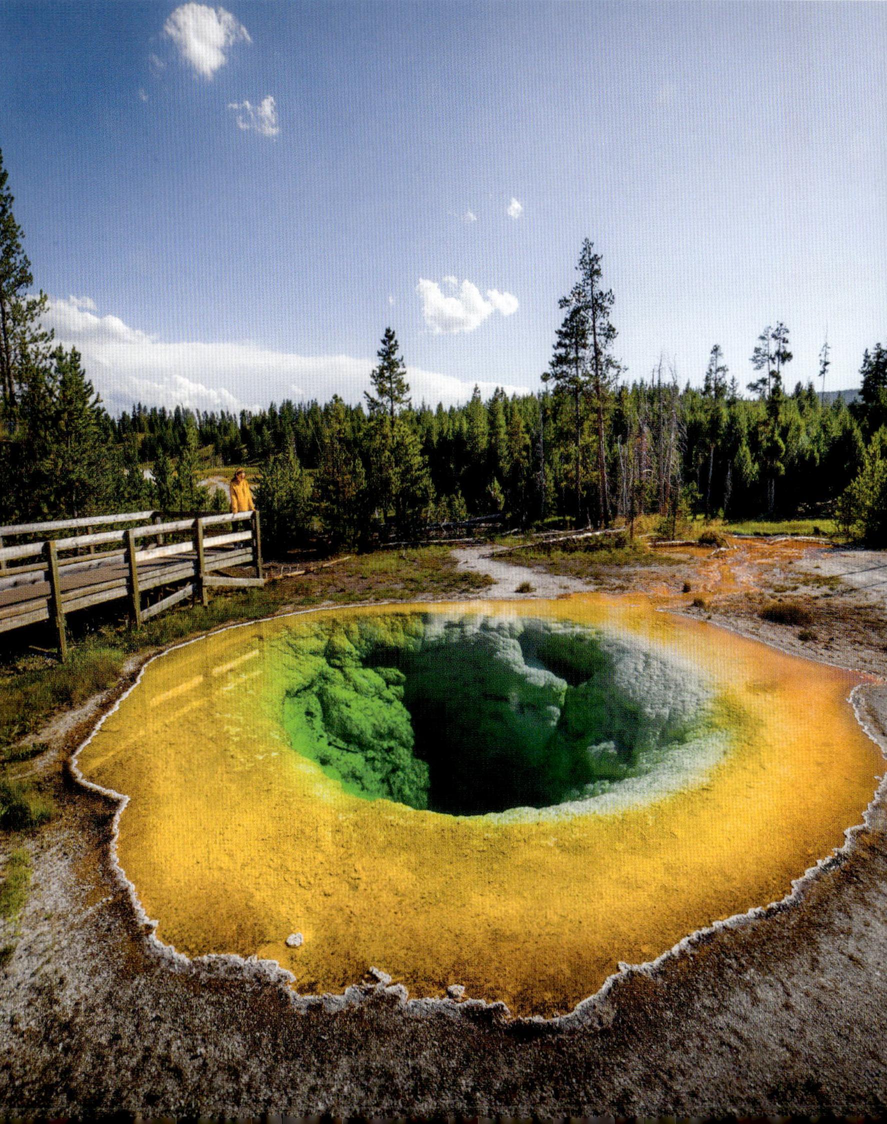

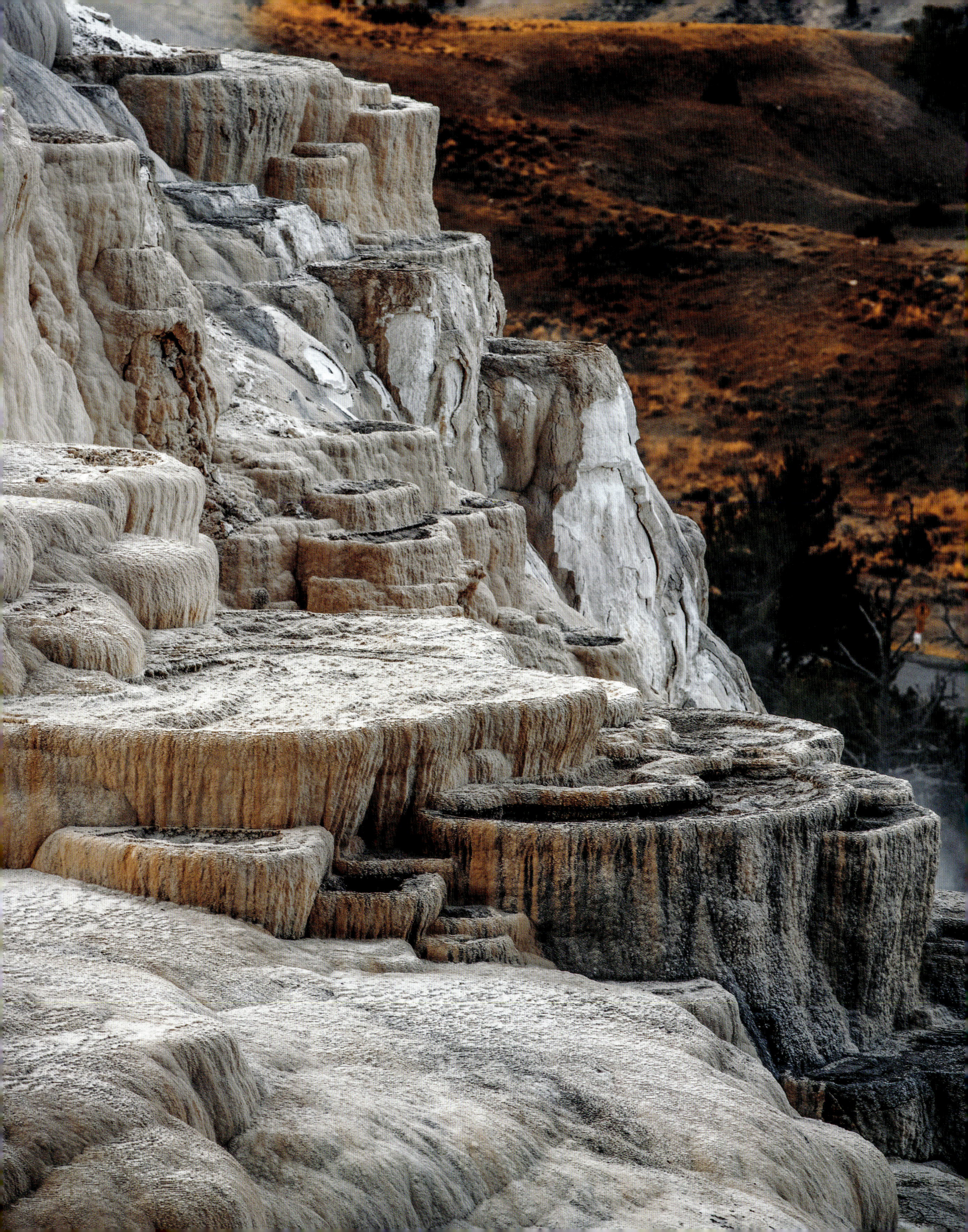

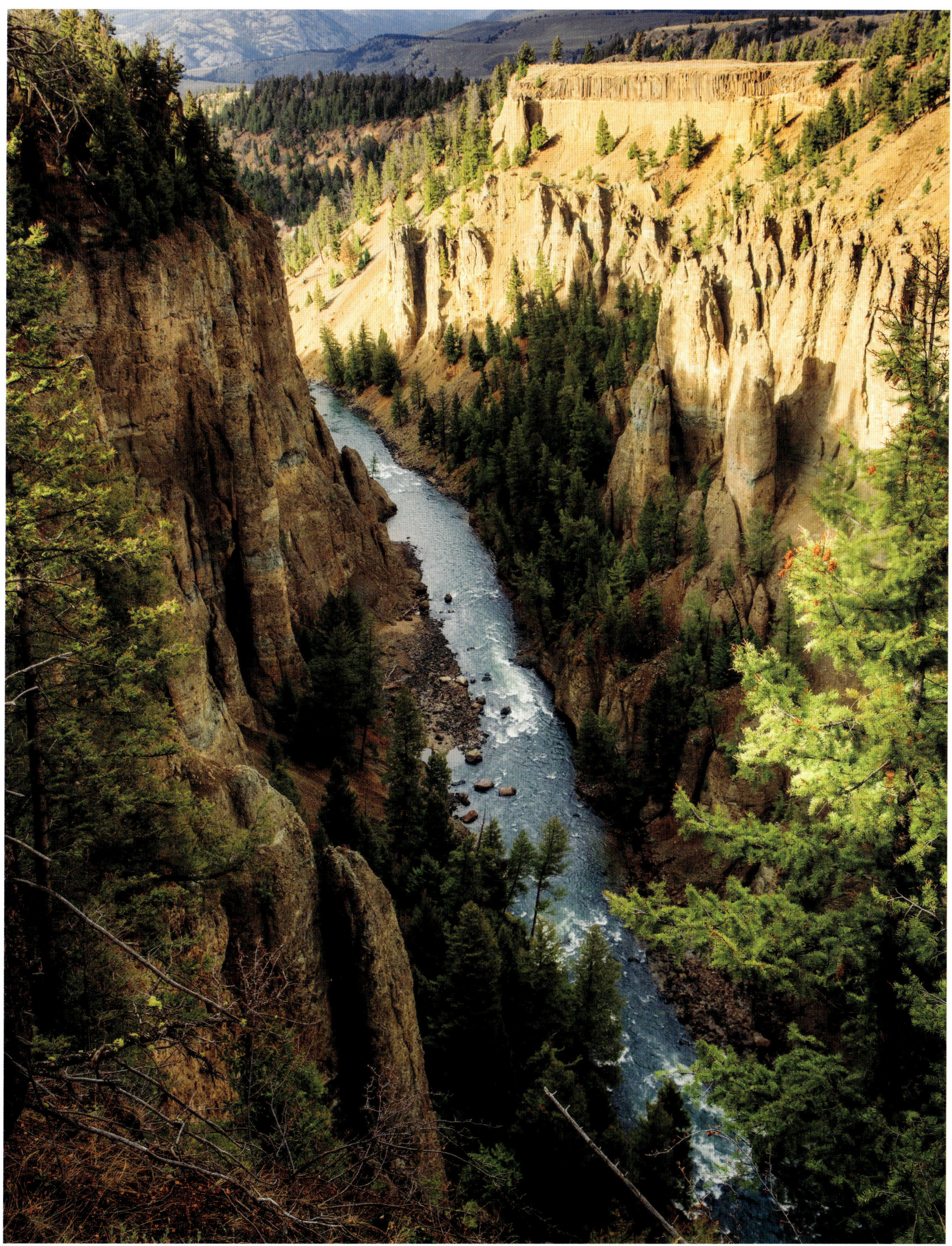

Above: Grand Canyon of the Yellowstone | Opposite: The Narrows, Yellowstone River

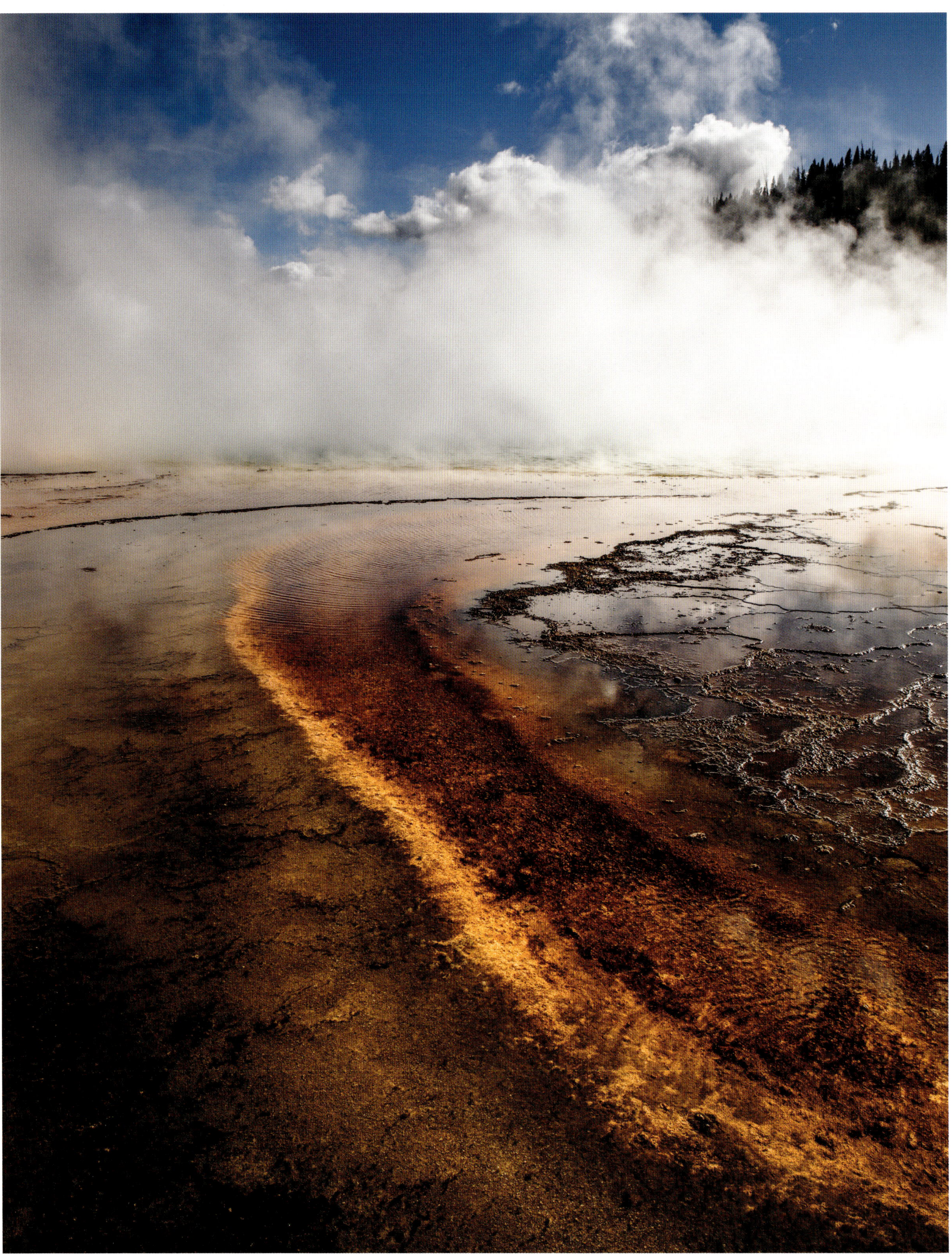

Above and opposite: Grand Prismatic Spring, Yellowstone National Park

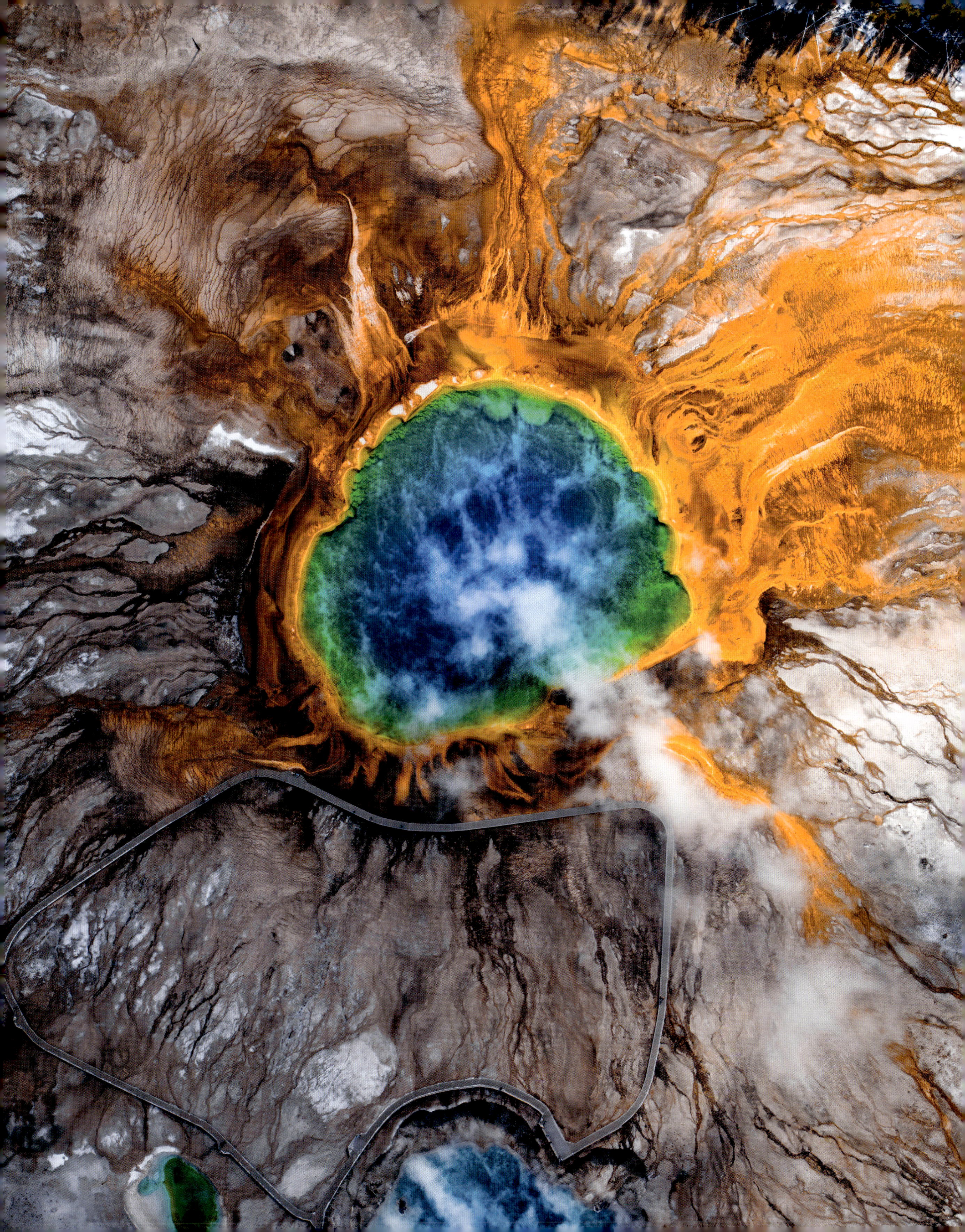

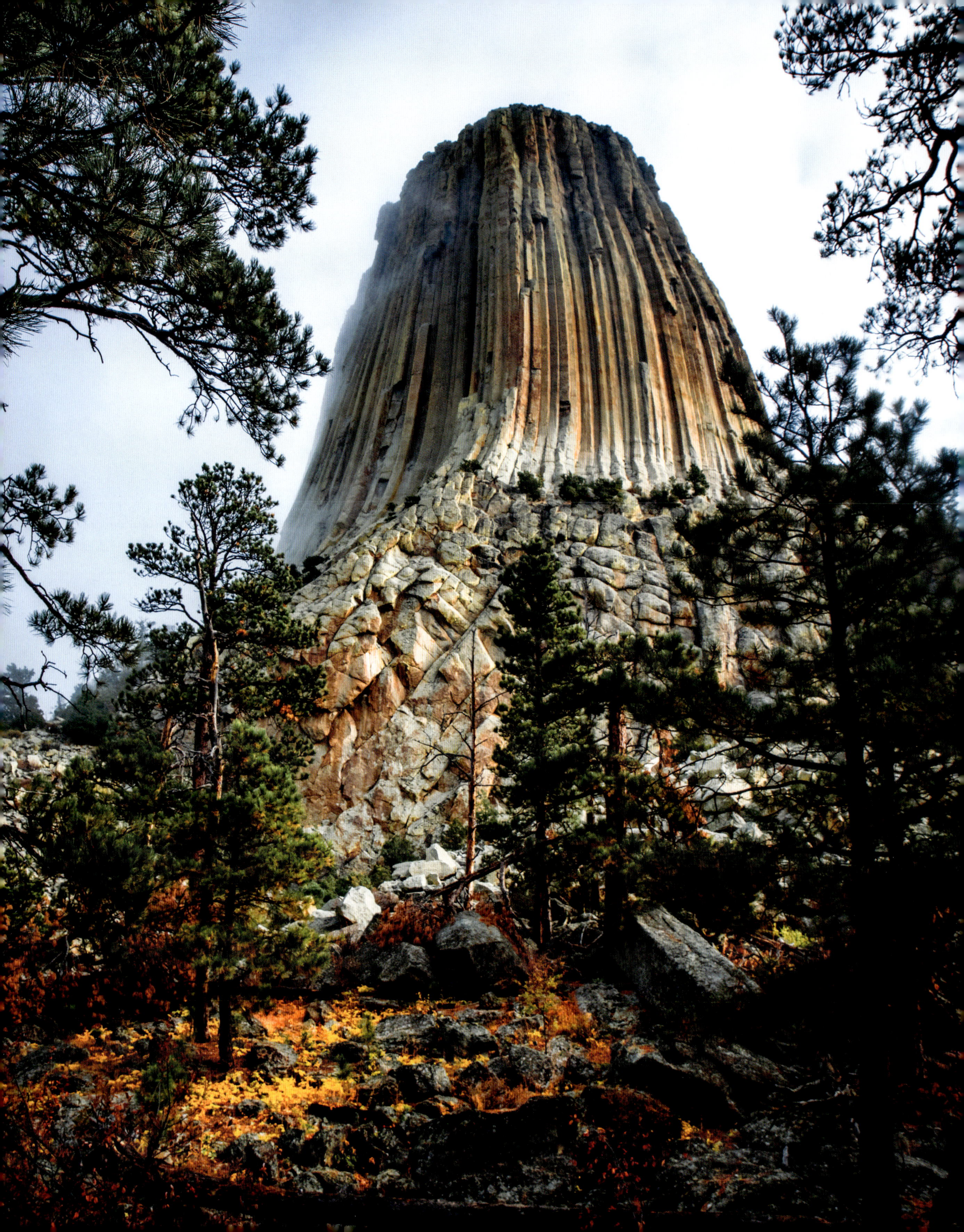

DEVILS TOWER NATIONAL MONUMENT

Devils Tower is a sacred site to many Indigenous tribes and was the first US national monument, designated in 1906. It rises dramatically from the rolling plains, making it a striking and mysterious landmark. Standing at the base of Devils Tower, it's impossible not to feel its presence; it looms over the landscape like something out of folklore. Walking the Tower Trail, I was struck by how massive and intricate the rock columns are up close, each one shaped over millions of years. I watched climbers inch their way up the sheer walls. At sunset, I hiked to Joyner Ridge, where the golden light cast long shadows across the hills. It's a place that feels both ancient and otherworldly, leaving you with a sense of awe long after you've left.

Region: Rocky Mountains

State: Wyoming

Coordinates: 44°35'24.7"N 104°42'52.6"W

Focal feature: Devils Tower, a massive, flat-topped volcanic formation with dramatic vertical columns

Formation attributes: The tower stands 867 feet (264m) from base to summit, with a total elevation of 5,112 feet (1,558m) above sea level. It was formed by the cooling and fracturing of igneous rock, though its exact origins are still debated.

Fun fact: Devils Tower is one of the premier crack-climbing destinations in North America, with hundreds of routes scaling its vertical columns.

Best time to visit: Spring and fall offer pleasant temperatures and fewer crowds, while summer brings peak visitation and hotter weather. Winter offers solitude but can be very cold.

How to access: Devils Tower is located in northeastern Wyoming, about an hour's drive from Sundance or two hours from Rapid City, South Dakota.

Things to consider: Be prepared for strong winds and rapidly changing weather, especially in the shoulder seasons. The monument is open year-round, and the visitor center provides insight into its geological and cultural history. Climbing is restricted in June out of respect for Indigenous ceremonies.

RECOMMENDED TRAILS:

Tower Trail: *1.6-mile (2.6km) loop; about 160 feet (49m) elevation gain; easy.* A paved loop encircling the base of Devils Tower, offering incredible close-up views and interpretive signs about its geology and cultural significance.

Red Beds Trail: *2.9-mile (4.7km) loop; about 500 feet (152m) elevation gain; moderate.* A scenic hike that provides sweeping views of the tower from different angles, as well as the surrounding valley and Belle Fourche River.

Joyner Ridge Trail: *1.5-mile (2.4km) loop; about 200 feet (61m) elevation gain; moderate.* A quieter, less-traveled trail with stunning panoramic views of Devils Tower from a distance, making it great for sunrise or sunset photography.

Tips for taking a great photo

- Sunrise and sunset offer the best lighting, casting warm golden hues on the tower's columns.
- Shoot from the Red Beds Trail or Joyner Ridge for wide-angle shots that capture the tower rising from the landscape.
- Devils Tower is a designated Dark Sky Park. Try astrophotography to capture the Milky Way above its silhouette.
- Look for prairie dogs near the base of the tower; they make great foreground subjects.

Opposite: Devils Tower

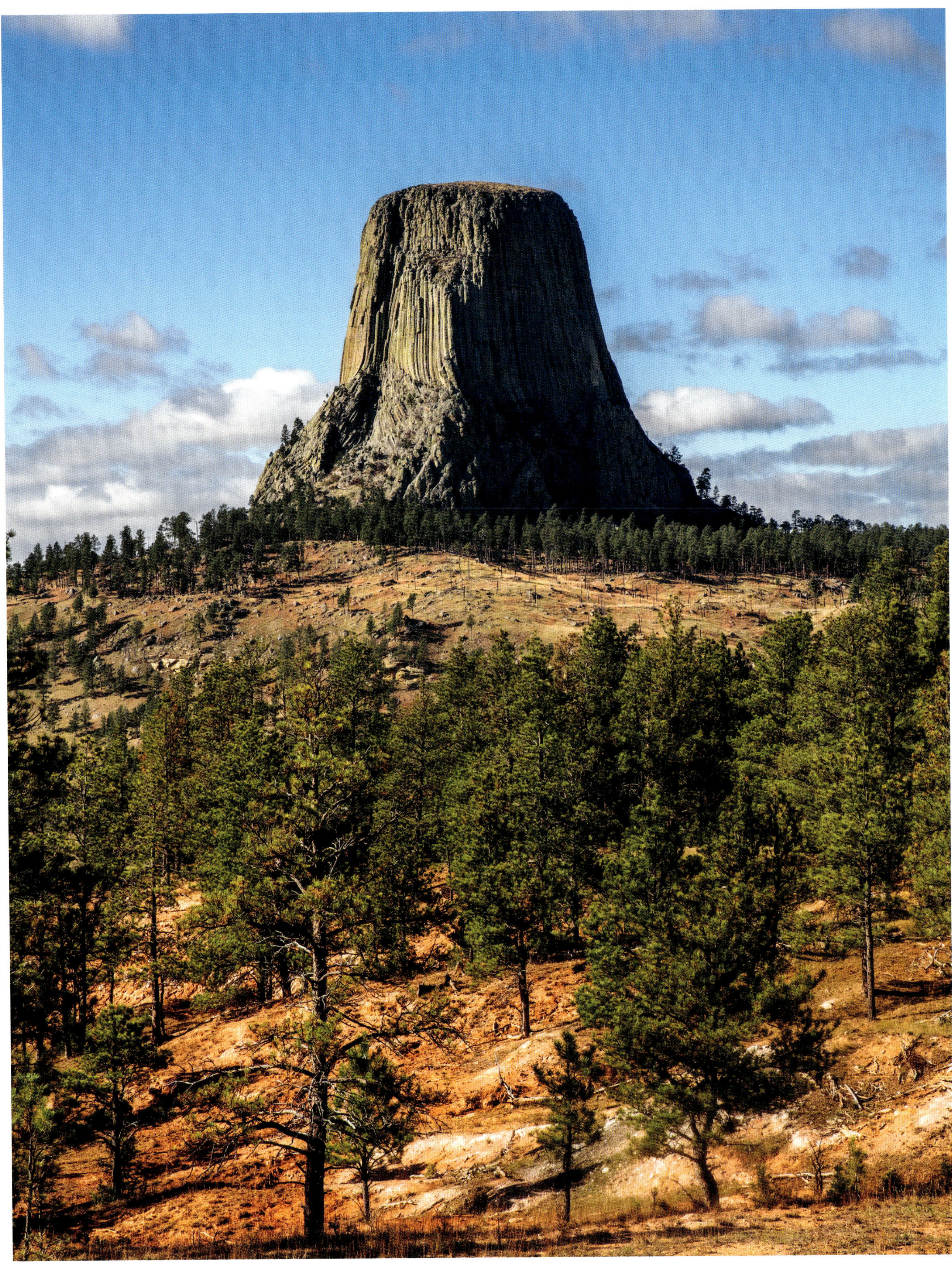

Above and opposite: Devils Tower

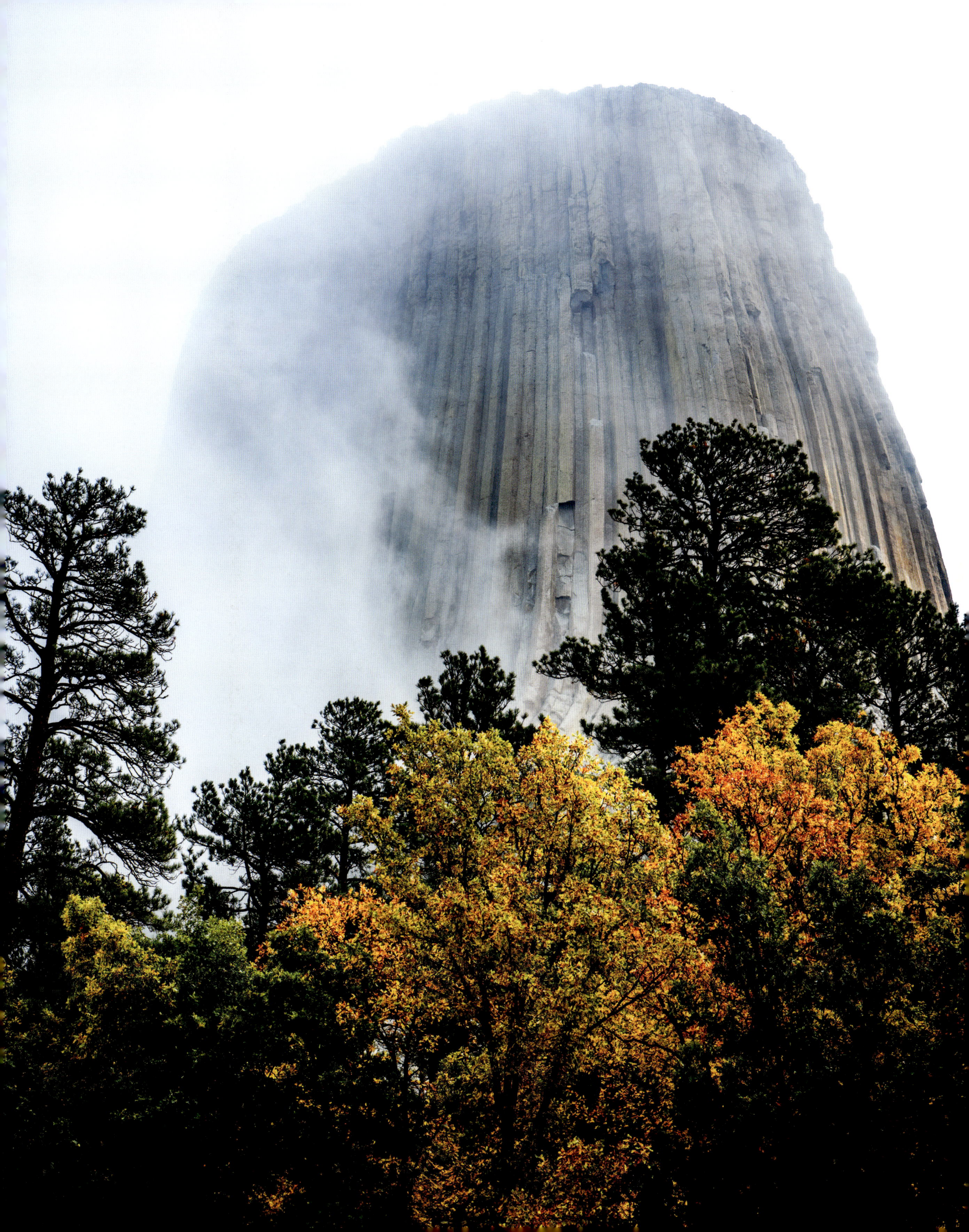

GRAND TETON NATIONAL PARK

The Tetons appeared suddenly, sharp and unreal against the morning sky. I stopped at Schwabacher Landing just as the first light hit the peaks, the mountains perfectly mirrored in the glassy water. As a solo traveler and photographer, moments like this are why I hit the road. Grand Teton National Park is a paradise for hikers, climbers, and photographers, with its jagged peaks, pristine alpine lakes, and abundant wildlife.

Region: Rocky Mountains

State: Wyoming

Coordinates: 43°47'25.4"N 110°40'54.5"W

Focal feature: The Teton Range, a stunning set of jagged peaks rising abruptly from the Jackson Hole valley

Formation attributes: The Tetons reach a height of 13,775 feet (4,199m) at Grand Teton, the tallest peak in the range, and were formed by seismic activity rather than volcanic eruptions like the neighboring Yellowstone region.

Fun fact: The park has no foothills, which makes the Tetons appear even more dramatic, as they rise almost straight up from the valley floor.

Best time to visit: June to September for the best hiking weather, though fall offers incredible foliage and fewer crowds. Winter transforms the park into a snowy wonderland, perfect for cross-country skiing and wildlife spotting.

How to access: The park is easily accessible from Jackson, Wyoming, via the John D. Rockefeller, Jr. Memorial Parkway. The nearest airport is Jackson Hole Airport, which is uniquely located within the park.

Things to consider: Be prepared for rapidly changing weather, especially at higher elevations.

RECOMMENDED TRAILS:

Schwabacher Landing: *0.5-mile (0.8km) round trip; minimal elevation gain; easy.* A peaceful riverside walk with stunning reflections of the Tetons in the water, often visited by moose.

Taggart Lake Loop: *3.8-mile (6.1km) round trip; about 400 feet (122m) elevation gain; moderate.* A scenic hike through meadows and forests leading to a beautiful alpine lake with the Tetons as a backdrop.

Paintbrush Canyon–Cascade Canyon Loop: *19-mile (31km) round trip; about 4,100 feet (1,250m) elevation gain; strenuous, multiday hike.* A breathtaking loop through wildflower-filled meadows, alpine lakes, and rugged mountain terrain.

Tips for taking a great photo

- Sunrise is ideal for capturing the first light hitting the peaks, especially at Schwabacher Landing and Oxbow Bend.
- Visit Jenny Lake or Taggart Lake early in the morning when the water is calm for the best mirrorlike reflections.
- The park is home to bears, moose, elk, and bison—bring a zoom lens to photograph them and keep a safe distance. Sunrise and sunset are ideal times for wildlife spotting.
- Use a wide-angle lens to capture the full scope of the towering peaks against the valley.

Opposite: The towering Teton Range

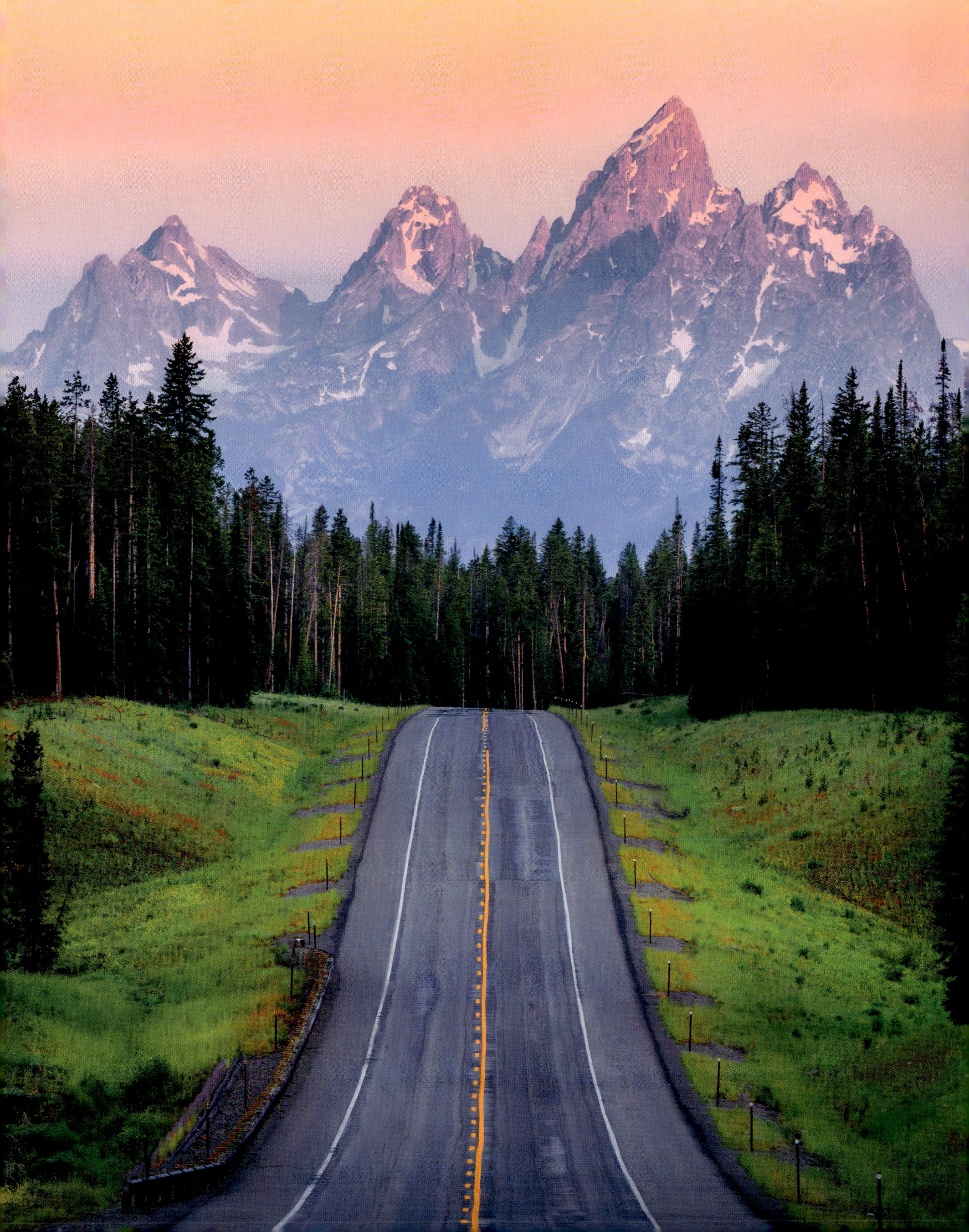

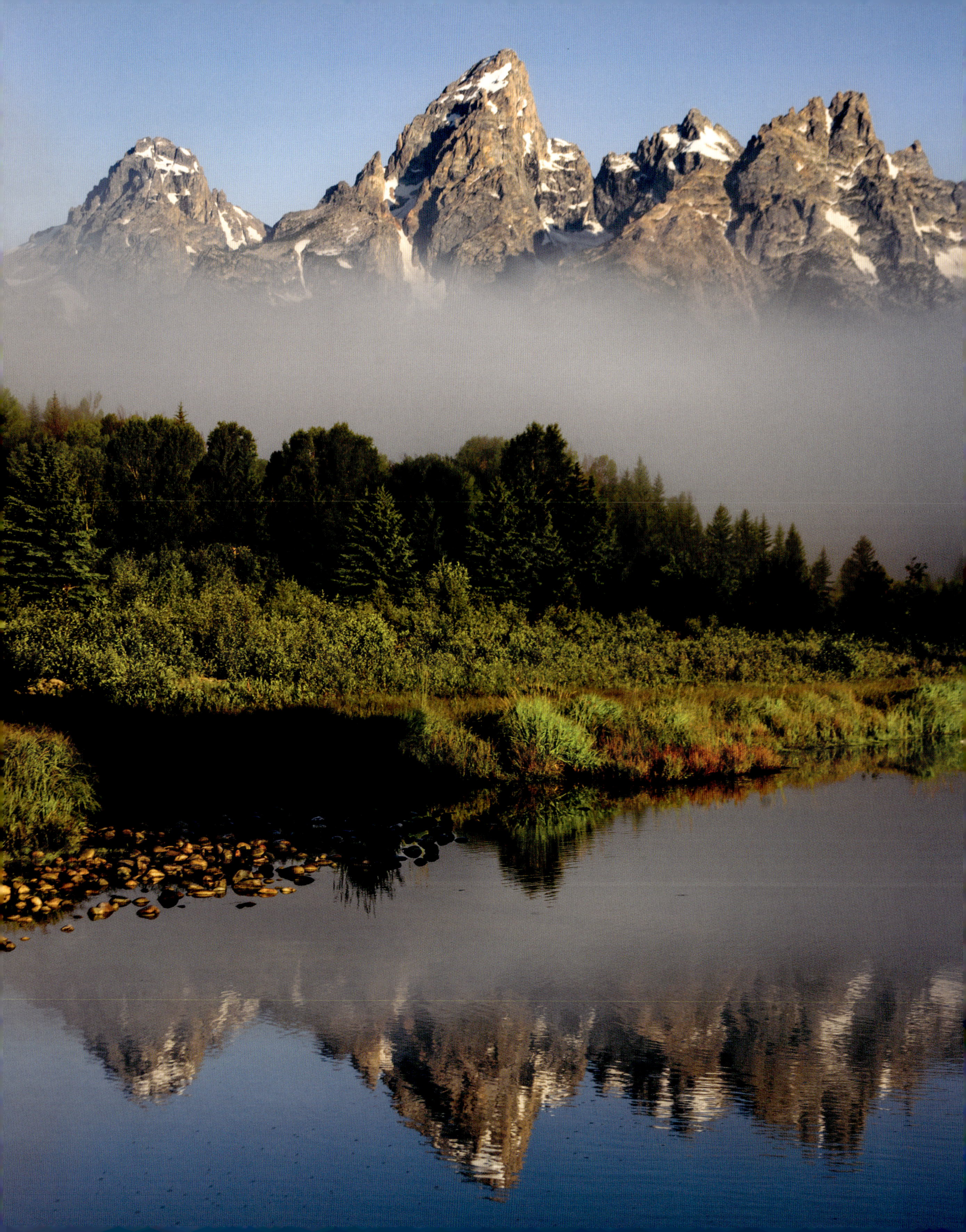

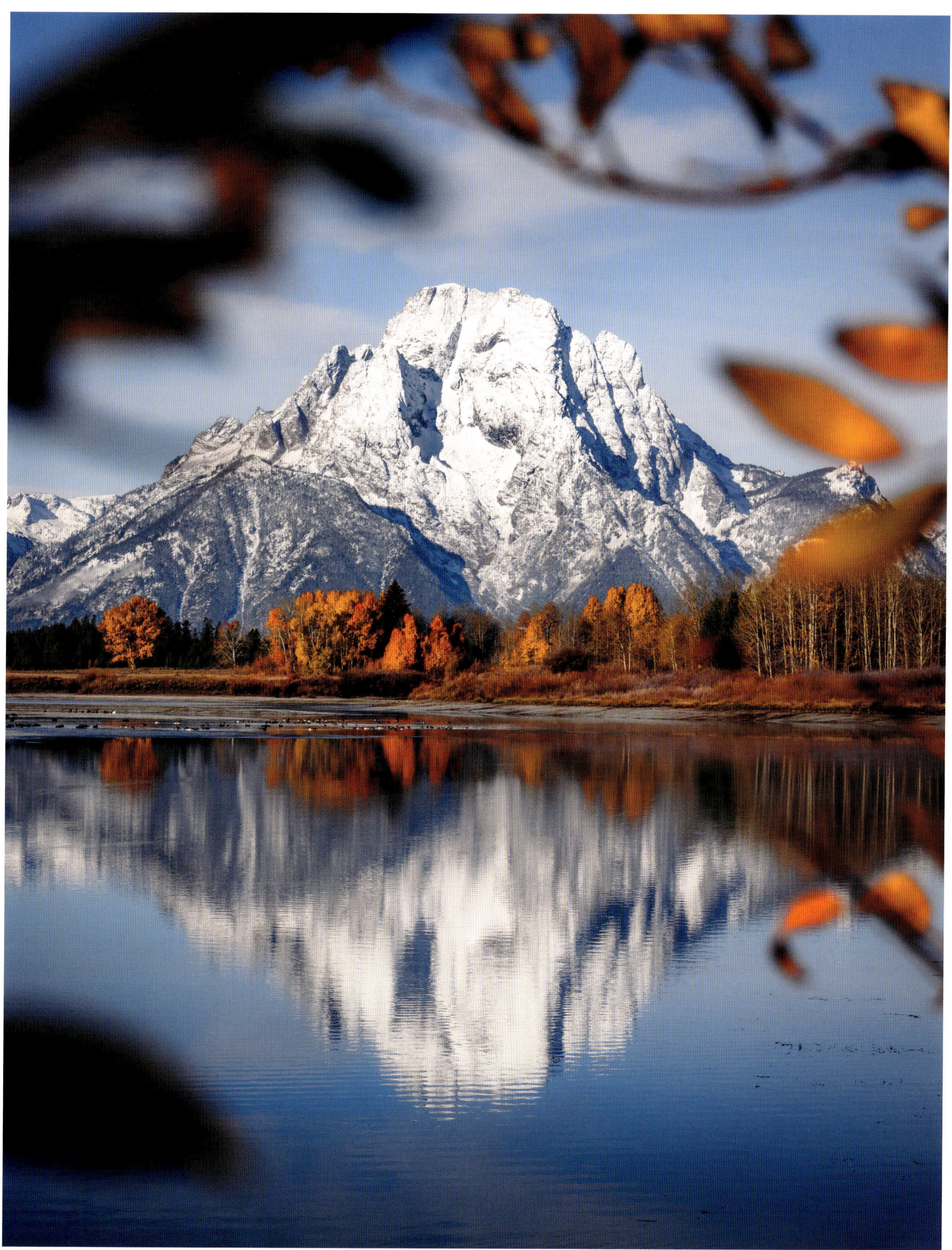

Above: Oxbow Bend, Grand Teton National Park | Opposite: Schwabacher Landing, Grand Teton National Park

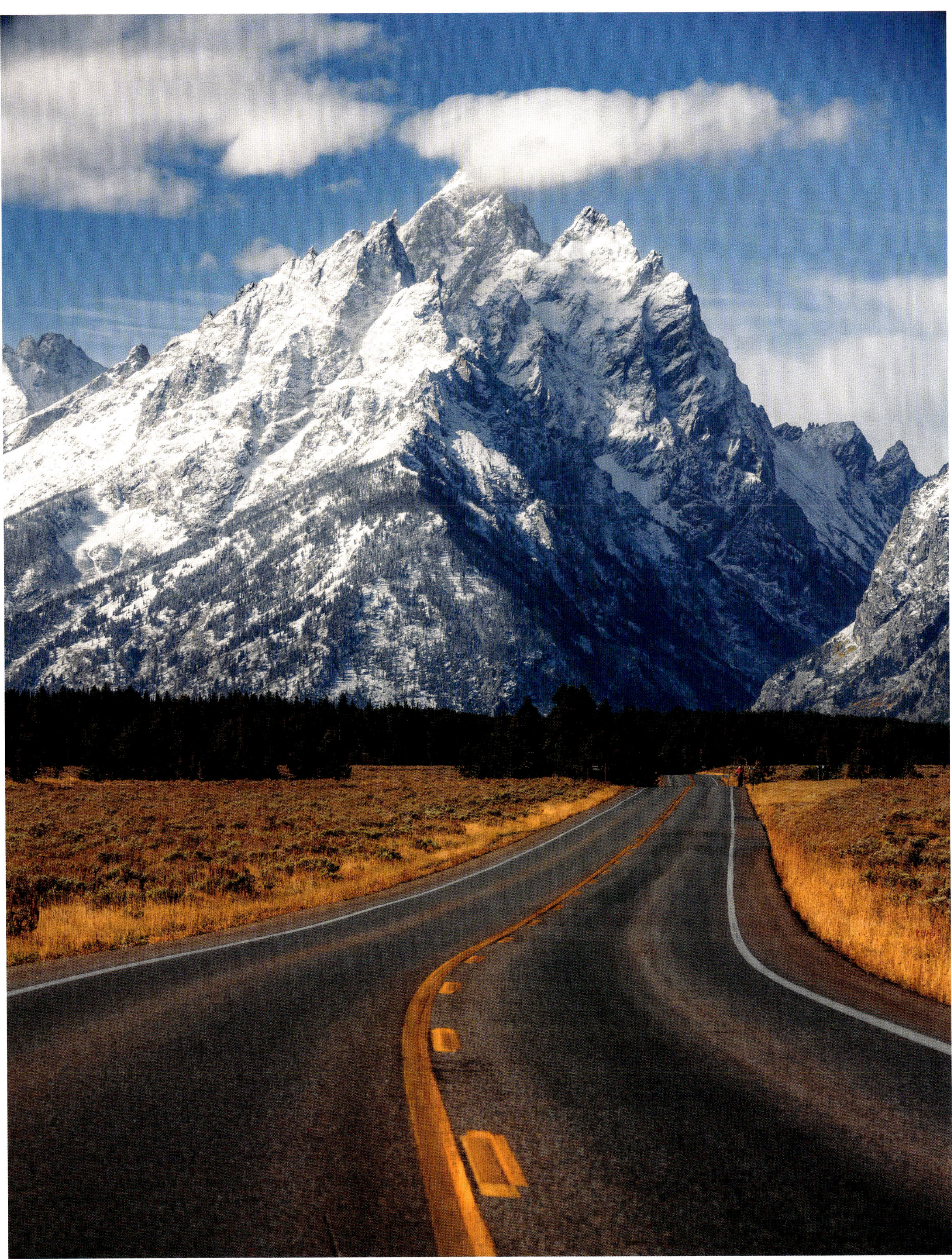

Above and opposite: Grand Teton National Park

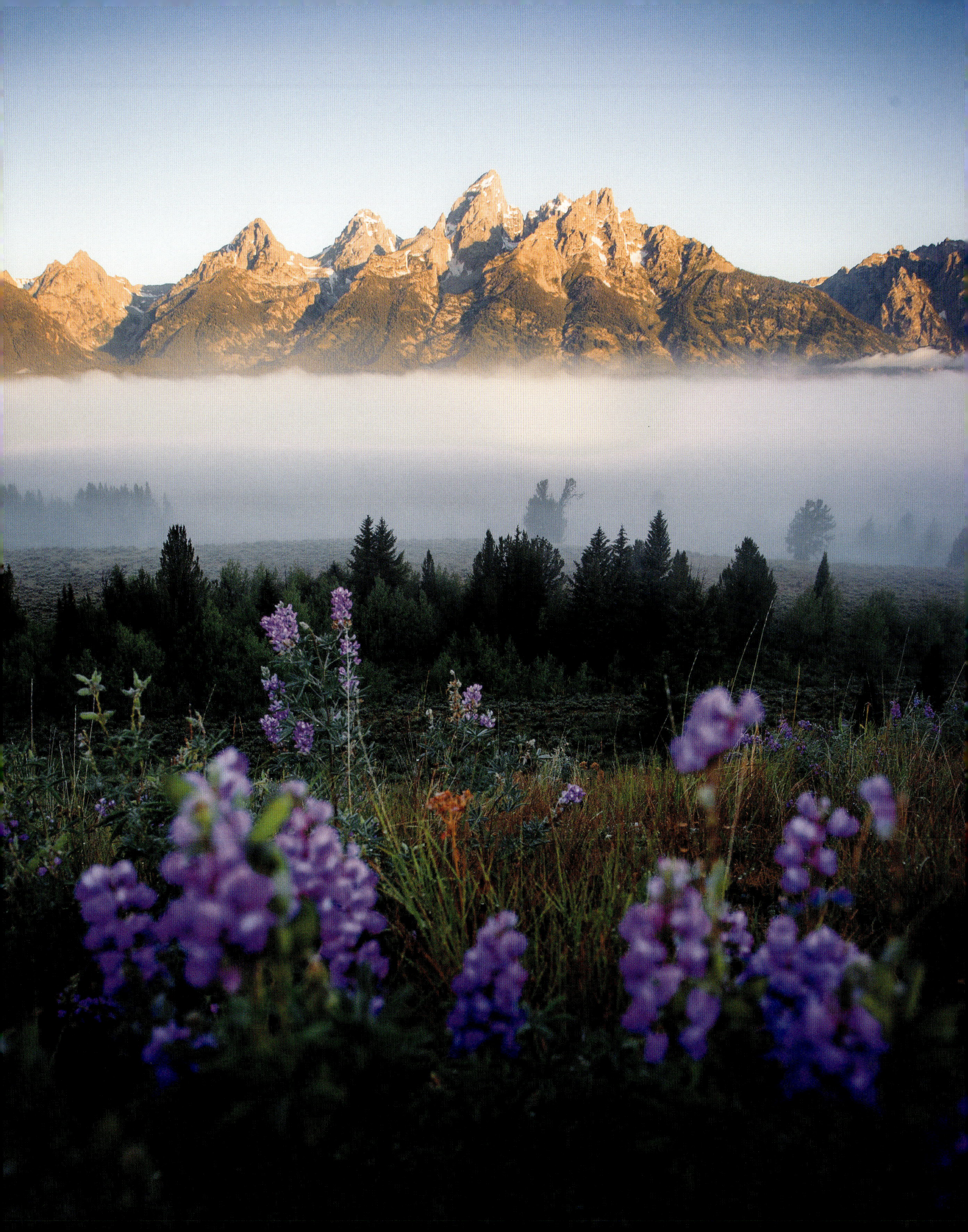

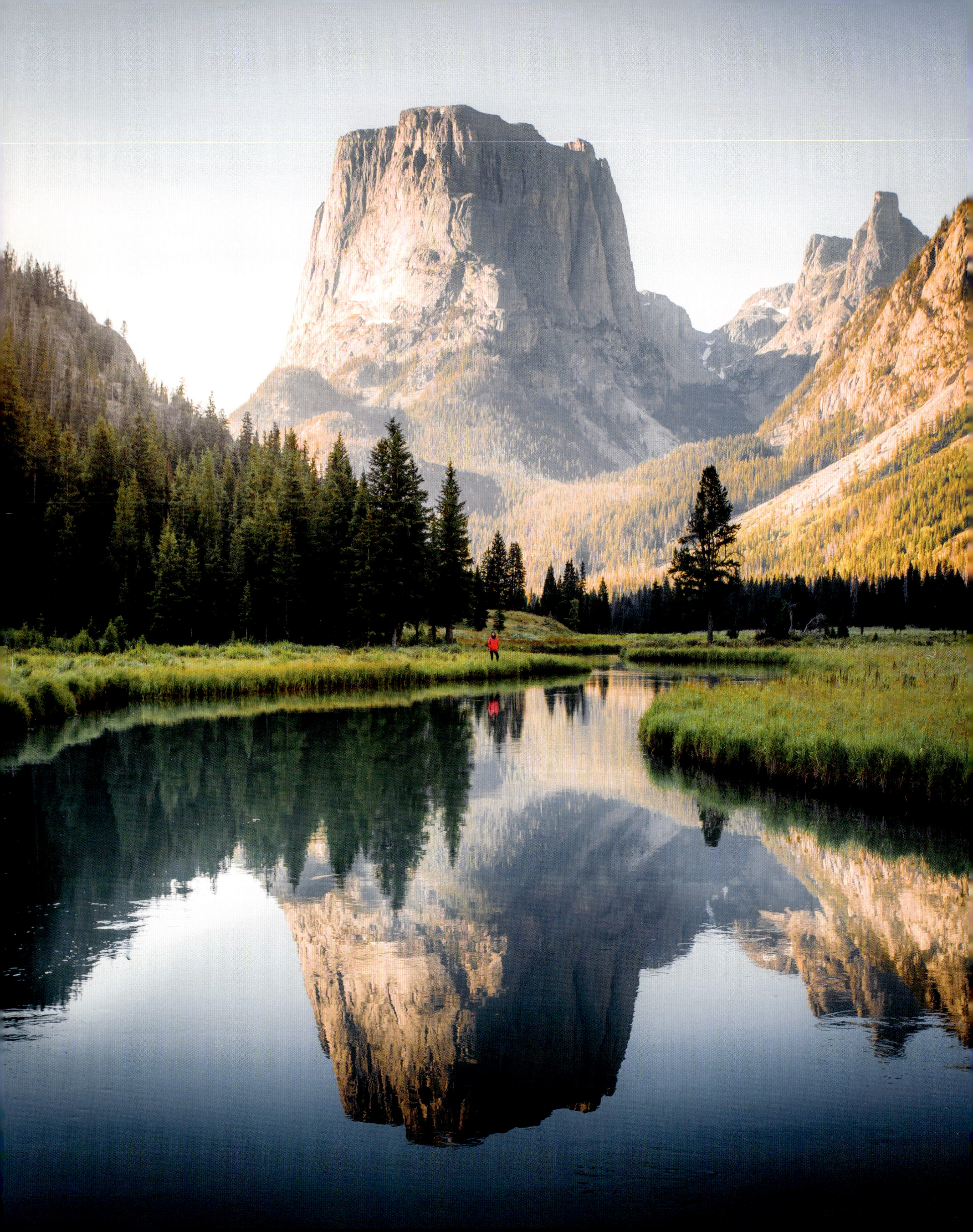

WIND RIVER RANGE

The Wind River Range pulled me in the moment I reached Green River Lakes. Squaretop Mountain towers over you and is one of the most unique peaks I've ever seen. I paused with my camera, watching a moose wade through the shallow river. Hiking deeper into the Bridger Wilderness, I spotted elk through the trees and a black bear in the distance, both gone before I could raise my lens. At dawn, near Vista Pass, marmots chirped as the peaks turned gold. I came chasing landscapes, but it was the unexpected wildlife—the quiet moments between shots—that stayed with me the longest. If you're looking for a hidden gem to backpack and explore, this is it.

Region: Rocky Mountains

State: Wyoming

Coordinates: 43°10'57.7"N 109°39'11.7"W

Focal features: Towering granite peaks and pristine alpine lakes

Formation attributes: The range stretches more than 100 miles (161km), with over forty peaks exceeding 13,000 feet (3,962m). Gannett Peak, Wyoming's highest mountain, rises to 13,810 feet (4,209m), and is also the largest glacier in the American Rockies.

Fun fact: The Wind River Range contains over 1,300 named lakes, many of which are stocked with trout, making it a paradise for backcountry fishing.

Best time to visit: Late July to September, when the snow has melted from the high passes and the mosquitoes have calmed down. Early summer can be beautiful but is often plagued by heavy snowpack and swarms of bugs.

How to access: The range can be accessed from multiple trailheads, with the most popular being Elkhart Park, Big Sandy, and Green River Lakes. Many trailheads require long drives on dirt roads.

Things to consider: Be prepared for unpredictable weather, high-altitude conditions, and possible bear encounters. Carrying bear-proof containers is required in many areas. There are no services, so come fully prepared.

RECOMMENDED TRAILS:

Sacred Rim Trail: *3.3-mile (5.3km) round trip; about 500 feet (152m) elevation gain; easy–moderate.* A short but stunning hike from Elkhart Park that provides panoramic views over the Wind River Range.

Big Sandy to Cirque of the Towers: *18-mile (29km) round trip; about 2,300 feet (701m) elevation gain; moderate–strenuous.* One of the most iconic hikes in the Winds, leading to a jaw-dropping cirque of sheer granite spires, popular among climbers and backpackers.

Titcomb Basin via Elkhart Park: *30+ miles (48+km) round trip; about 4,100 feet (1,250m) elevation gain; strenuous, multiday hike.* A challenging but rewarding trek deep into the range, featuring turquoise lakes, towering peaks, and potential glimpses of mountain goats.

Tips for taking a great photo

- Sunrise and sunset bring warm light to the granite peaks, creating incredible contrasts against the blue lakes.
- Early morning at Island Lake or Titcomb Basin often provides glassy water for perfect reflections of the mountains.
- Keep an eye out for moose near marshy areas and bighorn sheep on the high ridges.
- The Winds are far from light pollution, making them a fantastic place for astrophotography. Try capturing the Milky Way over Cirque of the Towers.

Opposite: Squaretop Mountain

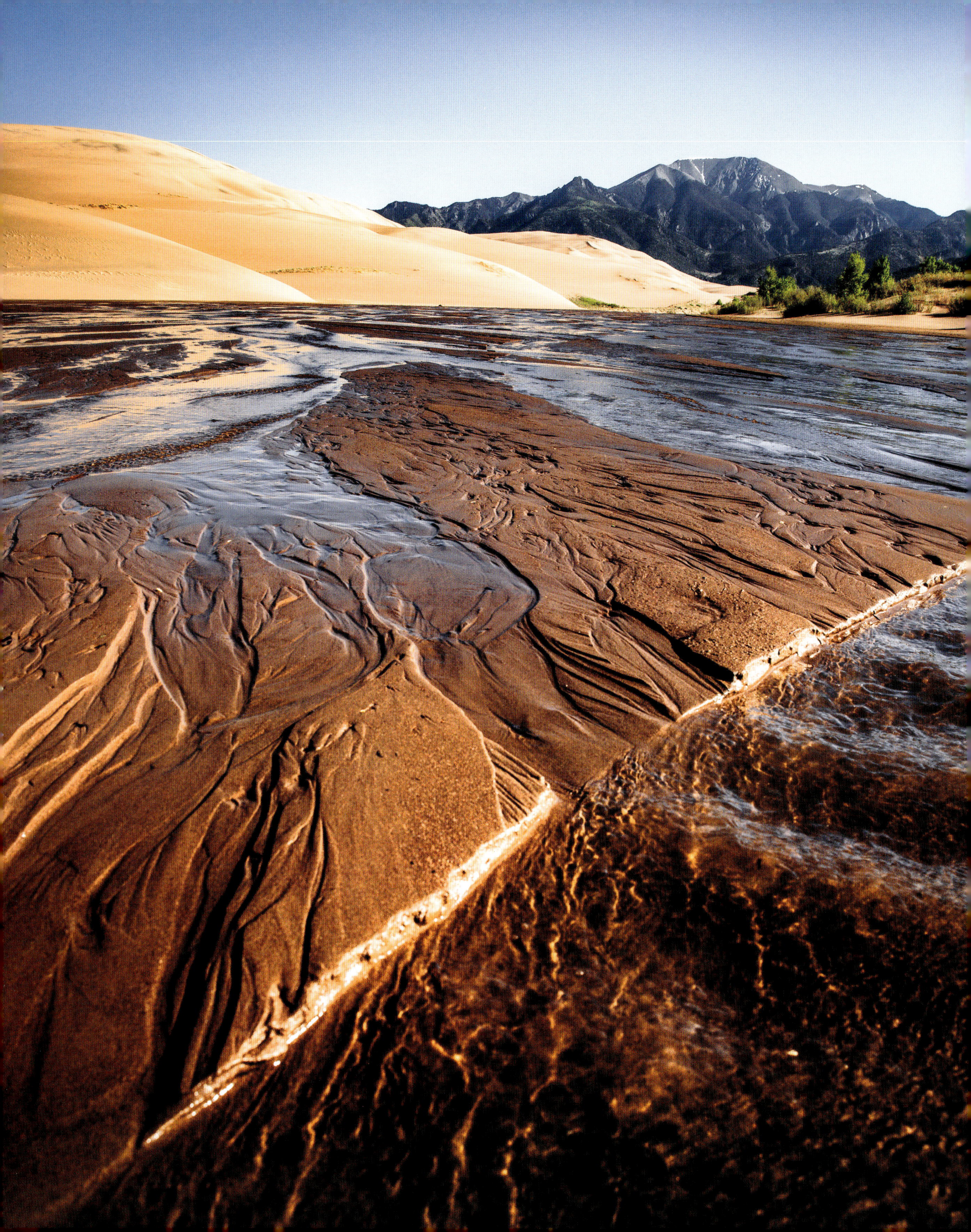

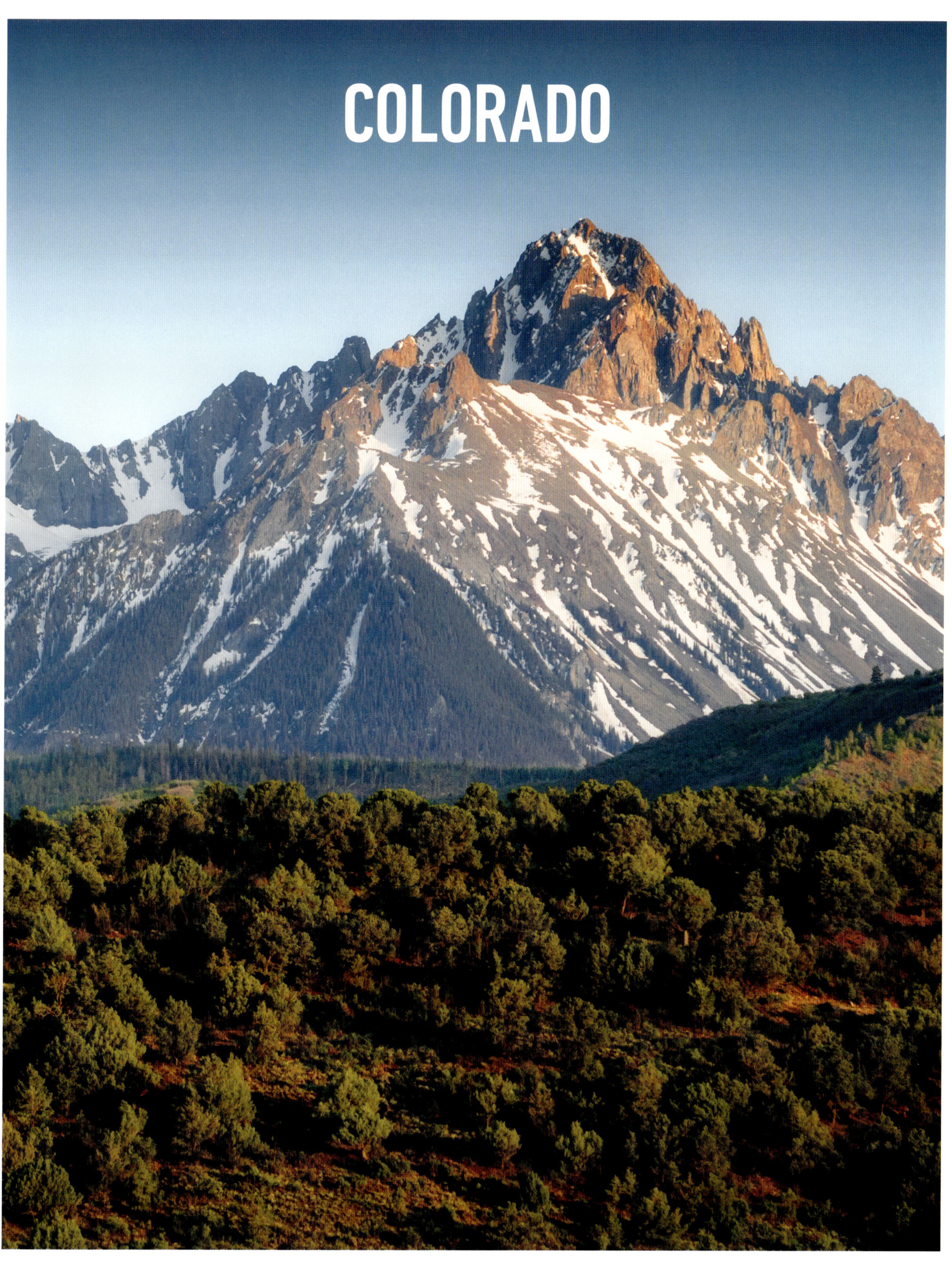
COLORADO

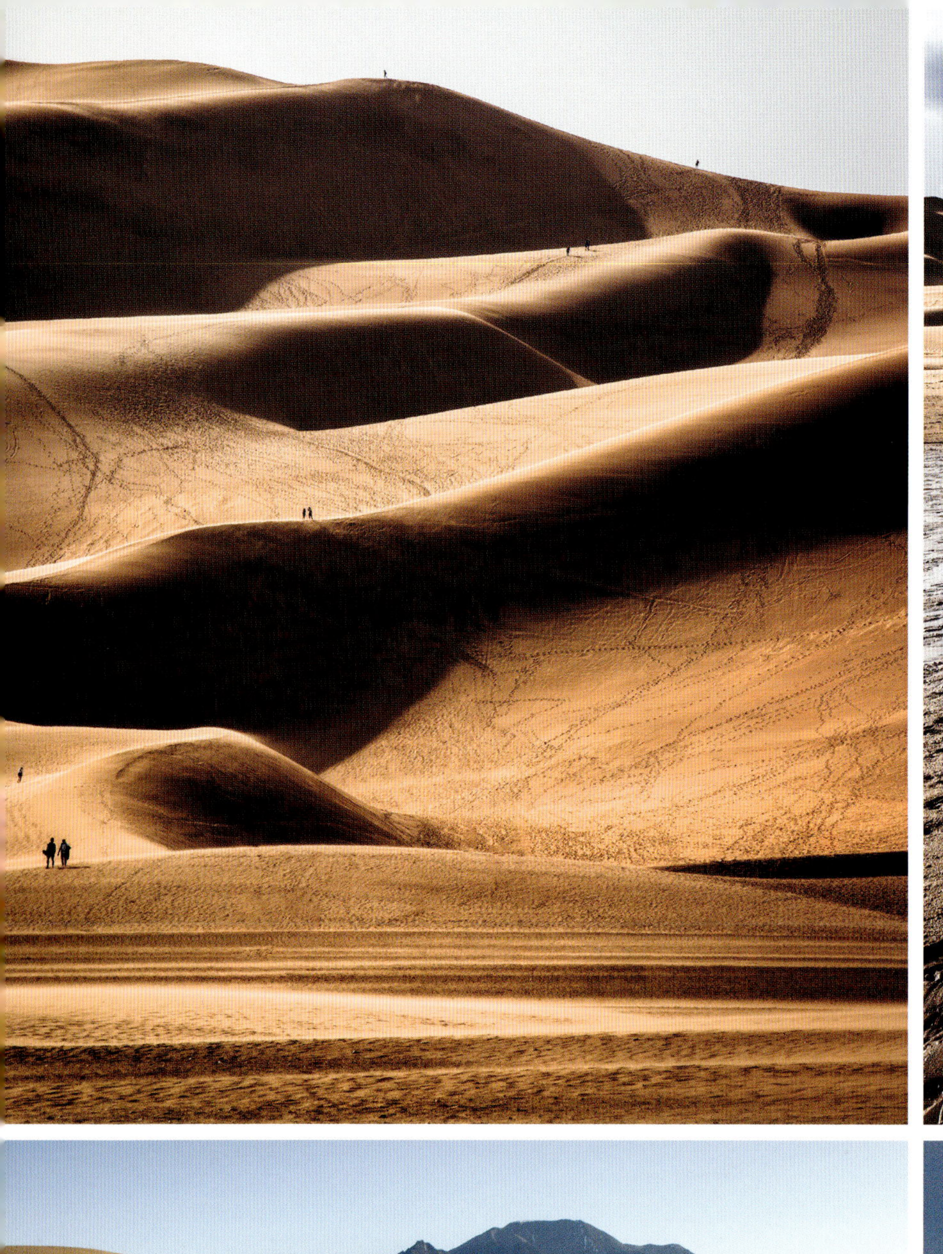
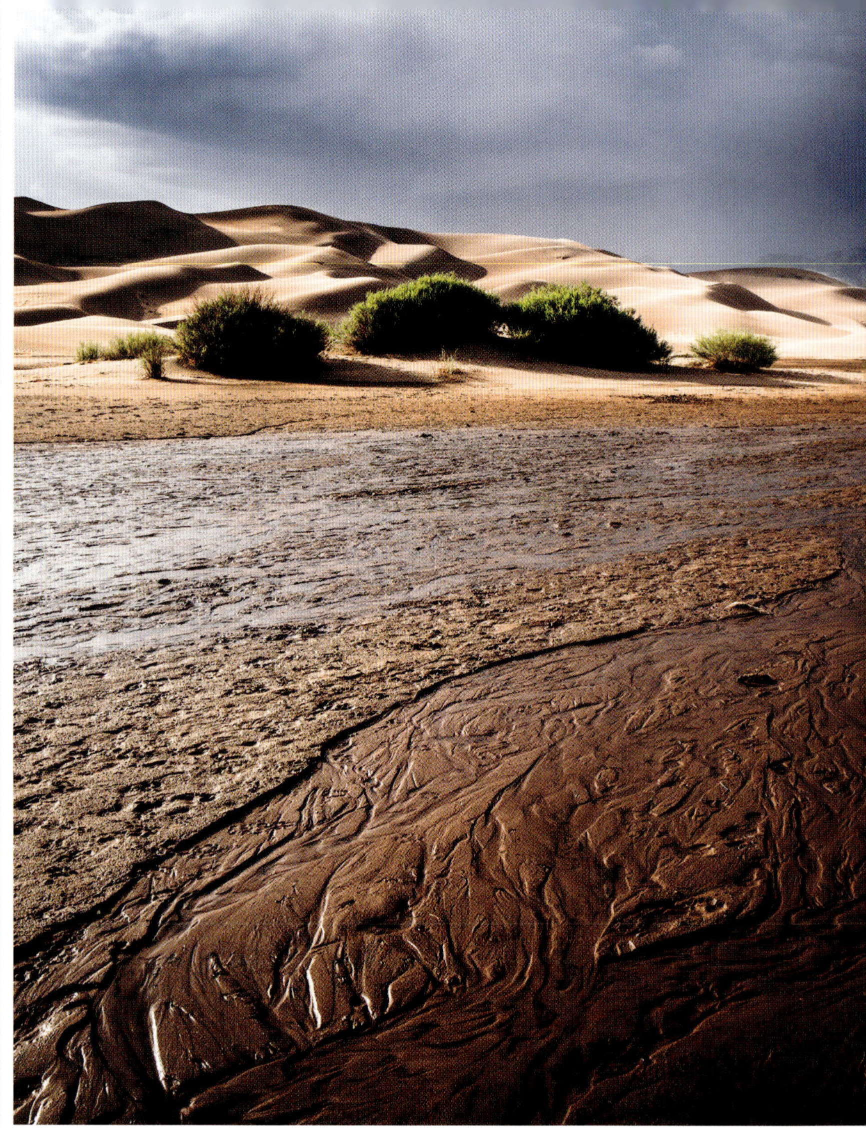
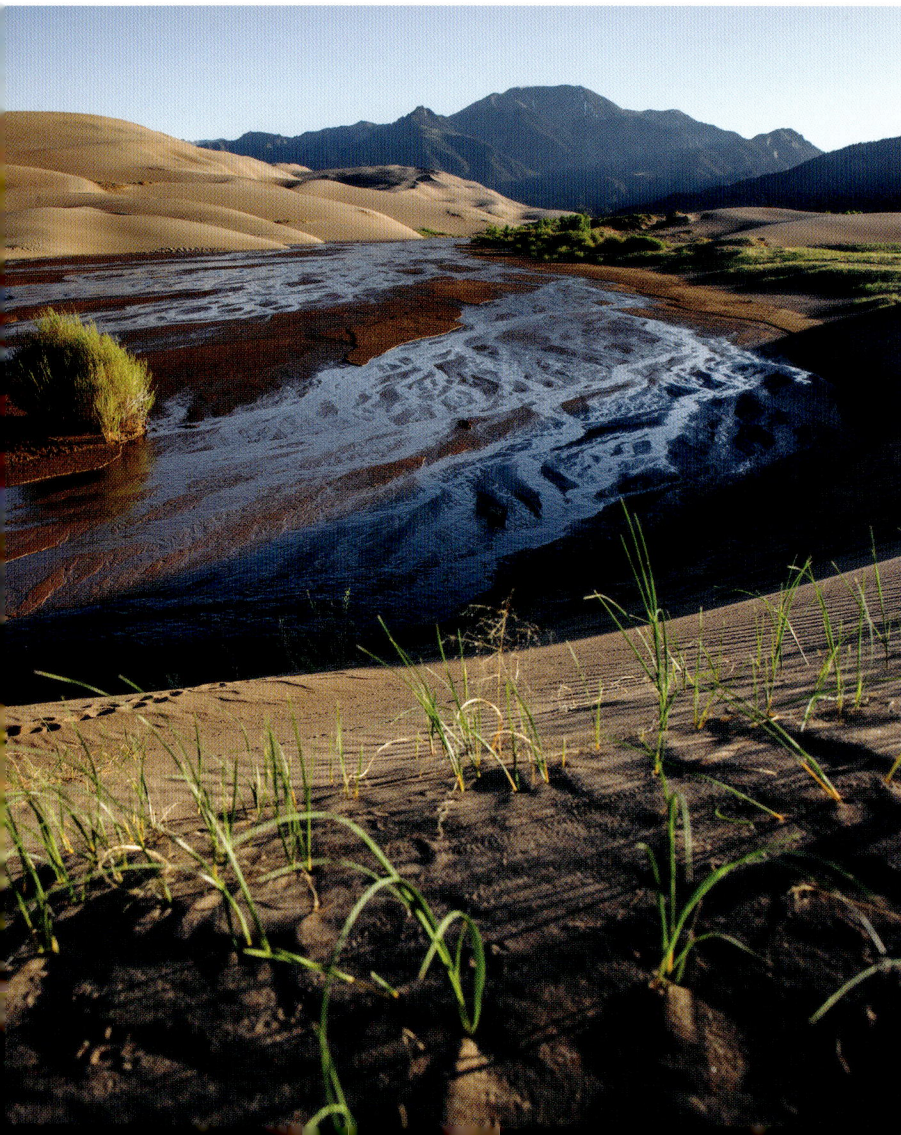
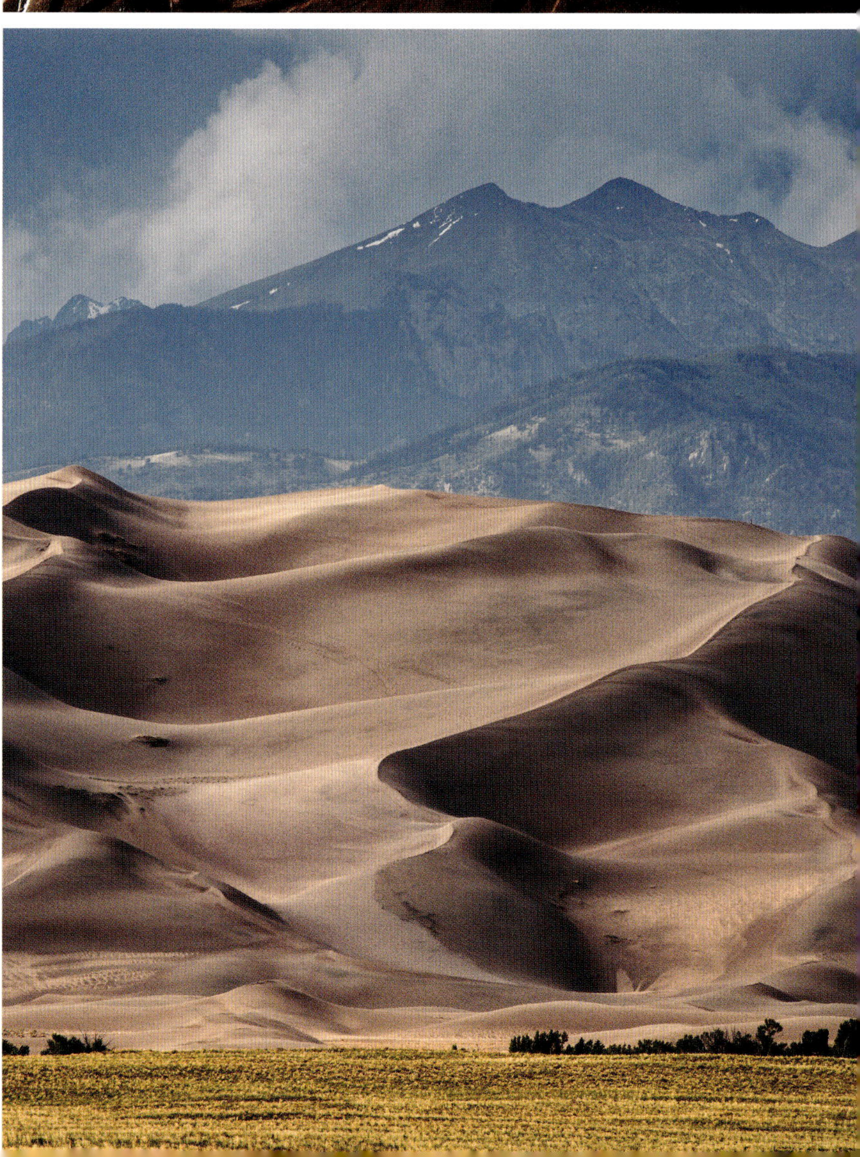

GREAT SAND DUNES NATIONAL PARK & PRESERVE

This park is home to the tallest sand dunes in North America, set against the dramatic backdrop of the Sangre de Cristo Mountains—a desert tucked up against mountains. Explore the towering dunes that rise like waves here and hike across them. You can also go sandboarding, or even just run barefoot down their sandy slopes. Nearby, you'll find cool creeks, alpine forests, and stunning mountain views. This park boasts an unexpected mix of landscapes all in one place.

Region: Rocky Mountains

State: Colorado

Coordinates: 37°47'33.4"N 105°35'39.5"W

Focal feature: Towering sand dunes with a striking mountain backdrop

Formation attributes: The dunes cover about 30 square miles (77.7km²), with the tallest, Star Dune, reaching approximately 750 feet (229m). They were formed over thousands of years as wind carried sand from the San Luis Valley and deposited it against the mountains.

Fun fact: The dunes constantly shift and change shape due to wind patterns, but their overall size and location remain relatively stable.

Best time to visit: Late spring and early fall offer the best conditions, with comfortable temperatures and seasonal water flow in Medano Creek. Summer visits should be planned for early morning or evening to avoid scorching sand.

How to access: The park is located about 3.5 hours southwest of Denver. The main access point is via State Highway 150 or County Road 6. Most of the park's major sites are accessible by regular vehicles, but high-clearance 4WD is required for Medano Pass.

Things to consider: Be prepared for extreme temperature shifts; summer sand temperatures can exceed 150°F (66°C), while nights can be quite cold. Bring plenty of water, sun protection, and consider visiting in the morning or evening to avoid the intense midday heat.

RECOMMENDED TRAILS:

Montville Nature Trail: *0.5-mile (0.8km) loop; about 100 feet (31m) elevation gain; easy.* A short but scenic loop with shade, offering views of the dunes and mountains.

Dunes Exploration: *Variable distance and elevation gain; easy–moderate.* Since there are no designated trails in the dunes, visitors are free to climb and explore at their own pace. Hiking to the top of High Dune (about 700 feet [213m] of elevation gain) offers sweeping views.

Star Dune Hike: *7.1-mile (11.4km) round trip; about 1,000 feet (305m) elevation gain; strenuous.* The tallest dune in North America, this trek requires endurance and strong legs as you climb through shifting sand.

Tips for taking a great photo

- Sunrise and sunset create dramatic shadows that emphasize the dunes' textures.
- Get low to capture the patterns and sand ripples created by the wind.
- Position the dunes with the Sangre de Cristo Mountains behind them for striking compositions.
- The park is an International Dark Sky Park. Try capturing the Milky Way over the dunes.

Page 170 and opposite: Great Sand Dunes National Park

Page 171: San Juan Mountains

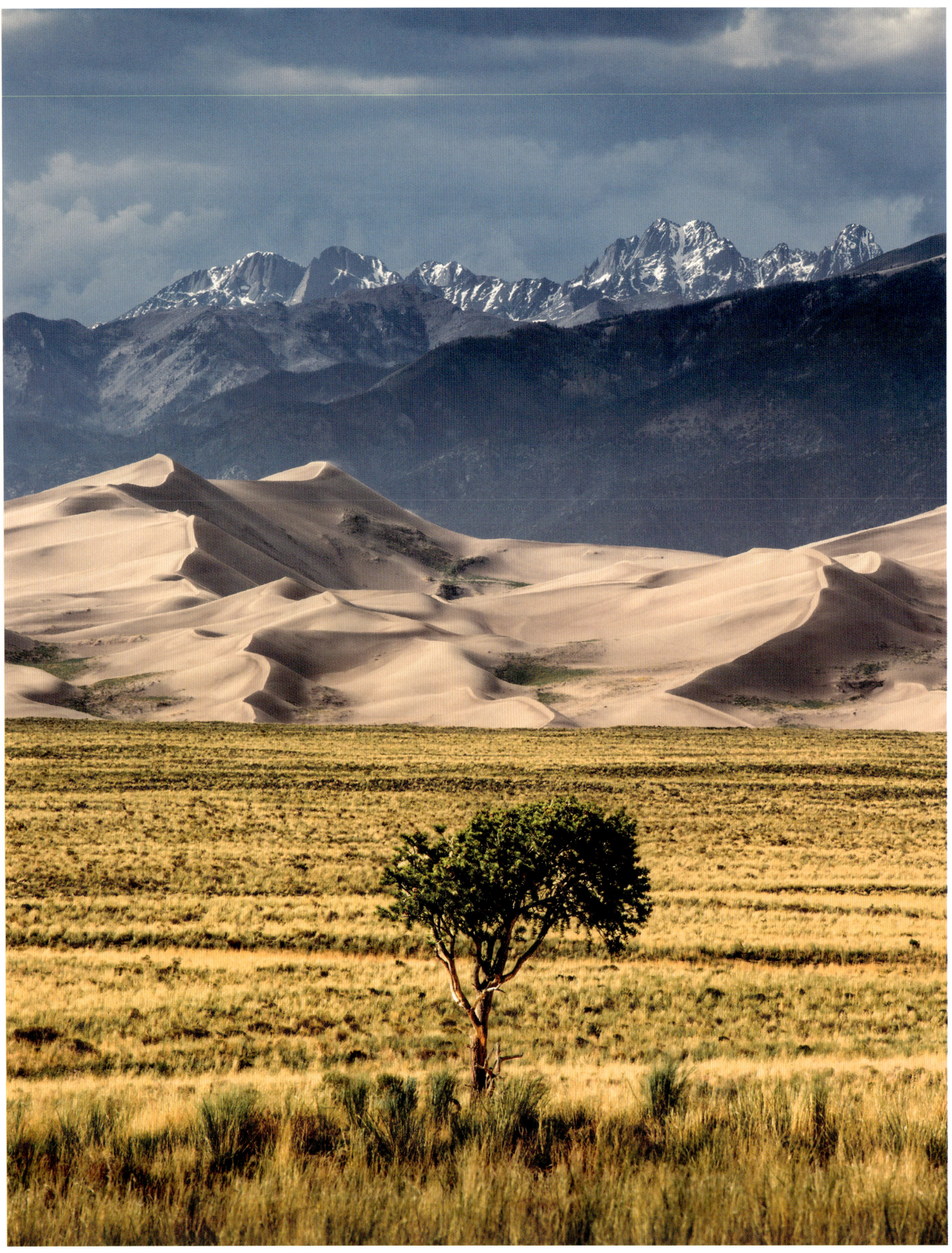

Above and opposite: Great Sand Dunes National Park

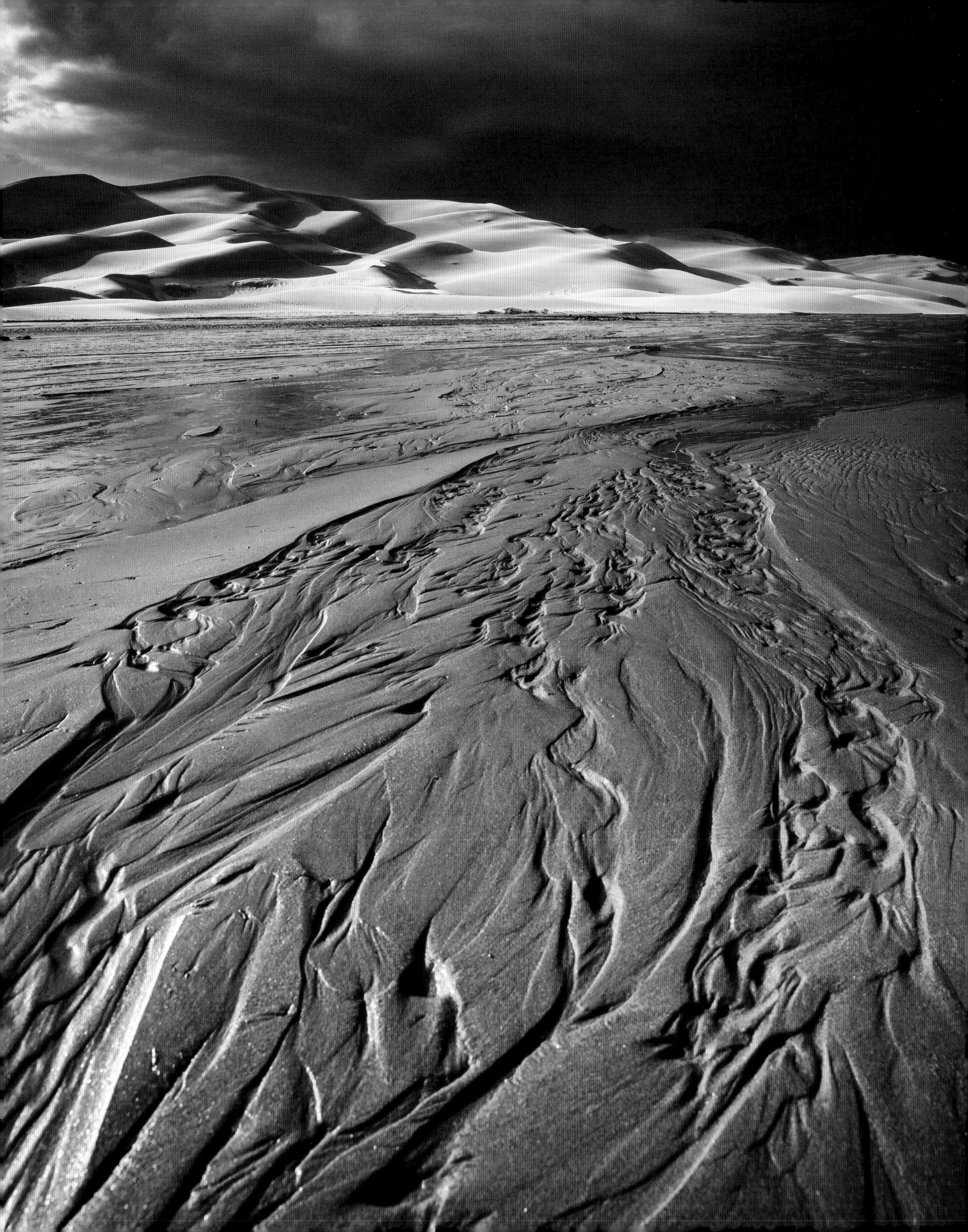

SOUTHWEST

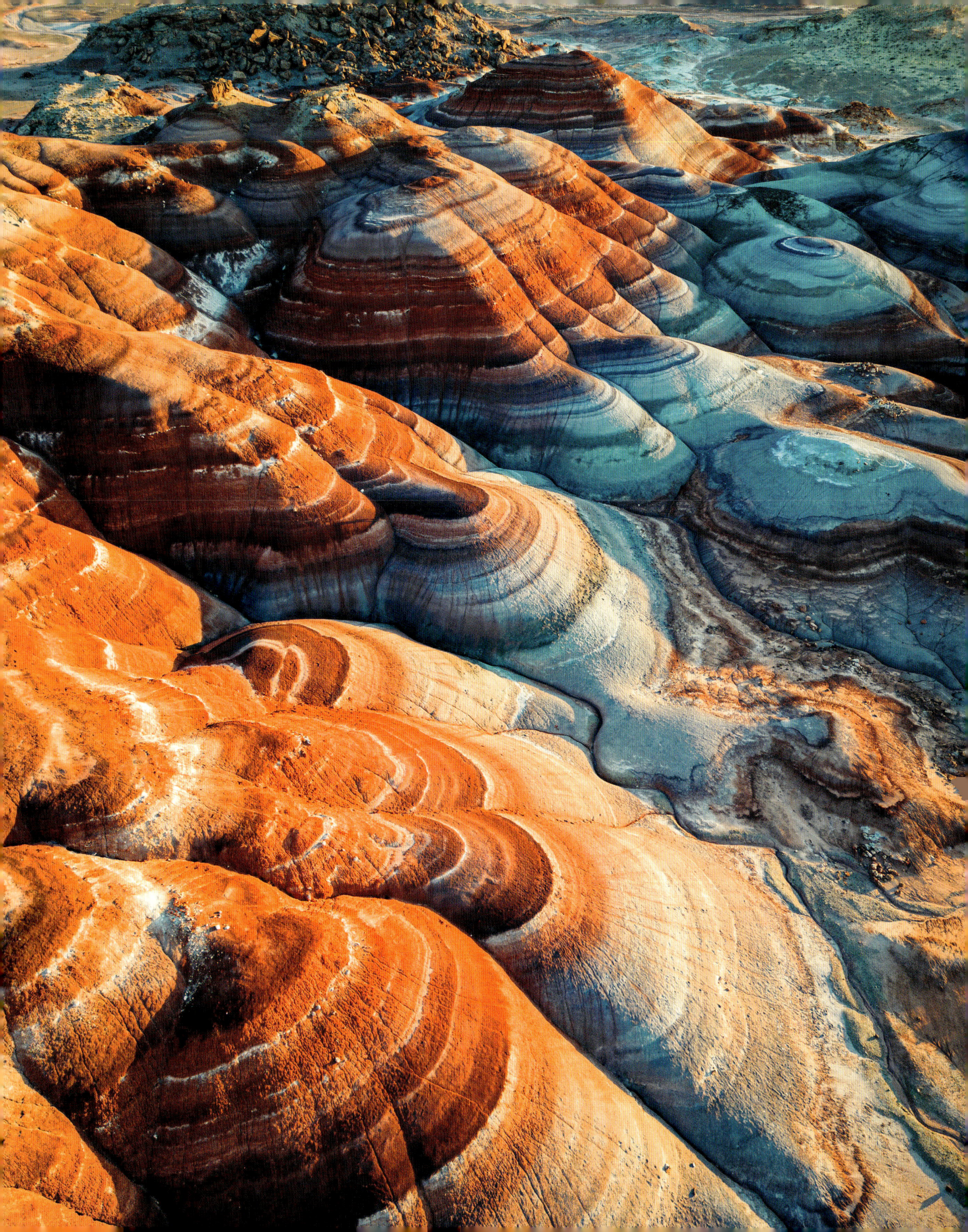

UTAH

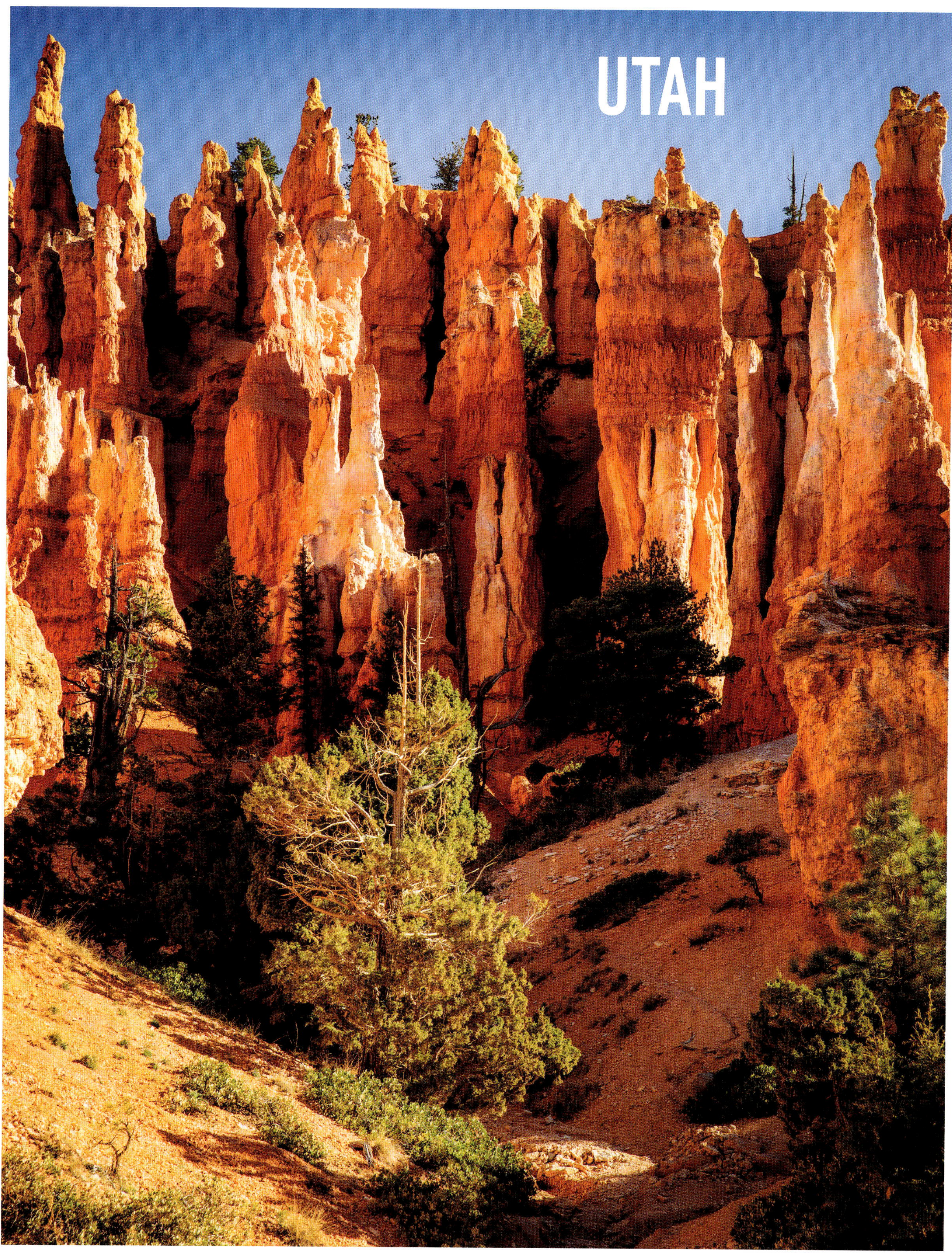

MOAB

There's something special about Moab. This small but amazing town is the hub to so many of my favorite places in Utah. If you're planning a road trip to the southwest, Moab has to be on the list as a paradise for van lifers and nomadic travelers like myself. Some of my favorite memories from life on the road come from this area.

Region: Southwest

State: Utah

Coordinates: 38°34'23.9"N 109°32'59.3"W

Focal feature: Outdoor recreation hub close to red-rock canyons, arches, and the Colorado River

Formation attributes: The region is characterized by sandstone formations shaped by erosion, including natural arches, towering spires, and deep canyons carved by the Colorado River.

Fun fact: Moab is home to the famous Slickrock Bike Trail, one of the most challenging and unique mountain-biking trails in the world.

Best time to visit: March to May and September to November offer the best weather, with cooler temperatures and fewer crowds. Summers can be extremely hot, while winter brings colder nights but quieter trails.

How to access: Moab is accessible via US Highway 191 and is about a four-hour drive from Salt Lake City. The town has a small regional airport, but most visitors drive in.

Things to consider: Moab serves as the gateway to both Arches and Canyonlands National Parks. The town is known for its red-rock landscapes, world-class mountain biking, off-roading, and river rafting. Expect hot summers and mild winters, and be prepared for limited water sources when hiking in the desert. Popular parks and trails can get crowded, so arriving early or visiting during the shoulder seasons helps avoid peak traffic.

RECOMMENDED TRAILS:

Corona Arch Trail: *2.3-mile (3.7km) round trip; about 500 feet (152m) elevation gain; easy.* A scenic hike to one of Moab's most impressive arches outside of the national parks, featuring stunning desert views.

Devils Garden Trail (Arches National Park): *8-mile (12.9km) round trip; about 1,100 feet (335m) elevation gain; moderate.* A spectacular hike showcasing multiple arches, including Landscape Arch, the longest in North America.

Fisher Towers Trail: *4.2-mile (6.8km) round trip; about 1,500 feet (457m) elevation gain; strenuous.* A challenging but rewarding trek through towering sandstone spires, offering incredible views of the Colorado River and surrounding canyonlands.

Tips for taking a great photo

- Sunrise and sunset provide the best lighting for capturing the deep reds and oranges of the rock formations.
- Arrive at Delicate Arch early to get a good spot, as this is one of the most photographed locations in Utah.
- Take advantage of still Colorado River waters in the morning for stunning reflections of the red cliffs.
- Moab has some of the darkest skies in the US, making it a great spot for capturing the Milky Way over iconic rock formations.

Page 178: Mars Desert Research Station

Page 179: Bryce Canyon National Park

Opposite: Double Arch, Arches National Park

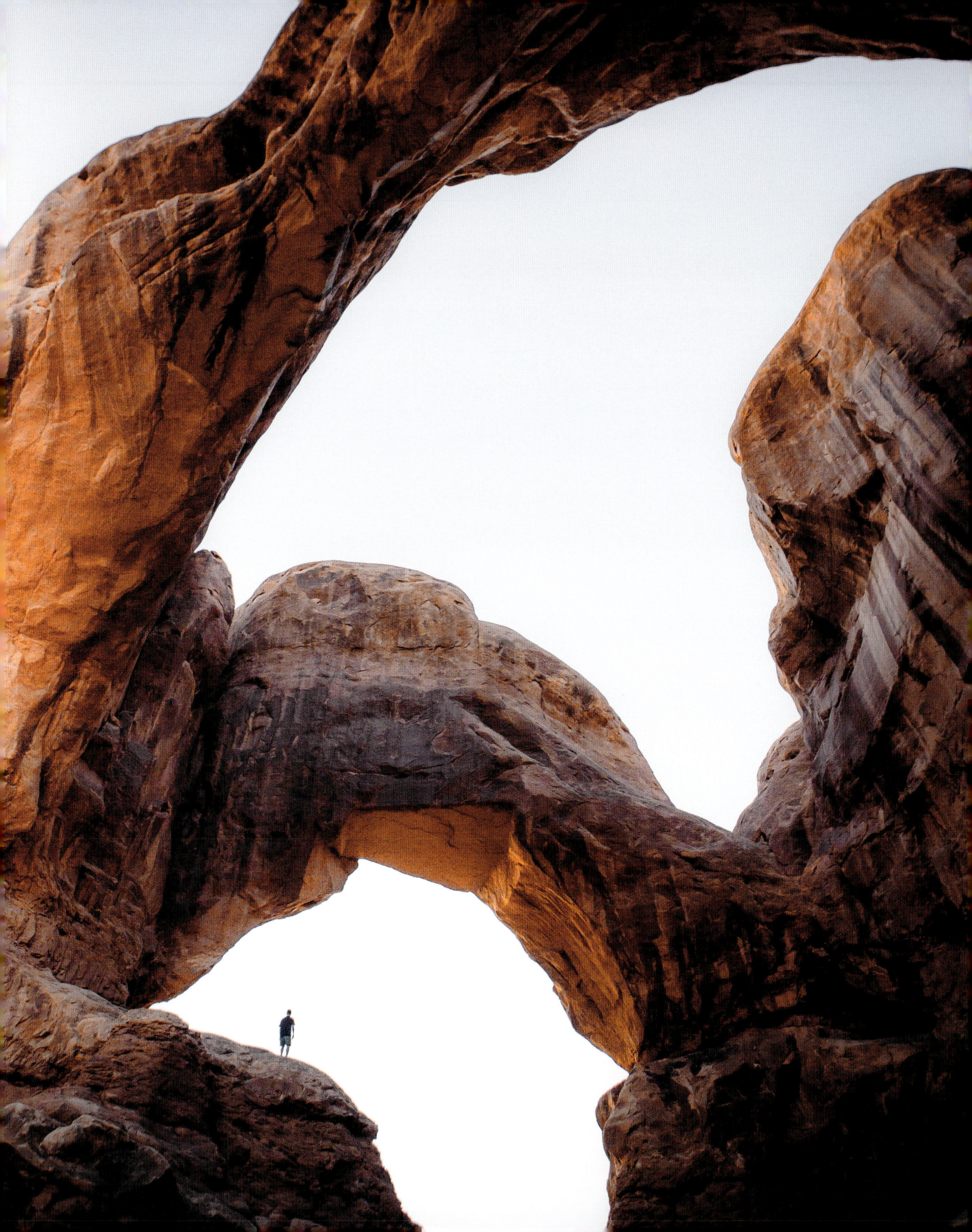

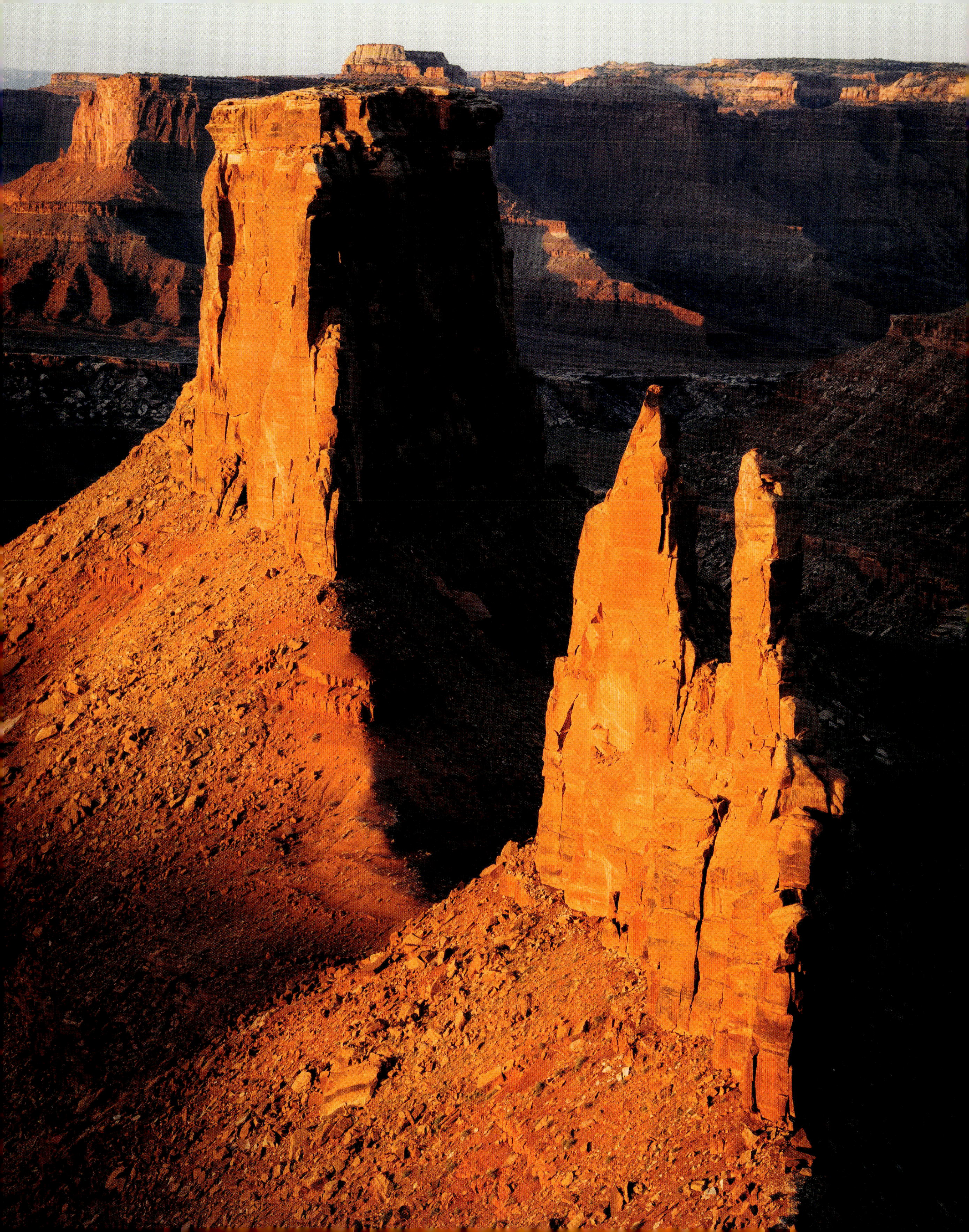

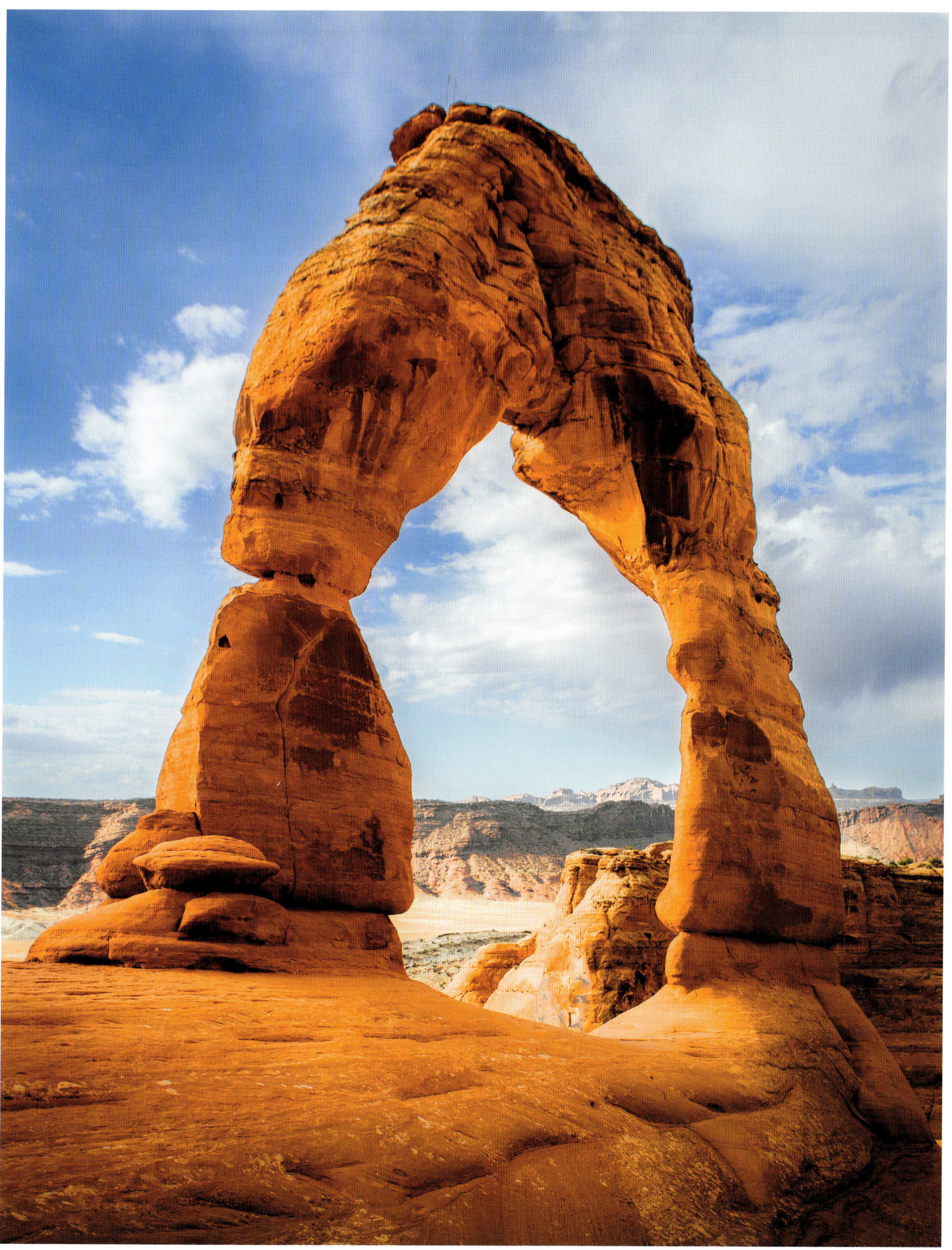

Above: Delicate Arch, Arches National Park | Opposite: Marlboro Point

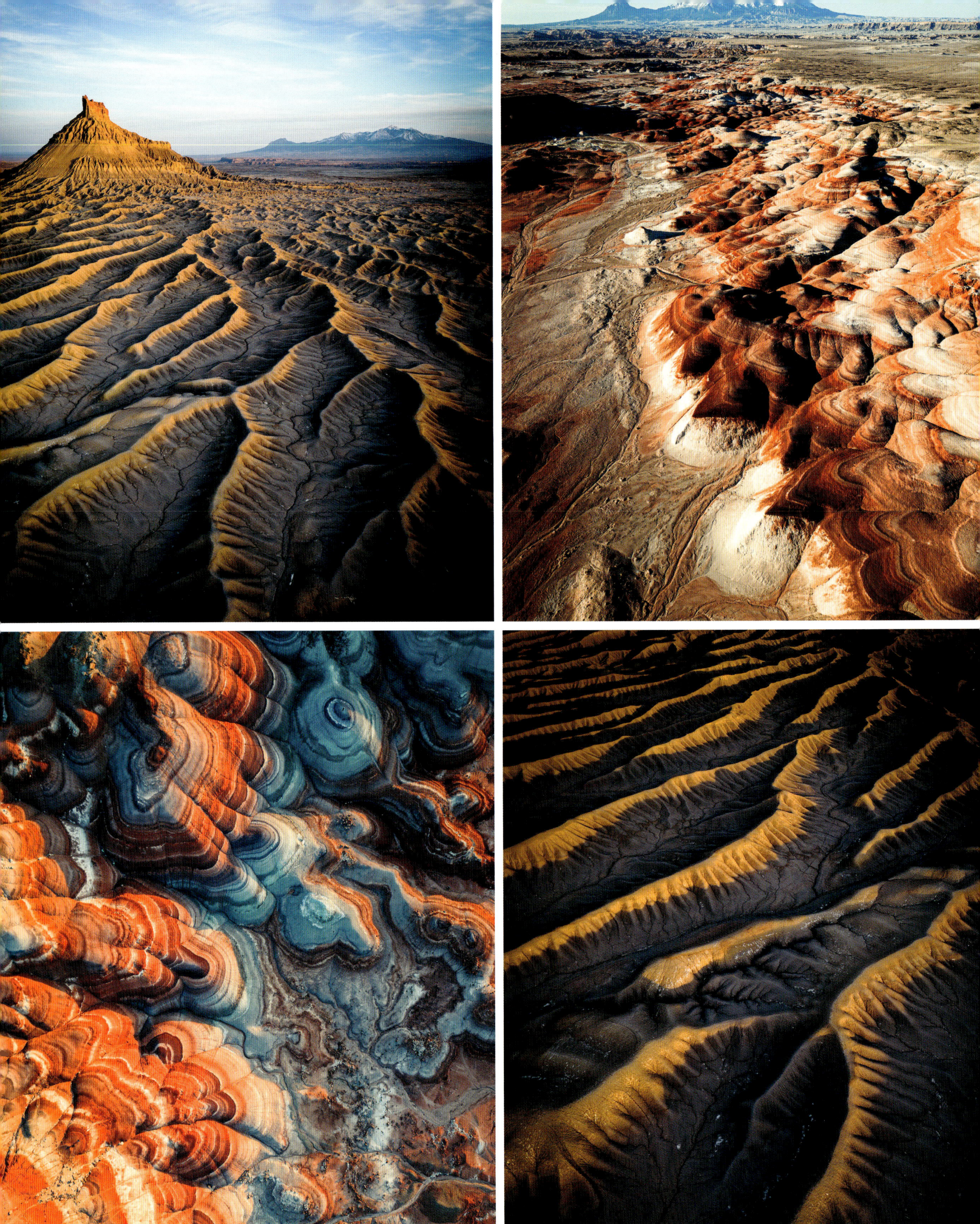

HANKSVILLE

There's something about the landscapes around Hanksville that makes you feel like you've left Earth behind. It's a remote desert town surrounded by otherworldly landscapes, from slot canyons and badlands to bizarre rock formations. The area is known for its Mars-like scenery, making it a popular destination for photographers, off-roaders, and adventurers. In my opinion, it's the most otherworldly place in America. Visit this place just once, and you'll know exactly what I mean.

Region: Southwest

State: Utah

Coordinates: 38°22'12.0"N 110°42'49.7"W

Focal features: Capitol Reef National Park, Goblin Valley State Park, and the surrounding Bureau of Land Management (BLM) public lands

Formation attributes: The region is shaped by millions of years of erosion, revealing layers of colorful rock, towering cliffs, and bizarre hoodoos. The surreal desert landscapes surrounding Hanksville include Mars-like badlands, slot canyons, and unique rock formations.

Fun fact: The Mars Desert Research Station, located just outside Hanksville, is used by scientists and astronauts to simulate missions to Mars.

Best time to visit: Spring and fall offer the most comfortable temperatures, while summer can be extremely hot. Winter is quieter but can bring occasional snow, creating dramatic desert contrasts.

How to access: Hanksville is located along Highway 24, about two hours from Moab or four hours from Salt Lake City. Many of the best sites require driving on dirt roads, some of which become impassable when wet. Check conditions and bring a high-clearance 4WD vehicle if venturing off the main roads.

Things to consider: Be sure to pack a lot of water when visiting here! There are little to no water sources in this area. The summer heat can be very intense, so be sure to pack sunscreen and a source of shade, if possible.

RECOMMENDED TRAILS:

Factory Butte Badlands: *Off-trail exploring; easy–moderate.* Not a designated trail, but the surrounding badlands near Factory Butte offer endless opportunities for hiking, photography, and scrambling over alien-like landscapes.

Little Wild Horse Canyon: *8.1-mile (13km) round trip; 800 feet (244m) elevation gain; moderate.* A stunning slot-canyon hike with narrow passageways, wavy rock walls, and incredible light play.

Lower Black Box (San Rafael River Gorge): *about a 12-mile (19.3km) round trip; 1,200 feet (366m) elevation gain; strenuous.* A remote and challenging slot canyon hike that requires wading or swimming through sections of the river.

Tips for taking a great photo

- Sunrise and sunset bring out the deep reds, purples, and blues in the badlands, creating a dramatic and surreal landscape.
- Use a telephoto lens to capture the intricate textures and ridgelines of Factory Butte.
- Midday light filtering through the narrow walls of slot canyons creates a stunning glow—just be aware of flash flood risks.
- With little light pollution, the area around Hanksville is perfect for astrophotography, especially near Goblin Valley and Factory Butte.

Top left and bottom right: Factory Butte | Top right and bottom left: Mars Desert Research Station

CANYONLANDS NATIONAL PARK

Canyonlands took me by surprise. I'd seen photos, of course—those vast red canyons and towering buttes—but nothing prepared me for the silence. I entered through the Island in the Sky district just after sunrise, the sky still cool and pale. Walking out to Mesa Arch, I felt like I was tiptoeing into a cathedral. When the sun finally cracked the horizon, it set the sandstone on fire, and for a moment, the whole canyon below looked like it was glowing from within. I didn't speak. No one did. We all just stood there, a small group of strangers, humbled into silence by the raw immensity of it all. Later, I took a solo hike along the Syncline Loop, which skirts the base of Upheaval Dome. The trail was rugged and quiet—no guardrails, no crowds, just slickrock and sky. Every turn offered a new, dramatic angle of the land, like walking through layers of time. Canyonlands didn't just show me beauty; it offered space to breathe.

Region: Southwest

State: Utah

Coordinates: 38°19'36.8"N 109°52'41.9"W

Focal features: The dramatic canyons, towering mesas, and winding rivers

Formation attributes: Shaped by the Colorado River and Green River over millions of years, the park features deep canyons, sandstone arches, and towering rock formations.

Fun fact: The Maze district of Canyonlands is one of the most remote and least accessible areas of any national park in the US, requiring serious preparation and self-sufficiency.

Best time to visit: March to May and September to November offer the most pleasant temperatures for hiking and exploring. Summer can be extremely hot, with temperatures often exceeding 100°F (38°C).

How to access: The most accessible area, Island in the Sky, is just a forty-minute drive from Moab. The Needles district requires a longer drive (about 1.5 hours from Moab), and the Maze is reachable only with a high-clearance 4WD vehicle and extensive planning.

Things to consider: Be prepared for extreme desert conditions, bring plenty of water, and check road conditions if heading into off-road areas.

RECOMMENDED TRAILS:

Mesa Arch Trail: *0.6-mile (1km) round trip; minimal elevation gain; easy.* A short walk to one of the most famous sunrise spots in the park, with the arch framing a breathtaking canyon view.

Chesler Park Loop: *10.2-mile (16.4km) loop; about 1,800 feet (549m) elevation gain; moderate.* A stunning hike through the Needles, featuring towering sandstone spires, slot canyons, and open desert views.

Druid Arch Trail: *10-mile (16.1km) round trip; 1,500 feet (457m) elevation gain; strenuous.* A challenging but rewarding hike leading to a massive rock arch resembling an ancient ruin.

Tips for taking a great photo

- Sunrise at Mesa Arch creates a glowing effect as the sun rises beneath the arch. Get there early to claim a good spot.
- Use a wide-angle lens to capture the vastness of the park's canyon landscapes.
- Sunrise or sunset brings out the deep red and orange hues in the sandstone spires of the Needles.
- With minimal light pollution, Canyonlands is one of the best places in the US for astrophotography.

Opposite: White Rim Overlook, Canyonlands National Park

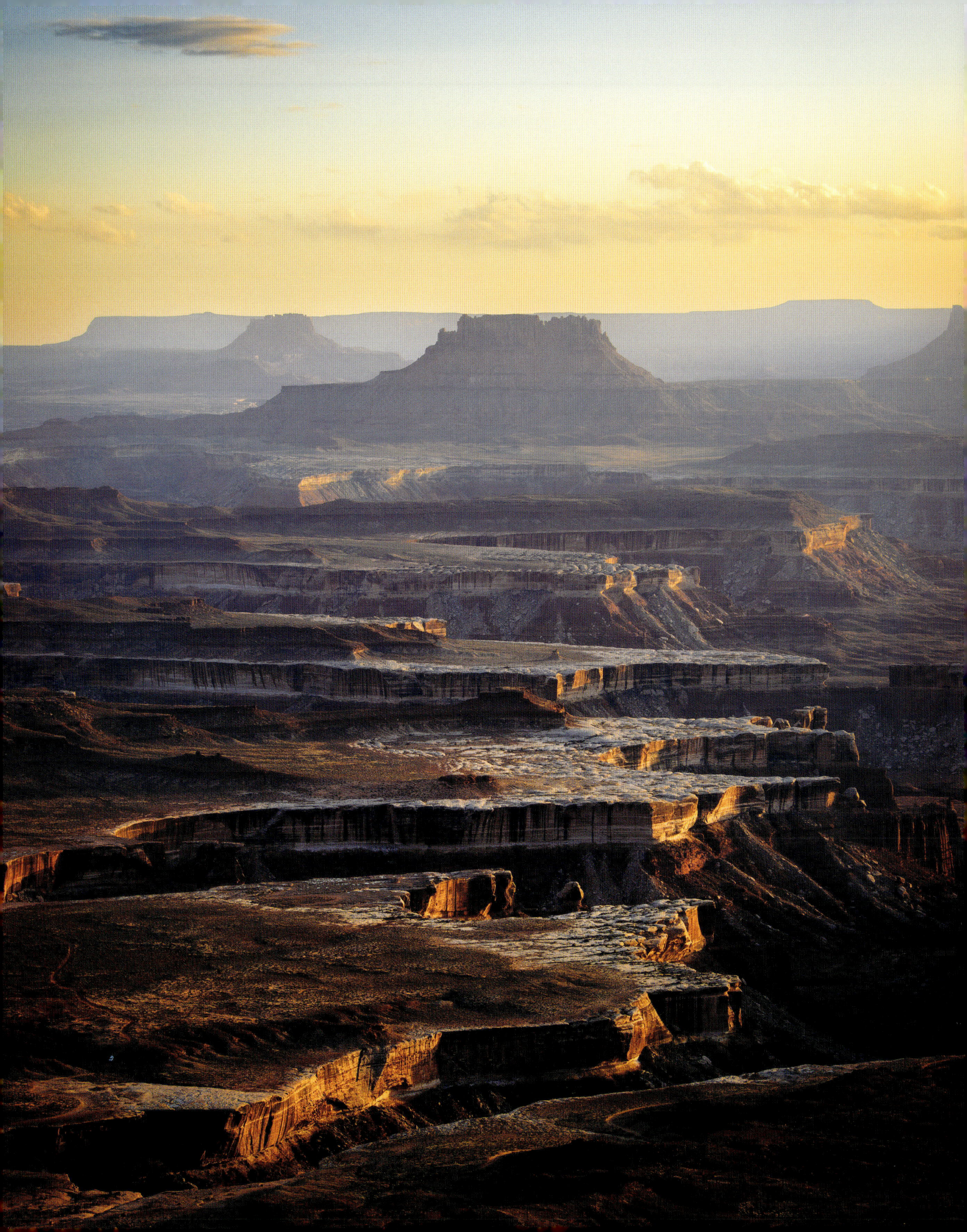

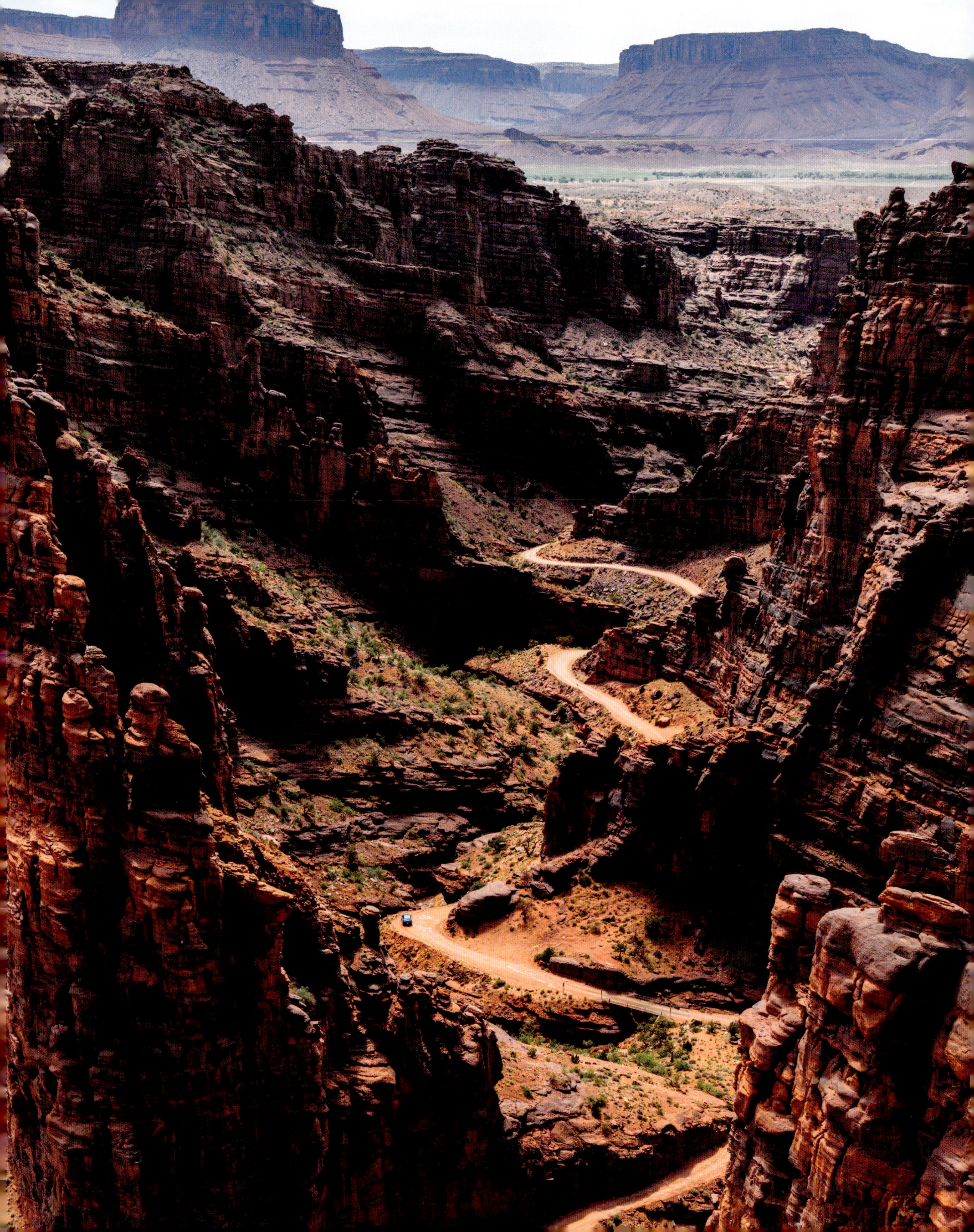

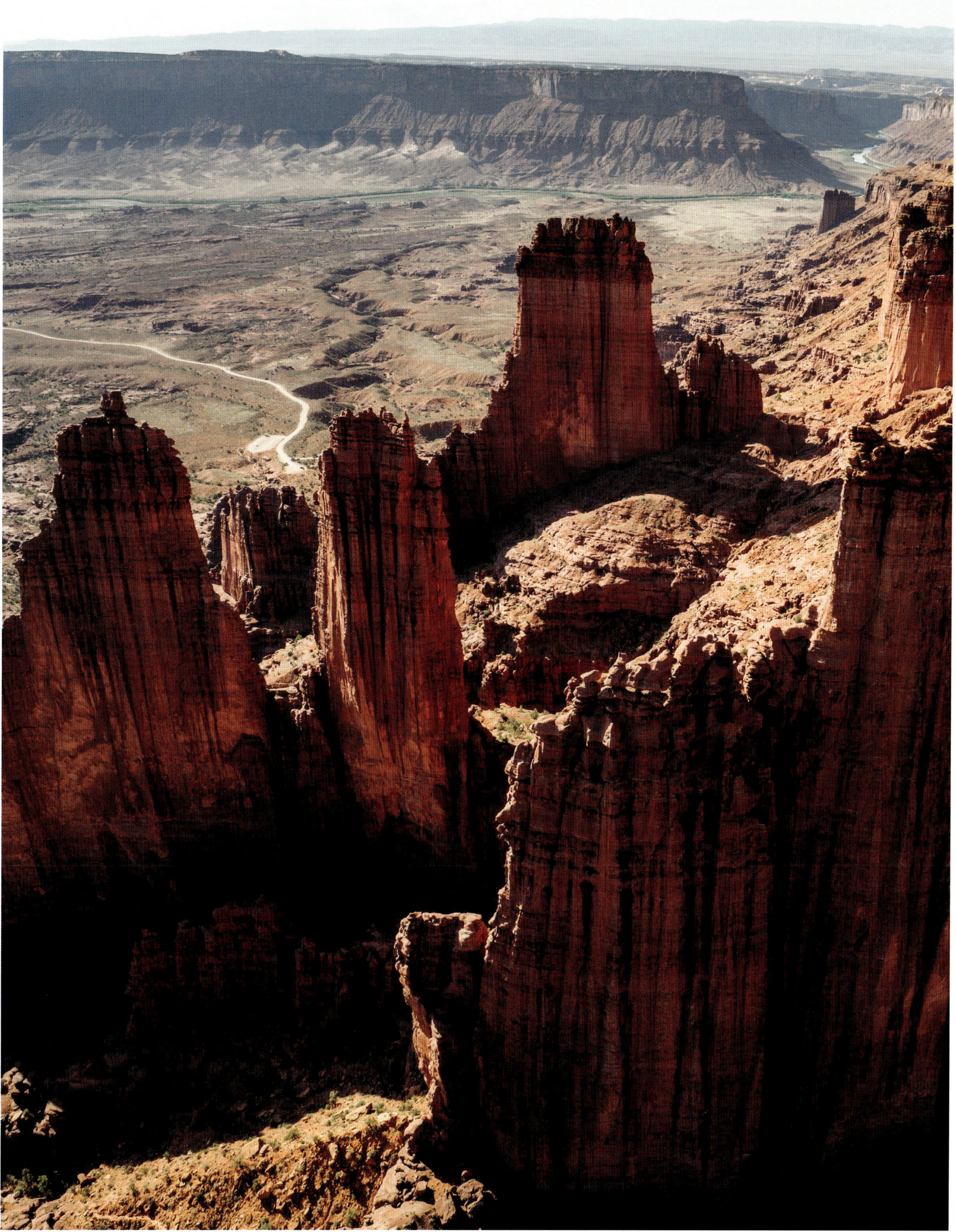

Above: Fisher Towers | Opposite: Near Onion Creek

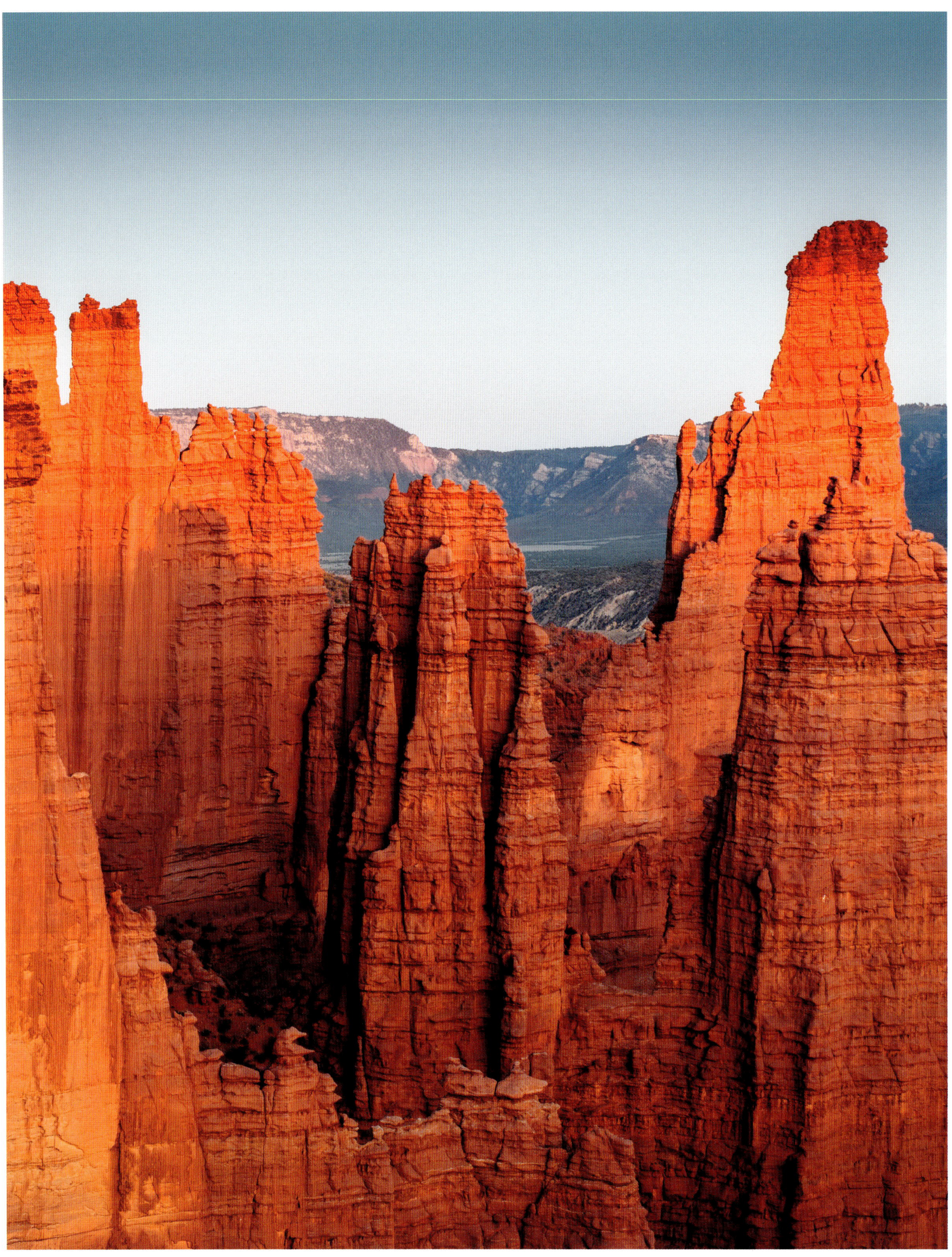

Above: Fisher Towers | Opposite: Dead Horse Point State Park

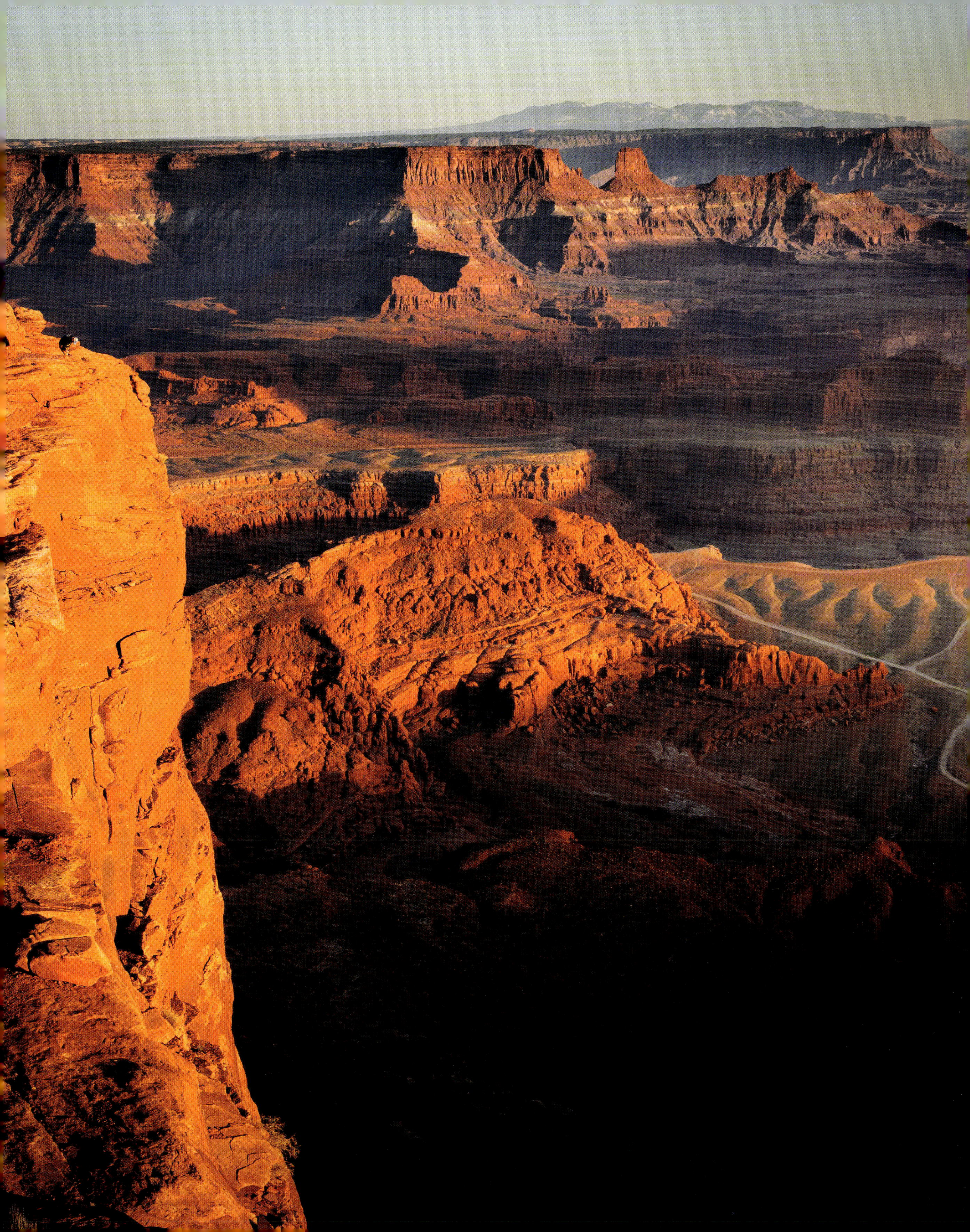

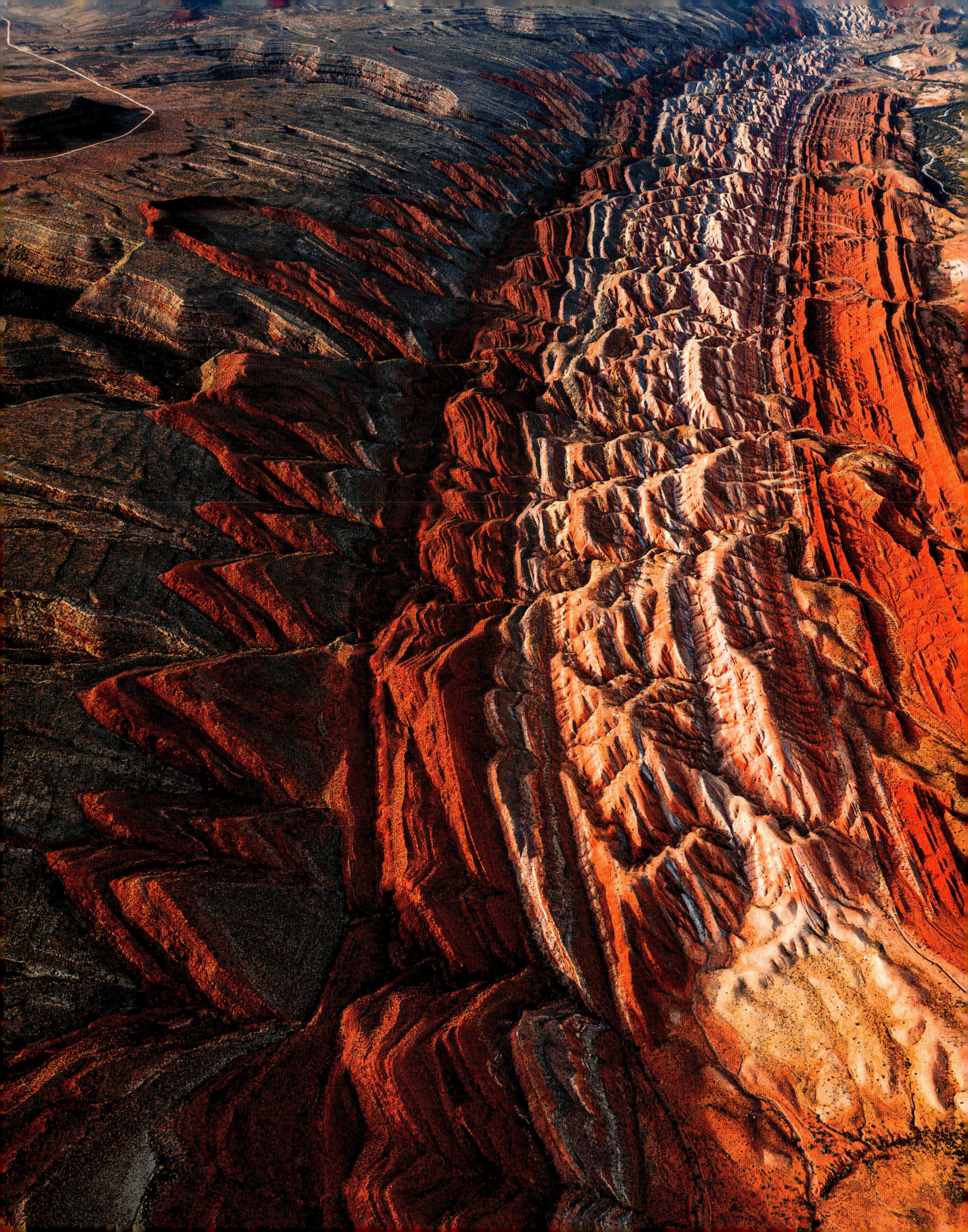

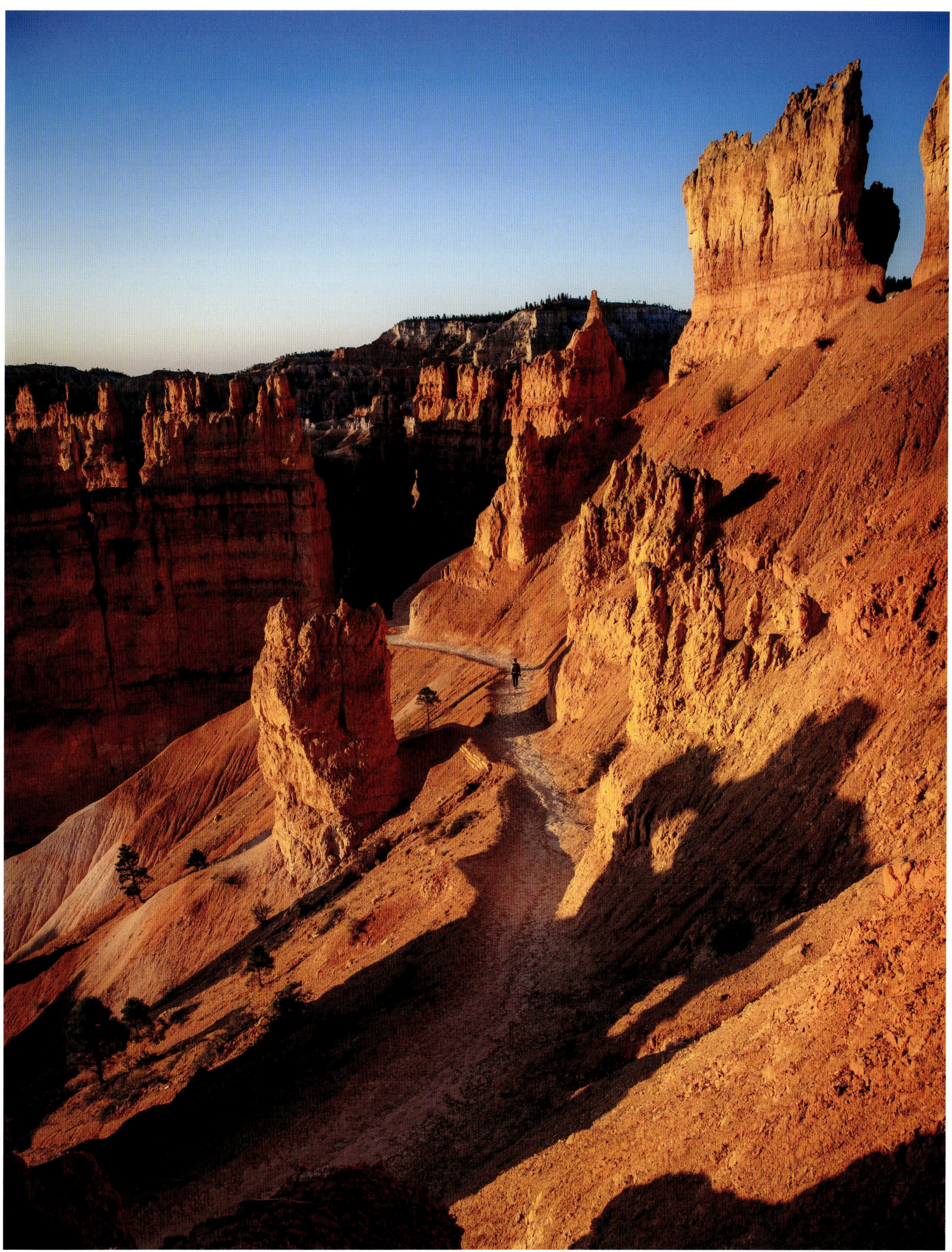

Above: Bryce Canyon National Park | Opposite: Near Mexican Hat

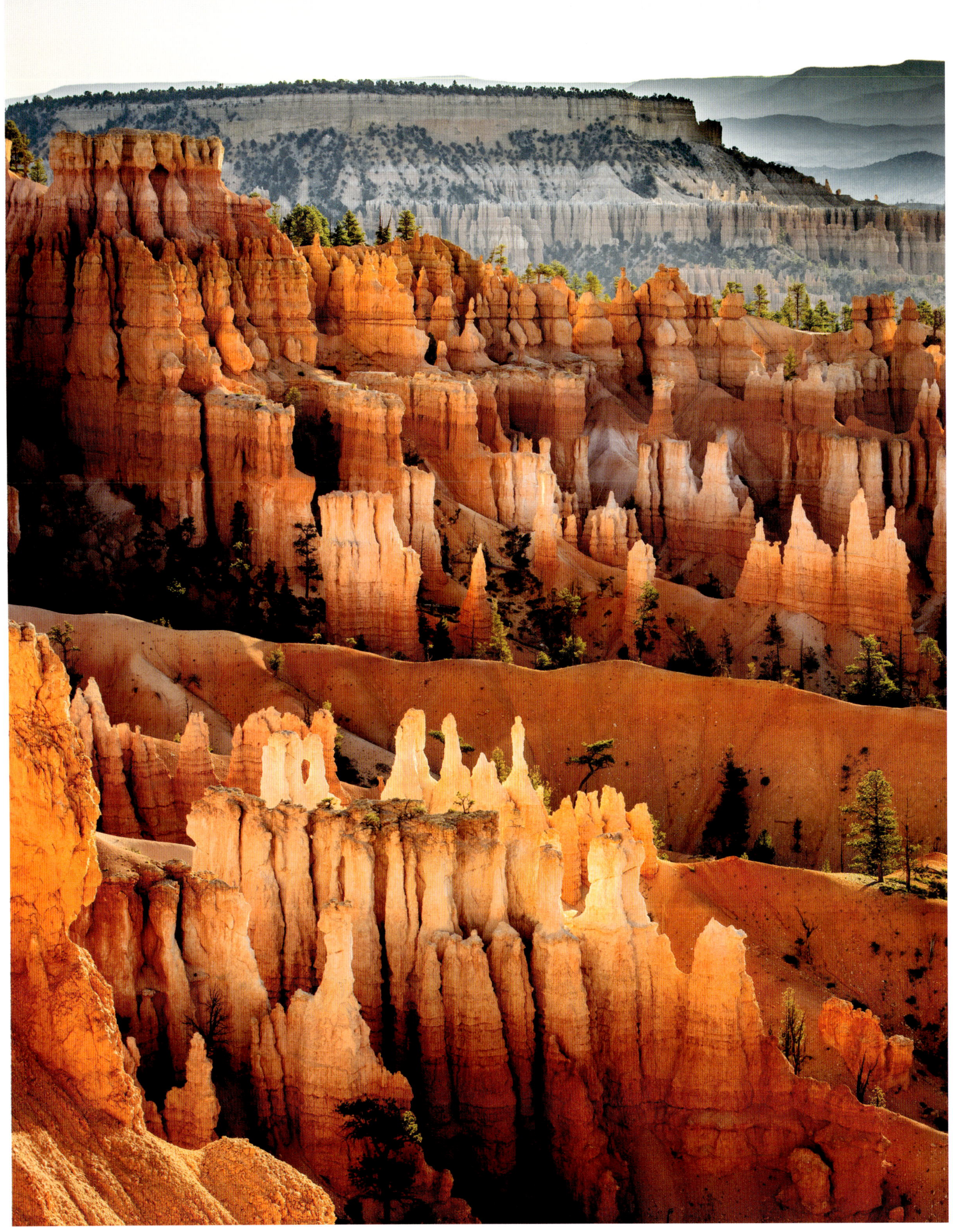

Above and opposite: Bryce Canyon National Park

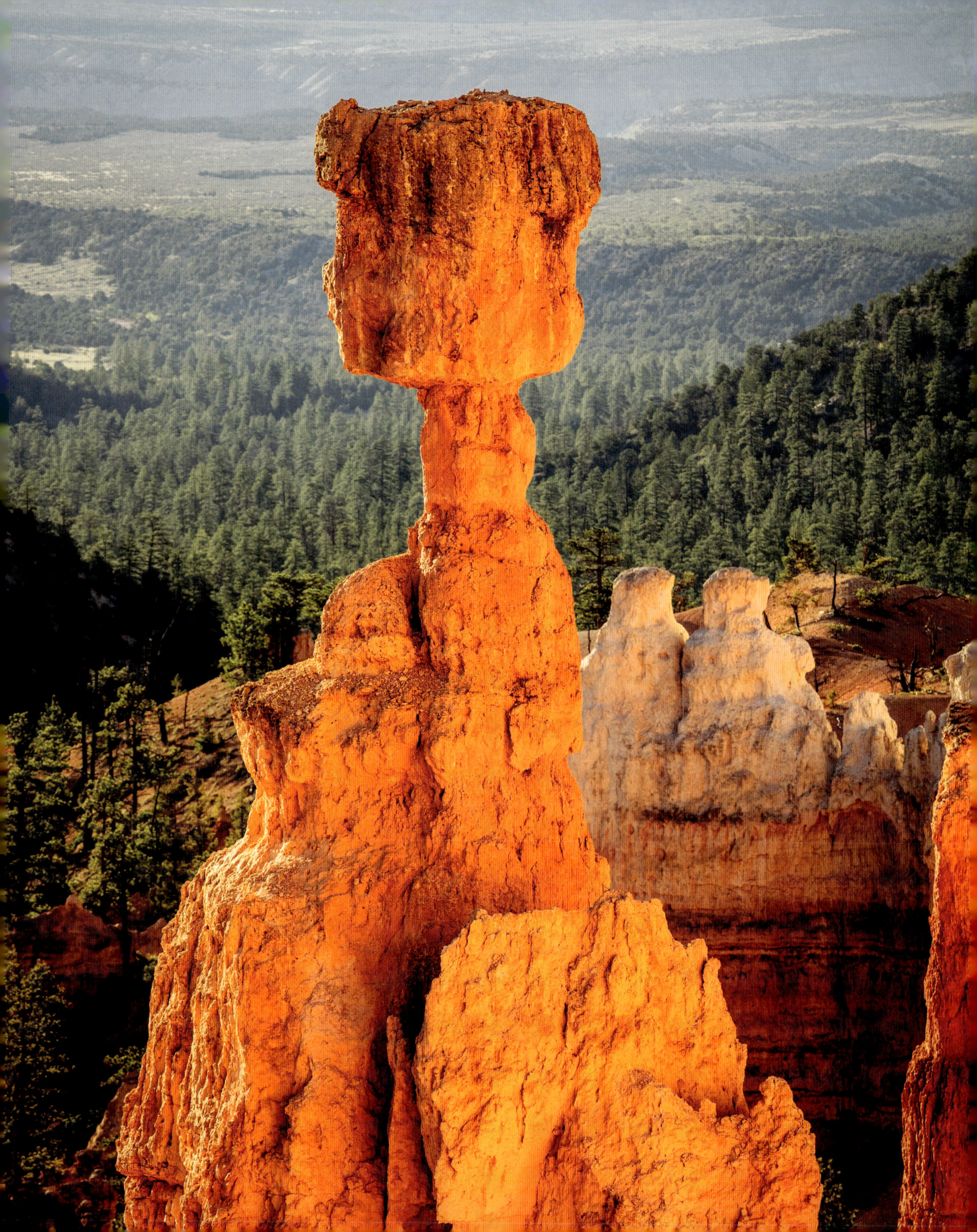

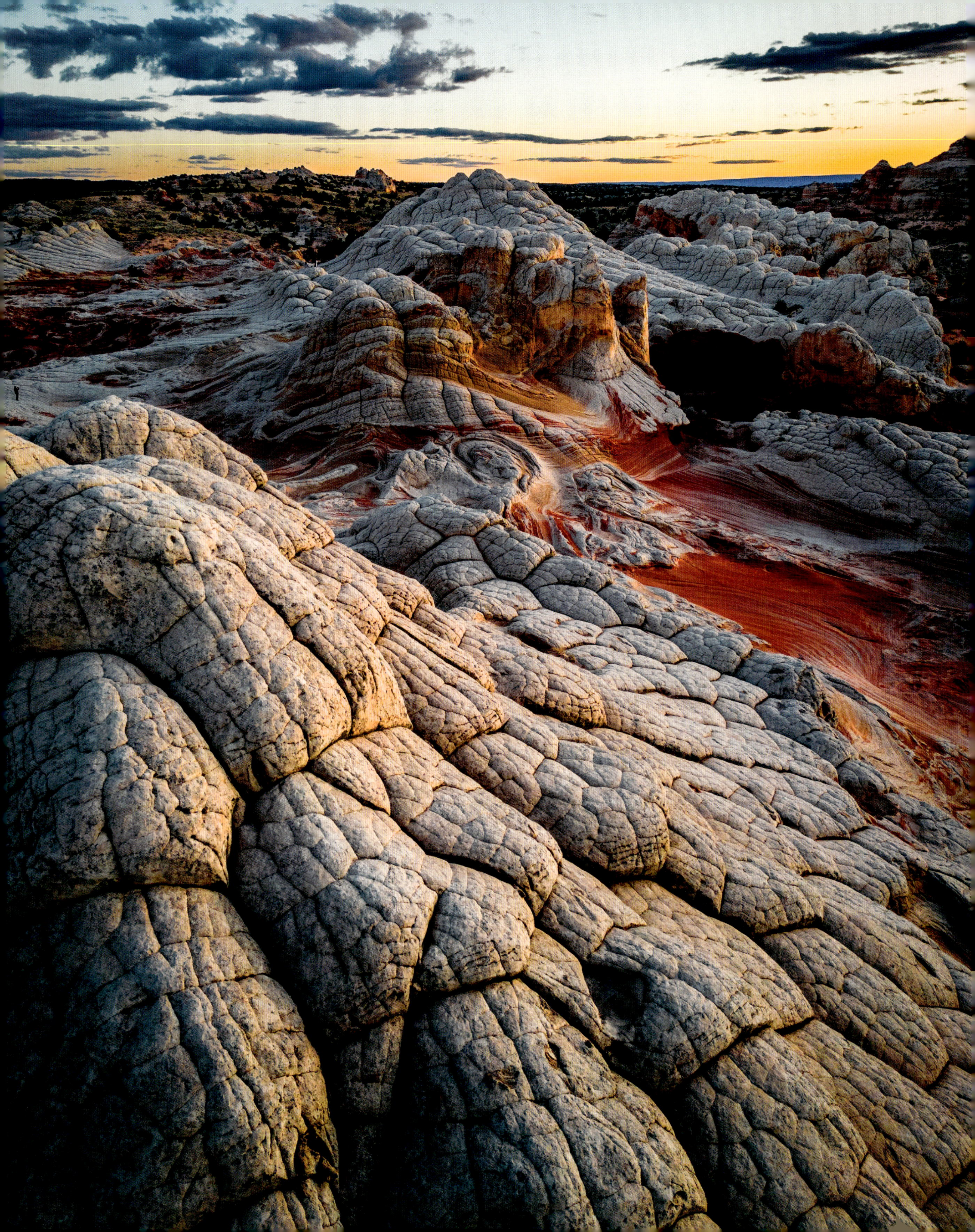

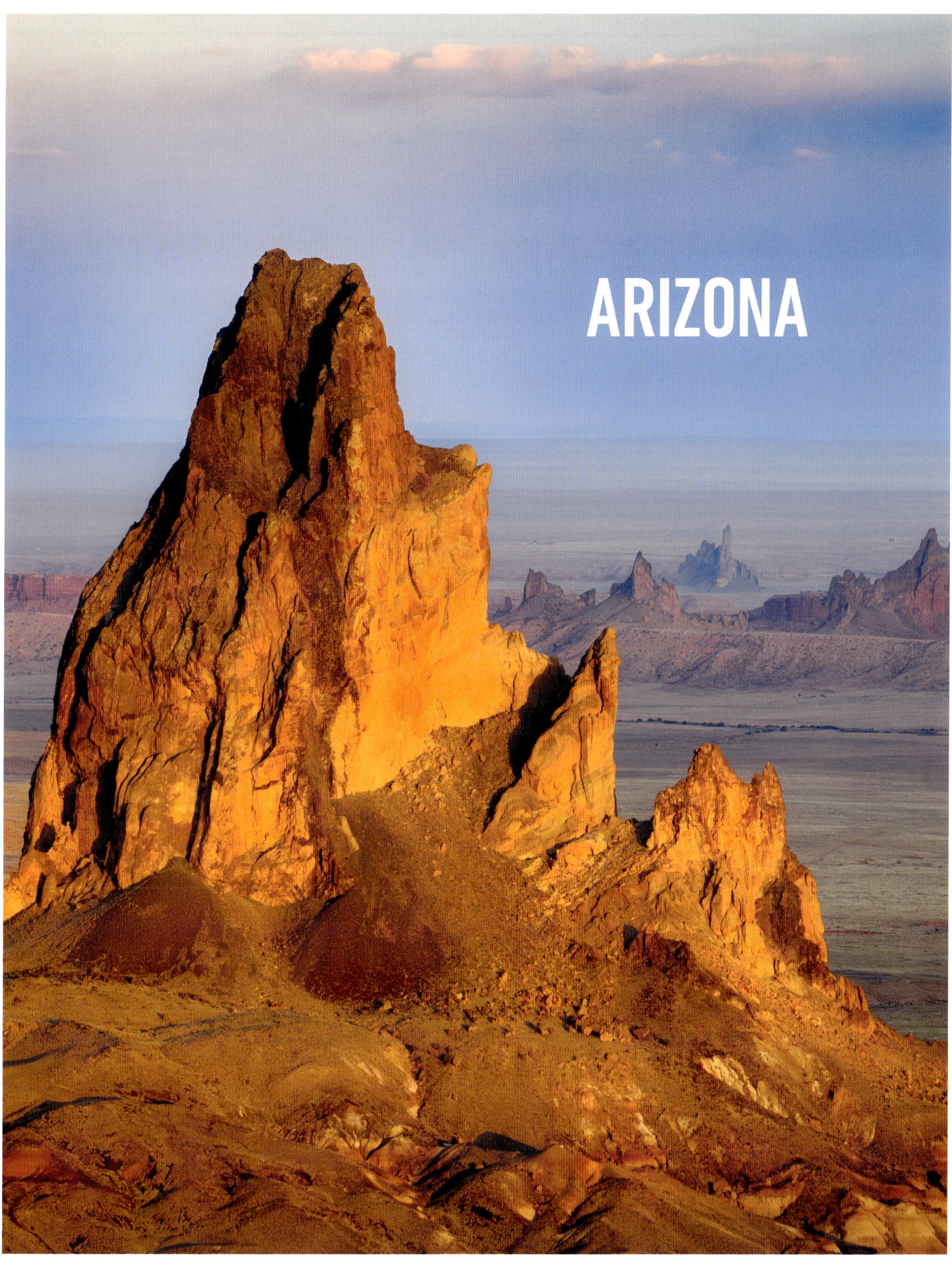
ARIZONA

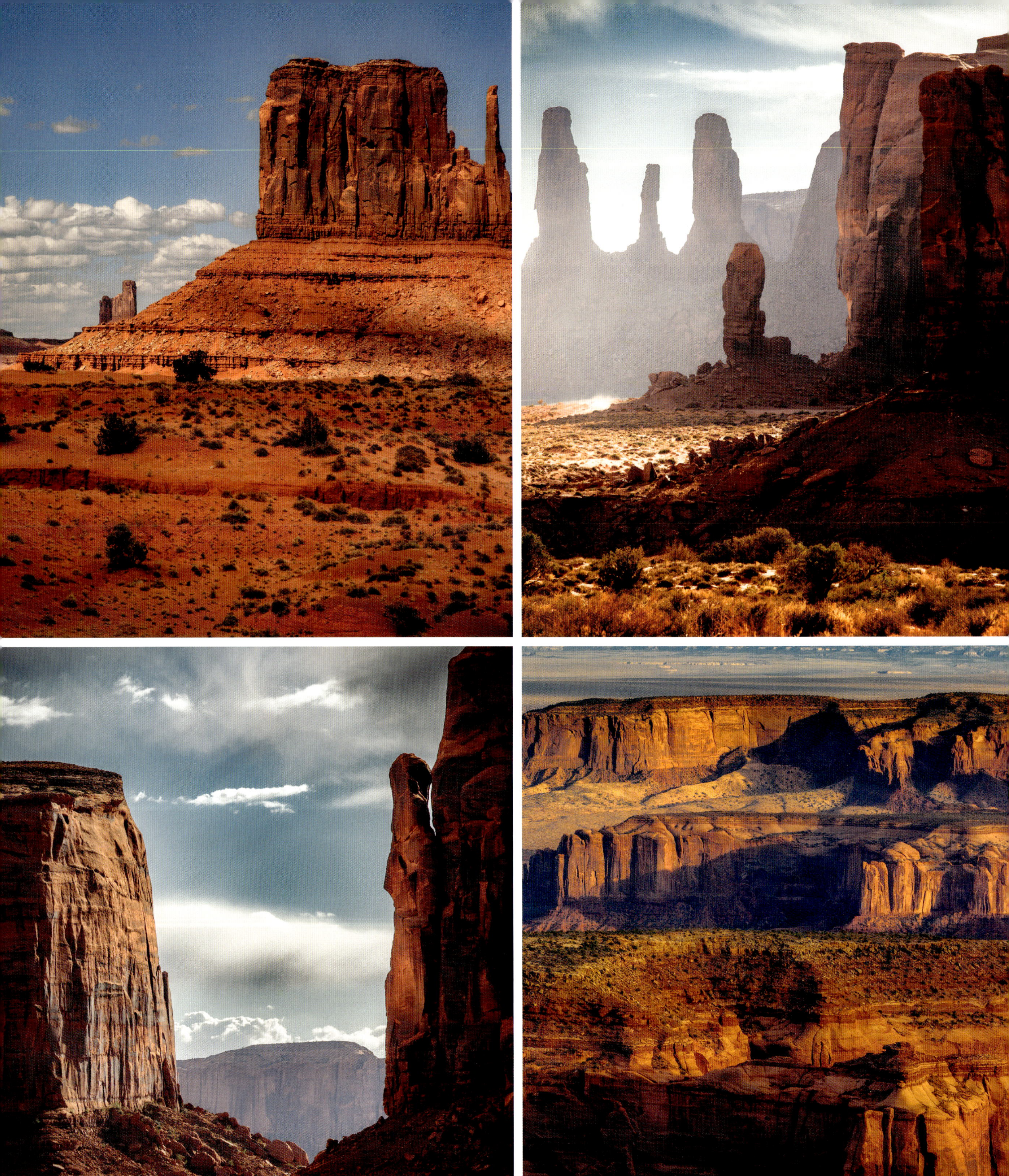

MONUMENT VALLEY

Driving into Monument Valley, I felt like I had stepped into a Western movie scene—towering buttes rose from the desert like sentinels. But what stuck with me most was the connection the Navajo share with this land. If you visit, hire a Navajo guide to learn about the history and significance of this place. It'll make you see it in a whole new way. To put it simply, this land is sacred.

Region: Southwest

States: Arizona and Utah

Coordinates: 37°00'17.6"N 110°05'54.2"W

Focal feature: Towering sandstone buttes rising from the desert floor of Monument Valley Navajo Tribal Park

Formation attributes: The iconic red-rock formations of Monument Valley are made of Navajo sandstone and reach heights of up to 1,000 feet (305m). Wind and water erosion have shaped these striking monoliths over millions of years.

Fun fact: Monument Valley has been featured in countless films, TV shows, and advertisements, most famously in classic Westerns directed by John Ford.

Best time to visit: March to May and September to November offer the best weather, with mild temperatures and clear skies. Summer can be extremely hot, and winter nights can be very cold.

How to access: The park is located along US Highway 163, near the town of Kayenta, Arizona. Visitors can drive the 17-mile (27km) scenic loop through the valley, but a high-clearance vehicle is recommended due to the rough unpaved road. For deeper exploration, guided tours are required.

Things to consider: Monument Valley is located on Navajo Nation land, and visiting the park requires an entry fee. Some areas are accessible only with a tour led by Navajo guides, offering a deeper cultural and historical perspective. Be prepared for limited services; bring water, snacks, and a full tank of gas.

RECOMMENDED TRAILS:

Hunt's Mesa Tour: *5–6-hour guided tour; strenuous*. This off-the-beaten-path adventure involves a guided 4WD tour and some hiking but rewards visitors with one of the most breathtaking panoramic views of Monument Valley.

Wildcat Trail: *4-mile (6.4km) round trip; about 400 feet (122m) elevation gain; moderate*. The only self-guided hiking trail in the park, this loop takes you around the iconic West and East Mitten Buttes, providing up-close views of the towering monoliths.

Mystery Valley Tour: *3.5-hour guided tour; moderate*. A fascinating journey through a less-visited part of the park, featuring ancient Ancestral Puebloan ruins, petroglyphs, and stunning rock formations.

Tips for taking a great photo

- Sunrise and sunset create stunning lighting on the buttes, with deep shadows and vibrant red hues.
- Visit John Ford Point for a sweeping view of the valley, great for capturing the vastness of the landscape.
- The golden hour right before sunset is perfect for dramatic shots of the buttes, featuring silhouettes and long shadows.
- With almost no light pollution, Monument Valley is an incredible place for astrophotography. Try capturing the Milky Way above the buttes.

Page 196: White Pocket, Vermilion Cliffs National Monument

Page 197: Agathla Peak

Opposite: Monument Valley

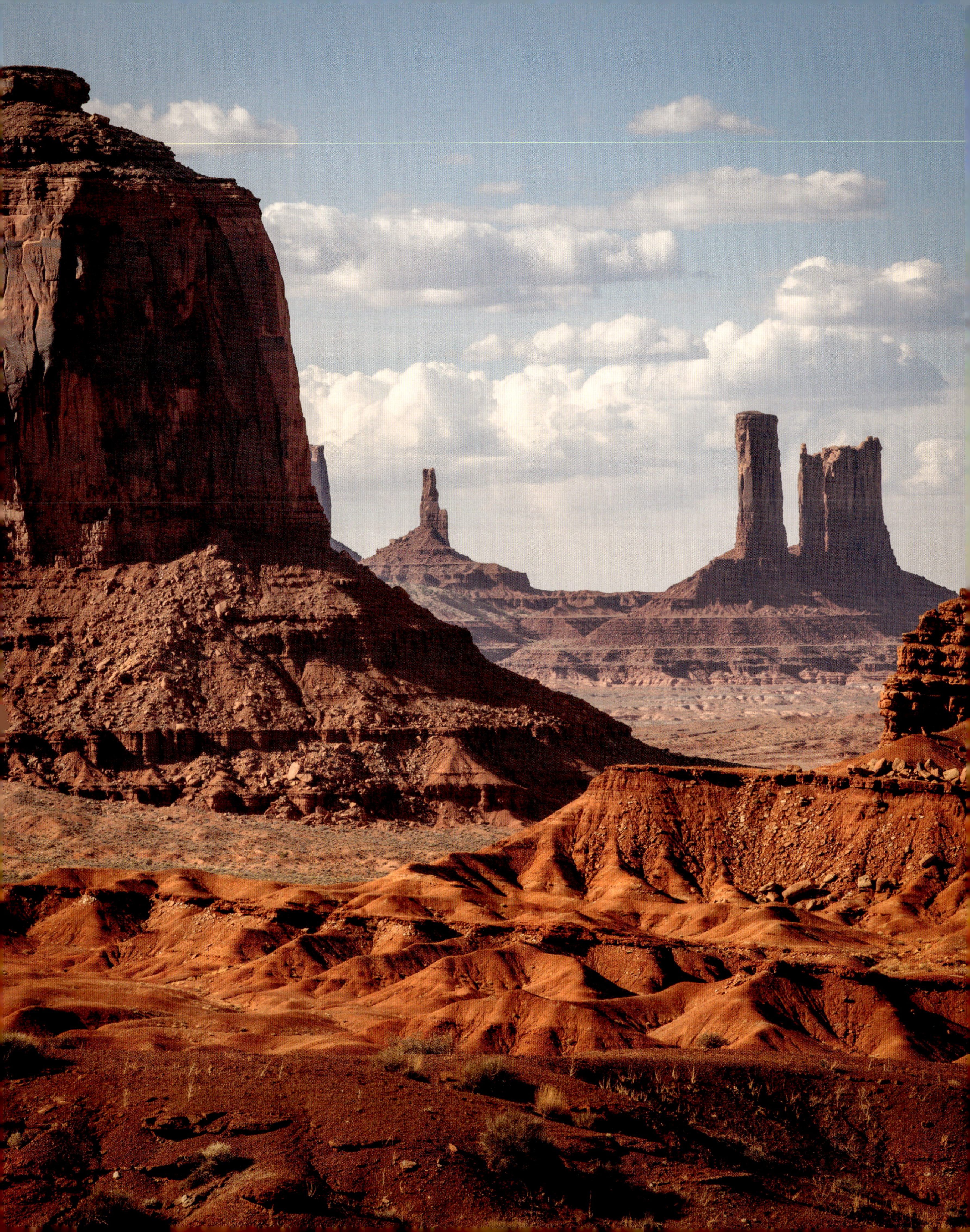

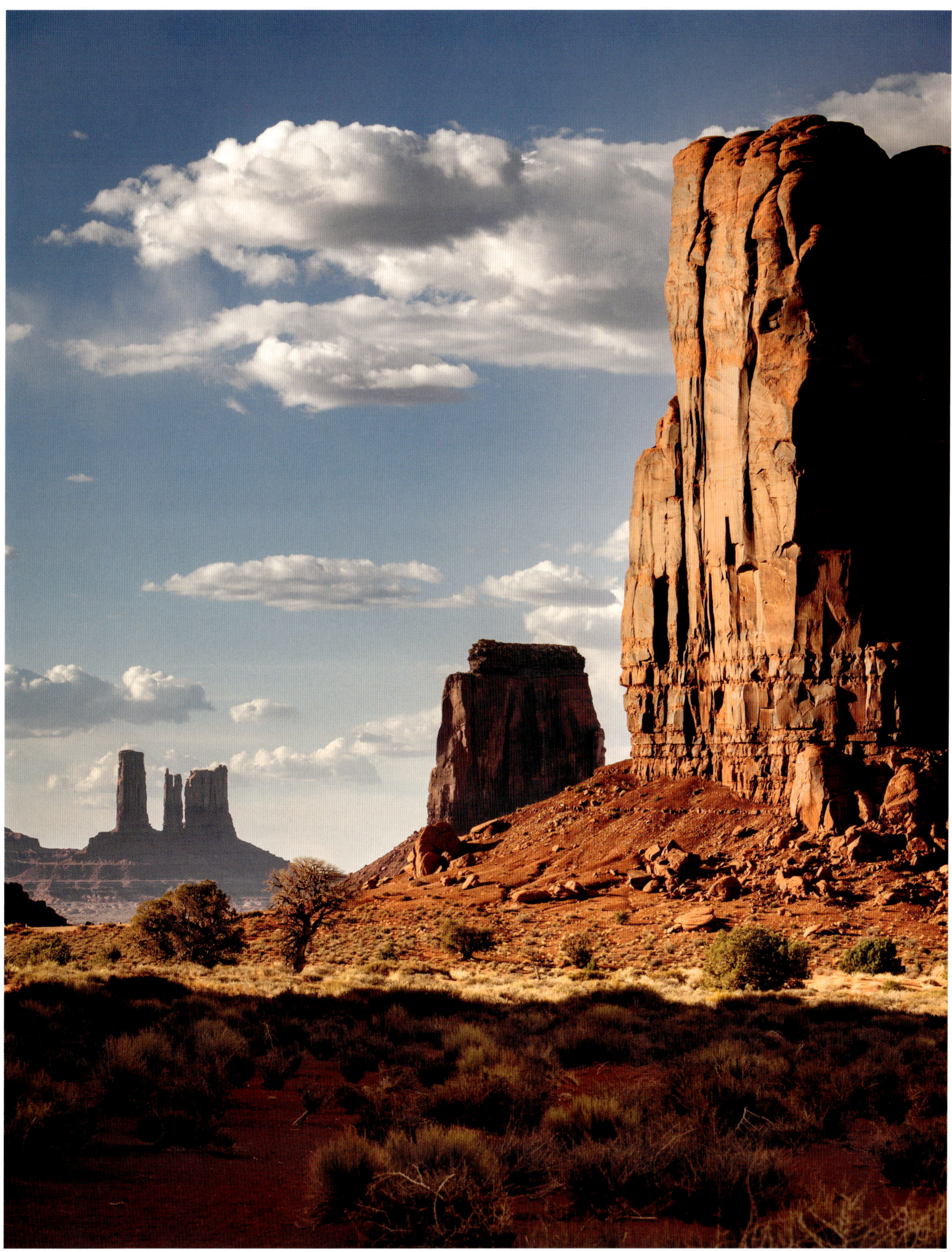

Above and opposite: Monument Valley

COYOTE BUTTES NORTH

Coyote Buttes North is home to the world-famous Wave, a surreal sandstone formation featuring flowing layers of red, orange, and yellow rock. After years of trying to get a permit, I finally stepped into the Wave. The first glimpse of its flowing sandstone ridges transported me into a painting. Although the permit is very hard to obtain, it's well worth the wait.

Region: Southwest

State: Arizona

Coordinates: 36°59'42.4"N 112°00'24.1"W

Focal feature: The Wave, a stunning sandstone formation with undulating rock patterns in Vermilion Cliffs National Monument

Formation attributes: Navajo Sandstone sculpted over millions of years by wind and water erosion, creating smooth, wavelike striations in vivid hues.

Fun fact: Only sixty-four people per day (as of recent regulations) are permitted to visit the Wave, making it one of the most exclusive hikes in the US.

Best time to visit: March to May and September to November offer the best weather. Summer temperatures can exceed 100°F (38°C), and winter storms can make roads impassable.

How to access: The hike to the Wave starts at the Wire Pass Trailhead along House Rock Valley Road, which is often impassable after rain. A high-clearance 4WD vehicle is strongly recommended.

Things to consider: Due to the fragile nature of the Wave, access is highly restricted, requiring a permit obtained through a competitive online and in-person lottery system. Visitors should be prepared for a rugged, exposed desert hike with no marked trails and limited shade. Bring plenty of water and navigation tools.

RECOMMENDED TRAILS:

Wire Pass to Buckskin Gulch: *5.6-mile (9km) round trip; about 400 feet (122m) elevation gain; easy*. A stunning slot canyon hike featuring towering sandstone walls and some of the longest, deepest slot canyons in the world.

The Wave Hike: *6.8-mile (10.9km) round trip; about 1,200 feet (366m) elevation gain; moderate*. A route-finding adventure across exposed slickrock, leading to the Wave's breathtaking swirls of red and gold sandstone.

The Wave and Beyond (Second Wave and Top Rock Arch): *8+ miles (13+km); variable elevation gain; strenuous*. A longer exploration past the Wave, featuring additional swirling rock formations, natural arches, and panoramic views of the Vermilion Cliffs.

Tips for taking a great photo

- Midmorning to early afternoon provides the best lighting inside the Wave, with deep shadows and vibrant rock colors.
- Use a wide-angle lens to capture the full scope of the Wave's mesmerizing curves and formations.
- After rain, small pools of water can form inside the Wave, creating incredible mirrorlike reflections.
- While midday light makes colors pop, it can create harsh shadows—try different angles for the best effect and to avoid midday glare.

Opposite: The Wave

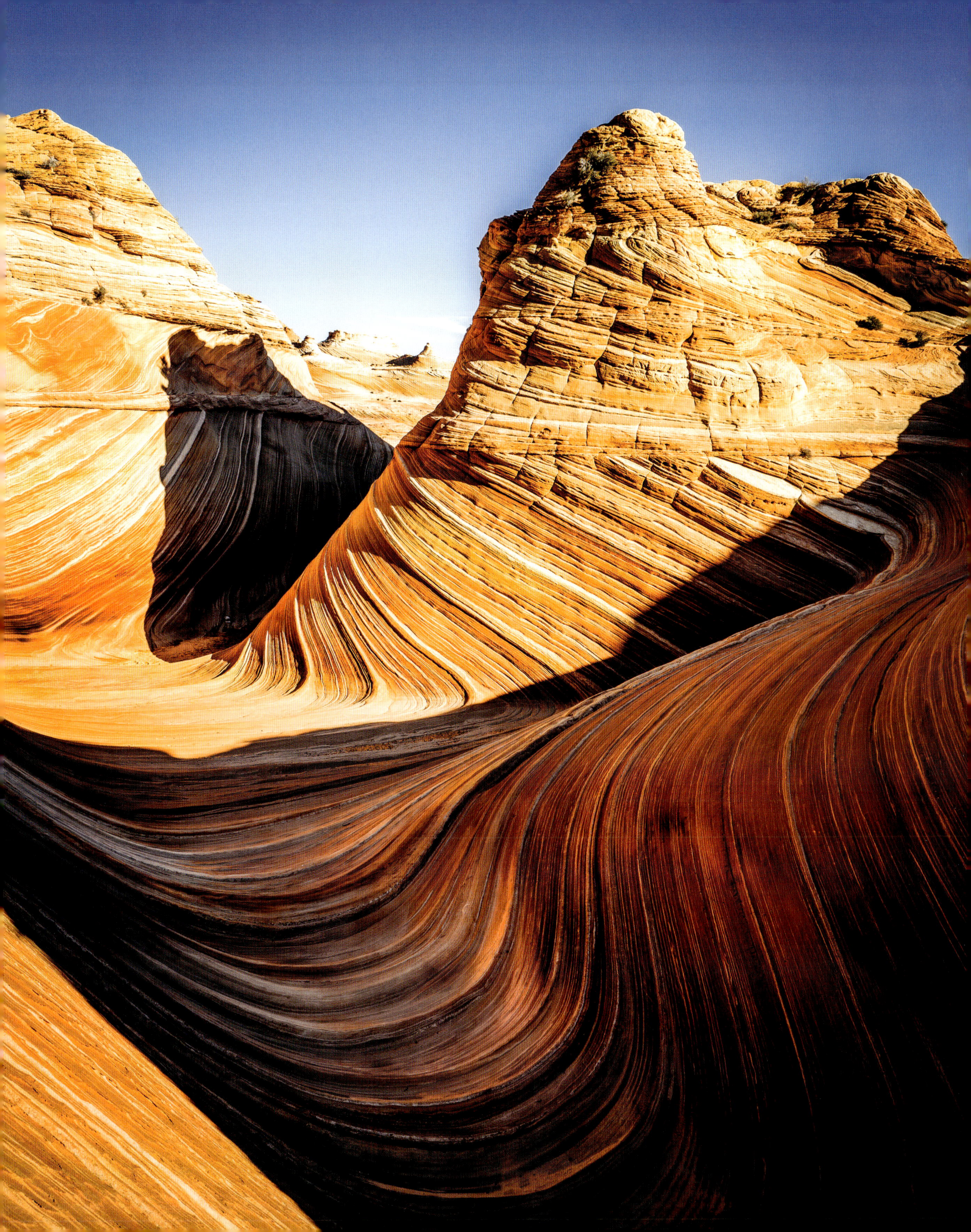

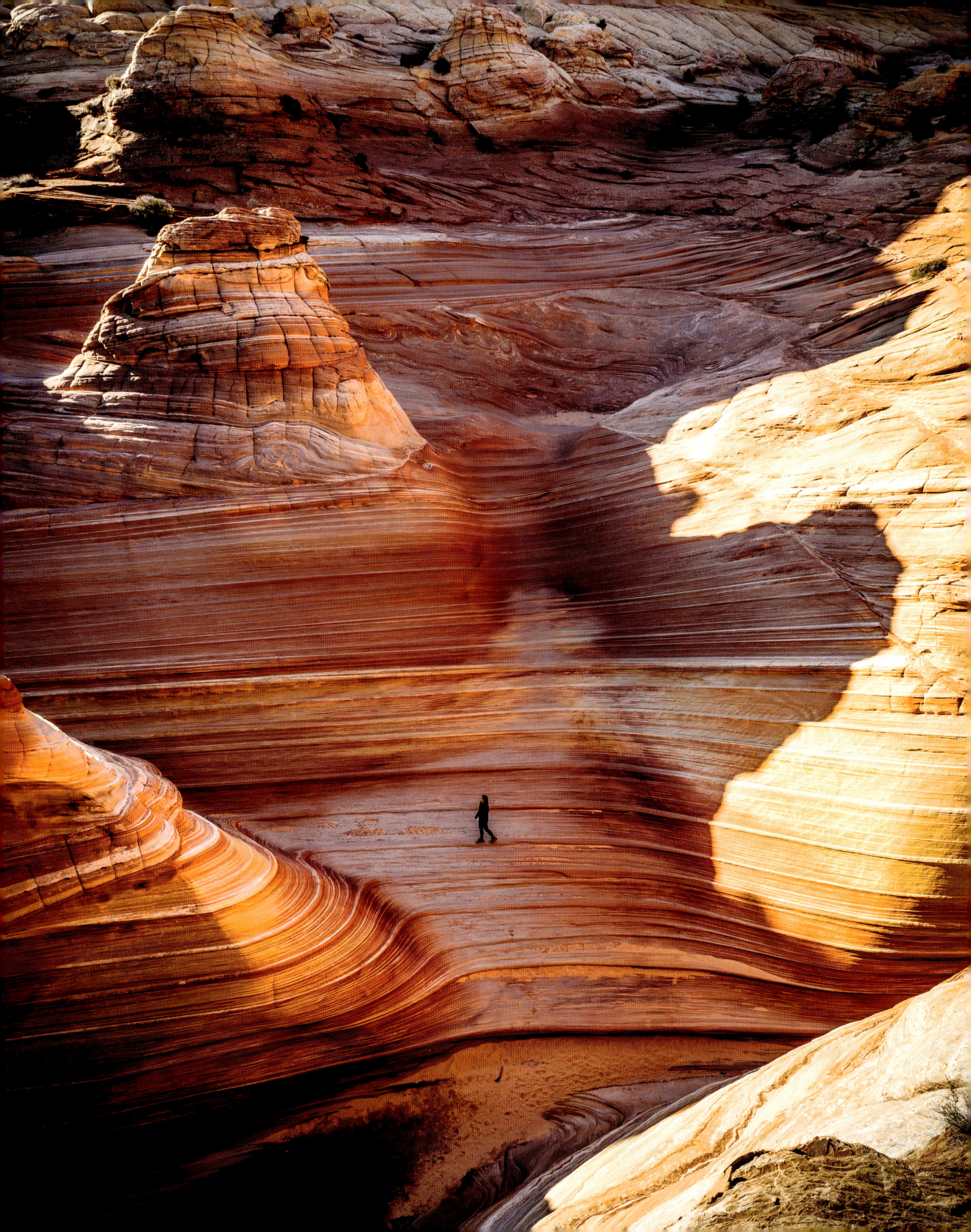

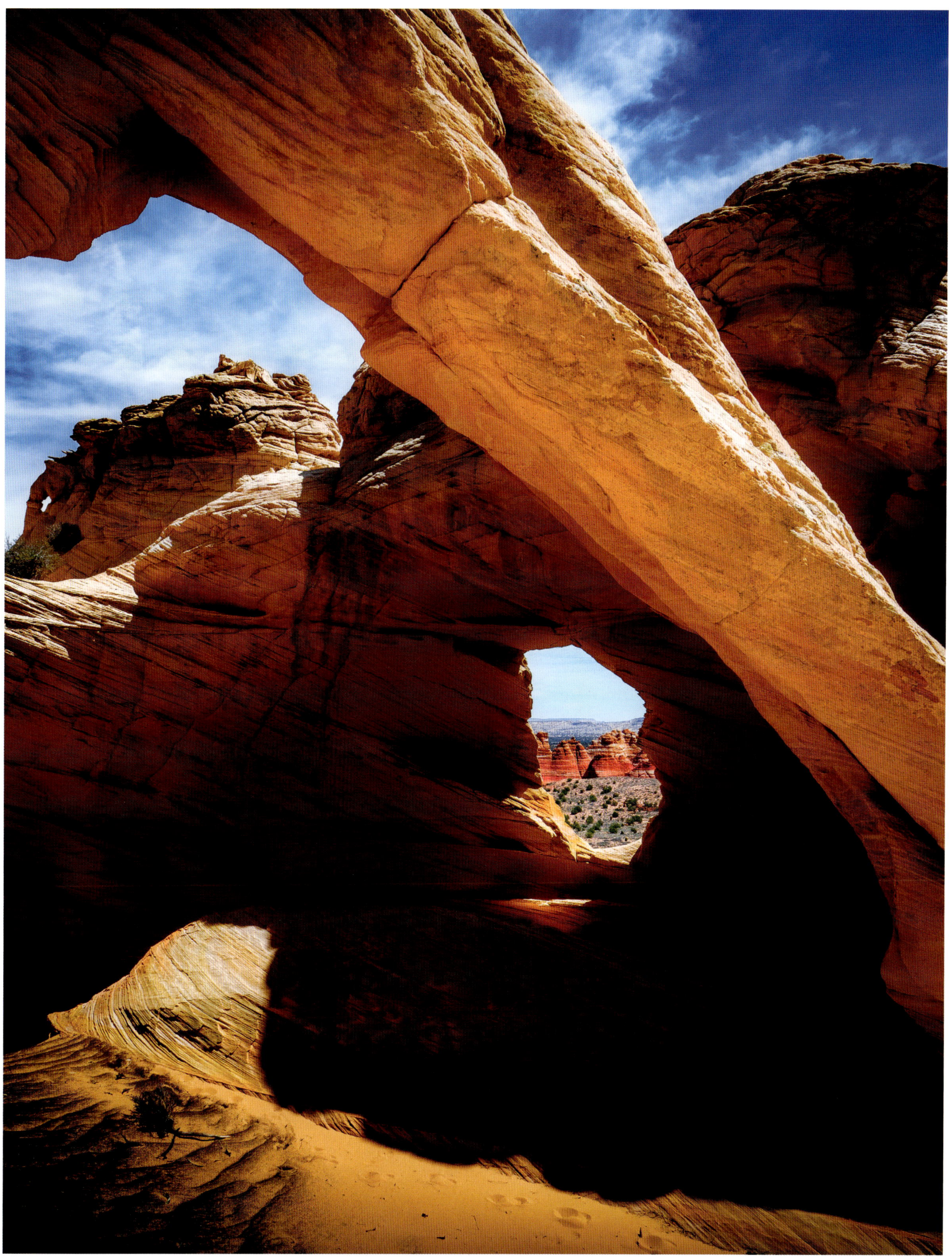

Above: Melody Arch | Opposite: The Wave

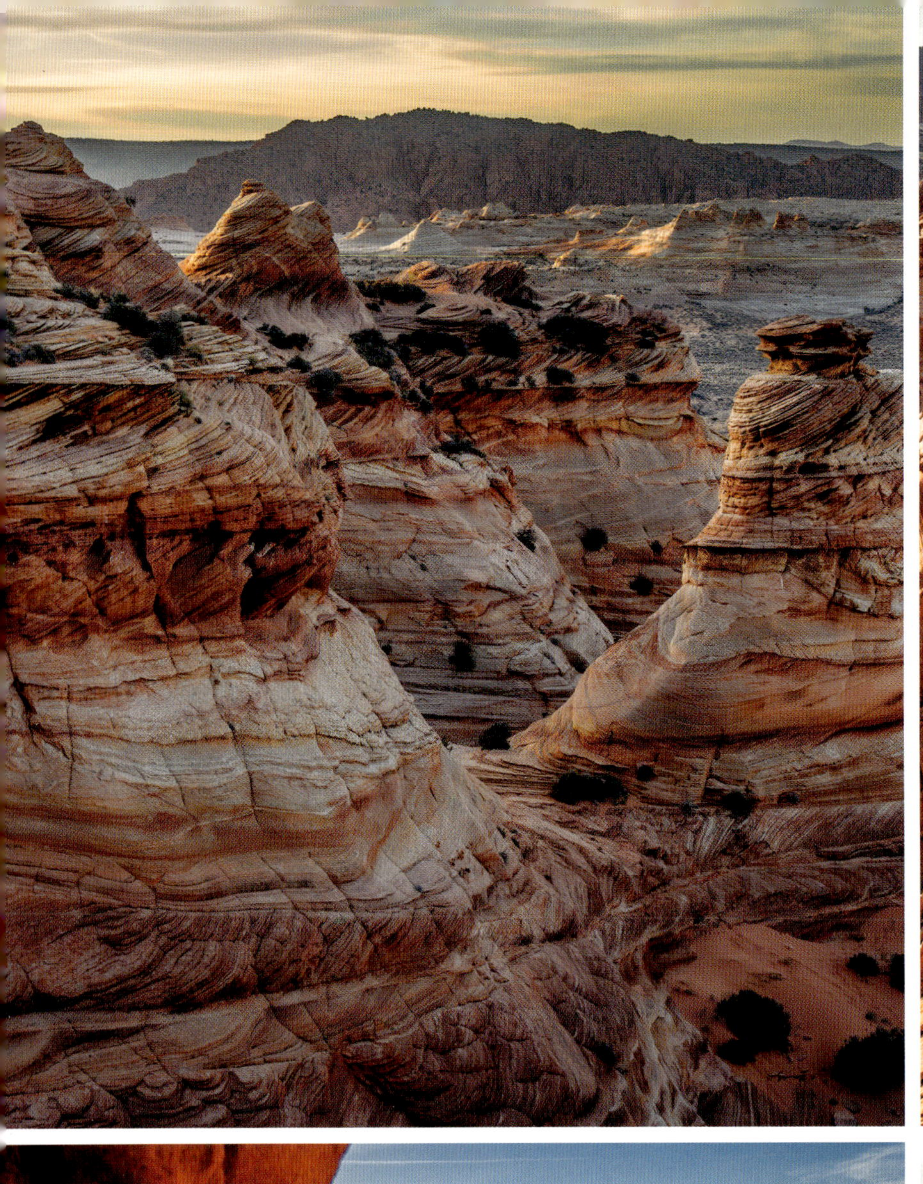
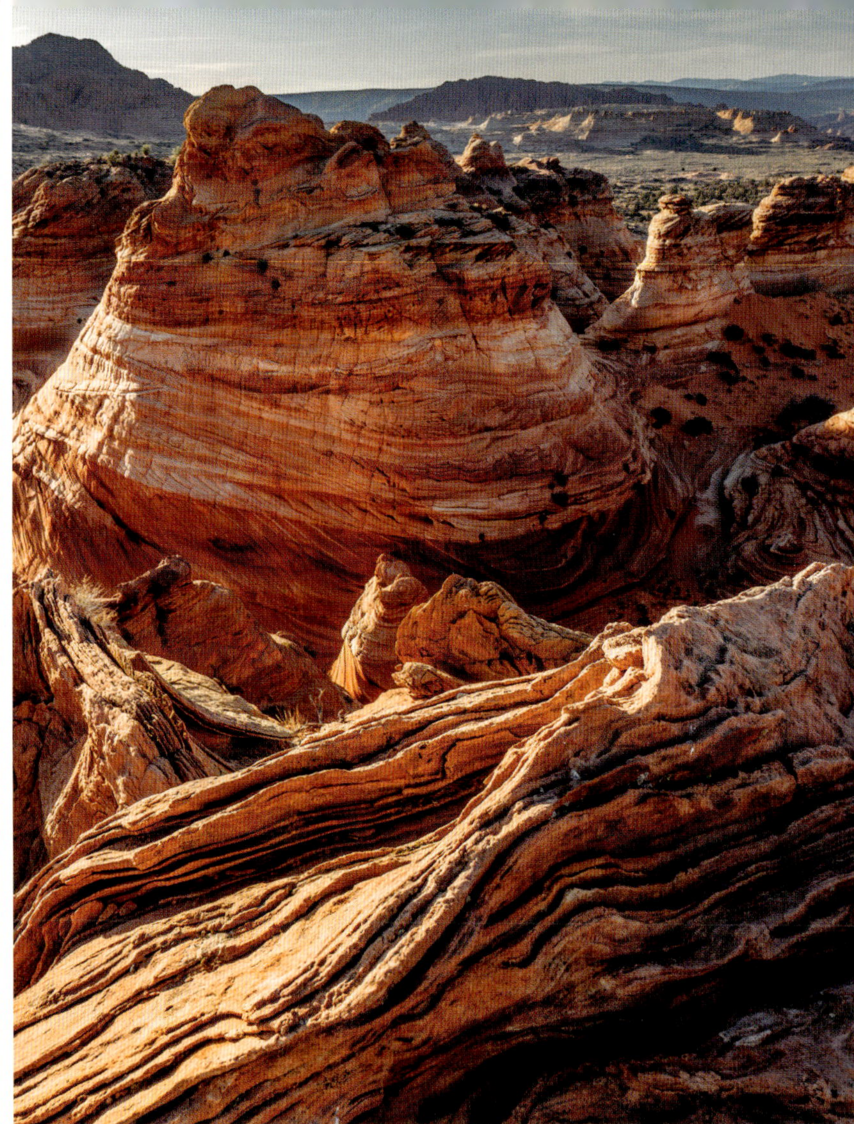
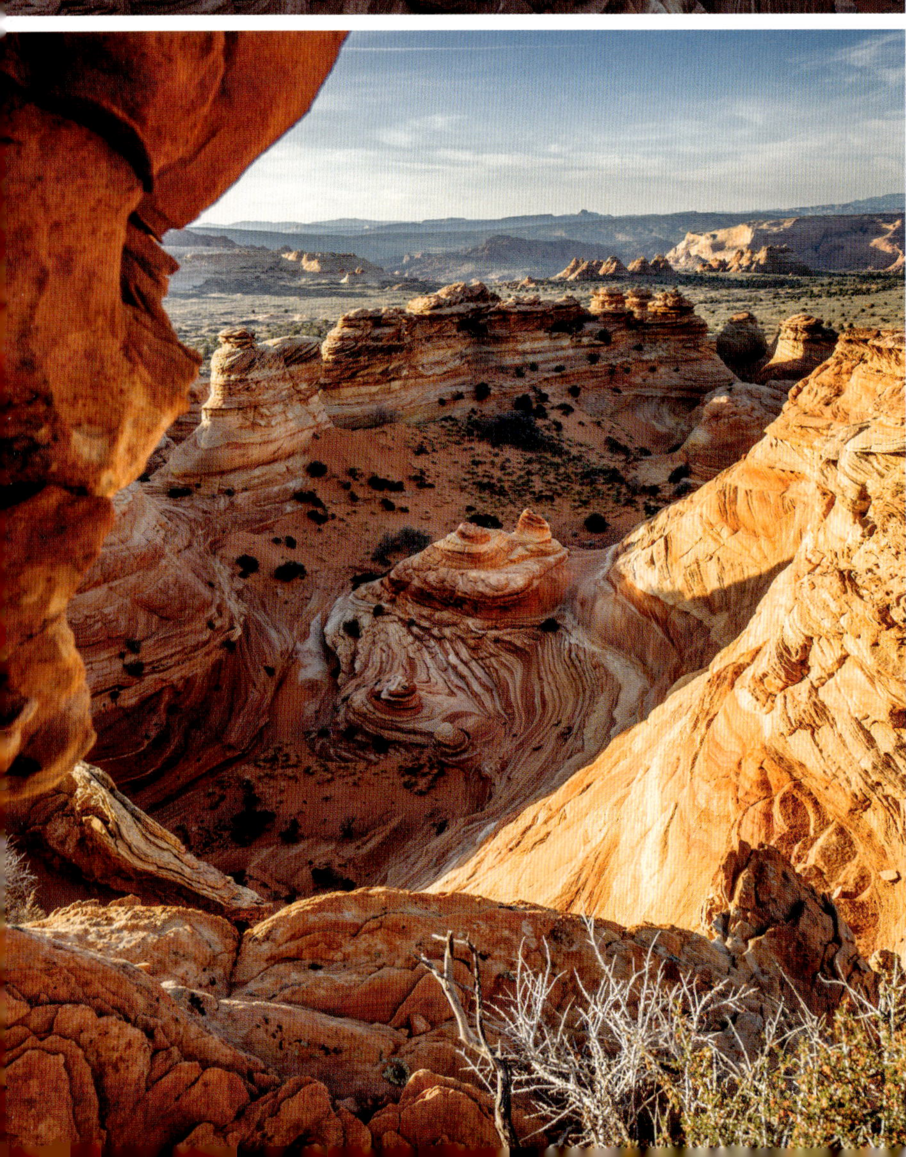
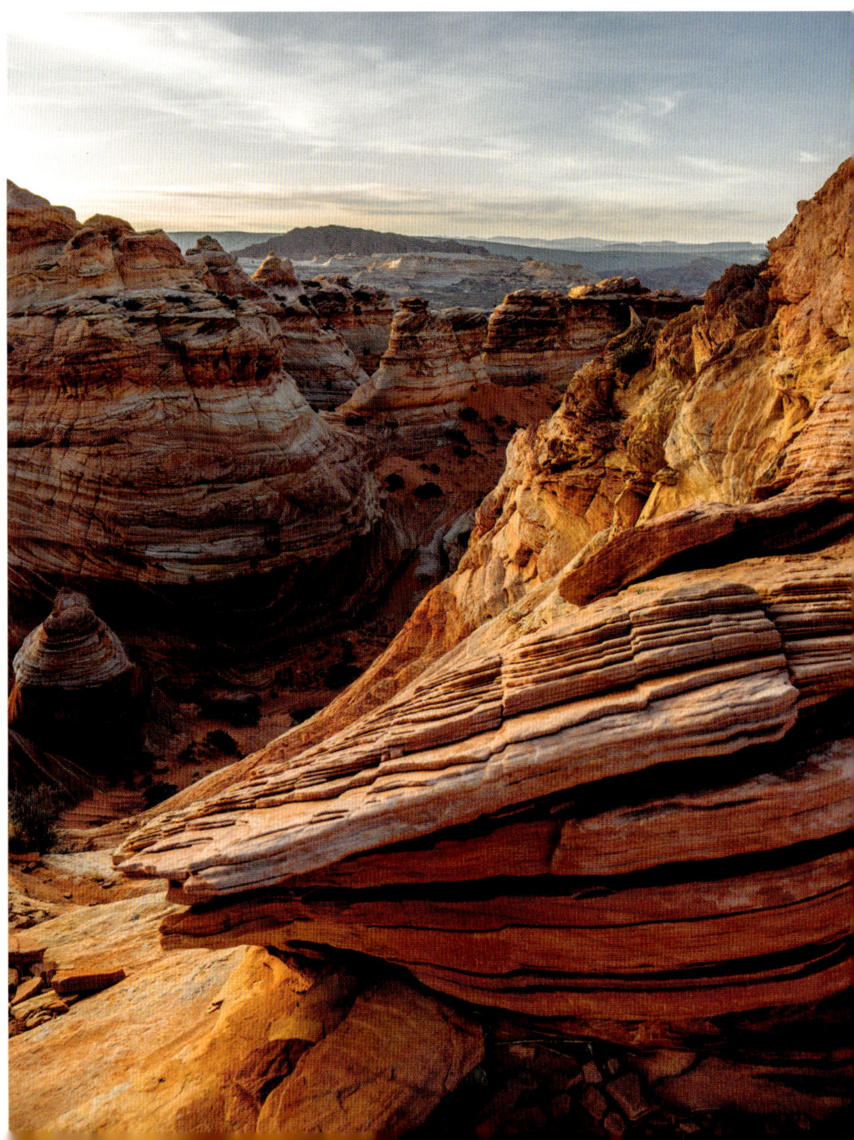

COYOTE BUTTES SOUTH

Coyote Buttes South is a lesser-known but equally stunning counterpart to the famous Wave in Coyote Buttes North. It features swirling sandstone formations, delicate hoodoos, and vibrant red, orange, and yellow rock layers. When you hike through Coyote Buttes South, you'll feel like you're stepping onto Mars. The colors in the sandstone seem alien, shifting in the light from deep reds to glowing oranges and yellows. The solitude makes it even more special. Unlike the crowds at the Wave, here, I had the entire landscape to myself.

Region: Southwest

State: Arizona

Coordinates: 36°57'34.9"N 112°00'08.6"W

Focal feature: Striking sandstone formations and colorful rock layers of Vermilion Cliffs National Monument

Formation attributes: Layers of Navajo Sandstone sculpted over millions of years by wind and water erosion, creating wavelike patterns, balanced rock formations, and delicate striations.

Fun fact: Coyote Buttes South is home to the stunning Cottonwood Cove area, where delicate rock formations and pastel swirls create a dreamlike landscape.

Best time to visit: March to May and September to November offer the best temperatures. Summer can be dangerously hot, and winter may bring unpredictable weather and impassable roads.

How to access: Access is via House Rock Valley Road, which is often impassable after rain.

Things to consider: A permit is required to visit Coyote Buttes South, and only a limited number are issued per day through a lottery system. Because of its remote location, a high-clearance 4WD vehicle is required, and visitors should be prepared for extreme desert conditions and carry plenty of water, as there are no services in the area.

RECOMMENDED TRAILS:

Cottonwood Cove Exploration: *Variable distance; minimal elevation gain; easy.* Wander through a wonderland of sculpted rock formations, colorful swirls, and delicate fins—perfect for photographers and those looking to explore at their own pace.

Paw Hole Trail: *1–2-mile (1.6–3.2km) round trip; about 200 feet (61m) elevation gain; moderate.* A short but sandy hike through dramatic red and orange sandstone formations, offering sweeping desert views.

Coyote Buttes South (from Cottonwood Teepees Trailhead): *3–5-mile (5–8km) loop; variable elevation gain; strenuous.* An off-trail adventure through rolling sandstone, featuring some of the most unique rock formations in the region.

Tips for taking a great photo

- Early morning or late afternoon provides the best lighting to enhance the deep reds and swirling rock patterns.
- The wavelike rock formations create natural curves that can make for striking compositions.
- Use side lighting to highlight the intricate sandstone layers and details.
- Use a wide-angle lens to help capture the expansive, otherworldly landscape.

Opposite: Cottonwood Cove, Coyote Buttes South

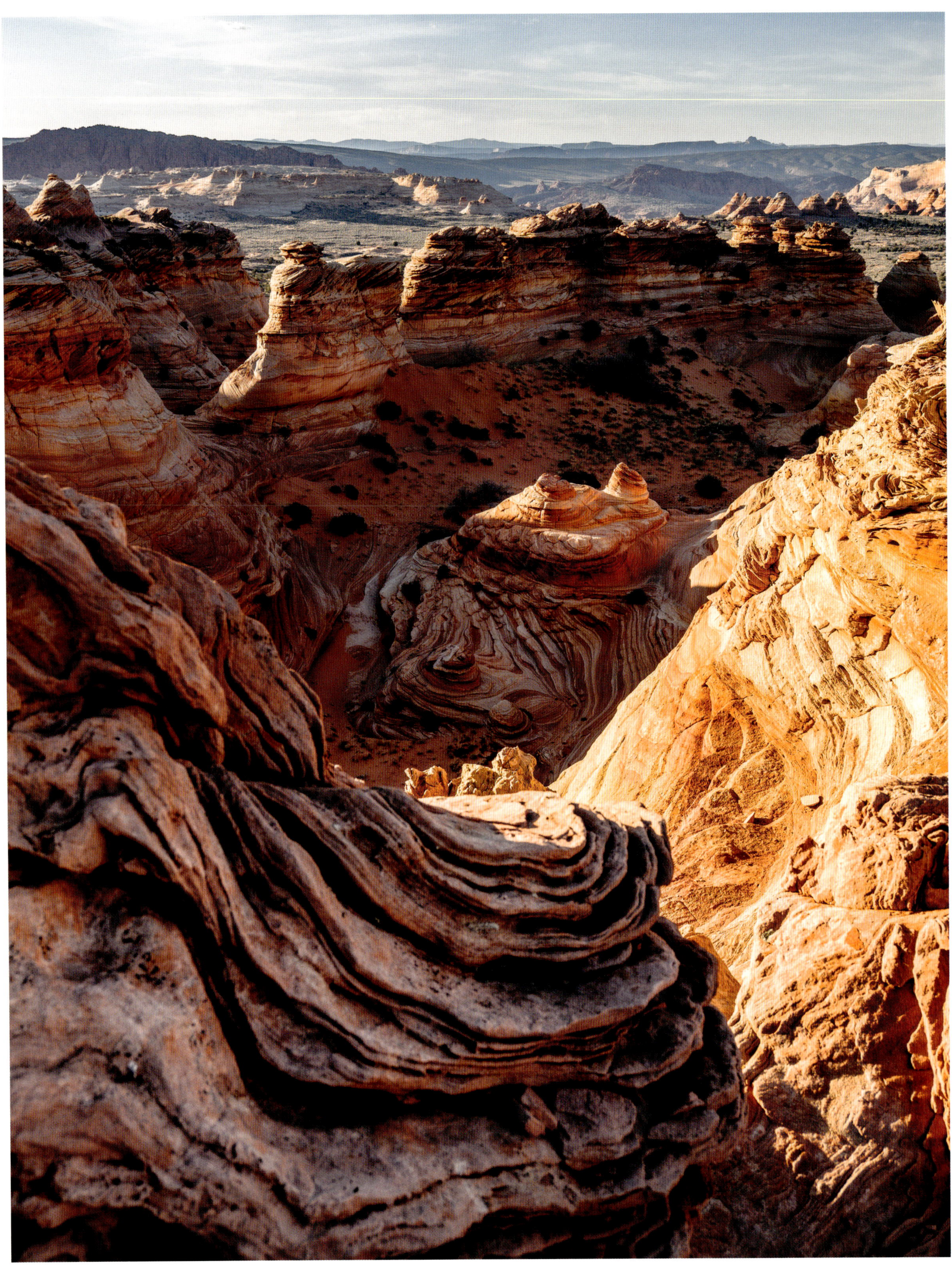

Above and opposite: Cottonwood Cove, Coyote Buttes South

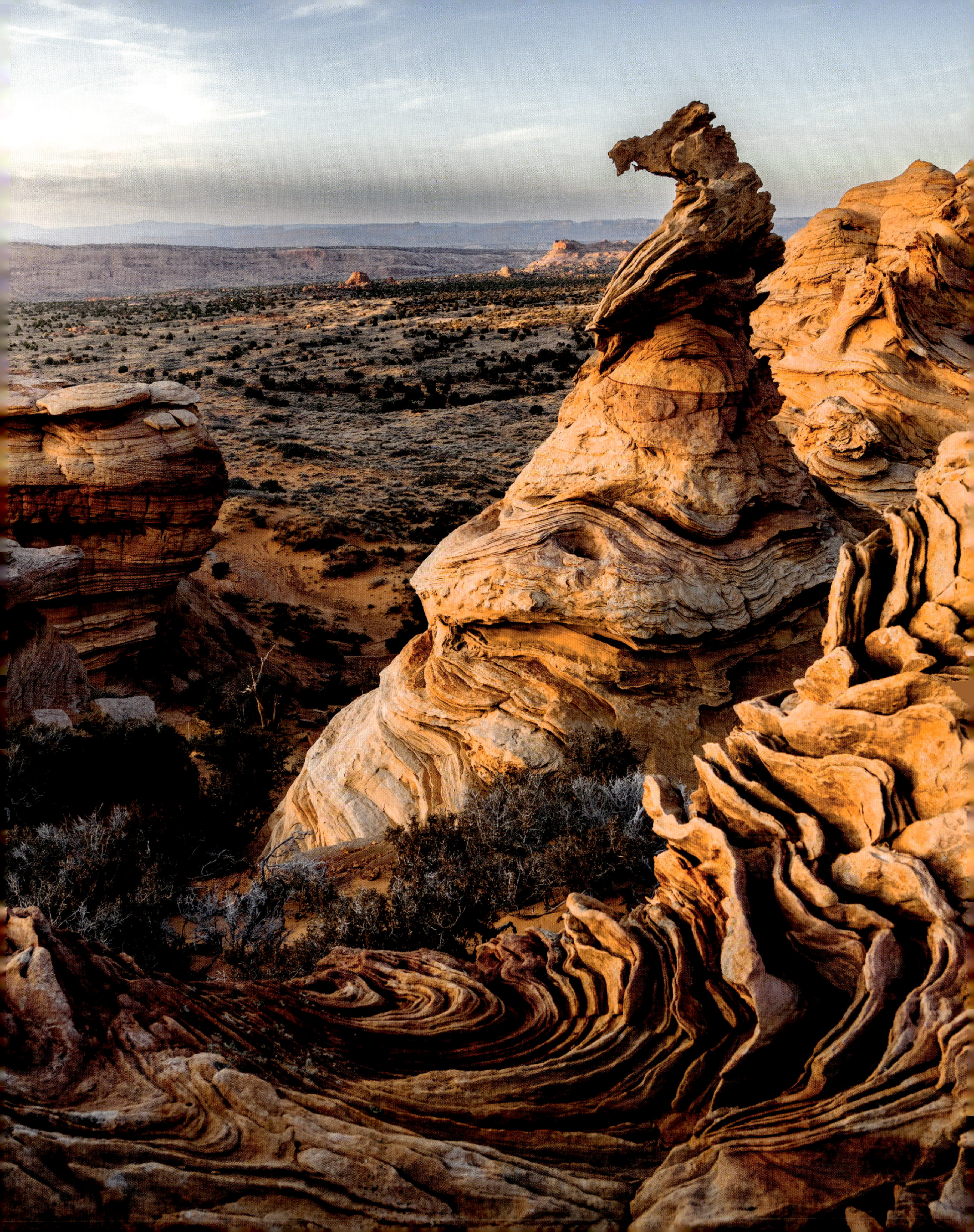

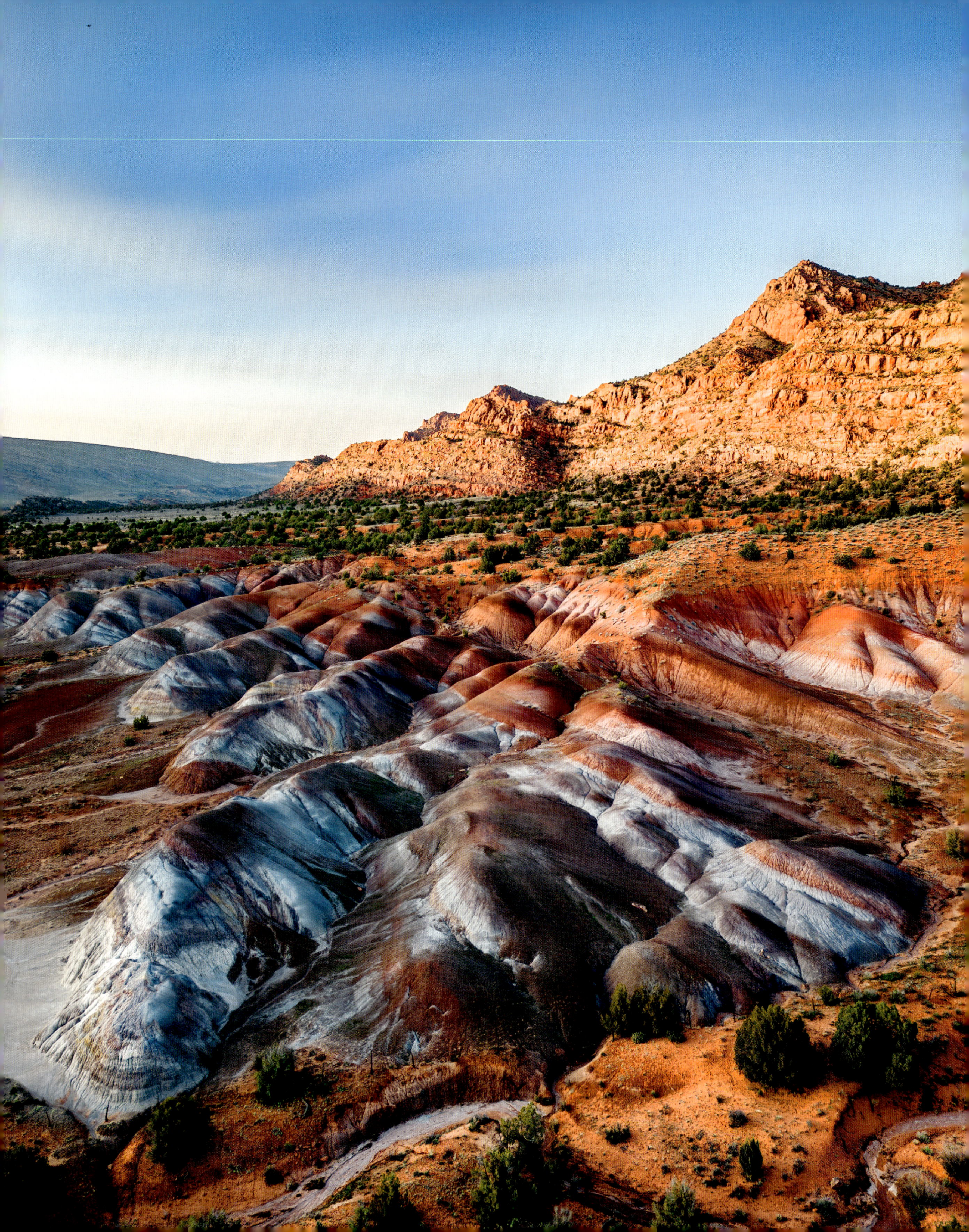

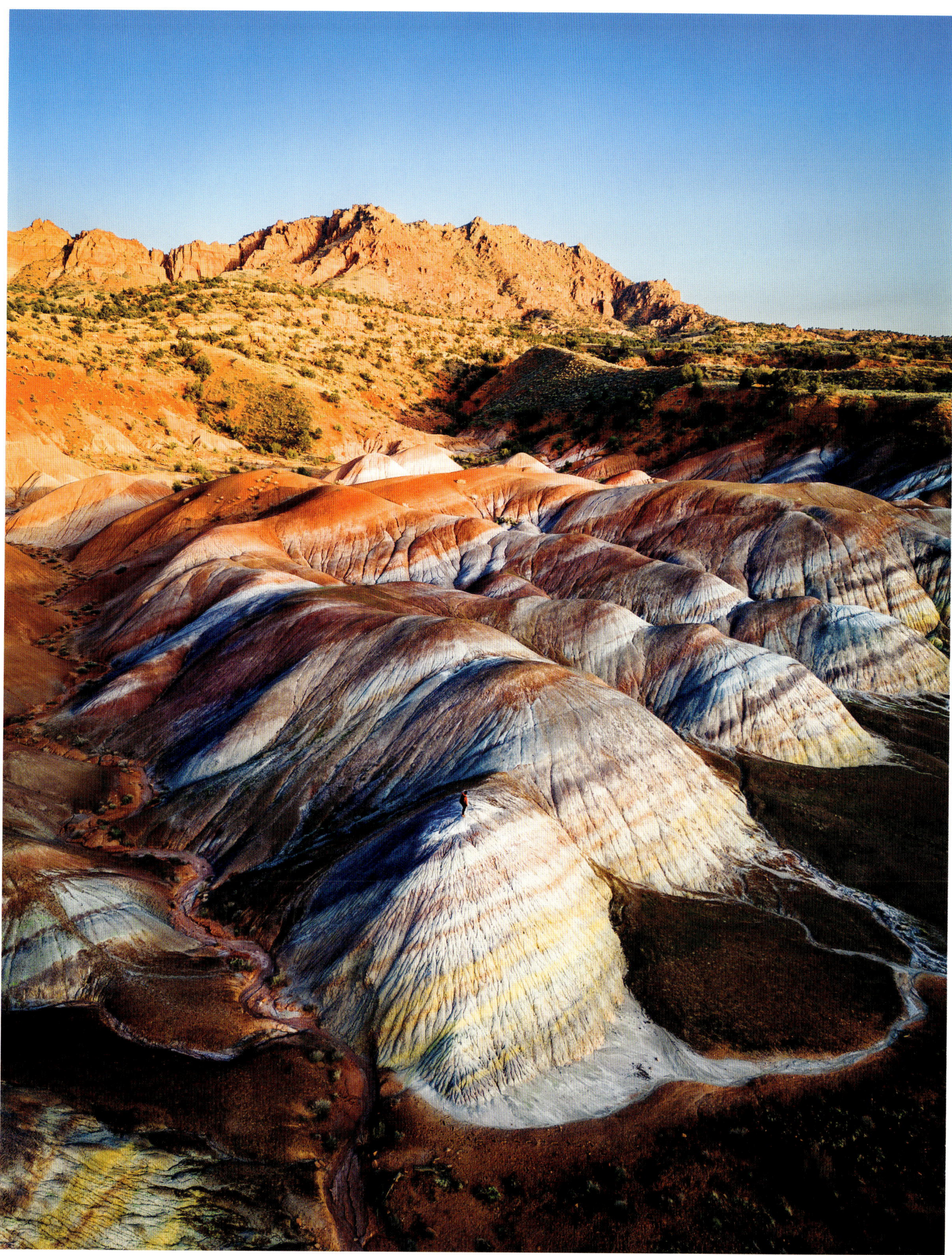

Above and opposite: Rainbow Valley

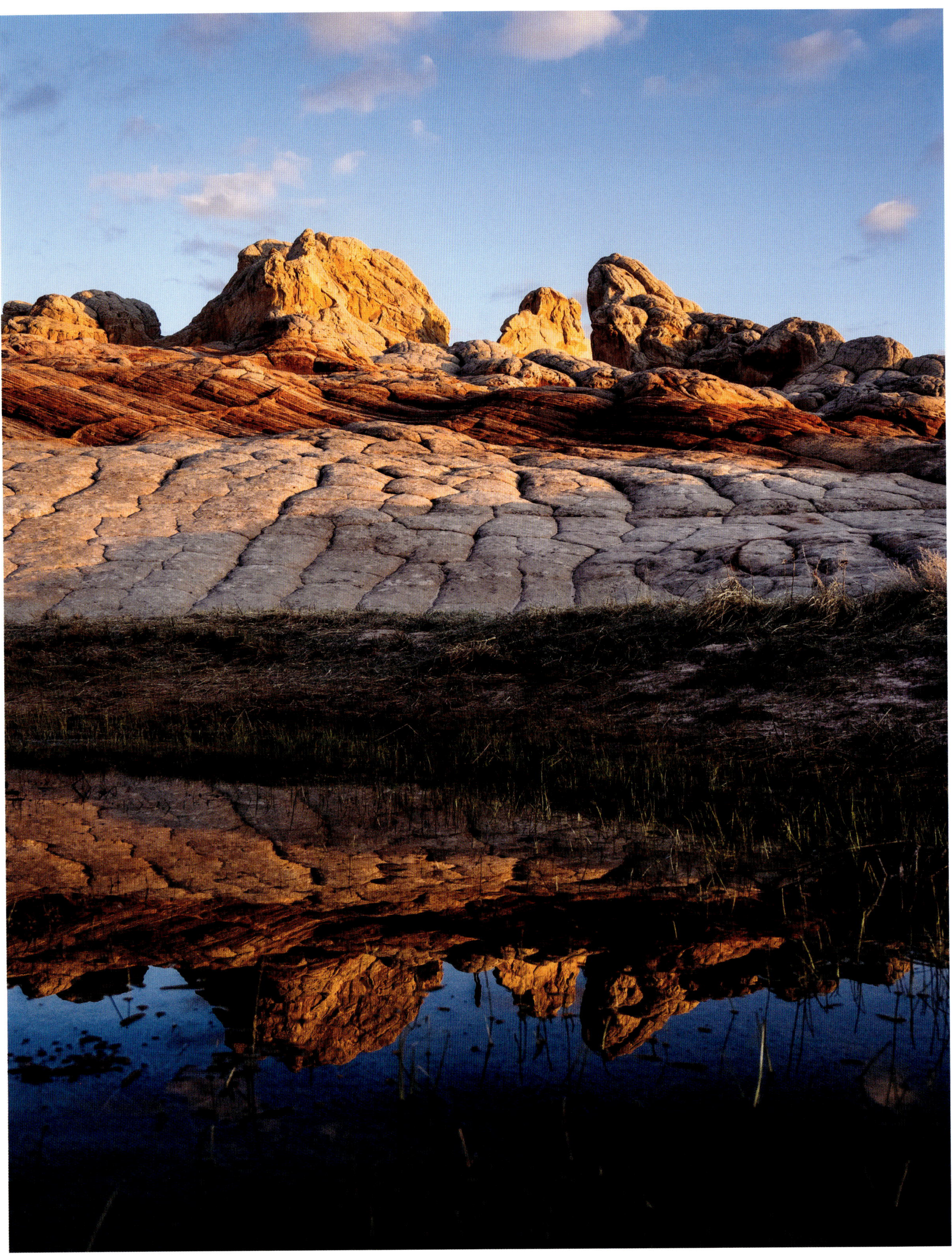

Above and opposite: White Pocket, Vermilion Cliffs National Monument

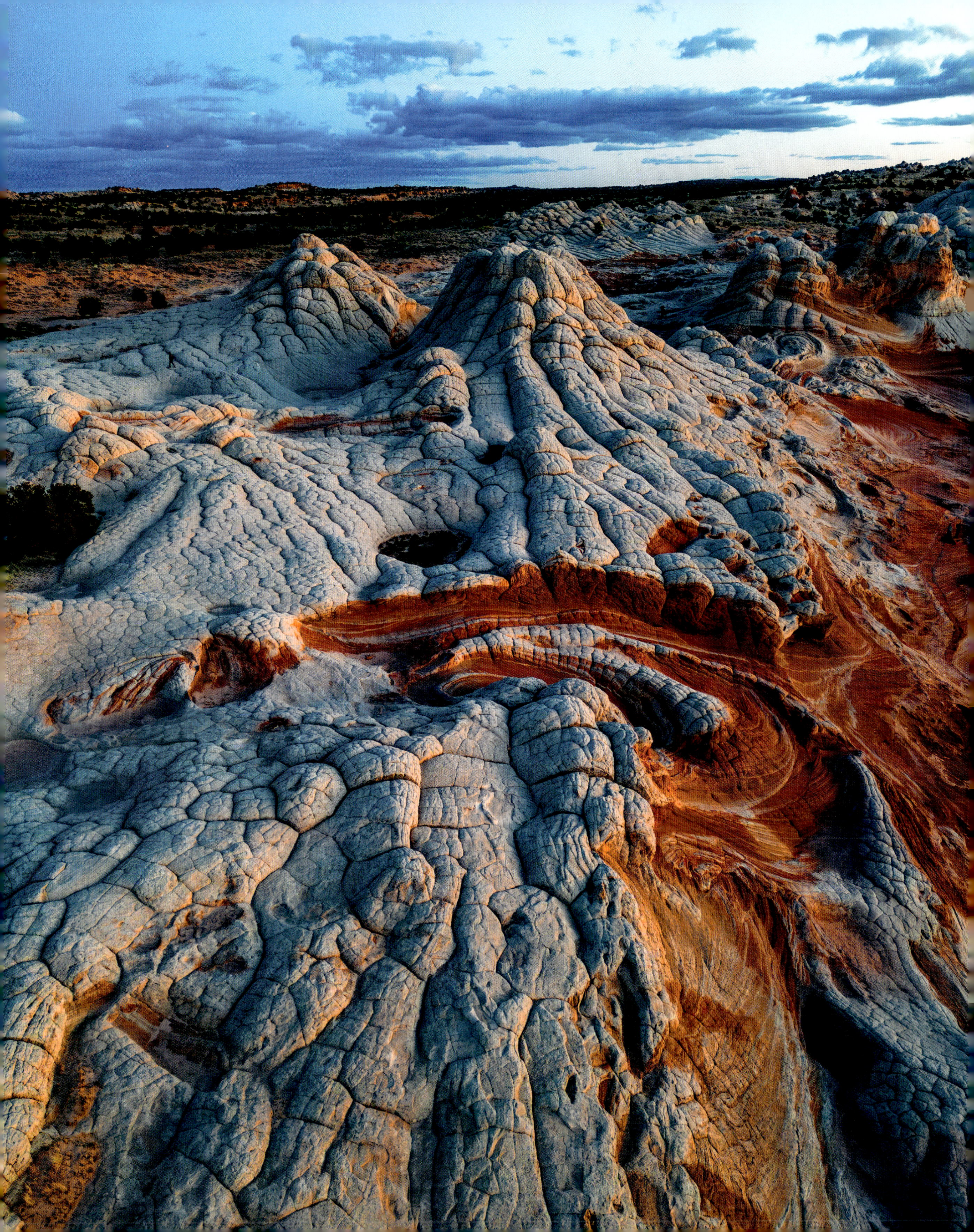

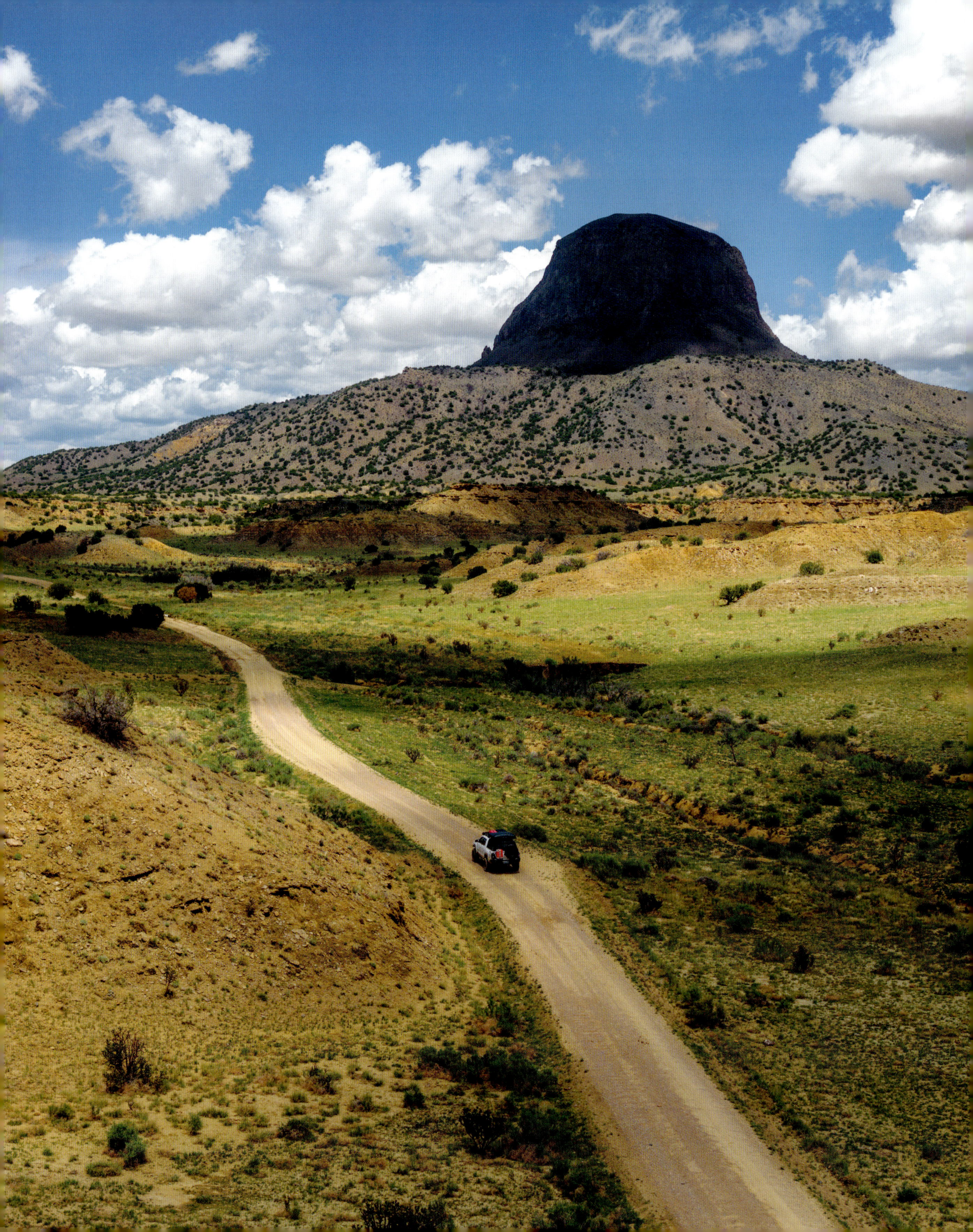

NEW MEXICO

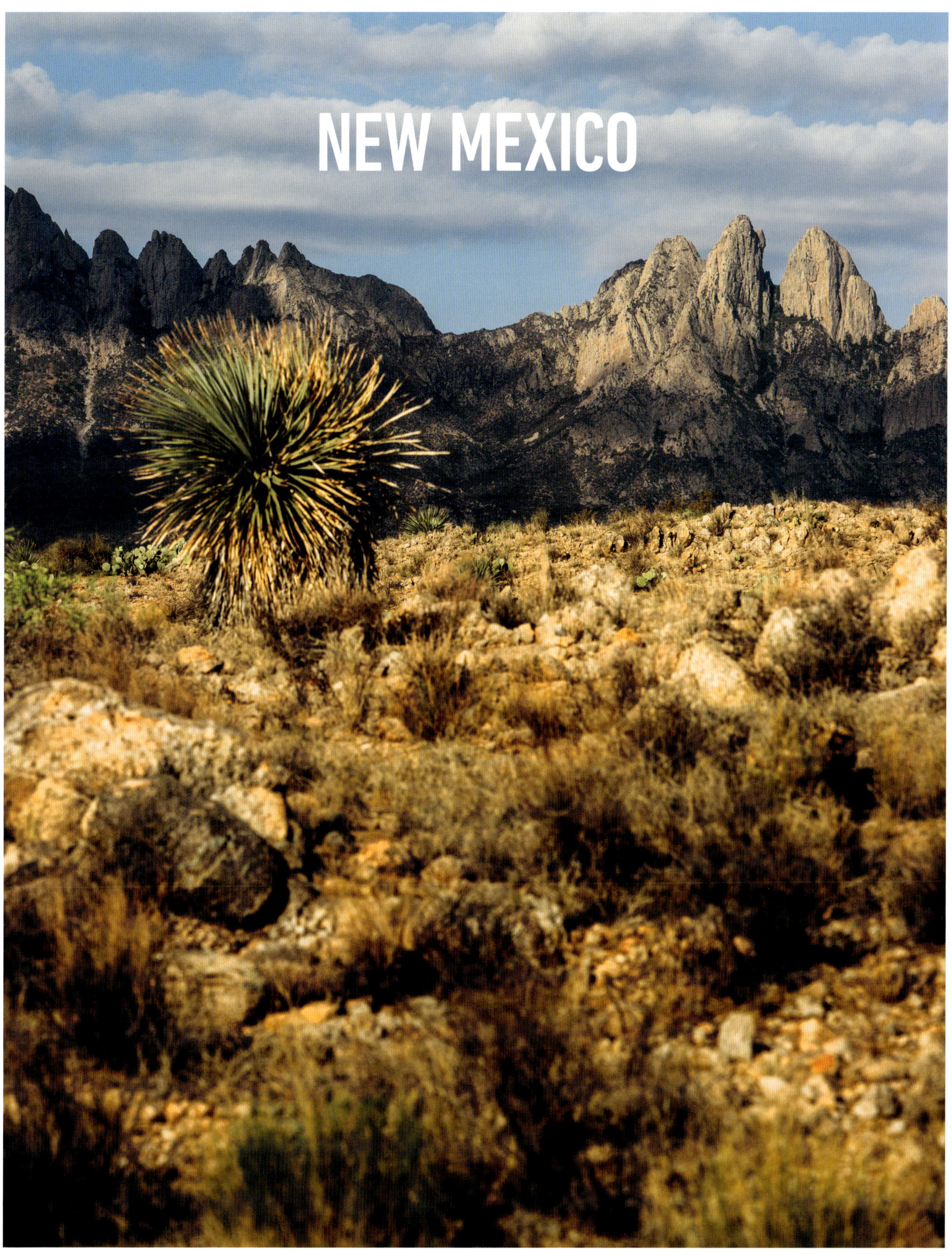

SHIP ROCK

Ship Rock is a sacred site to the Navajo Nation, known as "Tsé Bit'a'í," meaning "Rock with Wings." The towering monolith rises dramatically from the desert landscape, a striking remnant of an ancient volcanic eruption.

Region: Southwest

State: New Mexico

Coordinates: 36°40'57.0"N 108°50'24.0"W

Focal feature: A towering volcanic rock formation that dominates the surrounding desert

Formation attributes: Ship Rock stands at about 7,177 feet (2,188m) above sea level, rising roughly 1,583 feet (483m) above the surrounding desert floor. It is the remains of a volcanic throat, with long volcanic dikes extending outward.

Fun fact: Ship Rock is featured in Navajo legends as the remnants of a great bird that carried the Navajo people to safety. The formation has also been used in numerous movies, TV shows, and photographs due to its dramatic and isolated appearance.

Best time to visit: Spring and fall offer the best weather, with cooler temperatures and clear skies. Summer can be extremely hot, and winter may bring snow that adds a unique contrast to the dark volcanic rock.

How to access: Ship Rock is located in the northwestern corner of New Mexico, about 13 miles (21km) southwest of the town of Shiprock. The best views are from Indian Service Route 13 and Highway 491. Since the site is on Navajo Nation land, be respectful and avoid driving off-road or trespassing.

Things to consider: This area is off-limits to climbing or hiking due to its cultural significance, but visitors can view it from surrounding roads and nearby areas.

Page 214: Cabezon Peak

Page 215: Organ Mountains

Opposite: Ship Rock

RECOMMENDED ACTIVITIES:

There are no official trails, as hiking is not permitted on or around Ship Rock. The best way to experience it is from a distance, capturing its dramatic shape from different vantage points along the roads.

Tips for taking a great photo

- Sunrise and sunset create incredible lighting, with long shadows and vibrant desert colors.
- Use the surrounding desert and distant mountains to create a sense of scale.
- A backdrop of dark clouds or a lightning strike can make for an unforgettable shot.
- Ship Rock is an excellent location for astrophotography, with minimal light pollution allowing for stunning Milky Way shots.

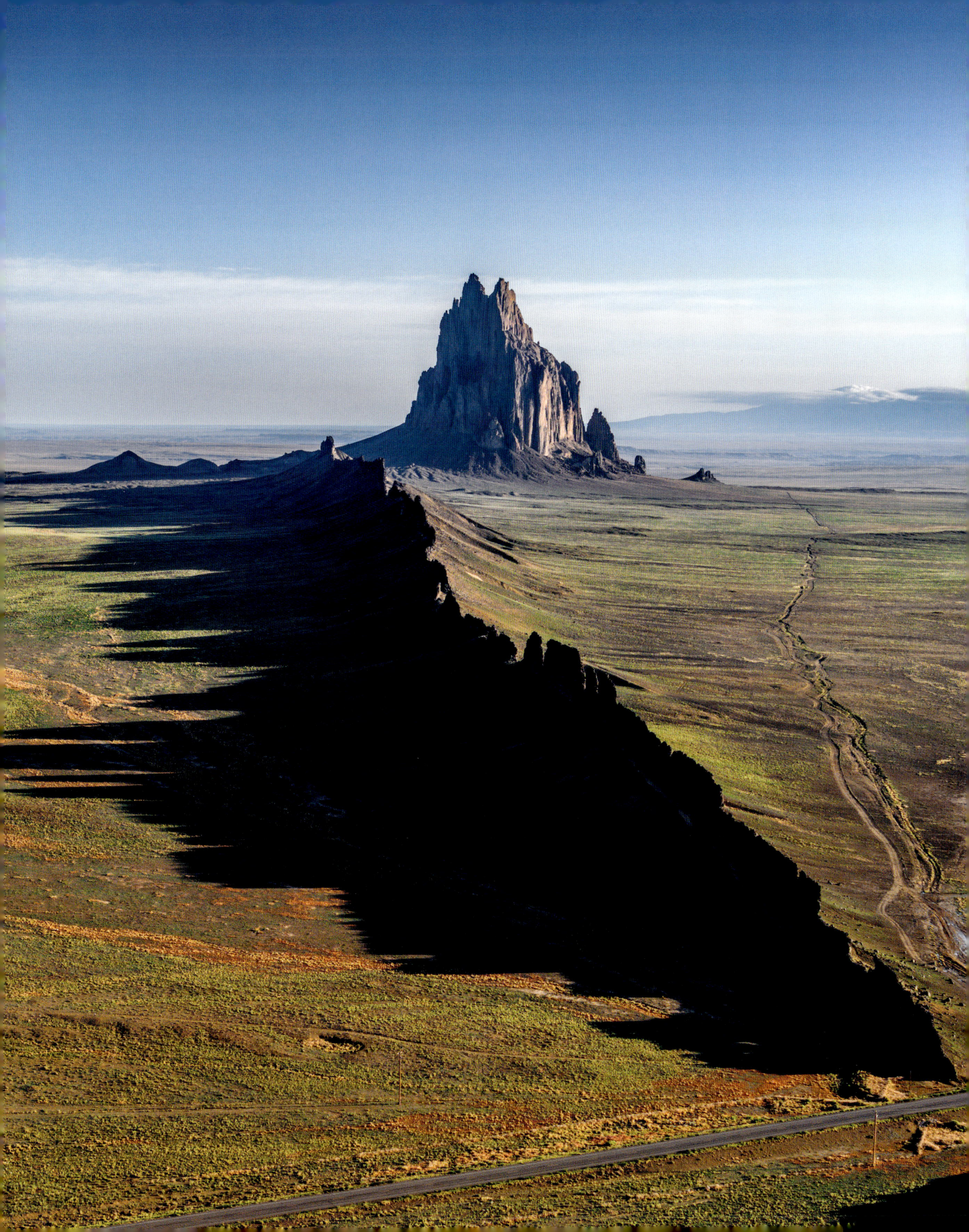

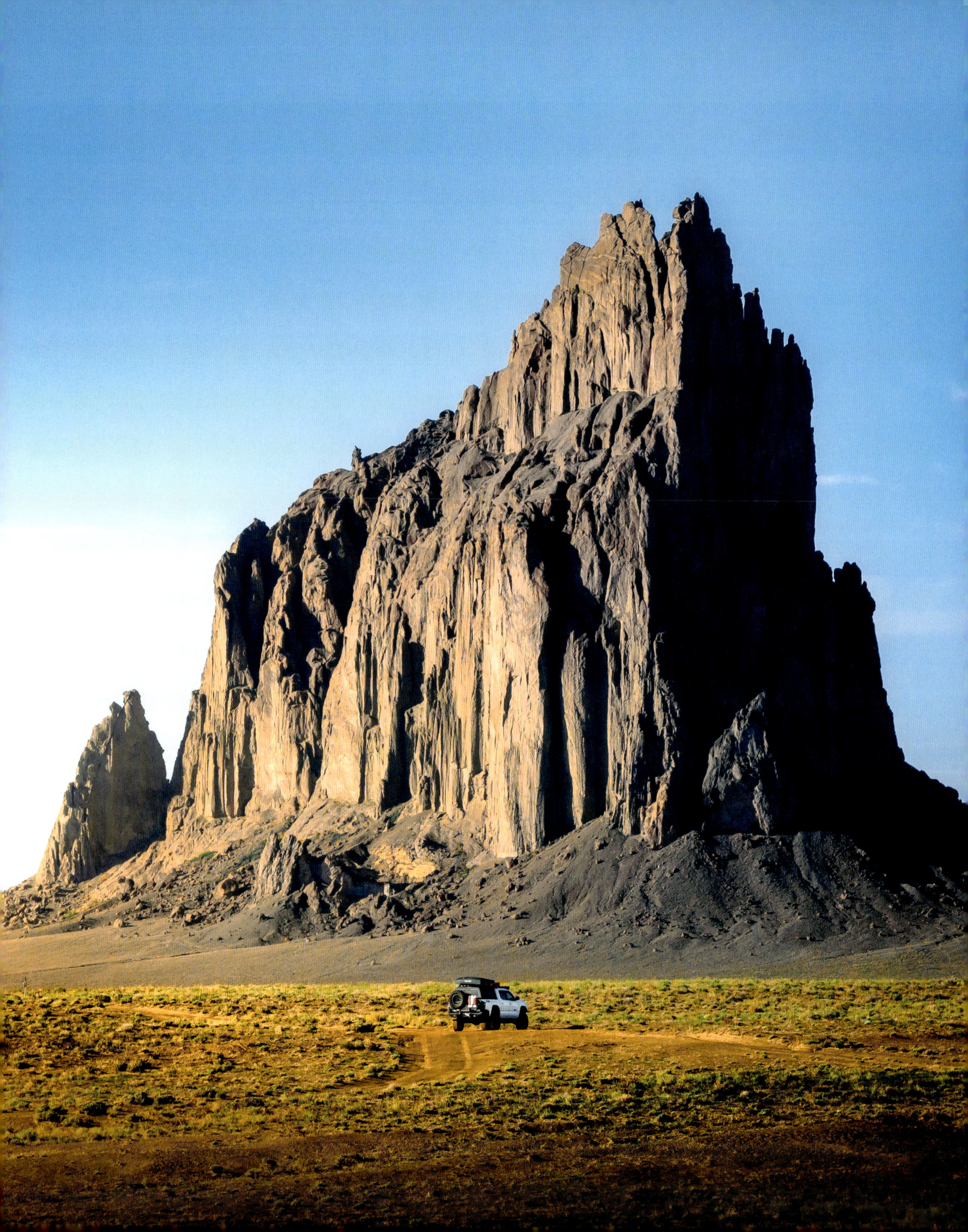

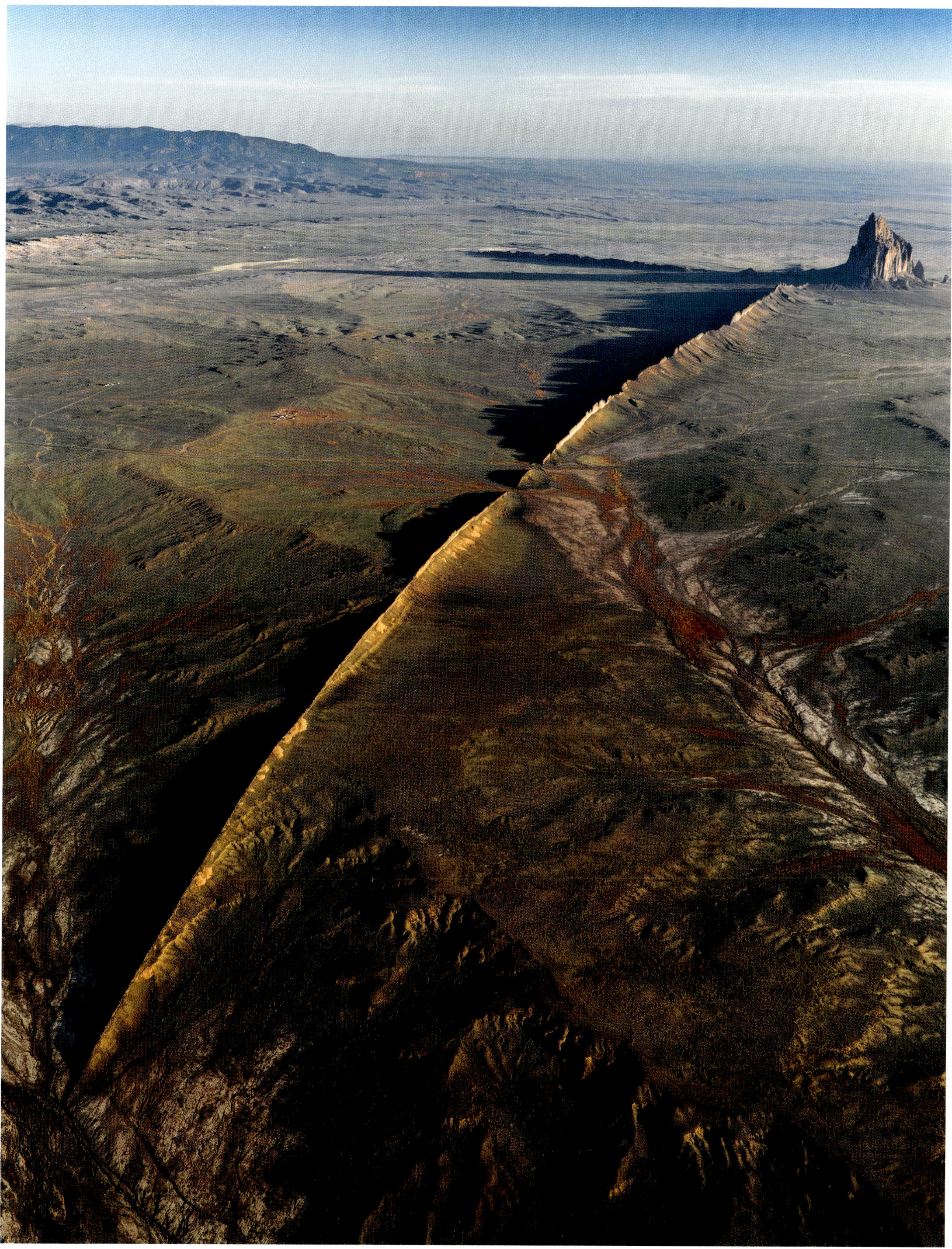

Above and opposite: Ship Rock

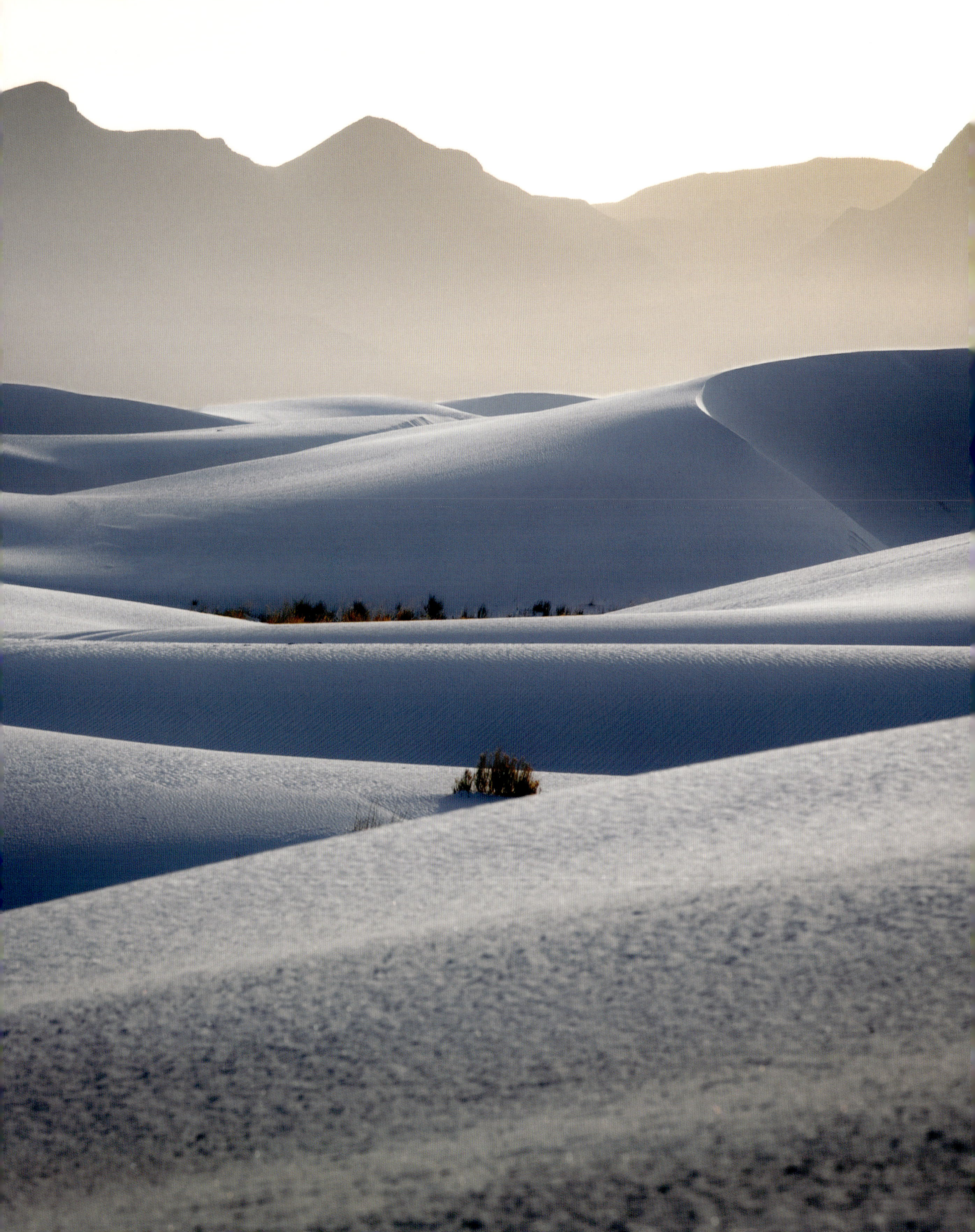

WHITE SANDS NATIONAL PARK

White Sands is home to the largest gypsum dune field in the world, covering 275 square miles (712km²) of stunning, otherworldly terrain. The bright white dunes create a surreal landscape that shifts and changes with the wind. Running up the soft, cool dunes at White Sands feels like playing in fresh snow—except it never melts! When I visited, I grabbed a sled and flew down a steep slope, laughing as fine gypsum dust trailed behind me like powder. Later, as the sun dipped lower, the dunes turned golden. Sitting atop one of the tallest dunes, I watched the sky shift through shades of pink and purple, the landscape stretching endlessly in every direction. Just me, the sand, and the sky.

Region: Southwest

State: New Mexico

Coordinates: 32°46'44.8"N 106°10'18.8"W

Focal feature: The vast expanse of white gypsum dunes

Formation attributes: The dunes are composed of gypsum, a mineral that dissolves in water but remains here due to the Tularosa Basin's unique lack of drainage, allowing the mineral to build up over time. The ever-shifting dunes can move up to 30 feet (9m) per year.

Fun fact: White Sands is so bright that it can be seen from space! It's one of the few places in the world where you can go sand sledding down gypsum dunes, and the sand stays cool to the touch, even on hot days, making it a unique place to explore barefoot.

Best time to visit: October to April, when temperatures are mild. Sunsets and full moon nights offer especially magical views.

How to access: The park is located off US Highway 70, about 15 miles (24km) southwest of Alamogordo, New Mexico. The main road, Dunes Drive, takes visitors into the heart of the park.

Things to consider: Be prepared for intense sun exposure, as there is little shade, and bring plenty of water, as there is none available beyond the visitor center. The park closes occasionally due to nearby missile testing at White Sands Missile Range—check the schedule in advance.

RECOMMENDED TRAILS:

Interdune Boardwalk: *0.4-mile (0.6km) round trip; minimal elevation gain; easy.* A short, accessible walk with interpretive signs explaining the unique desert ecosystem.

Dune Life Nature Trail: *1-mile (1.6km) loop; minimal elevation gain; moderate.* A marked trail that takes you through the rolling dunes, offering glimpses of hardy desert plants and wildlife.

Alkali Flat Trail: *5-mile (8km) round trip; minimal elevation gain; strenuous.* A challenging trek over the untouched dunes, with no shade or marked trails across a seemingly endless sea of white sand.

Tips for taking a great photo

- Sunrise and sunset cast long shadows that add depth and texture to the dunes, while midday light creates a bright, almost blinding effect.
- Use the curves and ripples of the sand to create striking, simple images with minimalist compositions.
- A deep blue sky or dramatic clouds provide a stunning contrast against the white sand.
- Try shooting untouched dunes for a pristine look or include footprints to add a sense of scale.

Opposite and pages 222–223: White Sands National Park

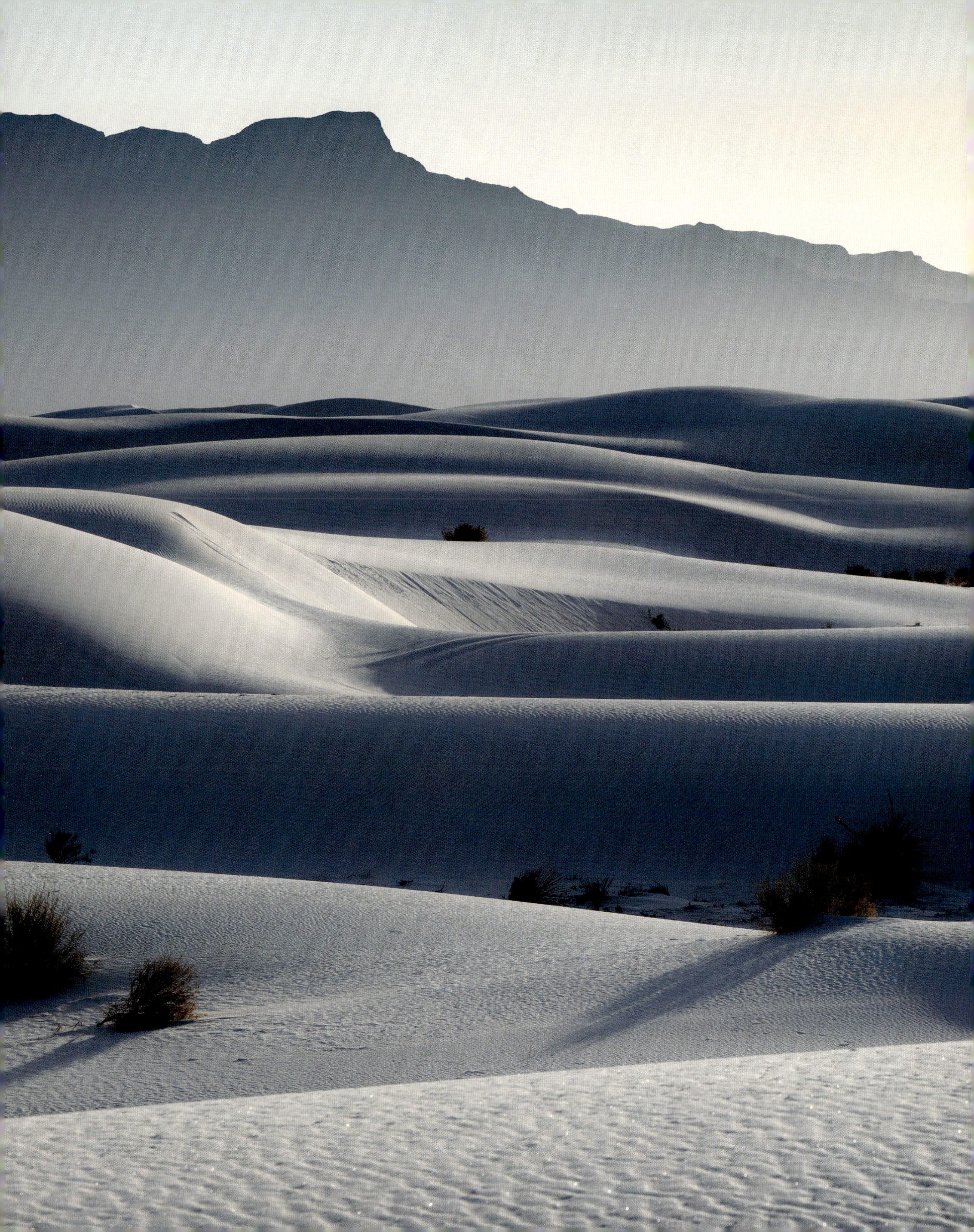

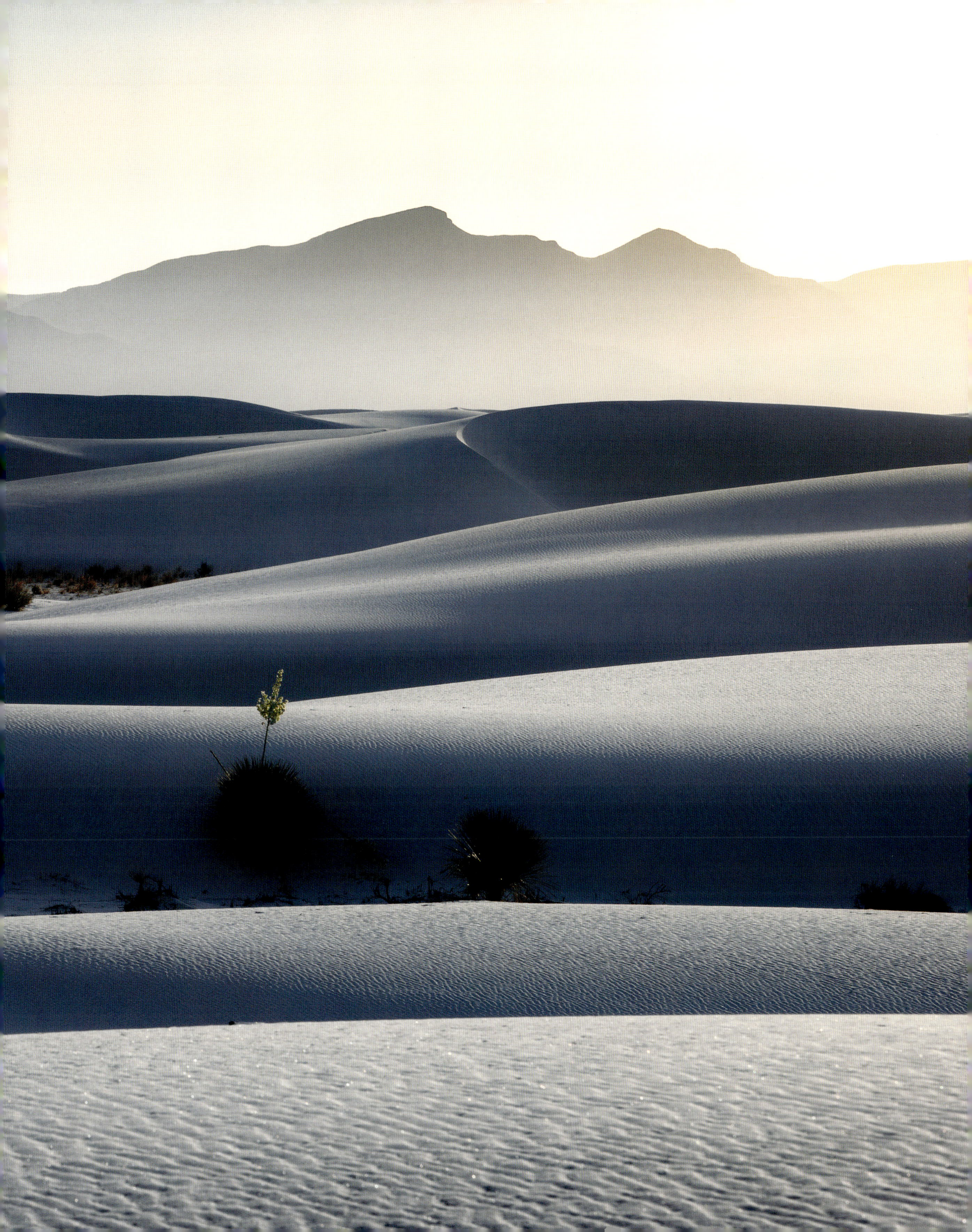

POTRILLO MOUNTAINS

A remote and rugged range in southern New Mexico, the Potrillo Mountains are less well-known but offer dramatic desert scenery, fascinating geological formations, and a sense of true solitude.

Region: Southwest

State: New Mexico

Coordinates: 31°56'24.6"N 107°11'01.9"W

Focal feature: A small but striking mountain range in the Chihuahuan Desert, surrounded by vast open landscapes

Formation attributes: The Potrillo Mountains rise abruptly from the desert floor, shaped by millions of years of erosion and tectonic activity. The region is characterized by rocky outcrops, deep arroyos, and dramatic ridgelines.

Fun fact: The area is home to unique desert flora and fauna, including ocotillo, yucca, and desert bighorn sheep. Its remote nature makes it an excellent place for stargazing.

Best time to visit: Fall through spring offers the best weather, as summer temperatures can be extreme, often exceeding 100°F (38°C).

How to access: The Potrillo Mountains are located in a remote part of southern New Mexico. Access is via dirt roads, which may require high-clearance 4WD vehicles, especially after rain.

Things to consider: There are no services nearby, so bring plenty of water, fuel, and supplies.

RECOMMENDED ACTIVITIES:

There are no official trails, but experienced hikers and explorers can navigate the rugged terrain. Be prepared for off-trail hiking and route-finding.

Tips for taking a great photo

- Early morning or late afternoon is the best time of day for soft, golden light on the rocky formations.
- Use foreground elements like desert vegetation or weathered rock formations to add depth to your shots.
- Monsoon season can bring dramatic clouds and lightning for striking landscape photos.
- The remoteness makes this an excellent location for Milky Way shots with little light pollution.

Opposite: Potrillo Mountains

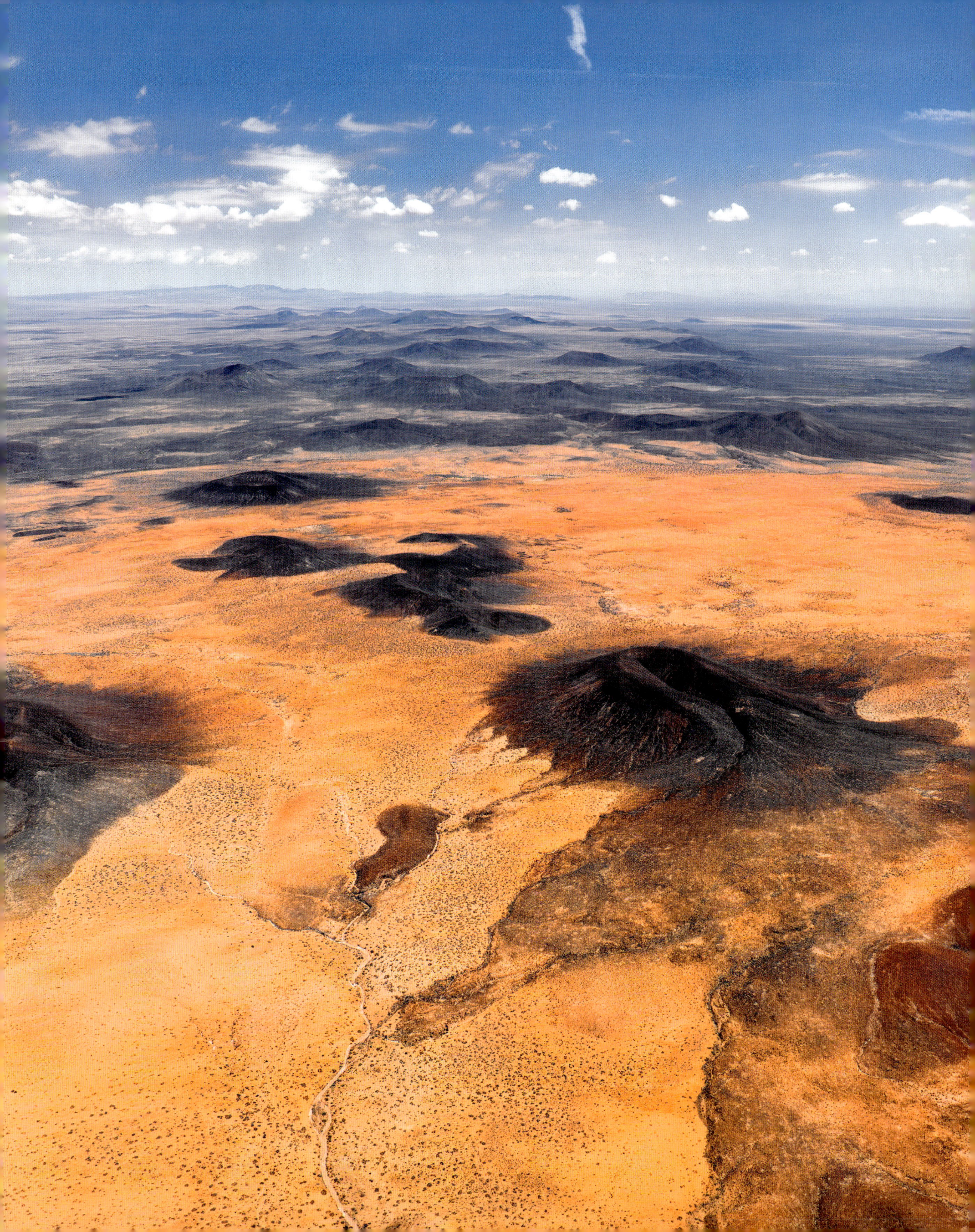

EAST

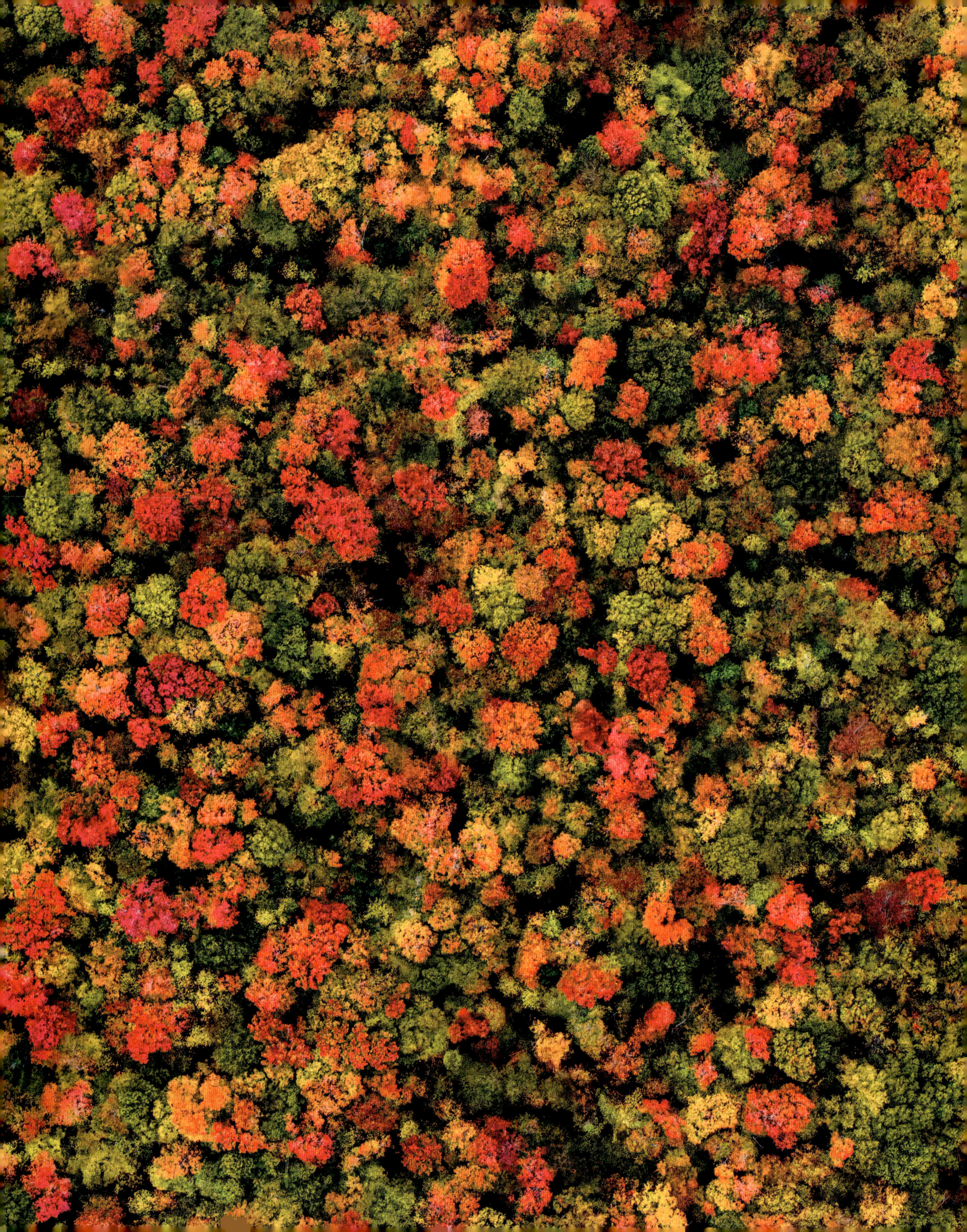

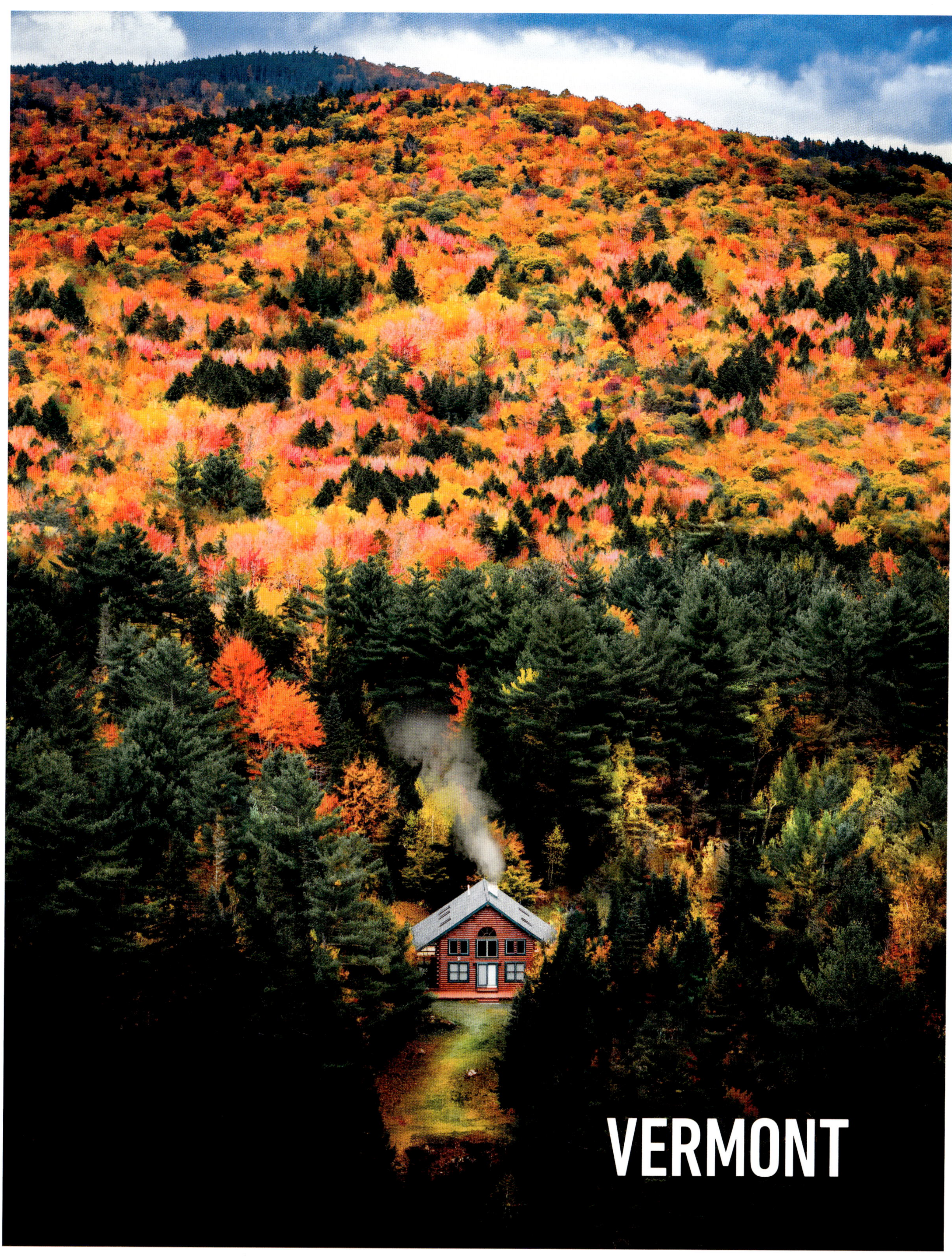

VERMONT

VERMONT

Hiking through Vermont in the fall is like stepping into a storybook. Near Woodstock, I took the Mount Tom trail, winding through forests bursting with red, orange, and gold. Seriously, the most vibrant fall colors I've ever seen. In Stowe, I hiked the Pinnacle Trail, a steeper climb. At the summit, I had a full view of the endless fall colors below. Vermont is famous for its spectacular fall foliage, charming small towns, and winding scenic roads lined with maple trees bursting in red, orange, and gold. The crisp autumn air, covered bridges, apple orchards, and farm stands selling fresh cider and donuts make fall in Vermont like something out of a postcard.

Region: Northeast

State: Vermont

Coordinates: Varies by location—popular spots include Stowe, Woodstock, and the Green Mountains

Focal feature: Vibrant autumn foliage covering rolling hills, mountains, and valleys

Formation attributes: Vermont's forests are primarily composed of sugar maples, which produce some of the most brilliant red and orange hues in the country.

Fun fact: Vermont has the highest concentration of maple trees in the US, and it's one of the top producers of maple syrup, which is best harvested in the spring but sold fresh year-round.

Best time to visit: Mid-September to early October in the northern and higher-elevation areas, while central and southern Vermont peak from early to mid-October.

How to access: Many of Vermont's best fall destinations are accessible by car via scenic byways like Route 100, the Green Mountain Byway, and the Mad River Byway. Burlington International Airport provides access to northern Vermont, while smaller airports in Rutland and Montpelier offer other options.

Things to consider: The weather can change quickly, so layering is key, and weekends can get crowded—aim for midweek visits for a quieter experience.

RECOMMENDED TRAILS:

Quechee Gorge Trail (Central Vermont): *1.3-mile (2km) round trip; about 200 feet (61m) elevation gain; easy.* A gentle trail leading to Vermont's "Little Grand Canyon," with stunning foliage views along the Ottauquechee River.

Sterling Pond Trail (Northern Vermont): *2.1-mile (3.4km) round trip; about 900 feet (273m) elevation gain; moderate.* A short but rewarding hike to a serene mountain pond surrounded by vibrant fall colors near Smugglers' Notch.

Camel's Hump Trail (Green Mountains): *6-mile (9.7km) round trip; about 2,600 feet (792m) elevation gain; strenuous.* A challenging hike leading to one of Vermont's most iconic peaks, offering panoramic views of fiery fall foliage stretching across the entire state.

Tips for taking a great photo

- Sunrise and late afternoon provide the best golden light, enhancing the warm tones of the leaves.
- Vermont has over a hundred covered bridges, which make for charming fall photo opportunities. Try the Middle Covered Bridge in Woodstock or Emily's Bridge near Stowe.
- Mount Mansfield, Lincoln Gap, and Hogback Mountain offer breathtaking panoramic views of Vermont's rolling hills covered in color.
- Chilly fall mornings often bring a layer of mist over valleys and rivers, creating an ethereal backdrop for photos.

Page 228, 229, and opposite: Fall colors near Lake Groton

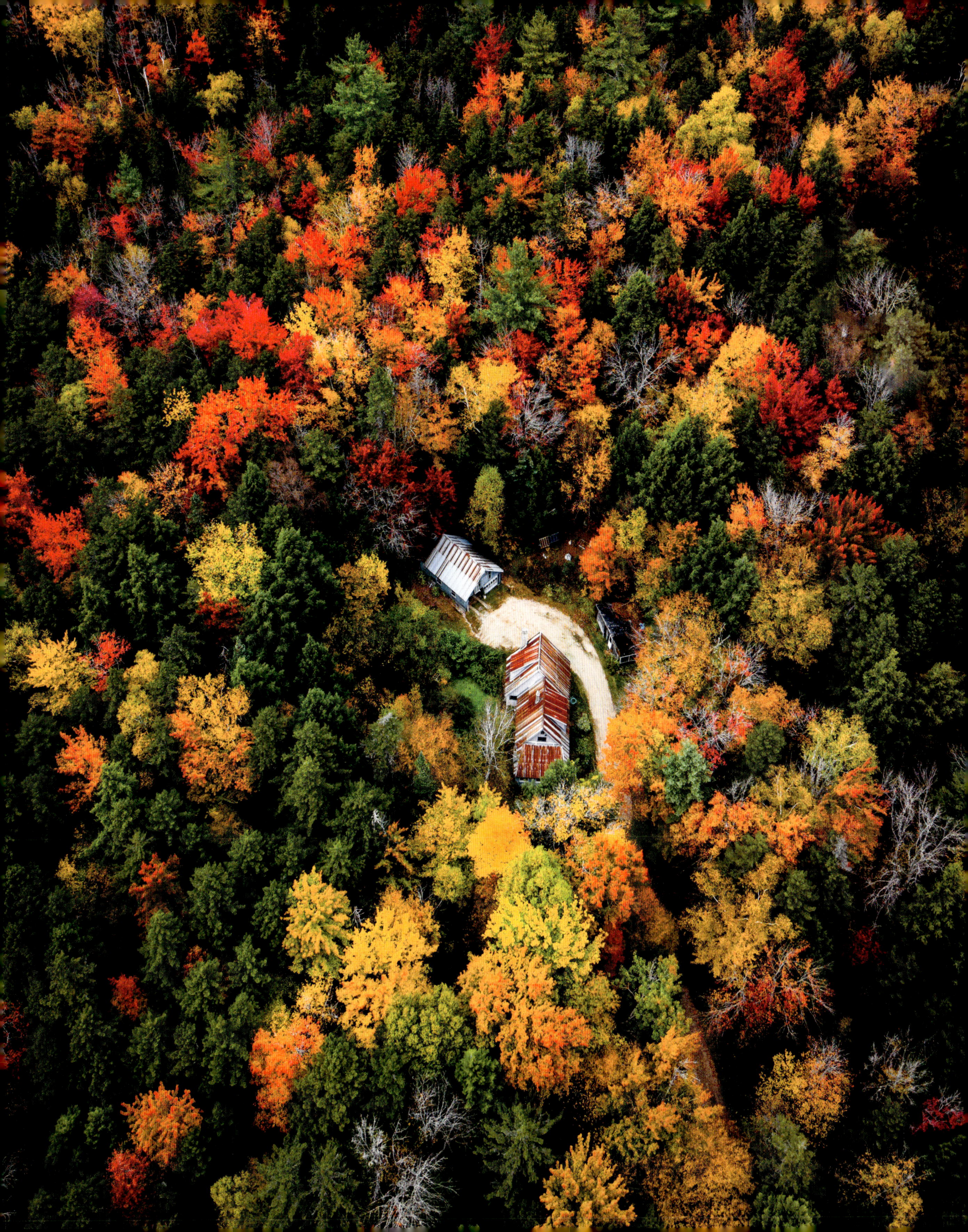

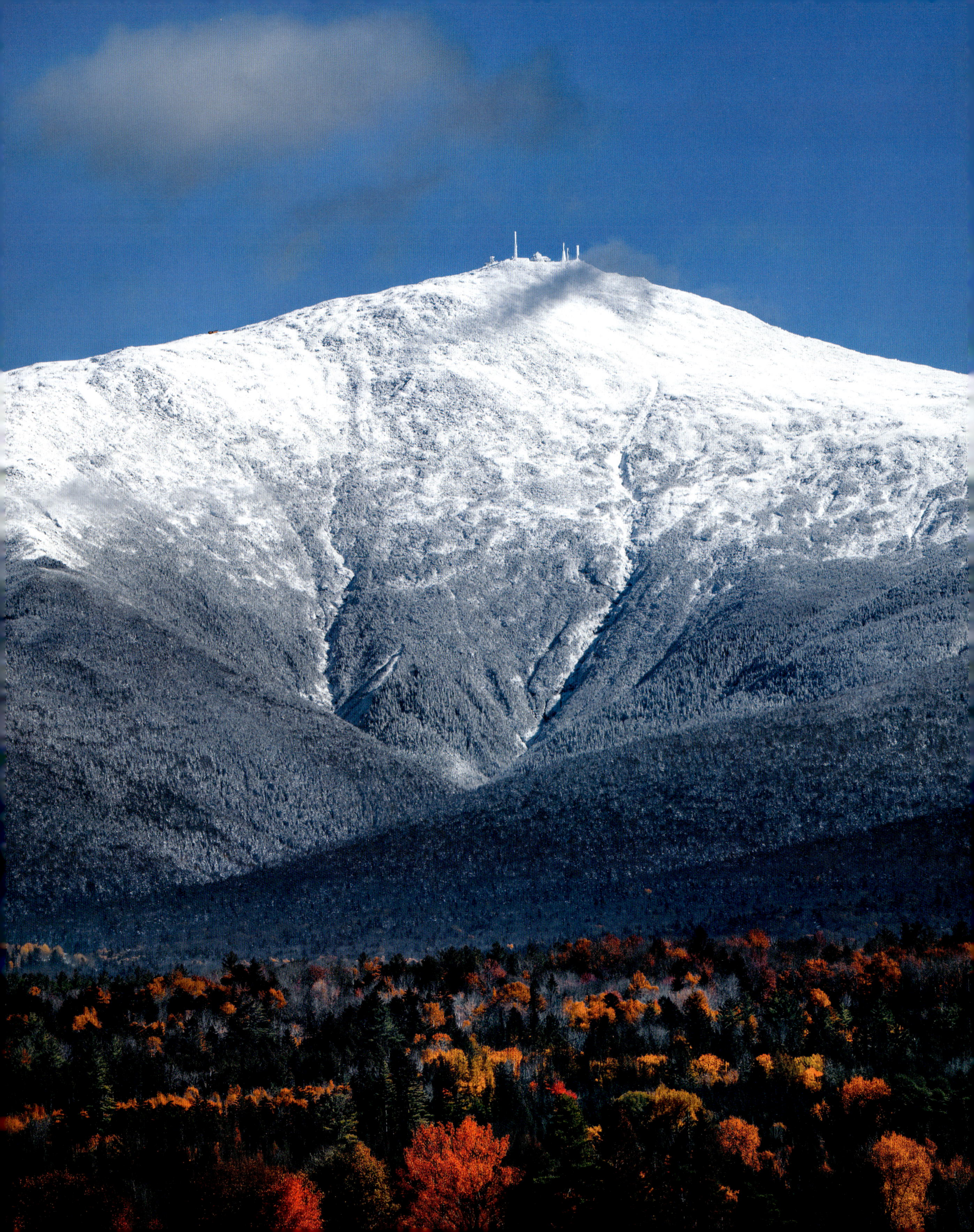

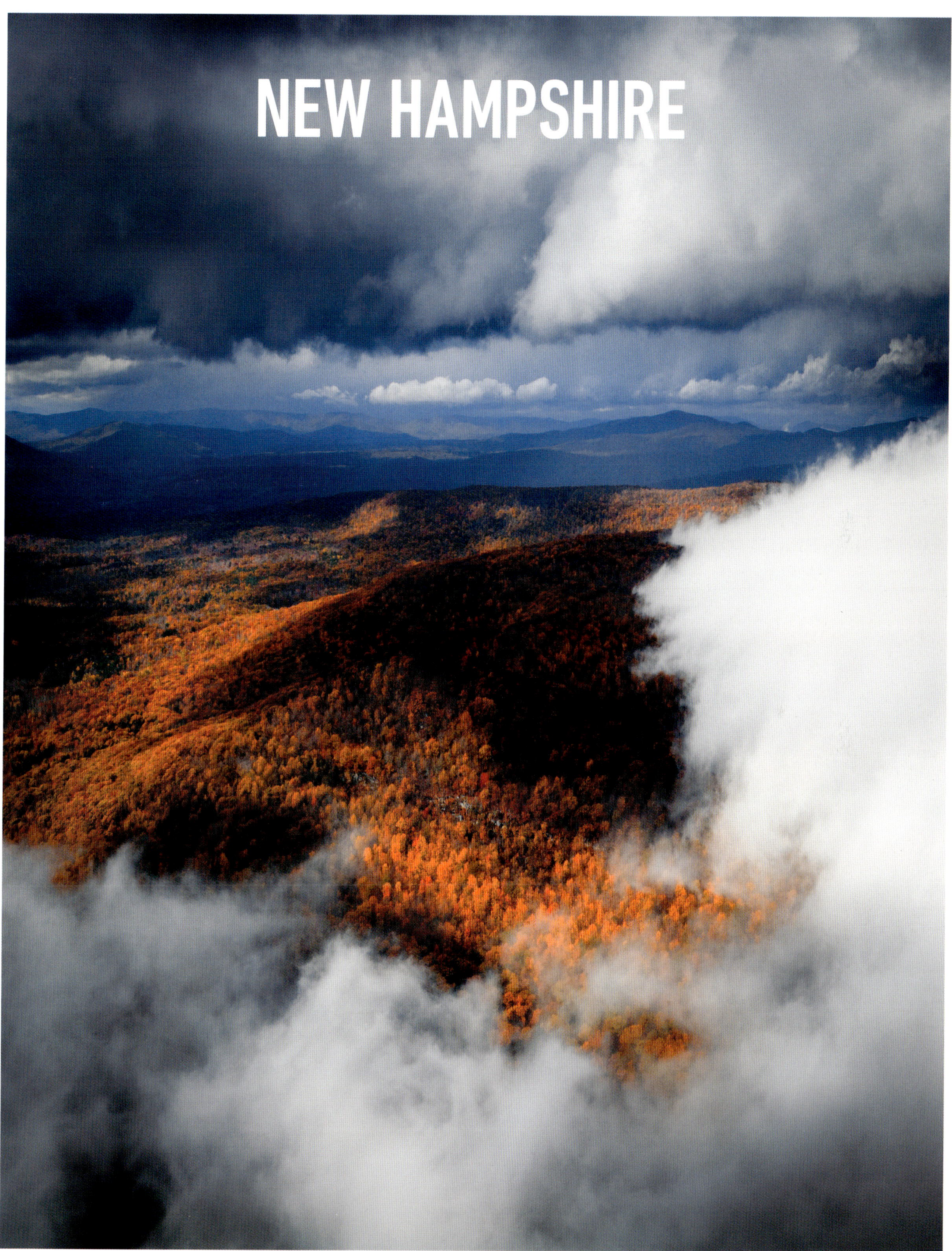
NEW HAMPSHIRE

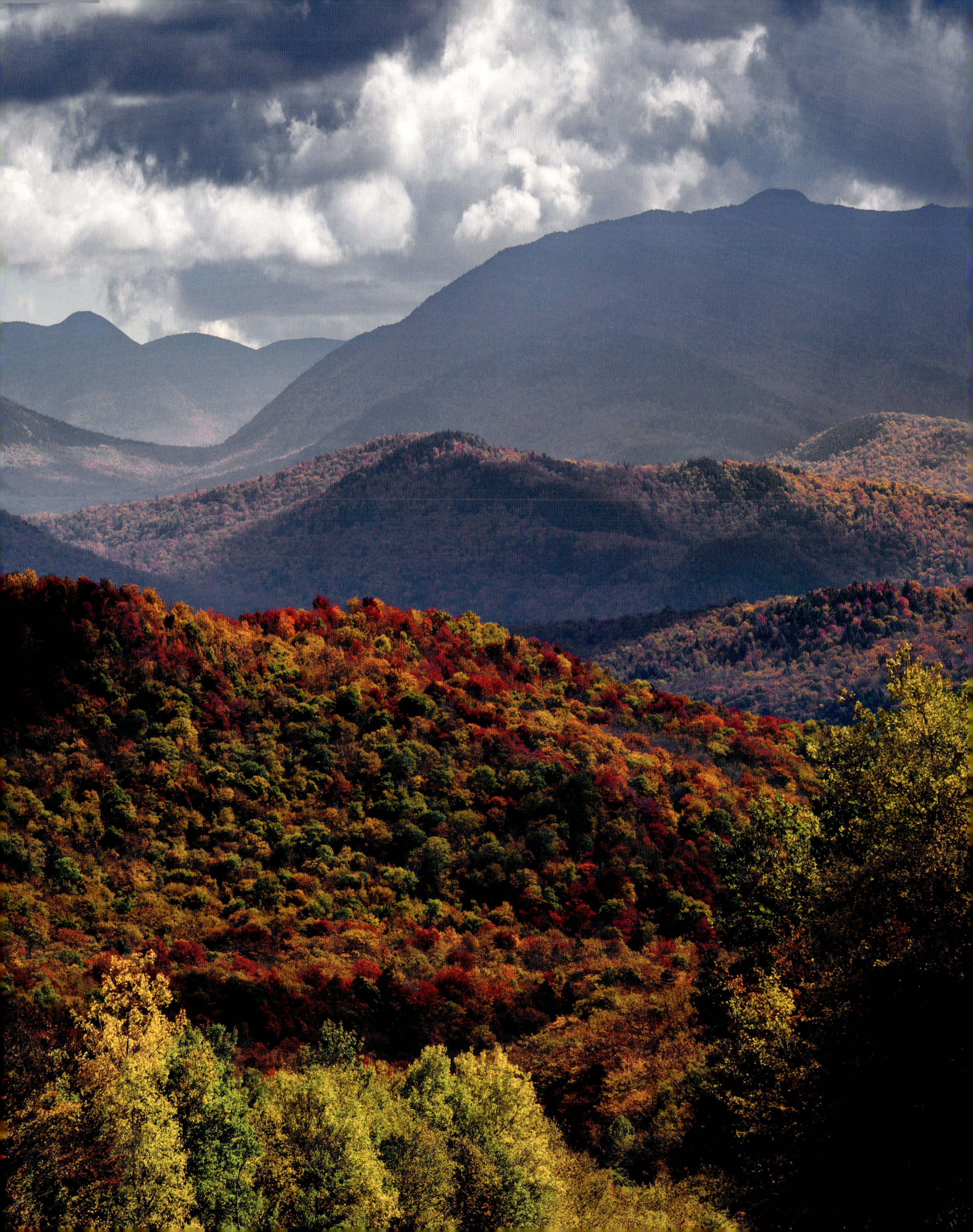

NEW HAMPSHIRE

Driving through the White Mountains in peak foliage season is unforgettable—the entire landscape transforms into a sea of reds and oranges. One of my favorite moments was hiking up to Artist's Bluff early in the morning. The air was crisp, and the view over Echo Lake was absolutely breathtaking. Whether it's a scenic drive along the Kancamagus Highway or simply sipping some warm apple cider at a roadside farm stand. Fall in the northeast is 10/10.

Region: Northeast

State: New Hampshire

Coordinates: Varies by location—some of the best areas include Franconia Notch, Kancamagus Highway, and the Mount Washington region

Focal feature: Stunning autumn foliage throughout the White Mountains, the Lakes Region, and the scenic byways

Formation attributes: The White Mountains rise over 6,000 feet (1,829m), creating breathtaking vantage points to view rolling hills blanketed in fall colors. New Hampshire is one of the best places in the US to experience fall, with its dramatic mountain landscapes, charming small towns, and winding scenic drives. The state's dense forests, filled with sugar maples, birch, and oaks, explode in brilliant shades of red, orange, and yellow.

Fun fact: The Kancamagus Highway, one of the most famous fall drives in the country, has no gas stations, restaurants, or lodges along its 34-mile (55km) stretch, making it a true escape into nature.

Best time to visit: Late September to early October in Northern New Hampshire and higher elevations; early to mid-October for central and southern areas.

How to access: Many of New Hampshire's best fall destinations are accessible by scenic drives, such as the Kancamagus Highway, Route 302, and the Mount Washington Auto Road. The closest major airport is in Manchester, with additional access from Boston.

Things to consider: The weather can shift quickly, so bring layers, and plan for weekend crowds at popular spots.

RECOMMENDED TRAILS:

Artist's Bluff Trail (White Mountains): *1.5-mile (2.4km) round trip; about 400 feet (122m) elevation gain; easy.* A short but rewarding hike that offers one of the most photographed fall views in New Hampshire, overlooking Echo Lake and the foliage-covered mountains.

Mount Willard Trail (Crawford Notch): *3.2-mile (5.1km) round trip; about 900 feet (274m) elevation gain; moderate.* A relatively easy hike with a breathtaking panoramic view of Crawford Notch, especially beautiful when the valley is ablaze with autumn colors.

Franconia Ridge Loop (Franconia Notch State Park): *9.1-mile (14.6km) round trip; about 3,900 feet (1,189m) elevation gain; strenuous.* One of the most spectacular hikes in New England, featuring a stunning ridgeline walk with 360-degree views of the White Mountains in peak fall colors.

Tips for taking a great photo

- Sunrise and sunset bring out the richest hues in the foliage, and early morning light creates soft, golden reflections on lakes and rivers.
- Visit Cathedral Ledge for a sweeping view over the valleys or drive up the Mount Washington Auto Road for the ultimate panoramic shot.
- New Hampshire has over fifty historic covered bridges. Albany Covered Bridge along the Kancamagus Highway and Flume Covered Bridge in Franconia Notch are two of the most photogenic.
- Crisp autumn mornings often bring mist over the lakes and valleys, adding a magical touch to fall landscape shots.

Page 232: Mount Washington, White Mountains

Page 233 and opposite: White Mountains

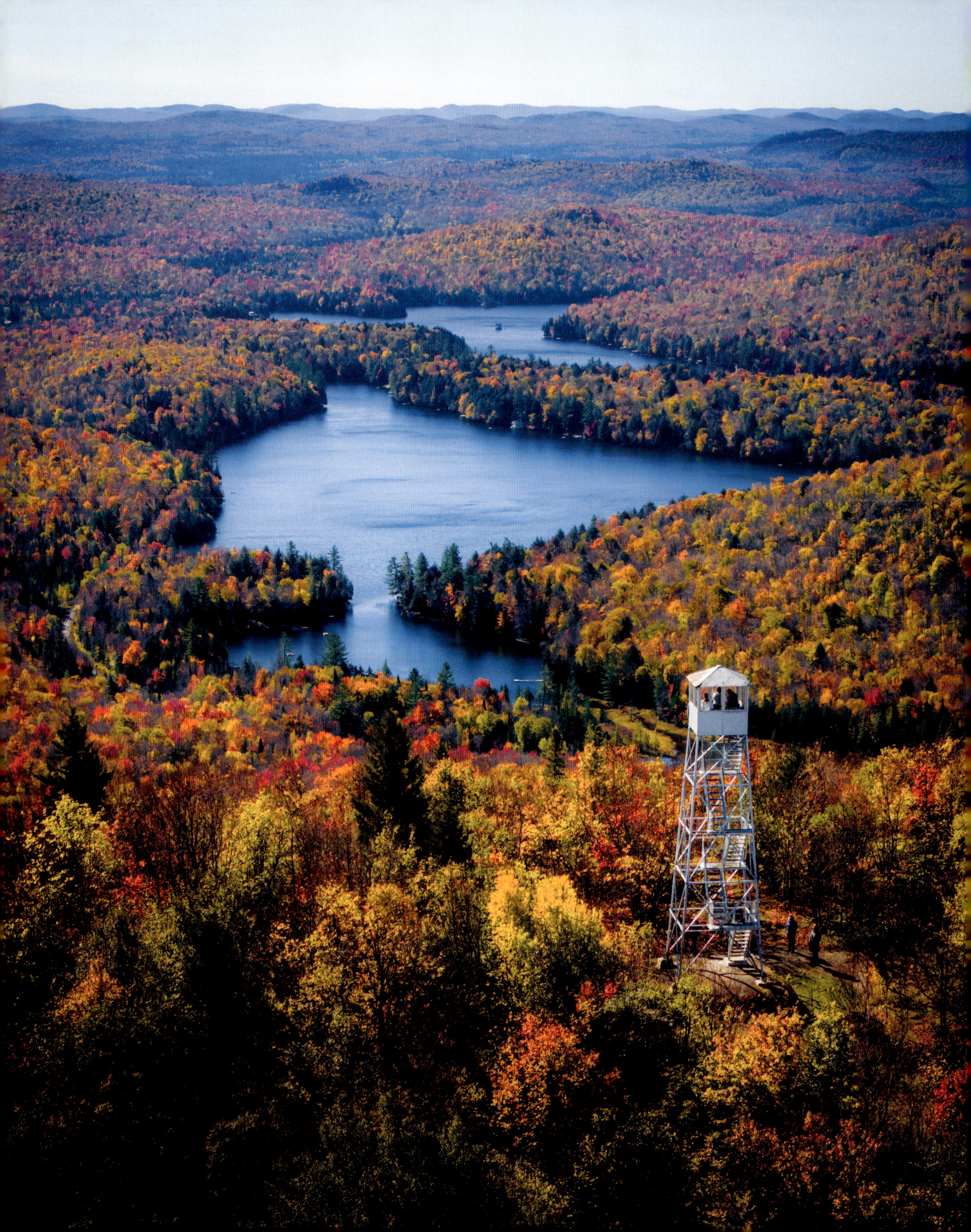

NEW YORK

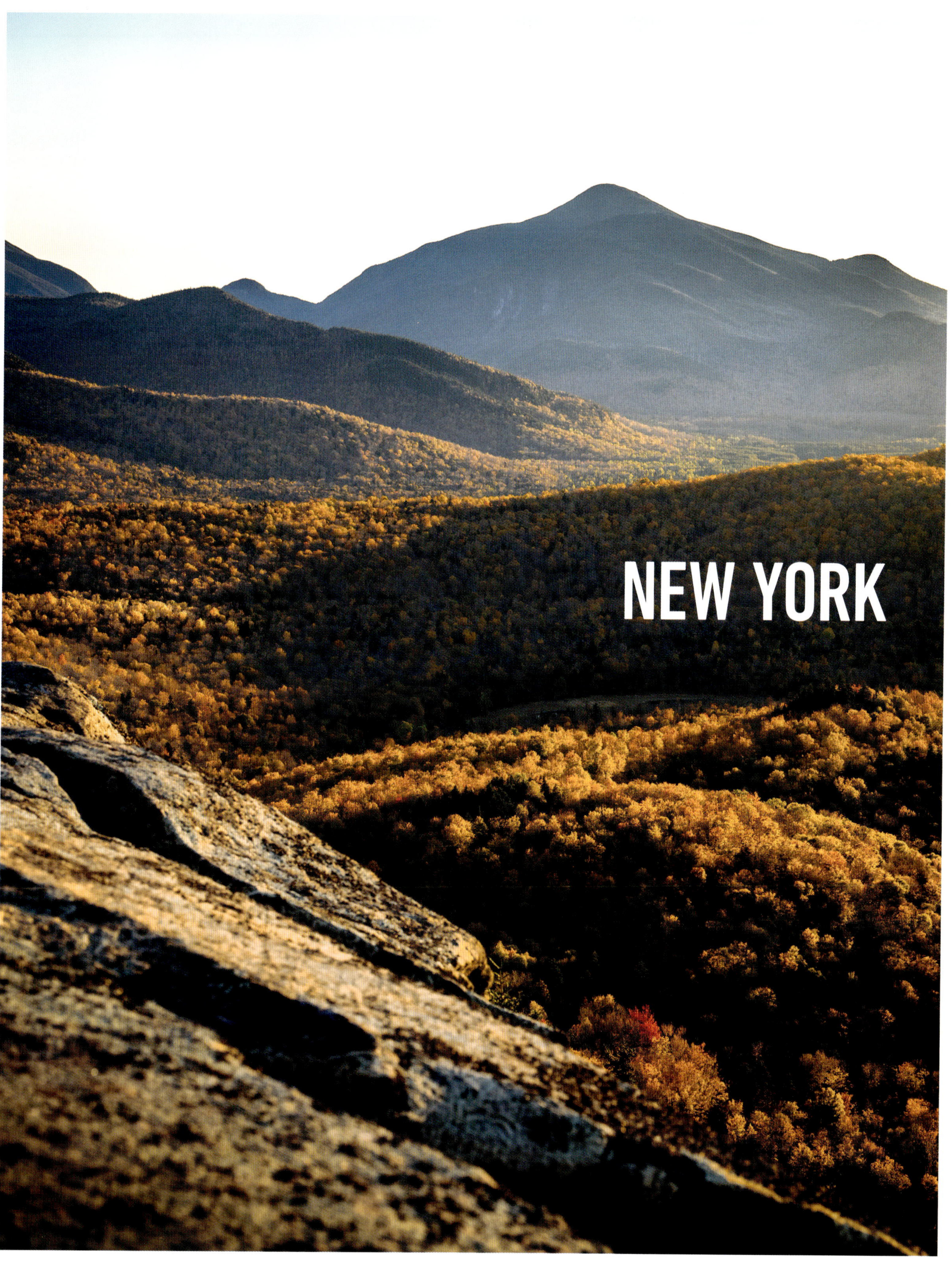

NEW YORK

I always pictured New York State as just a place with the biggest city, but when I finally visited upstate, I was completely blown away. New York is one of the best places in the country to experience fall, with vibrant foliage, crisp air, and scenic drives through the mountains and countryside. The state offers everything from charming small towns and apple orchards to dramatic mountain landscapes bursting with color. My favorites places are Indian Head Vista, Blue Mountain, and Elk Lake Lodge.

Region: Northeast

State: New York

Coordinates: Varies by location—Adirondacks, Catskills, and Hudson Valley are among the best regions for fall colors

Focal feature: Stunning autumn foliage across mountains, lakes, and forests

Formation attributes: New York's diverse forests include maple, oak, and birch trees, which turn brilliant shades of red, orange, and gold during peak fall.

Fun fact: The Adirondack Park is larger than Yellowstone, the Everglades, Grand Canyon, and Glacier National Parks combined, making it one of the best places for leaf-peeping in the US.

Best time to visit: Late September to mid-October in the Adirondacks and Catskills, while the Hudson Valley and New York City peak in mid-to-late October.

How to access: Many of the best fall destinations are easily accessible by car via scenic routes like the Catskill Mountains Scenic Byway and the Adirondack Northway (Interstate 87). If visiting from New York City, Metro-North and Amtrak offer train routes with stunning views along the Hudson River.

Things to consider: Be prepared for varying temperatures; early fall can be warm, while late fall brings chilly mornings and occasional frost.

RECOMMENDED TRAILS:

Kaaterskill Falls Trail (Catskills): *1.7-mile (2.7km) round trip; about 400 feet (122m) elevation gain; easy.* A short hike leading to one of New York's most famous waterfalls, surrounded by brilliant fall colors.

Mount Jo Trail (Adirondacks): *2.5-mile (4km) round trip; about 700 feet (213m) elevation gain; moderate.* A quick but rewarding hike with breathtaking views of the High Peaks region, especially stunning in autumn.

Giant Mountain via Ridge Trail (Adirondacks): *6-mile (9.6km) round trip; about 3,000 feet (914m) elevation gain; strenuous.* A challenging hike to one of the Adirondacks' best panoramic viewpoints, overlooking endless forests of fall foliage.

Tips for taking a great photo

- Early morning provides soft golden light and fewer crowds, while late afternoon can create dramatic, warm tones.
- Lakes and rivers, like Mirror Lake in Lake Placid, create stunning reflections of the colorful trees.
- Locations like Prospect Mountain and the Hudson Highlands offer sweeping valley views bursting with autumn hues.
- Chilly fall mornings often bring low-lying fog, which adds a dreamy atmosphere to mountain and forest shots.

Page 236: Mount Arab Lookout

Page 237 and opposite, top right: Adirondack Mountains

Opposite, top left and bottom right: Kaaterskill Falls

Opposite, bottom left: Bird Pond, Adirondacks

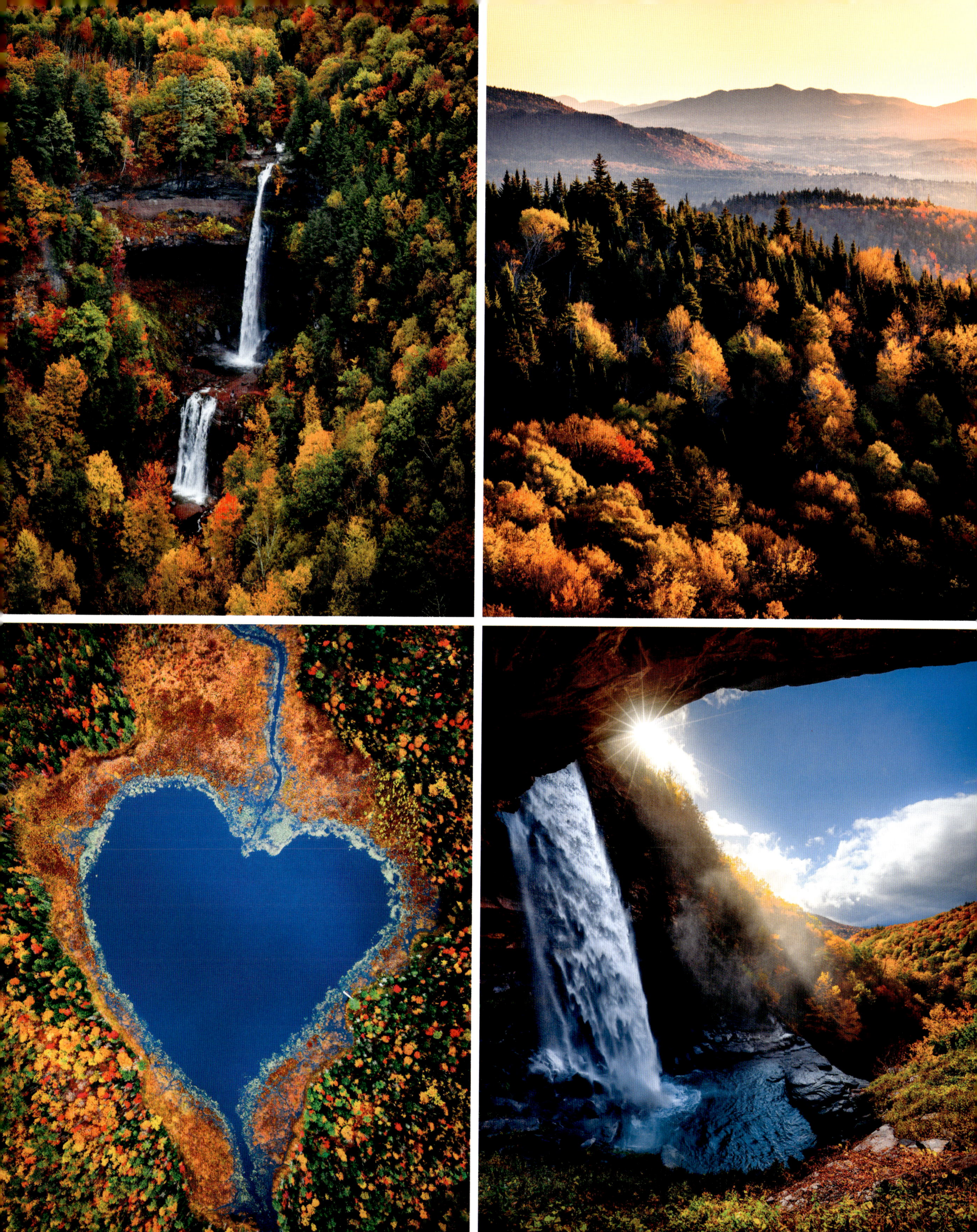

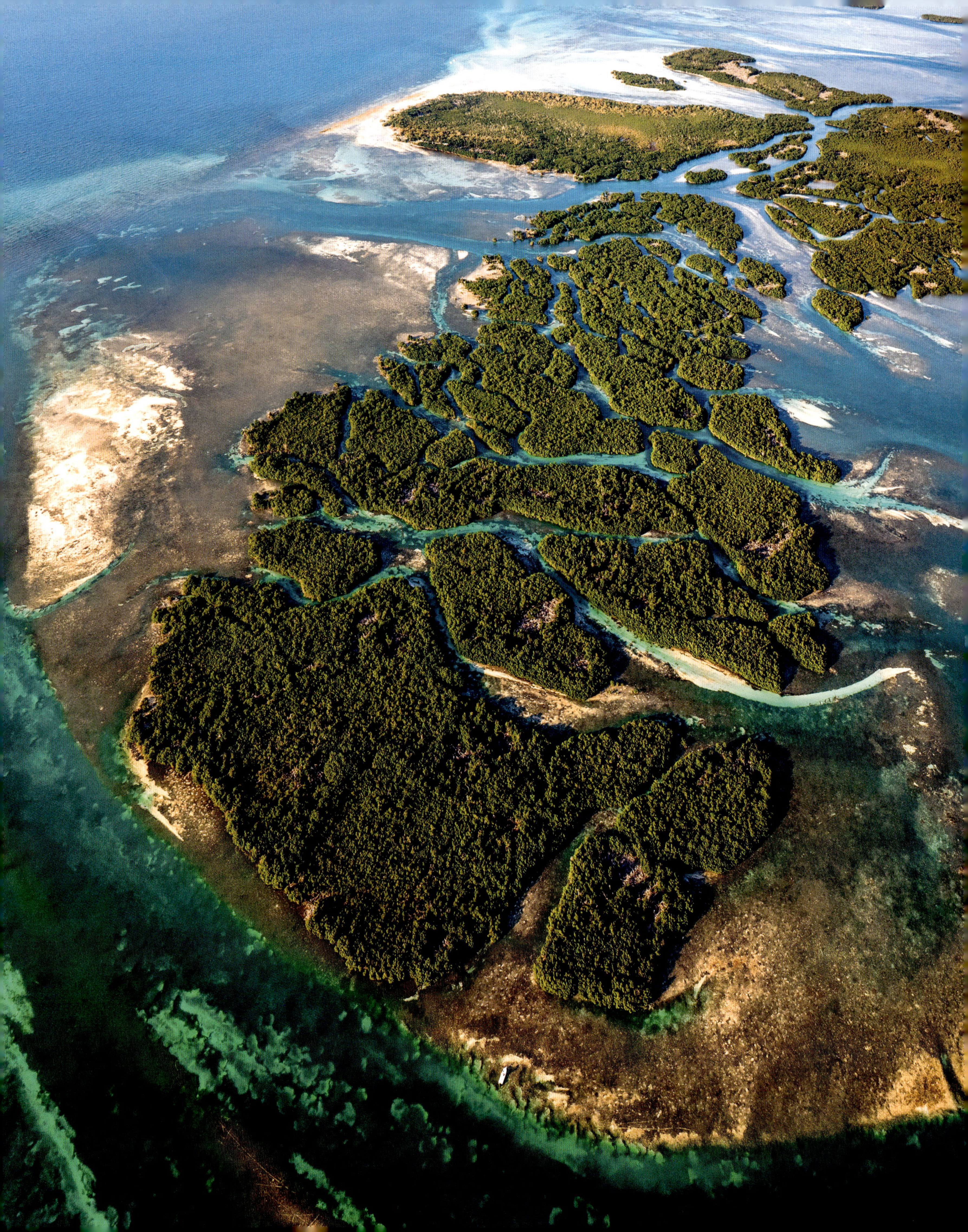

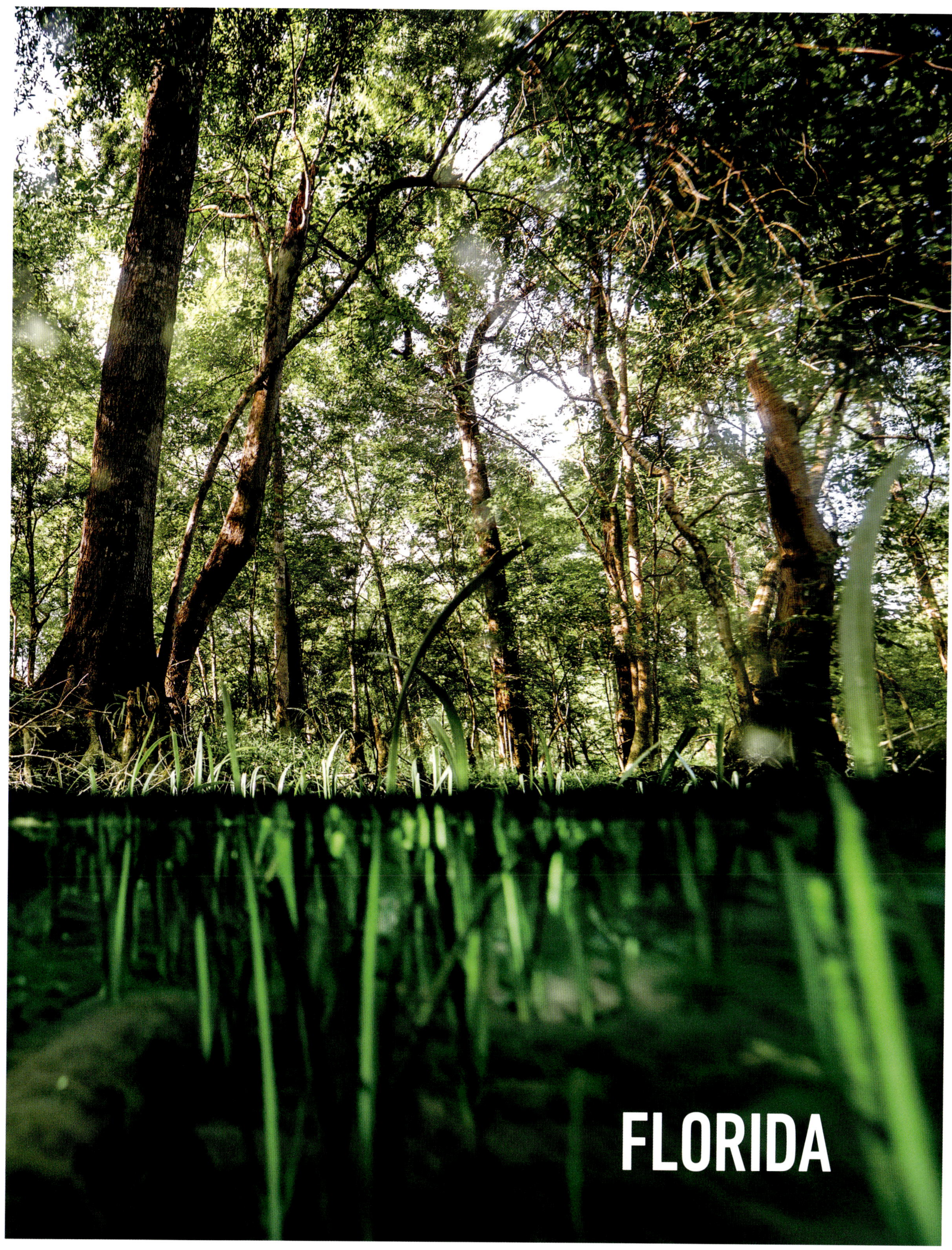
FLORIDA

THE EVERGLADES

Exploring the Everglades is like venturing into a timeless wilderness—vast, wild, and brimming with life. Explore endless mangrove tunnels and open grasslands, where alligators bask in the sun and colorful birds soar overhead. The park's remarkable biodiversity creates endless opportunities for photos.

Region: Southeast

State: Florida

Coordinates: 25°19'00.0"N 80°56'00.0"W

Focal feature: A unique subtropical wilderness composed of sawgrass marshes, mangrove forests, and diverse wildlife habitats

Formation attributes: Covers approximately 1.5 million acres, making it the largest subtropical wilderness in the US and the third-largest national park in the contiguous states.

Fun fact: The Everglades is the only place in the world where both alligators and crocodiles coexist in the wild!

Best time to visit: December to April for comfortable temperatures, fewer insects, and excellent wildlife-viewing opportunities.

How to access: Primary access points are through entrances at Ernest F. Coe Visitor Center near Homestead, Shark Valley Visitor Center along US Highway 41, and Gulf Coast Visitor Center in Everglades City. Be aware that there are no roads traversing the entire park, so exploring its diverse areas requires some planning.

Things to consider: Bring insect repellent, sunscreen, and ample water. Be mindful of wildlife and maintain safe distances.

RECOMMENDED TRAILS:

Anhinga Trail: *0.8-mile (1.3km) round trip; minimal elevation gain; easy.* An unchallenging walk along a boardwalk through a freshwater marsh ideal for wildlife viewing, particularly for alligators, herons, and turtles.

Gumbo Limbo Trail: *0.5-mile (0.8km) loop; minimal elevation gain; easy.* Wander through shaded hardwood hammock forests, perfect for observing flora and smaller wildlife species.

Shark Valley Tram Trail: *15-mile (24km) round trip; minimal elevation gain; moderate (primarily due to length).* A trail that can be explored via bicycle, tram, or foot, offering incredible panoramic views from the observation tower midway.

Tips for taking a great photo

- Early mornings offer calm waters that are ideal for reflections and soft lighting favorable for wildlife photography.
- Sunset is excellent for capturing silhouettes and vibrant skies reflected across the wetlands.
- Use telephoto lenses to safely capture close-ups of wildlife.
- Polarizing filters help reduce water glare, enhancing colors and clarity in your photographs.

Page 240: Mud Keys, Florida Keys

Page 241 and opposite: The Everglades

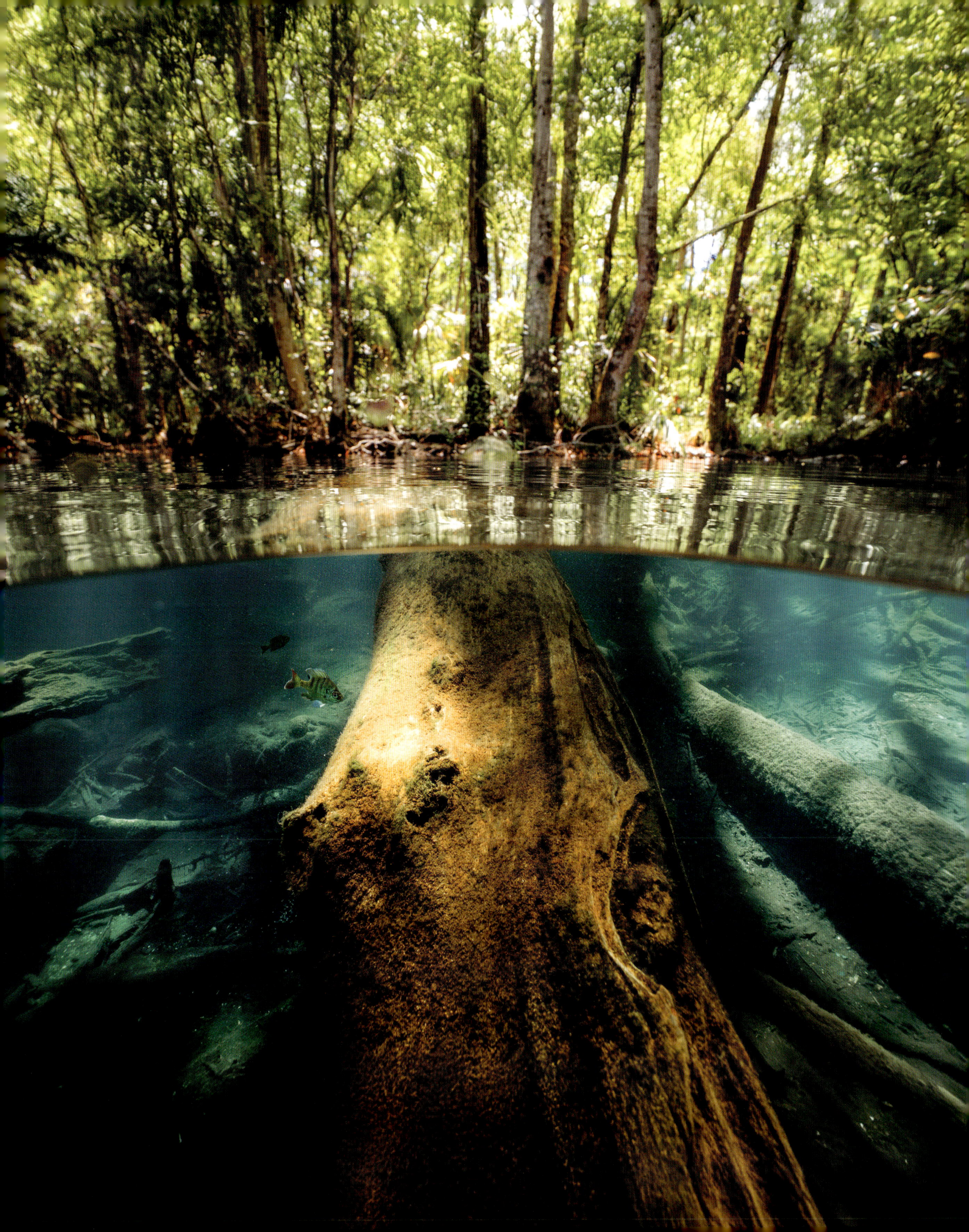

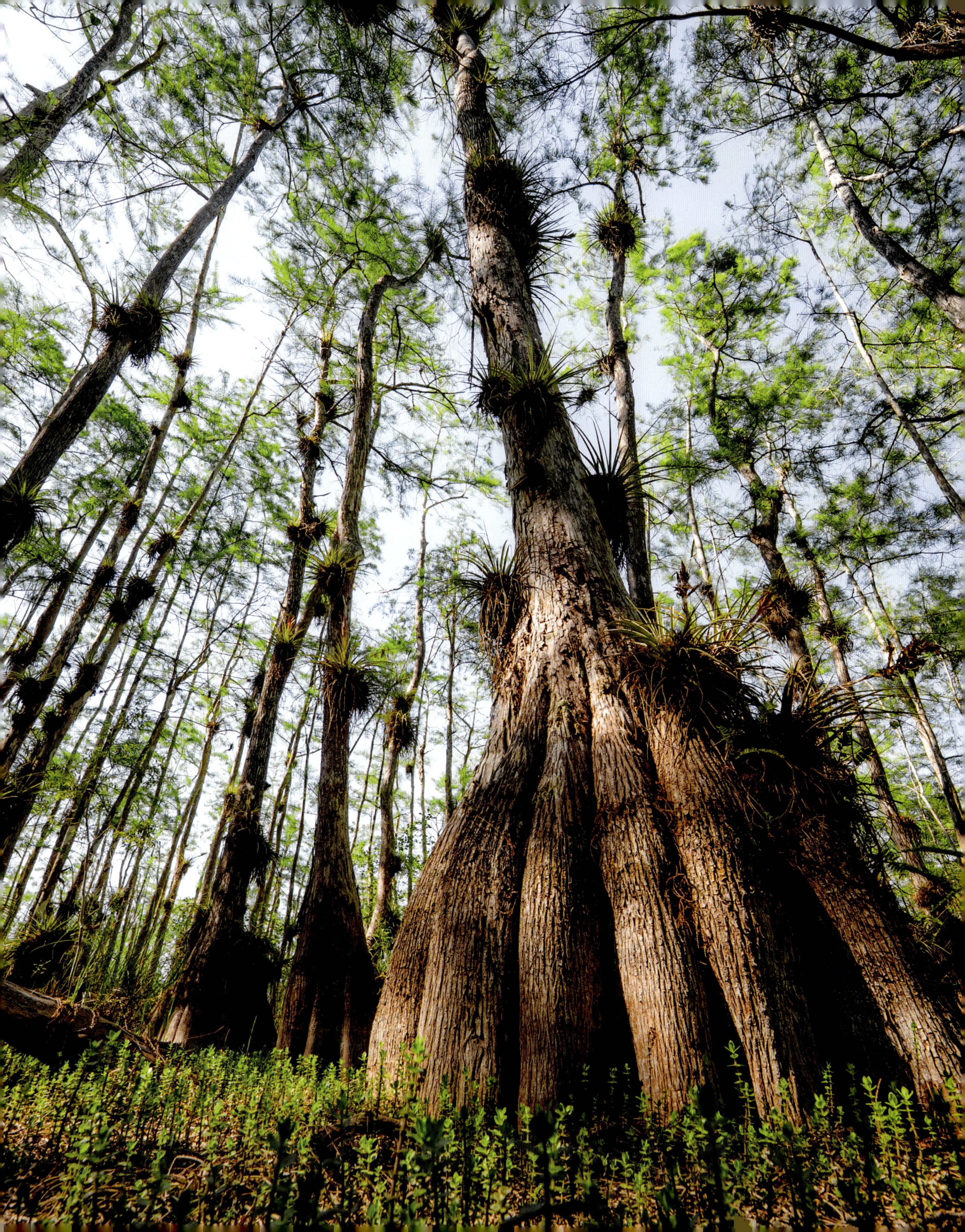

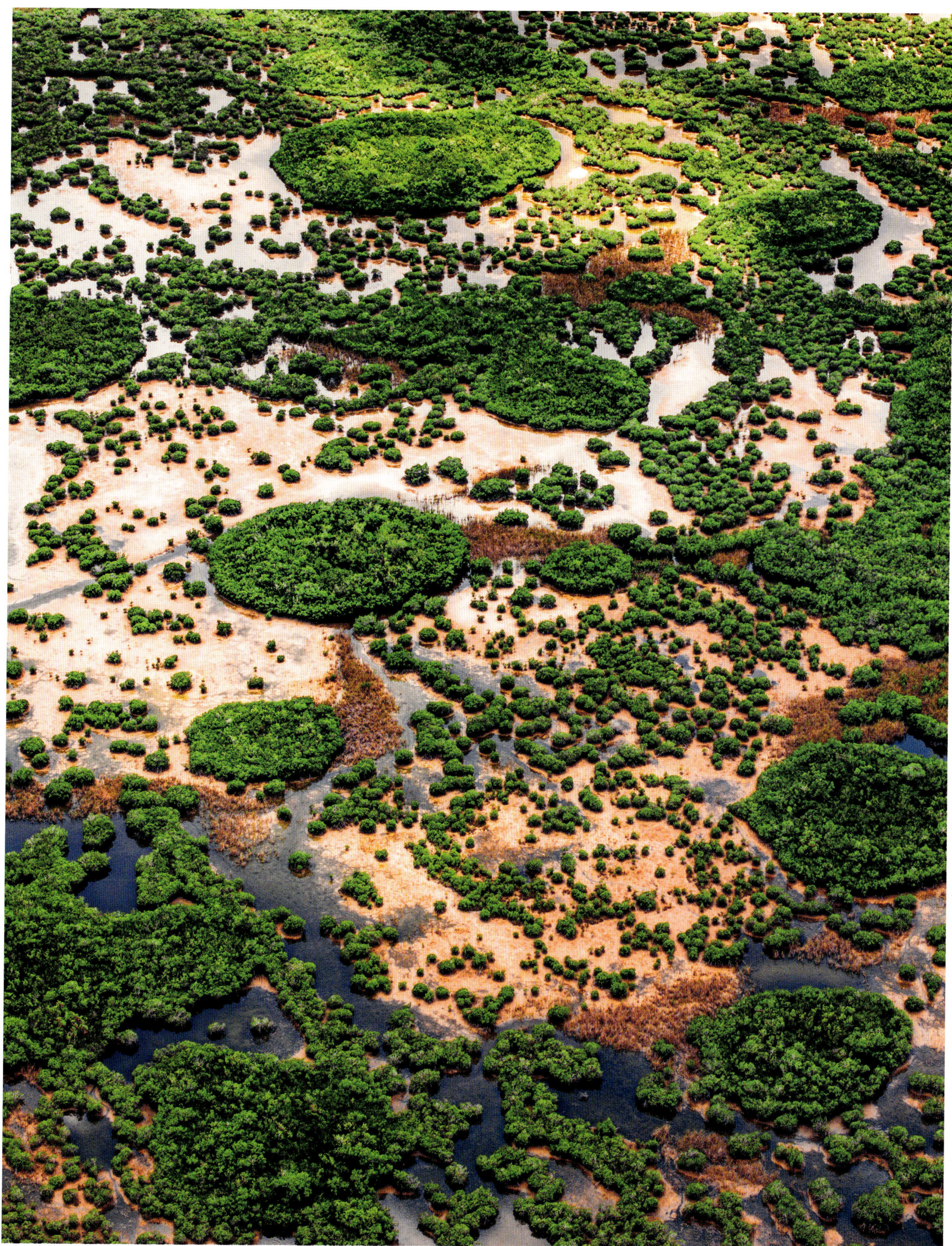

Above: Everglades National Park | Opposite: Big Cypress National Preserve

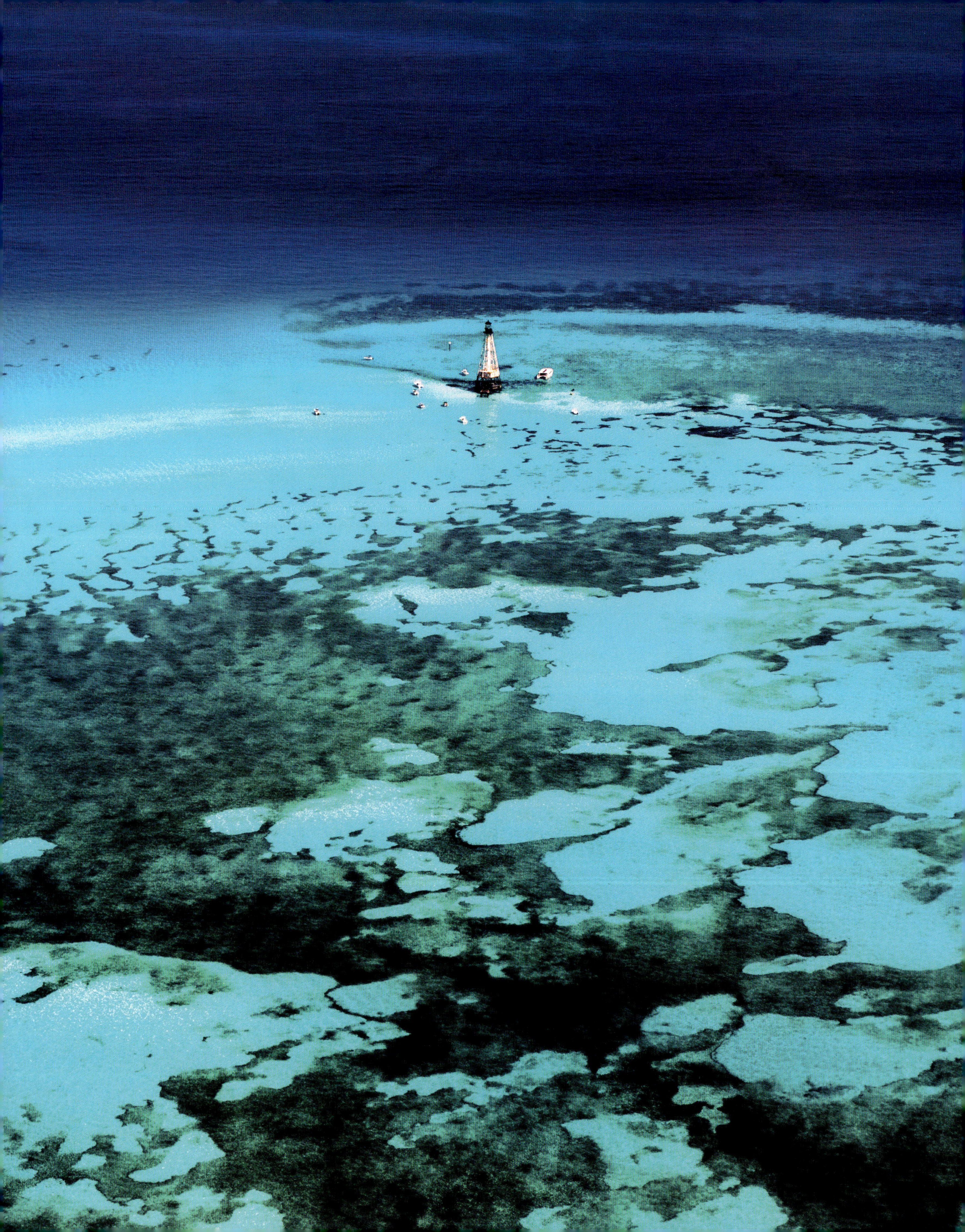

FLORIDA KEYS

The Florida Keys are a tropical paradise—turquoise waters and vibrant sunsets. Journey along the Overseas Highway, hopping from one idyllic island to the next, each offering unique charm and breathtaking scenery. The Keys' diverse marine life, coral reefs, and relaxed atmosphere make this an ideal destination for nature lovers and adventurers alike.

Region: Southeast

State: Florida

Coordinates: 24°33'00.0"N 81°47'00.0"W

Focal features: Crystal-clear waters, coral reefs, and a chain of tropical islands known for snorkeling, diving, and fishing

Formation attributes: Extends about 125 miles (200km) from Key Largo to Key West, connected by the iconic Overseas Highway (US Highway 1).

Fun fact: The Keys contain the third-largest barrier reef system in the world, offering incredible diving and snorkeling opportunities.

Best time to visit: November to April for warm, pleasant weather with lower humidity and excellent conditions for outdoor activities.

How to access: The Overseas Highway connects the mainland of Florida to Key West, passing through all the major Keys. Fly directly into Key West or drive down from Miami or Fort Lauderdale.

Things to consider: Sun protection is essential; bring sunscreen, hats, and sunglasses. Marine life is abundant, so follow guidelines for safe and responsible wildlife interactions.

RECOMMENDED AREAS:

John Pennekamp Coral Reef State Park (Key Largo): Famous for snorkeling and diving, with vibrant coral reefs and marine life.

Bahia Honda State Park (Bahia Honda Key): Known for pristine beaches, clear waters, and excellent opportunities for swimming and kayaking.

Dry Tortugas National Park: Home to historic Fort Jefferson and spectacular snorkeling in crystal-clear waters. Accessible by ferry or seaplane from Key West.

Tips for taking a great photo

- Capture sunrise or sunset for stunning colors and dramatic coastal views.
- Use an underwater camera or waterproof housing to photograph marine life and coral reefs.
- Use a polarizing filter to enhance water clarity and reduce reflections.
- Early mornings often provide calmer waters, ideal for clear shots of marine wildlife.

Opposite: Alligator Reef Lighthouse, Florida Keys

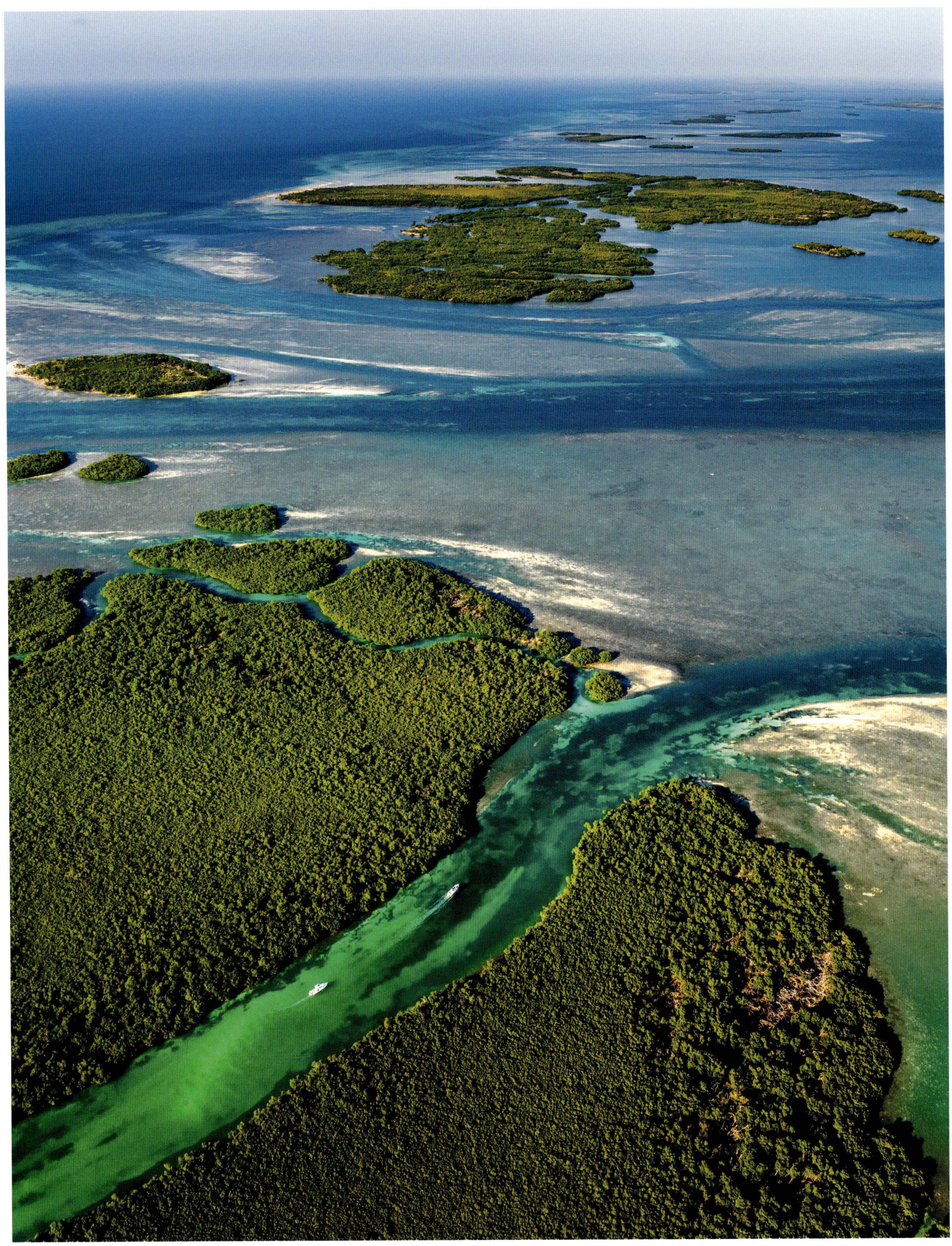

Above and opposite: Mud Keys, Florida Keys

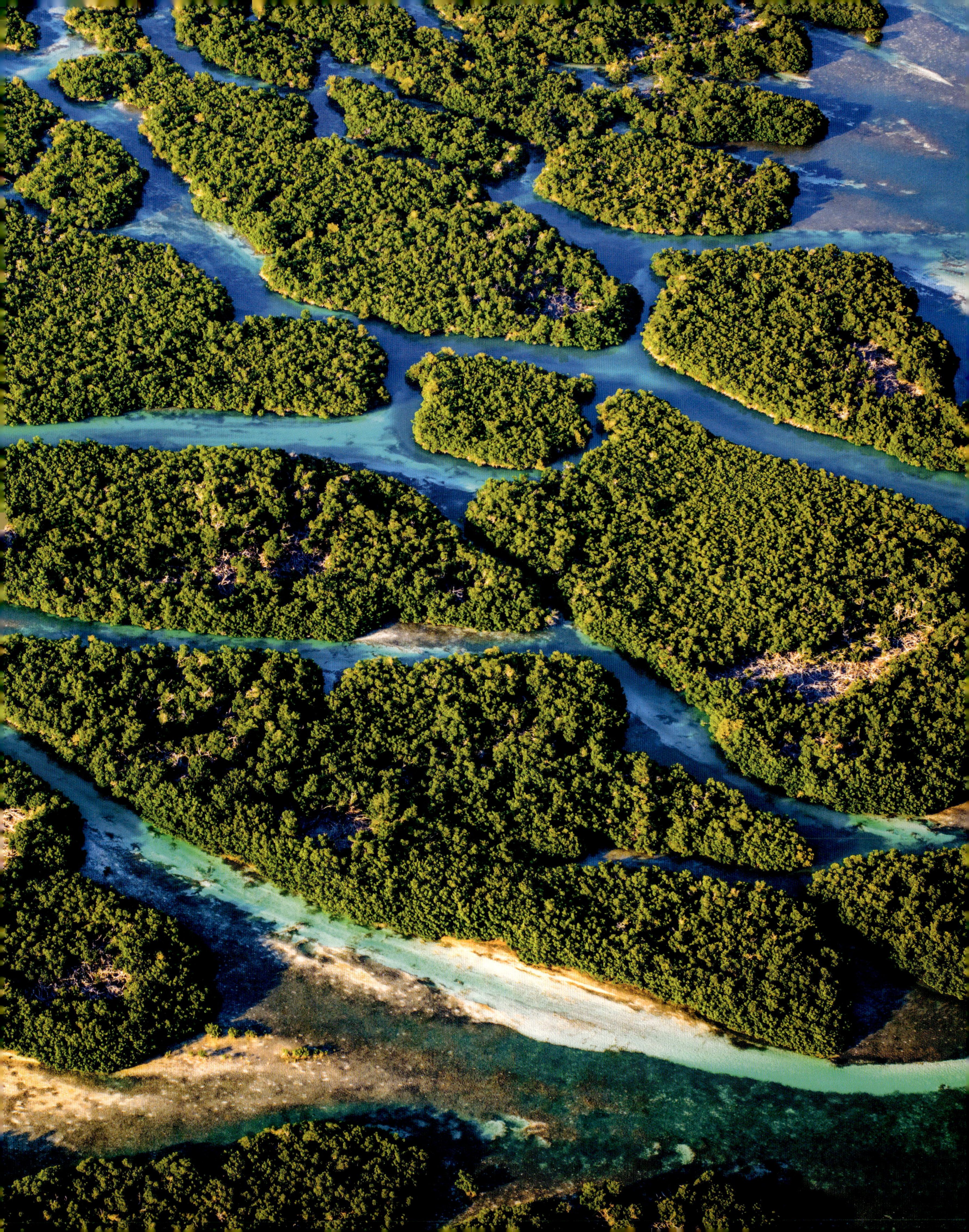

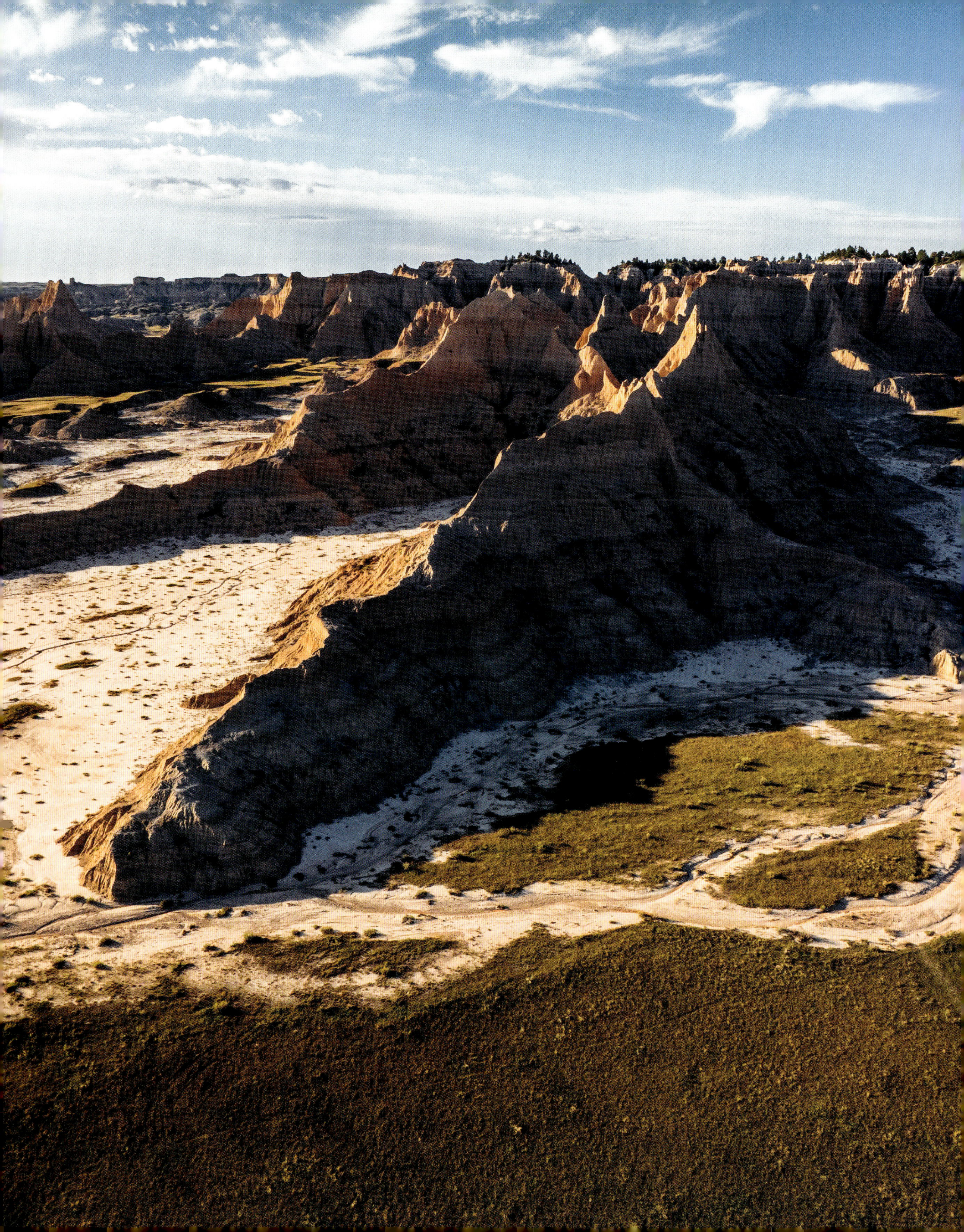

Acknowledgments

I'd like to start by thanking the millions of strangers online who have supported my work over the years. I never thought that sharing my photos on an app would lead me here. You've completely changed my life, and I'm forever grateful for all the love and support you've shown me. This book is for you.

Ever since I was little, doing arts and crafts on my Grandma Corryn's dining room table, it's been my dream to make a book. I wasn't quite sure what the book would be about back then, but when I found my passion for photography ten years ago, having my own photography book became the dream.

So when I received an email from my editor, Alexander Rigby, saying he wanted to help make that dream a reality, my heart practically exploded with excitement. Not only would I have an amazing editor, but I'd be working with the #1 publisher in the world. Thank you, Alex, for everything. Without you, there would be no book. You shaped my unorganized photo collection into something beautiful, all while dealing with my pea-sized attention span. You paved the way for me, and I am so grateful.

Thank you to the entire DK team and Penguin Random House for all the hard work that went into creating and sharing this book with the world. You are all amazing—truly the best in the business. Thank you for all your help! You've made one of my dreams come true. It's crazy to say that I'm now a published author.

To my sponsors and partners at DJI Global and Sony Alpha: thank you for supporting my career and supplying me with the best gear to capture the photos in this book.

Thank you to my wonderful family—my mom, Stephanie; my stepdad, Josh; and all of my amazing grandparents. Thank you for putting up with me and helping me get to the finish line.

To my best friend, Cole Hilton—thank you for being there every step of the way. We went on some crazy adventures for this book! I couldn't have done this without you, buddy.

To my amazing and incredibly supportive friends—Colton, Taylor, Brady, Sam, Brian, Juliah, Tyson, Chandler, and Lacey—thank you. You've been my escape and have helped me in more ways than you'll ever know. I love you all so much.

To my AP art and ceramics teachers at Cascade High School, Ms. Melby and Ms. Morgan: you were the spark that lit this fire.

Opposite: Badlands National Park

Index

About the Author

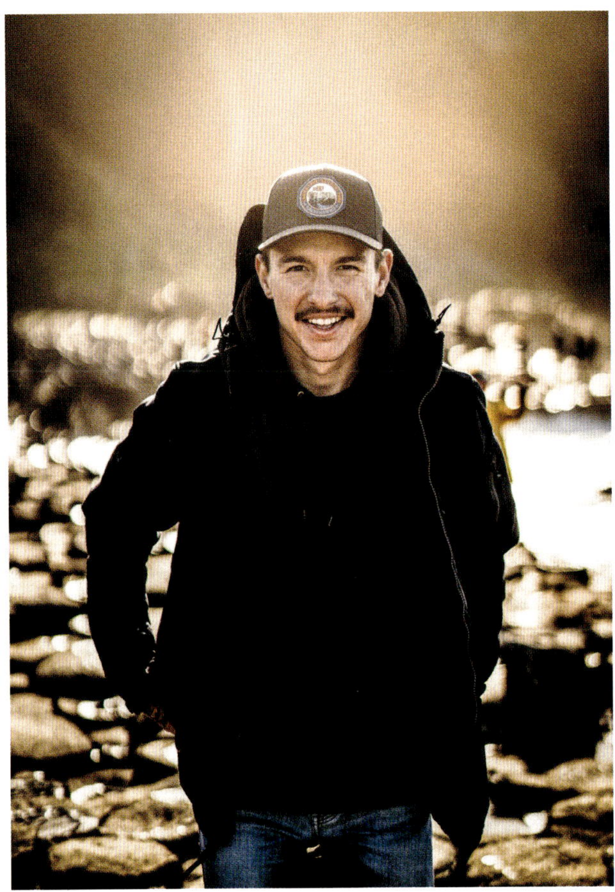

Jake Guzman is a professional outdoor adventure photographer and filmmaker based in Seattle, Washington. His distinct editing style, approach to photography, and storytelling has garnered the attention of millions across social media. Jake strives to push the boundaries with his images, carefully scouting the globe for his next composition. He hopes to inspire others and is always ready for the next big adventure.